HISTORY

OF

THE CONQUEST OF SPAIN

BY

THE ARAB-MOORS.

———◆———

IN TWO VOLUMES, VOL. I.

. . . beatis nunc Arabum invides
Gazis, et acrem militiam paras
Non ante devictis Sabææ
Regibus.
          HORAT. *Carm. Lib.* i. xxix.

"This book contains an account of the Conquest of Andalus by the
Moslems . . . and how that country became the arena wherein their
noble steeds raced, and the halting-place wherein their camels laid down
their burdens and grazed; . . . drawn from various sources, and the
accounts of historians compared together."

          AL MAKKARI, *Hist. Mohamm. Dyn.*,
                    Vol. I., Book IV., Ch.

HISTORY

OF THE

CONQUEST OF SPAIN

BY

THE ARAB-MOORS.

WITH

A SKETCH OF THE CIVILIZATION WHICH THEY ACHIEVED, AND IMPARTED TO EUROPE.

BY

HENRY COPPÉE.

VOL. I.

GORGIAS PRESS
2002

ISBN 1-931956-93-6 (Volume 1)
ISBN 1-931956-94-4 (Volume 2)

GORGIAS PRESS
46 Orris Ave., Piscataway, NJ 08854 USA
www.gorgiaspress.com

While I was looking for a patron to whom, with due humility, I might dedicate my work, a hand was stretched out to me from the Infinite, and across the great water.

No one will look upon these volumes with more affectionate interest, and a less critical eye, — as soon as he is able to read them, — than my dear little grandson and namesake,

HENRY COPPÉE THURSTON,

who was born at Meran, in the Austrian Tyrol, on the 8th of June, 1880, just as my manuscript was going into the publishers' hands.

PREFACE.

IT is proper that I should set before the reader the motives which prompted me to write this book; the scope and divisions of the subject, and the principal authorities from which I have derived my information.

I have always, since a sojourn of more than two years in Mexico, from 1846 to 1848, been greatly interested in Spanish history. The valiant deeds of the *Conquistadores* led me back to the mother country of such heroes, and to the earlier days of its romantic and brilliant annals, especially under the dominion of the Arab-Moors. The interest thus excited was greatly increased by a brief visit to Spain in 1870, with a special purpose to obtain those glimpses of scenery, and of classic localities, which are to the student revelations, giving system to what he has read, and enlightening him in his later studies. In that romantic land, Nature has played a large part in the history: the mountains and rivers teem

with the remains and the memories of the
olden time.   No one can thoroughly comprehend the varied drama of the Spanish
annals without visiting the scenes in which
the principal events were enacted.

When Washington Irving had written his
"History of Mahomet and his Successors,"
which brings the Arabians to the Pillars of
Hercules, and leaves them there contemplat-
ing the invasion of Spain, he closed his labors
with these words: "Whether it will be our
lot to resume the theme, to cross with the
Moslem hosts the strait of Hercules, and to
narrate their memorable conquest of Gothic
Spain, is one of those uncertainties of mortal
life and aspirations of literary zeal which be-
guile us with agreeable dreams, but too often
end in disappointment."   He did not accomplish this task.   In some desultory Spanish
papers he has presented a few legends of the
conquest, and in his "Conquest of Granada"
he has given a splendid but fanciful picture
of the last act of that eventful history.   Had
he been able to carry out his wishes, it is
hardly necessary to say that I should not have
presumed to write these volumes; but, as he
left the ground untouched, I have endeavored,
not without unfeigned diffidence, to present

a succinct and connected narrative of a great event, which exerted a powerful influence over a long and important period in the early history of modern Europe, and with which the general reader is not as familiar as with the other portions of western history. This period is synchronous in the West with most of the time of which Gibbon has given us the annals of eastern Europe, from the eighth to the fifteenth century. The history of the Eastern Empire from the reign of Heraclius to the fall of Constantinople is familiar to all: the Mohammedan dynasties in Spain are known to few; to most persons they are enveloped in a party-colored mist, and the glimpses are like the scenes in the "Arabian Nights' Entertainments," charming but unreal.

Another motive which presented itself to my mind is to be found in the very romantic and picturesque character of the subject, so long shrouded in these shining mists of legend, poetry, and tradition. Here the duty of the historian is not only to find and collate the facts, but to interpret fiction, which is often founded on fact. My interest has increased at every step; and the desire has grown stronger to reclaim the men and the events from legends and allegories, and re-

store them to veritable history. Besides, I
have been pleased to find myself more and
more confident, at every stage of my labors,
that the story would thus lose little of its pic-
turesqueness when the truth was told.   In
cases of doubt, or where there are conflicting
statements of a fact, I have not hesitated to
present the legends, offering, where it seemed
necessary, my judgment on the question, and
sometimes, where the interpretation seemed
clear, leaving the reader to make it for
himself. Sedulous to avoid partisanship, I
have followed those Spanish scholars who, like
the learned and judicious Gayangos, have
honestly attempted to repair the great wrong
done by many historians in ignoring or ma-
ligning the Moslems of Spain.

These were the principal motives which
prompted me to write. A word is necessary
as to the scope and character of the subject
when brought under the rules of historical
composition. When I began to study the
history of Spain, I was surprised to find that
it was in reality not one history, but two,
clearly distinct from each other, and each requiring a separate and different treatment.
Let me illustrate and explain.

In the history of England we have a suc-

cessive movement of races, in a normal and
logical order, according to the migrations of
men from the great generatrix in Asia. First
came the Kelts and Kymry, who occupied the
country. These were invaded and conquered
by the Romans; and when they were abandoned by the imperial legions, the Teutonic
wave swept across the channel in the form of
the Anglo-Saxons, who obtained a lasting
supremacy in the islands. The Danes and
the Normans were still Teutonic tribes of the
Scandinavian branch moving westward, the
former not making good their hold upon
England; the latter modifying and even
thus strengthening the Anglo-Saxon power;
and thus we reach the end and the present
status of the races of men in English history. In France the problem was similar.
The original Kelts, called Galli, who owned
the land were conquered and ruled by the
Romans. At the breaking up of the western
empire, as in England, they were invaded by
Teutons, — Goths and Burgundians, — who
were in turn overmastered by the fierce confederation of the Franks, — themselves Teutons, — and thus the tale of races is completed:
in the opinion of Augustin Thierry, the Gauls
and Franks are still "two nations on one

soil, inimical in their reminiscences, irreconcilable in their projects."

When we turn to Spain we find the same steps of invasion and conquest. The Celtiberians were dominated for four hundred years by the ubiquitous Romans, who in turn were overrun by northern Teutonic tribes; first the Alans, Vandals, and Suevi, and, in the second wave, — as in the other cases, — the Goths, who, full of Teutonic energy, conquered the whole Peninsula, oppressed alike the large population of Hispano-Romans, and the scattered, roving bands of their immediate Teutonic predecessors, and established a grand Visigothic empire in the fifth century, which extended over Aquitania, Septimania, and the whole of Spain.

Thus far the history of Spain closely resembles that of England and that of France. But, after this, another important and unexpected element appears: the logical order is no longer preserved. The permanence of the Gothic monarchy seemed assured, when strange rumors began to come that a Shemitic race, entirely unknown to the Goths, inhabiting a country of which the West was in almost as entire ignorance as if it belonged to some other sphere, had been united by the power of a new creed, and had declared a purpose to conquer the world. After magnificent conquests at the East, they were now coming with unexampled celerity to the West. They had converted and gathered into their armies the North African tribes; then they crossed the strait, so long guarded by the Pillars of Hercules, and in one decisive battle overthrew the unprepared and effeminate Goths, and made themselves masters of the Peninsula. A little more than a century after the death of the Prophet, Spain became a supreme Khalifate, independent of the East, strong and opulent, and ready to introduce the best culture in letters and science to western Europe.

I have said they conquered the entire Peninsula. To be more exact, it must be observed that there was a little congeries of Christians, who, as fugitives from the fatal battle, were huddling together like frightened sheep in the northwest; first faintly hoping for life; then resisting the attempts to dislodge them, and finally, as they grew in strength and numbers, marching out to attack the Moslem invaders. The conquest of Spain by the Arab-Moors was hardly established before it was thus confronted by the elements of a reconquest.

No sooner, therefore, had I contemplated writing the story of the Arabian conquest, than I said to myself, the history of Spain is essentially a dual history, a conquest and a reconquest. It must therefore be written from two distinct points of view. The historian of the conquest must take his place beside Musa and Tarik, Abdu-r-rahmán and Al-hakem. He must make his stand with Mohammed An-násir at the battle of Las Navas, and be expelled from Granada with Boabdil el Chico.

The historian of the reconquest must hide with Pelayo in La Cueva de Covadonga; must besiege Toledo with Alfonso VI., and join Alfonso VIII. in the crusade of Las Navas. He must be wise with Alfonso el Sabio; he must be in the councils of *los Reyes Catolicos*, and move to the conquest of Granada in the stately train of Ferdinand and Isabella.

Of the two, the conquest is far the more concentrated, simple, and compact; rapid in its development, brilliant as it approaches its culmination, precipitate in its decline. Its annals are full of Arabian romance and Oriental imagery. The reconquest is a larger and more diversified, but not less attractive theme. It may be divided into numerous periods, which would require, in their details, many distinct, almost monographic works. The closing period is the subject of Prescott's "Ferdinand and Isabella," and Irving's "Conquest of Granada." Thus the history of Spain is not a current chronicle, but a composite structure.

I have only attempted to depict the conquest. In laying out my plan, it seemed necessary to present an outline of the rise and progress of Islám as the great motive, and then to give more in detail the advance upon Spain, the treason of Ilyan; the crossing of the strait, the sad fate of Roderik after the initial and final battle in the plains of Medina Sidonia, and the spread of the Arab-Moors like summer fire over the Peninsula. I have dwelt at some length upon the great battle between Abdu-r-rahmán and Charles Martel near Tours, and the later efforts of Charlemagne, in spite of "the dolorous rout" of Roncesvalles, to erect a Spanish march in the northeast. The firm establishment of the Ommeyan dynasty brings the material conquest to its completion; but, beyond this, I have brought this dominion to its culminating point under Al-hakem II., and have exhibited its decline, stayed for a brief space by the

splendid usurpation of power by Al-mansúr,
analogous to that of the Peppins and Charleses
in France.

Then, with much less detail, I have only
proposed to give an outline of the remaining
history, which tells of the extinction of the
Ommeyades, the breaking up of their dominion
into petty kingdoms, the incursions and temporary sway of the Almoravides and Almo-
hades, the establishment of the kingdom of
Granada, and its final extinction in 1492.
These I have not intended to elaborate;
accepting my premises, the reader will see
that the chief interest of this later history
belongs to the reconquest, and must be left to
its historian. I beg to state this plainly, lest
any reader should be disappointed who looks
for careful details in this part of the history.

As to the remaining portion of the work, I
have sought to protect myself by calling it by
its right name, "A sketch of the civilization
which they achieved and imparted to Europe."
It is only a *sketch*, conveying what Bacon calls
" forth-showing instances," which will indicate
the great value of their achievements in every
department of culture, and claim for them a
credit, which, for many reasons, has long been
withheld from them.

With regard to the authorities which have been consulted and referred to, I shall not present a bibliographical list, but only mention those of greatest importance, leaving the rest to the foot-notes. The Arabian history, in chronological order, is most readily consulted, although presented briefly and often in a desultory way, in "The History of the Mohammedan Dynasties in Spain," collated rather than written by Ahmed Ibn Mohammed Al Makkarí; translated and annotated by Don Pascual de Gayangos, an elegant and critical Arabic scholar. The work was published by the Oriental Translation Fund, London, 1843. The notes of Gayangos are more voluminous and far more valuable than his author's work; and the reader regrets, at every page, that he did not expend his great labors upon an original history, which would have rendered such volumes as mine unnecessary, and, I may add, impertinent. How much I have owed to Gayangos and his translation, will appear on many pages of this work.

Next to this, and in parts far more detailed, is J. A. Condé's "Historia de la Dominacion de los Arabes en España," of which Gayangos speaks as "the only complete history of the

Spanish Moslems drawn entirely from Arabian sources;" but, owing to untoward circumstances, it is full of mistakes and repetitions, against which the student must be constantly on his guard. It supplies, however, to the cautious reader very much which is given briefly, or passed over in silence, by Al Makkarí.

I have sparingly consulted the work of Cardonne, "Histoire de l'Afrique et de l'Espagne," which for some time enjoyed great celebrity, but which the later researches have demonstrated to contain many errors and much carelessness.

So much for the current histories from Arabian sources. If we seek for contemporary writers, they are very few: documents, of course, there are none. Of the time just before the conquest we have the writings of Isidorus Hispalensis, bishop of Seville; especially his "Historia de Regibus Gothorum, Uvandalorum et Suevorum," which presents a rather highly colored picture of the Gothic rule, but is valuable in that he was an eyewitness of much that he describes. He died in 636.

Next in order is Isidorus Pacensis, Bishop of Béja or Badajos, who was a contemporary of the conquest, and who may be regarded as a continuator of Isidor of Seville. Notices of his writings will be found in the text of this work.

The other, and the only other, exactly contemporary record is found in the " Chronicon Biclarense," by el Abad de Vallclara, San Juan. Of this there is a " continuation " by a later hand.

The works of all these earlier writers were collected in the eighteenth century by Don Enrique Florez, in a work called " España Sagrada; Theatro geographico-historico de la Iglesia de España." The writers are chiefly ecclesiastics of different periods, and the purpose of the work is to give a history of the church in the various dioceses. The work is in forty-seven volumes; and so intimate were the relations of the church to the state in Spain, that the chronicles are invaluable to the secular historian. Copies of this work are in the Astor Library, and in Mr. Ticknor's collection in the Boston Public Library.

For the eastern history in connection with the conquest, I have consulted, among other works, the "Annales Moslemici" of Abulfeda.

Notices of all the writers on Spanish history are to be found in a voluminous work in

two parts, entitled "Bibliotheca Hispana Vetus," and "Hispana Nova." It is in four folio
volumes, published at Madrid in 1783, by Don
Nicholas Antonio, of Seville. The copy which
I have consulted is the property of the Smith-
sonian Institution, in the keeping of the Con-
gressional Library at Washington. I believe
it is rare.

With regard to the numerous Spanish historians of later times, I would say that I have
been very glad to avail myself of their aid, for
various and often widely different reasons.
The "Historia General de España," of Padre
Juan Mariana, which has been edited and annotated by numerous scholars since he wrote
it, is chiefly of value because he was a Jesuit
priest, and regards the conquest from the point
of view of the church; but when the question
was of the claims of the church herself, he was
bold enough to be honest, and his history fell
for a time under the ban. He died in 1623,
at the great age of eighty-seven. In his urgent claims for the recognition of Spanish
greatness, one cannot fail to see a regretful
suspicion that her halcyon days were passing
away.

The learned work of Masdeu, "Historia
Critica de España y de la Cultura Española,"

written at the close of the last century, well deserves its title. It was the first critical history of Spain ever written; he seeks to penetrate every doubtful question, and his work must be consulted not only for its facts and philosophy, but for its spirit. Arabian Spain is treated in the volumes from the twelfth to the fifteenth. Always critical, Masdeu is often censorious.

I have for the current history availed myself most frequently, however, of the excellent work of Don Modesto La Fuente, chiefly the first ten volumes. It bears the name, "Historia General de España, desde los tiempos mas remotos hasta nuestros dias." In the narrative it is clear and interesting; philosophical in moral deductions, free from superstition and bias, laborious in the collection of authorities, and liberal and fearless in its judgments.

The reader will observe that I have not scrupled to quote from these authors even as to early facts. This has been sometimes because I had no other authority to offer, sometimes to corroborate an opinion, but more generally to exhibit the view influenced by the time, profession, and circumstances of the writer, — as, for example, the zealous bigotry

of Mariana, the occasional censoriousness of
Masdeu, and the philosophical conclusions of
La Fuente. I have frequently quoted from
Ford's Hand-book (original edition). This is
no ordinary guide-book, but a treasure-house
of knowledge, statistical, archæological, philosophical, and æsthetic. The author knew more
of Spain and Spanish affairs than any other
foreigner, and than most Spanish scholars.

Nothing I think remains to be said but that,
while I have honestly endeavored to sift the
materials at my command, presenting in every
case, and perhaps sometimes unnecessarily,
my authorities, my chief purpose has been to
write a work for the general public, who have
not these authorities within easy reach, and
to put in popular form before American and
English readers a history of great interest in
itself, parts of which have been written before
in our mother tongue, but which, I believe, as
a connected whole, has never before appeared
in an English dress.

Painfully conscious that there are many
faults of omission, for which I must plead lack
of space, and knowing also how much better
the work might have been done had it been
undertaken by one of our distinguished historical writers, such as it is I commit it to the

reading world, in the fair dress given to it
by my eminent publishers, with the hope that,
whatever its defects, it will still be found instructive and entertaining to many hitherto
unacquainted with the attractive story.

THE LEHIGH UNIVERSITY,
    DEC. 1, 1880.

CONTENTS OF VOLUME I.

BOOK I.

FROM MECCA TO THE PILLARS OF HERCULES.

CHAPTER I.

MOHAMMED AND HIS MISSION.

CHAPTER II.

THE CREED OF THE PROPHET.

CHAPTER VIII.

SOME ALLEGORICAL LEGENDS.

BOOK III.

THE ARABIAN INVASION OF SPAIN.

CHAPTER I.

THE GREAT EXPEDITION OF TARIK EL TUERTO.

CHAPTER II.

THE ARMIES IN ARRAY; THE FIELD OF BATTLE.

CHAPTER III.

THE BATTLE IN THE PLAINS OF MEDINA SIDONIA, COMMONLY CALLED THE BATTLE OF THE GUADALETE.

CHAPTER IV.

THE RAPID AND BRILLIANT PROGRESS OF TARIK.

CHAPTER V.

MUSA CROSSES THE STRAIT AND CAPTURES MANY CITIES.

CHAPTER VI.

MUSA'S TREATMENT OF TARIK.

BOOK IV.

THE ADVERSE FORTUNES OF THE MOSLEM CONQUERORS.

CHAPTER I.

MUSA AND TARIK ORDERED TO DAMASCUS.

CHAPTER II.

THE PUNISHMENT OF MUSA.

BOOK V.

HISTORY

OF

THE CONQUEST OF SPAIN

BY

THE ARAB-MOORS.

THE CONQUEST OF SPAIN BY THE ARAB–MOORS.

———•———

BOOK I.

FROM MECCA TO THE PILLARS OF HERCULES.

CHAPTER I.

MOHAMMED AND HIS MISSION.

IN undertaking to write the history of a conquest, it is necessary, at the outset, to present the personality, individual and social, of the people who achieved it, — their habits, customs, and modes of thought and expression, — and to set forth, with such attention to detail as may be requisite to a clear understanding, the grand *motive* of their purposes and exploits.

The people who achieved the conquest of Spain in the eighth century were the Arabians, reinforced by such tribes of Northern Africa as they converted and gathered in their train. Their principal motive is found in the religion of Mohammed, the faith of Islám.

A few pages of this volume must therefore be devoted to the early history of the Arabians, — their rise from ignorance and inaction at the call of their prophet; their eager adoption of Islám; and the principles and formularies of that remarkable creed, the inspiring influence of which carried them from their primitive seats with a powerful momentum to the East and to the West, and with a constantly developing purpose to conquer the entire world.

On Friday, the 16th of July, A.D. 622, Mohammed, in great danger of his life at the hands of his wrathful kinsmen, the Koreish, fled from Mecca. After concealments and adventures on his perilous

El Hijra, or the emigration. journey, he arrived at the city called Yathreb, with the inhabitants of which some of his adherents had already formed a secret league. It was also on Friday, two weeks later, that he entered this protecting town. From the former day, called el Hijra, or the emigration, the Mohammedans date the beginning of their calendar. From the coincidence of the two they established that day of the week, Friday, as Yawn Al Joma, the day of assembly for prayer.[1]

Yathreb, which received the persecuted prophet, became *Medinatu-'l-Nabi*, the city of the prophet, or, more concisely, Medina, *the city* by pre-eminence. The Arabian chroniclers also speak of it as *Medina esh-sherefa*, the noble city.

---

[1] The Korán, note to ch. lxii. An additional reason given by Al Beidâwi for the adoption of Friday is that God finished his creation on that day. It is a common superstition that Friday is the most fortunate day in the week, while with us it is the most unlucky. The annual calendar before Mohammed was computed from an Ethiopian war, "the arrival of the lords of the Alfil, or elephant." Condé, Dominacion de los Arabes en España, I., ch. ii.

The event thus celebrated is the greatest in the Arabian annals, — one of the greatest in the history of mankind. It changed the condition of the Eastern world; it revolutionized Asia, and was fraught with the most momentous consequences to Its consequences. Southern and Western Europe. Just eighty-nine years after the flight of Mohammed, when Syria, Persia, and Northern Africa had all been subdued, a Moslem host stood upon the southern coast of the Strait of Gibraltar, ready for the invasion of Spain.

It is in view of these rapid results that an Arabian writer says: "For our part we consider Andalus as the prize of the race won by the horsemen who, at the utmost speed of their chargers, subdued the regions of the East and the West, . . . and that country became the arena in which their noble steeds raced, and the halting-place wherein their camels laid down their burden and grazed." [1]

Never in history had so sudden a change been wrought in a nation, and such marvellous results produced by the genius and fortunes of a single man.

The origin of the Arabians is enveloped in the swathing-bands of tradition. Their own The origin of the Arabians. account is that they descend from two sources. The pure Arabs, Arab-al-Ariba, trace their origin to Joctán, also called Kahtán, the son of Eber; while the so-called naturalized tribes are said to have sprung from Adnan, a descendant of Ishmael, the son of Hagar, who, according to the Korán, was commissioned by God, with his father Abraham, to take

[1] Al Makkari, Mohammedan Dynasties in Spain, translated by Don Pascual de Gayangos, Vol. I. pp. 13, 17, 250.

charge of the Kaaba and keep it clean.[1]   The two
streams were, however, mingled by the marriage of
Ishmael with a daughter of Modad, who was
ninth in descent from Joctán, and of the
family that ruled in Hejaz.   The descendants of Ishmael were called Arab-al-Mostareba, or naturalized
Arabs,[2] and were proud of their lineage through him
from Abraham, one of the four great prophets to be
acknowledged by Mohammed, and "the father of
many people."   The bar sinister in their escutcheon
did not detract from the honor of their ancestor; but
the blood thus derived seemed eminently adapted to
the nature of their country and their conditions of life.

Two streams.

All their antecedents made them ready to receive
a new creed and a new form of government from the
hands of the remarkable man who now proposed
and expounded them as a direct revelation from
Heaven.   The voice of Mohammed, like a current of
electricity, galvanized the incoherent mass of dark
puppets, and with this vital force came coherence and
a new nationality.

Let us dwell for a moment upon their condition
before this great transformation came.   Before the
advent of the prophet Arabia was of little
importance to history.   Hardly known to
the western world, it was to the more eastern nations *Ereb*, the far West.   It had thus been placed
between two distinct civilizations; and if it had
shared the benefits of neither, it had to a great de-

The age of ignorance.

---

[1] The Korán, ch. lxii.

[2] Sale's Preliminary Discourse contains genealogical tables of
both.

gree escaped the national vices, as well as the cruel devastations of both the East and the West. The reports of its genial climate, and the fertility of a portion of its territory, afterwards known as Arabia Felix, had reached the ears and tempted the cupidity of Alexander the Great, who, according to Dionysius Perieges, formed the design, just after the return from his eastern expedition, to establish his royal residence and court there, as a more central position from which to govern his newly acquired dominions. But his early and sudden death put an end to this scheme of conquest, and his successors did not further attempt it.

Its peninsular form, its desert expanses in the central portion, and its stony barriers at the north, largely protected it against the incursions of the later Greeks and the Romans; portions of Hejaz, of which Yemen was the most fruitful, produced enough for their subsistence. It was thus a sheltered and secure Geography home, in which, surrounded by the tumults of Arabia. of a world in arms, threatened by universal subjugation to Roman power, a race was being trained and fostered for some mighty enterprise, whenever a man should arise who could inspire, unite, and lead them. Assyria, Media, Persia, Egypt, had been overrun by Grecian and by Roman armies, but it was the boast of the Arabians that their country had preserved her unity and independence since the Flood.[1]

[1] See Sale's "Preliminary Discourse to the Korán," in which the numerous efforts to conquer Arabia and her successful resistance are set forth in detail.

It was mainly due to this freedom of admixture with other nations, that they could also glory in the possession of an ancient and powerful language, very little contaminated by surrounding dialects, and capable of a varied and noble literature ; of which, indeed, before the birth of Mohammed they already had a promising beginning. The poetical capacity of their language, at once harmonious, copious, and expressive, is displayed in the *Moallakât*, seven of the most celebrated poems which had obtained prizes at the annual fairs, and which, inscribed in letters of gold upon Egyptian silk, were so called because they were *suspended* on the walls in the Kaaba at Mecca ; they were also known as Modhahabât, the golden verses. These poems are of great historical value, in that they contain pictures of love and war, and present striking glimpses of the individual habits and social customs of the Arabs in the period when they were written and applauded.

Language and poetry.

The Arabians were divided, by the diversity of their territory, — desert, mountain, and fertile spots, — into numerous *kabilahs*, or tribes, each under the patriarchal government of its own sheik.[1] These tribes, incited by jealousy and greed of gain, were making cunning and constant raids upon each other, and were yet romantically endeavoring to reconcile the stratagems of banditti with a factitious and often embarrassing hospitality. This hospitality was cherished as a popular trait, and sent down as a

Kabilahs, or tribes.

[1] Sheyk, or sheik, means an *elder*. In later times it has been used as a title of respect — only applied to Moslems — corresponding to our *Mister*.

national inheritance, inculcated and carried by the Arab wherever he went. Respect for guests is enjoined by the Korán. A stranger came to the first house or tent, and a carpet was spread for him and a meal prepared. The breaking of bread and the eating of salt together were a pact of peace, even between enemies.

The social instinct and the popular needs led to the building of towns, as the gathering-places of caravans and the markets of trade; and thus a new division was formed into town-people and tent-people. The former could not fail to make some approaches toward civilization, in domestic comforts, and in the way of local and municipal law; but the borders of the deserts, the oases upon the sands, and the mountain passes, were alive with roving bands, most of them on horseback, half-warriors, half-herdsmen, tending scant flocks and herds, and making predatory war upon the neighboring tribes or taking violent tribute from the caravans.

Town-people and tent-people.

These "sons of the desert" were the primitive Bedouins (Bedawees), who lived, in their long, low, black or striped tents of camel's hair, — like those which may be seen to-day in the East, — the life which had been predicted for the descendants of the bond-maiden: they were "wild men"; their hand was "against every man, and every man's hand against" them.

The town-people had little influence for good upon the tent-people; while the condition and actions of the latter could not fail to retard the civilization which comes with streets and market-places. The

Bedouin life seemed an unmitigated evil to Arabia, but it was not so; it had its excellent uses. This wild, roving existence kept the race from stagnation, of which the town life was in danger. The muscles of the tent-people were always in full exercise. Thus the Arabians of all tribes and classes presented an excellent type of primitive manhood. They were strong, sinewy, and active in body, and especially remarkable for their powers of endurance. They were extremely frugal. Their principal food was bread, dates, milk, and, as an occasional relish, camel's flesh, to which some of their physicians attributed their vindictive and bloodthirsty disposition,—"that creature being the most malicious and tenacious of anger."[1] Constantly using weapons in the chase and in their quarrels, they became from boyhood skilful in handling sword, lance, bow, and dagger. They were more at home on horseback than on foot; the horse was their friend, companion, child; they lived and talked with him, and he was not only the recipient of their affection, but the creature of their superstition.[2]

They were receptive and quick in mind, and gifted

Natural gifts. with a poetic imagination. They were thus unconsciously but eminently ready for a better and wider fortune when the auspicious day should dawn; they were capable of aspiring to the

---

[1] Sale's Preliminary Discourse, sect. i.

[2] Horses, according to Mohammed, had lucky and unlucky marks and colors. "The best horses are black with white foreheads and upper lips. . . . Prosperity is with sorrel horses." — *Mishkât-el-Masâbceh,* II. 250, 252, quoted by Poole, Arabian Nights, ch. ix. p. 50.

conquest of the world. What they now needed was that union which comes with an attractive aim, to silence their jarring discords, to awaken their cupidity, to confederate their tribes into a united and prosperous nation.

One religious nucleus was acknowledged and reverenced by every Arabian; it was that magical wellspring in the province of Hejaz, which, by an *The well Zem-zem.* expressive onomatopœia, to represent the gurgling of the waters, they called Zem-zem.[1] It had, according to their tradition, miraculously burst forth from the desert sand, to slake the thirst of their progenitor, Ishmael, when he and his mother Hagar were fainting in the fierce noontide heat. It was believed to have miraculous virtues; it was used medicinally, and sprinkled upon grave-clothes. To those who could not come to the well, the waters were carried by pilgrims, and were a most acceptable present.

To this sacred and healing spring, laying aside at stated times their differences and animosities, the tribes congregated from far and near to worship; and a city rose, called from these assemblages *Mecca, "the place of concourse."* Mecca (Mekkeh), *the place of concourse.* The attraction was purely of religious sentiment, for it happens that Mecca, although cinctured at some distance by fertile country, is, as to its immediate locality, very barren; and of Zem-zem it must be said that

---

[1] Sale's Preliminary Discourse, sect. i. This is the generally received derivation. There is, however, a legend to the effect that when the well-spring burst forth, the flow was so rapid that Hagar could not drink until Abraham commanded it to glide more gently, using the word "zem-zem" for that purpose.

it is only the least brackish of the numerous bitter springs in and around the city.

In a consecrated enclosure, fondly fabled to have been laid out by Abraham and Ishmael, stood the *Kaaba*, or square, built of unhewn stones laid without mortar, the chief temple of the Arabian worship, before and after the coming of the prophet. The Kaaba and the black stone. In the Kaaba there was enshrined a black stone of mysterious origin and virtue. It fell from Paradise when Adam fell. According to their credulous traditions, it had been once white, but had changed its color, partly on account of the sins of men, and partly from the kisses of its worshippers.[1] It was set in silver, and was placed in the southeastern corner of the temple, about four feet from the ground. This was the palladium of the nation, and was confided to the watchful care of priests selected from the kabilah of the Koreish, the most elevated of their tribes in national rank. The chief family of the Koreish was that of Hisham or Hashem. This kabilah also had the guardianship of the sacred language in which was set forth the formularies for the worship of the three hundred and sixty graven and molten images — one deposited by each tribe — collected in the Kaaba. The sanctity of the Kaaba and the reverence for the holy stone were confirmed by Mohammed in his new creed;

---

[1] "Or perhaps from the frequent burnings of the temple." — Dozy, *L'Islamisme*, p. 8. Travellers who have seen the stone declare it to be of volcanic basalt, with dottings of feldspar. It has been frequently broken, and is now in a dozen pieces, which are collected as nearly as possible in the original form. Many consider it an aerolith.

and wherever Arabian arms penetrated, the Faithful were to turn to them in their prayers.

Such a religion as the Arabians had in these days of ignorance they claimed to have received from Abraham and Ishmael. In truth, it was a very vague, desultory, and discordant creed, The early religion. drawn chiefly from nature, and poetized by the ardent fancy of the votaries. As with the Greeks and Romans, the powers of nature were deified; but this idolatrous process seems to have been, as with other nations, a departure from a primitive monotheism. They had once believed in a single God, whom they still called Allah Taâla, the Most High, but their fears and their fancies led them to propitiate the forces of earth, air, fire, and water; and thus they lapsed into idolatry. The minor deities they called Al Ilahât, the goddesses; then they extended their worship to the stars, — *Saba*, the host of heaven, — upon the rising and setting of which they based their prognostics of agriculture and navigation. Soon these idols became more sacred than Allah Taâla; for not only, when the gifts were made, did the idol receive an equal share with Allah, but if it was found that the latter had fared best, his better share was exchanged with that of the idol.

They adored angels, and worshipped their images; they believed the angels to be interceders for them with their very distant Most High God. Three of these — Allat, Al Uzza, and Manah — were called by pre-eminence the daughters of God; and one of these was adopted by each tribe as a patron saint: Allat by the kabilah of Thakif, Al Uzza by the

Koreish and Kenana, and Mana by the tribes of
Hodhail and Khozâah.

We find that as idolatry multiplies objects of
adoration, it creates diversities of belief.   There were
many conflicting sects among them, and religious
intolerance found numerous illustrations.   Some of
these, not content with the antiquity of the faith
which came from Abraham and Ishmael, cherished
Noah's   not only idols, but antediluvian idols, against
preaching.   which Noah had preached in those evil
days.   "They devised," says the prophet, in speaking of the days before the flood, "a dangerous plot
against Noah, and the chief men said to the others,
'Ye shall by no means leave your gods, neither shall
ye forsake *Wadd* nor *Saiva,* nor *Yaghuth* nor *Nesr,* . . .
and Noah said, ' Lord, leave not any of the family of
the unbelievers on the earth.' " [1]   These were the antediluvian idols which, although they had tended to the
destruction of the world, the Arabs still cherished.   The
denunciations of Noah were repeated by Mohammed.
Wadd was represented in the likeness of a man, Saiva
as a woman, Yaguth as a lion, and Nesr as an eagle.

But this was not the extent of the idolatry from
which Mohammed was coming to reclaim them.   Besides these public gods they seem to have created
at will and fancy their household gods : these *lares
et penates* were very numerous, and some of them
very grotesque.   A portion of the tribe of Hanifeh
— which was afterwards to furnish one of the most
renowned and orthodox doctors and expounders of
Mohammedan law [2] — worshipped a lump of dough.

[1] Korán, ch. lxxi.   [2] Abu Hanifeh an Nóman Ibn Thabet.

In their own way they were devout. Prayer was straitly enjoined upon all at stated times during the day; burnt sacrifices were prescribed, and pilgrimages were made to a spot near Harran, where special sacrifices were offered.

Their treatment of women was barbarous in the extreme. Women were virtually slaves, instruments for the comfort and pleasure of their masters. Barbarous treatment of It was considered a misfortune for men women. to have daughters. Some, to keep up the number needed in their social economy, were permitted to live; some were killed at birth; others were left, in doubtful probation, until the age of six; and then, if not needed as substitutes for those removed by accident or disease, after this long period of harrowing expectancy, the mother heard from the father's lips the fatal words: "Perfume her and adorn her that I may carry her to her mothers," and she was buried alive; or, if frantic prayers prevailed, and the child was well and strong, she was clothed in a garment of wool or hair, and sent to the desert to keep camels or sheep.[1]

The difficulty encountered by Mohammed in putting a stop to these inhuman practices and in overcoming this repugnance is illustrated in many passages of the Korán. "When any of them is told the news of the birth of a female, his face becometh black, and he is deeply affected: he hideth himself from the people, because of the ill-tidings that have been told him, whether he shall keep it with disgrace, or whether he shall bury it in the dust; do

[1] Sale's Preliminary Discourse, sect. v.

they not make an ill judgment?"[1]   "When the girl
who has been buried alive shall be asked for what
crime she was put to death, . . . every soul shall
know what it hath wrought."[2]   "They attribute
daughters unto God (far be it from him), but unto
themselves children of the sex which they desire."[3]

Their heterogeneous creed contained more than a
tincture of Judaism; for, elsewhere perse-

Judaism.

cuted and despised, more than once the children of Israel in considerable bodies had taken shelter
in Arabia; the heirs of promise were beholden to the
descendants of Hagar. Especially had they sought
that protection after the devastation of Judæa by the
Romans. There they had made many proselytes;
princes, or sheyks, and entire tribes, embracing the law
of Moses. Thus tenets of the Jewish faith and practices of the Jewish worship had been insensibly
adopted by the idolatrous Arabians, and led them
towards that belief in one only God which Mohammed was to enounce as the vital principle of his
religion.

Christianity was not unknown or inoperative
among them. Tradition asserts that it had been
preached in Arabia by St. Paul, and Ara-

Christianity.

bians are mentioned in that motley crowd
which heard the tongues and beheld with astonishment the outpouring of the Spirit on the first Christian Pentecost. In the beginning of the third century
large numbers of Christians, fleeing from the perse-

[1] Korán, ch. xvi.
[2] Ibid., ch. lxxxi., a chapter of comminations.
[3] Ibid.

cutions of Rome and the disorders of the Eastern Empire, settled in what was then pre-eminently the "country of liberty,"[1] where they were even allowed to hold public disputations with the Jews. And when, under Constantine, Christianity became the accepted creed of the all-absorbing Roman state, there was really established an *imperium in imperio*; its claims were more widely known and more powerfully championized, and its doctrines were seriously discussed by the wisest Arabian minds.[2]

It would be more difficult to trace the influence of the Magian religion of Persia upon the Arabian mind, but the vicinity of its seats and the intellectual force of its system are known to have been felt and acknowledged long before the coming of Mohammed: this very contiguity was also an element of hostility, and the Persians looked with contempt upon such specimens of the wandering Arabians as they came in contact with.[3]

Magian tenets.

I have been thus particular in describing this untutored man, and presenting the conditions of his home life before the advent of the prophet, that we may see him in the rough, — in the age of ignorance, — and then observe him as he passes through the

[1] Sale's Preliminary Discourse, sect. ii.

[2] Ibid., sect. i.

[3] It seems to me to be a clear case of judging the many by the few, — the men of the city by the frontiermen, — which led an envoy to Yesdejird, King of Persia, to say of the Arabians before the coming of Mohammed, that "their food was green lizards; they buried their daughters alive; some of them feasted on dead carcasses and drank blood, while others slew their relations. They made no distinction between that which is lawful and that which is unlawful." — MALCOLM, *History of Persia*, I. 172.

processes of instruction and refinement, until we can place in strong contrast his achievements under the inspiring voice and at the command of the man who called himself, and whom they believed to be, the prophet of God, the seal, the greatest and last of the prophets.

It was upon this condition of the Arabian people, and in this period of their history, — called, in contrast with that which was to follow, the Age

The coming of Mohammed.

of Ignorance, — that Mohammed appeared like a splendid luminary. There was independence, but little union ; there was even fraternity and a pride of common ancestry, but no real nationality.

His gifted and philosophic mind grasped at once the data of the problem. From acute observation in his travels as a trader he formed a just idea of the state of the world, — the torpor of the East, the effeminacy of the Eastern Empire, the barbarism of the West. He studied silently and carefully the capabilities and needs of his own people, and with a prophetic eye discerned, as in a vision, the glorious future which lay open to their well-directed enterprise and ardor. In this way the wisest men are prophets without inspiration ; we call them far-seeing ; they plan and devise, and reason to distant and magnificent results.

Mohammed was born in Mecca, in the province of Hejaz, about the year 571 of our era. He was of one

His family.

of the principal families of the Koreish, that of Hashem ; and a direct descendant, through ten unbroken generations, of that Fehr, surnamed Koreish, from whose loins a new prophet, should one arise, would be expected to spring.[1] Abd-al Motalleb, his grandfather, had thirteen sons, of whom Abdullah, the father of the prophet, was the seventh. Mohammed was the only son of his father.[2] His uncle Abu Taleb, the first son of Abd-al Motalleb, was the father of that Ali who became the son-in-law of Mohammed, and the most valiant champion of the new faith.

It is worthy of note in this place that Al Abbas, the second son of Abd-al Motalleb, was the progenitor of the later family and powerful dynasty of the Abbassides, the Khalifs of Baghdad.

The mother of Mohammed, Amina, was also, by a lateral branch, of the same stock of the Koreish, through Kelab, the ancestor at four removes of the prophet's grandfather.

The name of the prophet, Mohammed, which means "greatly praised," lends some slight color to the stories which have been told of the miracles which accompanied his birth and infancy, but which, it is only just to say, were not creations of his own fancy.[3]

Left an orphan at an early age, he first received the care of his grandfather, and afterwards that of his uncle Abu Taleb. Thus his cousin Ali became

---

[1] See the genealogical table, Sale's Preliminary Discourse, sect. i.

[2] "Obiit [Abdullah], unicum filium relinquens, nostrum Muhammedem." — ABULFEDA, Annales Moslemici, I.

[3] "Some authors tell us that when the angels ripped up his belly [when he was an infant], they took out his heart, and squeezed out of it the black drop which is, they believe, the consequence of original sin . . . being found in the heart of every person descended from Adam, except only the Virgin Mary and her son Jesus." — OCKLEY, History of the Saracens, p. 8.

to him as a brother. This intimacy had much to
do with the early fortunes of Islam and the fate of
Ali, upon whom the magnetism of Mohammed seems
to have been more powerful than upon all others.

Like most men who have swayed the wills and determined the conduct of masses of men Mohammed
His person- was endowed with a remarkable personality. ality; he was "greatly praised" by all with
whom he came in contact. Women loved him and
men trusted him; and, apart from his personal
charms, one strong element of popularity is found
in the fact that he represented all classes and denounced caste. He was soldier, trader, law-maker,
high-priest, and prophet, and he sought through his
creed to elevate all men to an equality in the sight
of Allah.

His features shine clearly through the mists of the
intervening centuries. His person was well formed:
he had an oval face; hooked nose; long and arched
eyebrows, nearly meeting; large, restless black eyes;
smooth skin; clear olive complexion; full dark hair
and beard; and an elastic, springy step.

If he was ambitious, in the ordinary affairs of life
he was extremely unselfish; he seldom had money,
and cared nothing for it; he swept his own house and
mended his clothes and shoes. In his dealings with
men he was truthful and honest. Very temperate
and frugal in his diet, he had few wants. He was
no respecter of persons, but incorruptible and fearless; the friend of the poor and needy.[1] He was
extremely fond of children.

---

[1] "Ubi juris et æquitatis res ageretur eodem in loco habebat affi-

His beautiful smile and impressive manners, so attractive to all around him, may have been the first suggestion of that "prophetic light" which The prophetic light. his followers declared they had seen in his face.   There can be no doubt that his remarkable personality had great efficacy in preparing the immediate circle of his friends to receive with confidence and devotion the creed he was about to propose. His intimate companion, Abu Horaira, declared that he never saw a more beautiful man than the prophet.[1]

Without venturing upon those details which Gibbon has not rendered more acceptable by the Latin veil which only partially conceals them, the number of his wives, specially permitted by a revelation, and his well-known amours, substantiate the assertion that he was extremely amorous.   Perfumes and women were his chief delight; but the incontinence which with us is a stain, it must be remembered, was in that day a boast and a power in the East

When his personal magnetism had disappeared from among men, his creed was to stand on its own merits ; and yet in that he still appears as the chief agent, the mediator, the ex-cathedra announcer and denouncer.   He claimed for his religion entire freedom from idolatry : I have always thought the failing case to be the godlike importance of the prophet himself ;

nes et alienos, potentes et infirmos, amabat pauperes neque sperne-
bat egenum ob egestatem neque timebat principem ob circumfusam
potestatem." — ABULFEDA, Annales Moslemici, I. 57 ; where also
may be found a full description of his person and the miracles which
attended his birth and early life.

[1] Ockley, History of the Saracens, p. 62.

his simple adherents worshipped him. "Whenever he made the ablution to say his prayers, they ran and caught the water he had used; whenever he spat, they immediately licked up the spittle; they gathered every hair that fell from him with great superstition;"[1] and ever since that time, in all parts of the world, if Allah rules the Moslem heaven, on earth no name is so powerful as the name of the prophet.

In the excogitation of his creed he presents a most curious problem. He was a devotee alike to his convictions and his fancies, which were singularly commingled. He saw strange visions coming and passing like fever dreams. In the stillness of the night His inspiration. he heard spirit voices, and high among them that of the angel Gabriel, calling upon him to rise and cry aloud in the name of the Lord,[2] and he answered, like the truer prophet of the Scriptures, "What shall I cry?"

The well-known events of his career would be out of place in this historical summary. It must suffice to say that this man — whom a hero-worshipper has selected as the representative hero-prophet;[3] who was indeed a hero, and not a prophet at all in the Chris-

---

[1] Abulfeda, Annales Moslemici.

[2] "Veniebat ad ipsum Angelus Gabriel illa nocte . . . jubebatque prophetam recitare. At quid recitabo? interrogat Muhammed. Recita, inquit Gabriel, verba hæc: In nomine Domini tui, qui creavit omnia, creavit hominem e grumo sanguinis; Recita; Dominus tuus est spectabilissimus et beneficentissimus, qui docuit calamum, docuit hominem id quod non norat." — ABULFEDA, *Annales Moslemici*, I. 8.

[3] "He is by no means the truest of prophets, but I do esteem him a true one." — CARLYLE, *Heroes and Hero-Worship*, Lect. II.

tian sense of the word, but rather a poet, a dreamer, and a man of singularly acute judgment withal — availed himself of his own transcendent powers, his epileptic visions, his ardent fancy, the condition of the surrounding world, and the state of his own people, to undertake the task of creating and composing a new creed, not for the Arabians alone, but for the whole world ; an instrument which should contain a body of canon and civil laws applicable to the greatest numbers and the largest interests of humanity. How well he accomplished that task the grand successes of Islam must attest.

CHAPTER II.

THE CREED OF THE PROPHET.

HE called it *Islám* (resignation to God's will), and we find it set forth in the Korán. He expressly declared that it was not a new religion, but a restoration of the only true religion. The Jews he considered as having held the true faith until the coming of Christ. He asserted that the Pentateuch, the Psalms, and the Gospels had been corrupted, and that a clear prophecy of his own coming and mission had been expunged from the last.

The Korán.

So we find in the Korán the Jewish history and the Jewish prophets. In it there are given, with fanciful variations, the faith of Abraham, the matchless story of Joseph, bedecked to the Arabian taste, as in the story of Potiphar's wife, whom he calls *Zuleikha;* the giving of the Law by Moses; the checkered life of David; the wisdom and folly of Solomon, — in a word, the romantic and instructive history of the children of Israel. It acknowledges the mission of Jesus as a prophet and apostle, but not as God or the Son of God;[1] it sets forth the immaculate conception of the Virgin Mary, and the annunciation. Using and altering the Gospel of St. Barnabas, the Korán accepts the

[1] "The Christians say Christ is the son of God. They imitate the saying of those who were unbelievers in former times : may God resist them." — *Korán,* ch. ix., also ch. iii.

miraculous birth of Jesus, asserts that he performed
miracles in his infancy, adopts the Basilidian heresy
that he was not really crucified, — Simon the Cyrenian
being his substitute, — but that "God took him up
unto himself," [1] and declares that he shall return to
the earth, kill Antichrist, and then, embracing Islám,
establish peace and happiness forever among men.[2]

From the Magian system Mohammed borrowed
many principles and institutions already domiciled in
Arabia;[3] and he prudently retained, for the same
reasons, such features and practices of the Sabæan
worship as did not conflict with monotheism. He
catered to the time-honored veneration of the Arabians for the well Zem-zem and the black stone of
the Kaaba, and though at first he thought of making
Jerusalem the holy city of the Moslem world, he
changed his mind and exalted Mecca to that distinction,
making it the chief place of pilgrimage and concourse.

These various but not conflicting elements he combined in a harmonious and logical system of doctrine
and practice, irradiated throughout with that The unity of
greatest of all truths, the unity and person- God.
ality of God, — a truth which destroyed at once the
idolatrous worship which was the characteristic of the
existing faith, and with it much of the superstition
which bound the people.

And this new creed, let it be borne in mind, was
not the work of a learned philosopher in his study,
consulting the wisdom of former ages, and construct-
ing his intellectual mosaics with æsthetic skill and

[1] Korán, ch. iv.   [2] Sale's Korán, note to ch. iv.
[3] Sale's Preliminary Discourse, 16.

satisfaction. He was a thinker, but not a scholar. He fasted in solitude ; he meditated and prayed, with groans and tears ; and then, emerging from his seclusion, an enthusiast and a fanatic, but at this period not an impostor, he boldly proclaimed his great scheme of faith and worship. He declared it to be a revelation, in detached utterances, from Heaven. Some of these he showed to his friends, as they had been written down, but he depended chiefly upon his simple and magnetic eloquence. He preached it to his wife and nearest kinsmen, giving them " line upon line and precept upon precept "; for the Korán in its present complete form contains much that was revealed at a later day, and is a compilation and arrangement by his successors of what he left and taught.

Great as were the changes he proposed, and dangerous as was the self-imposed task, he uttered no uncertain note. Every sermon that he preached, like every chapter of the Korán but one, began with the auspicatory formula, *Bismillah*, — " In the name of the most merciful Allah." [1]

He called his religion Islám, which means· self-

---

[1] The ninth chapter lacks the opening formula ; but this must certainly be an accidental omission. It was the last chapter revealed to the prophet, and as he died very soon after, it is probable that he left no directions as to the place it should occupy or the mode of its introduction. Some writers have considered it a continuation of the preceding chapter. At his death the Korán consisted of numerous scraps of paper and mutton bones upon which the several revelations were written. These were all deposited in a chest which he left in charge of one of his wives, Hafsa. Efforts were made to reduce these to system by his first successor, Abu-Bekr ; but the establishment of the single text is due to Othman, who had a new copy of the Hafsa made, and destroyed all others.

devotion or resignation to God, and the corner-stone of the structure is found in the announcement, *La I 'laha illa Allah, Muhammed resoul Allah,* — "There is no God but Allah; Mohammed is the prophet of Allah."

Islám is set forth in articles of faith and practice, a glance at which will at once reveal its modern and composite character, although, to endue it with the reverence belonging to antiquity, its founder declared that it had been the true religion from the fall of Adam to the death of Abel.[1] It consists of two distinct, but interdependent parts, — *Imán*, faith, and *Din*, practice, or doctrine and ritual.

Faith is divided into six branches or articles: 1. Belief in God; 2. Belief in angels; 3. Belief in the scriptures of the Korán; 4. Belief in the prophets; 5. Belief in the resurrection and final judgment; 6. Belief in predestination.

Articles of faith.

The cardinal doctrine and great strength of this creed, its high revolutionary characteristic, is found in the first of these articles, a belief in one only God in opposition to the time-honored Arabian practice, to the "gods many" of heathenism, and to idolatry in all its forms. In this announcement of God and his attributes the Korán is as clear as the Bible itself: "God! there is no God but he — the living, the self-subsisting; neither slumber nor sleep seizeth him; to him belongeth whatsoever is in heaven and on earth." "He knoweth that which is past, and that which is to come unto them, and they shall not comprehend anything of his knowledge, but so far as he pleaseth.

[1] Sale's Korán, note to ch. x.

His throne is extended over heaven and earth, and the preservation of both is no burden to him; he is the high, the mighty." The Korán abounds also in denunciations of idolatry, and "it is not allowed to the prophet, or those who are true believers, that they pray for idolaters, though they be of kin"; and this was subjected to a crucial test which forbade all future criticism. It is recorded that when Mohammed stood at the grave of his mother Amina, he burst into tears and said, "I asked leave of God to visit my mother's tomb, and he granted it me; but when I asked leave to pray for her, it was denied me." [1]

The belief in one only God opposed also, in the eyes of the Arabians, the orthodox Christian doctrine of Opposed to the Trinity. They would not regard it as a the Christian doctrine of mystery; to their reason it presented three the Trinity. Gods. "Believe therefore in God and his apostles, and say not there are three Gods; forbear this; it will be better for you." [2] With reference to the sonship of Christ, the Korán says, "They say God hath begotten children; God forbid." [3] Their vague ideas with reference to the angels were derived from the Jewish and Christian Scriptures, but the images thus presented were imbued with new features by their fancy. The angels were created of light, and were impeccable beings, employed by God as mes-

---

[1] Al Beidâwi ; note to Sale's Koran, ch. ix.

[2] Korán, ch. iv. ; also ch. v. passim. Pococke gives (Specimen Historiæ Arabum, Oxon., 1648–50) the interpretation, at length, of the first article and of its connection with the mission of Mohammed, by Al Ghazali, one of the most famous of the commentators.

[3] Korán, ch. ii.

sengers to perform his will among men. Highest
in rank were four archangels: Gabriel (Jebraeel)
was the august medium of his revelations;
Michael (Meehál), the friend of the Jews; *Angels.*
Azraeel, the messenger of death; and Israfeel, who
will sound the trumpet of the resurrection.

Azaleel, once among the nearest to the throne of
Allah, of whom the traditions are doubtful whether
he was by origin an angel, or a Jann captured when
young and brought up among the angels,[1] fell from
his high estate, and was called *Eblis*, the devil, whose
name means *despair*. There were a countless throng
of angelic beings, among whom these were the chief.

The Korán adopted from the former faith of the
Arabians a belief in genii (Jinn or Jann), who were
peccable beings of supernatural power, created of smokeless fire; the devils were evil *Genii.*
Jinn. The orders of these supernatural beings were
numerous; among them were the Sheytans, or evil
genii; the Efreets, who are very powerful for evil; and
the Ghools, who eat corpses and even living men.

From the omnipotence and omniscience of God was
deduced the doctrine of predestination, — as baldly
enunciated, an absolute fatalism, which has *Predestina-*
produced the most opposite results in his- *tion.*
tory. It leads contemplative souls to inaction; it
makes the less thoughtful but impetuous men who
adopt it, by a heedlessness of consequences, to the
wildest and most perilous adventures.

[1] The Korán should settle the dispute: " Remember when they
said unto the angels, Worship ye Adam; and they all worshipped
him except Eblis, *who was one of the genii.*" — Ch. xviii.

Incompatible as it seems with other parts of Islám, — the efficacy of prayer, for example, — it is explicitly taught in the Korán. "God has secretly predetermined not only the adverse and prosperous fortune of every person in this world, in the most minute particulars, but also his faith or infidelity, his obedience or disobedience, and consequently his everlasting happiness or misery after death ; which fate or predestination it is not possible by any foresight or wisdom to avoid."[1] "The fate of every man have we bound about his neck."[2]   Attempts have been made to modify this extreme view. Mr. Lane, the accomplished Arabian scholar, speaking of modern opinions in Egypt, says: "I have found it to be the opinion of my Muslim friends that God may be induced by supplication to change certain of his decrees."[3]   This is certainly a great departure from the teaching of the Korán. We shall find, in considering the progress of Islám, that what was at first but a guiding rein has become in later days a strangling cord.

The other articles of belief need little comment. Everything necessary to salvation was to be found in the Korán. This name, from the Arabic *Karaa*, to read, has the force of the Greek *Biblia*, the books, and of the Latin *scripturæ*, the writings. The inspired readings of the Korán contain the Pentateuch of Moses, the Psalms of David, and the Gospels of Jesus Christ, all restored from their corruption ; and, so to speak, the Korán not only surpasses, but abrogates

[1] Sale's Preliminary Discourse, p. 74.
[2] Korán, ch. xvii.
[3] Arabian Nights, note to ch. i., Vol. I. p. 53.

these. The prophets are Adam, Seth, Noah, Abraham, Moses, Jesus, and Mohammed.

In presenting the earlier portions, as he claimed to receive them by successive revelations, Mohammed conceded that God had made known his will to the earlier prophets, — Adam, Seth, Enoch, and Abraham, — but that these Scriptures had been lost. By divine inspiration Moses wrote the Pentateuch, and David many of the Psalms. The record of Jesus, the Son of Mary, was presented in the Christian Gospels; but these, as I have said, were all greatly corrupted, and now Mohammed had been commissioned to restore them to their original purity, as the last of the Apostles and the seal of the prophets; and was thus presenting to the world the former revelations in their truth, together with the latest revelations of God to mankind. He did not substantiate his claims by working miracles, whatever his infatuated followers might assert of signs and wonders performed by him; "for," he said, "are not the leaves of the Korán the greatest of miracles?"[1]

The general resurrection and judgment were to be followed by rewards and punishments, chiefly sensual On a white stone of immense size, placed near the throne of the Almighty, and concealed by the excess

---

[1] "When he was called upon to work miracles in proof of his divine mission, he excused himself by various pretences, and appealed to the Korán as a standing miracle." — OCKLEY, *History of the Saracens*, pp. 65, 66. Abulfeda (Annales Moslemici, I. 16) gives a list of the principal miracles claimed for him by his adherents. Some of them compute the number at four thousand four hundred and fifty. Among them are his night-journey to heaven, and his calling the moon down and passing it through his sleeve.

of light from all other eyes, every act and every event
in the lives of men were inscribed, running parallel

Rewards
and punish-
ments.
with their destiny, which was as inflexible
and irremediable as that sung by the Parcæ
of an older mythology to their revolving spindles, —
stabili fatorum numine; and yet for their actions
men were judged, and rewarded or punished. This
relentless law was beyond the control of Allah himself. It was but another version of that Fatum, or
spoken word, which, when uttered, was superior to
Zeus himself.[1]

In arranging his system of future rewards and punishments, he catered to the tastes and the fears of a
people remarkable for their keen enjoyment of certain
sensual pleasures, and at the same time sensitive to

Paradise and
the houris.
corporal pain. He conceived a paradise
which would intensify and prolong these
pleasures. To the desert born, rivers of cool and
limpid water, of wine, of milk, and of clarified honey;
to the weary souls, that " they shall repose on couches,
the lining of which shall be of thick silk, interwoven
with gold, and the fruit of the two shady gardens shall
be near at hand to gather. Therein shall receive
them beauteous damsels [hooreeyahs] refraining their
eyes from beholding any besides their spouses, . . .
having complexions like rubies and pearls. Therein
shall they delight themselves, lying on green cushions
and beautiful carpets."[2]

[1] μοῖραι τρίμορφοι, μνήμονές τ᾽ Ἐρινύες.
τούτων ἄρα Ζεύς ἐστιν ἀσθενέστερος
οὔκουν ἂν ἐκφύγοι γε τὴν πεπρωμένην.
                                AESCHYLUS, Προμ. Δεσ., 515.

[2] Korán, ch. xxii., lvi., lxx.

To deter men from sin and unbelief, he provided a hell, horrible and eternal, — garments of fire, boiling waters poured upon their heads and down their throats, ceaseless blows from maces of Hell. iron. "Woe (especially) be on that day to those who accused the prophet of imposture. It shall be said unto them, 'Go ye to the punishment which ye denied as a falsehood; go ye into the shadow of the smoke of hell, which shall ascend in three columns, and shall not shade you from the heat, neither shall it be of service against the flame; but it shall cast forth sparks as big as towers, resembling yellow camels in color.'" [1] Above this terrible hell is a bridge (Al Sirát) over which all must pass: it is finer than a hair and sharper than a sword; and the wicked, burdened with their sins, fall from it into the flames.

Complementary to the tenets of faith, and pointing out the duties by which man may gain heaven and avoid hell, are the following Practice. titles of practice: I. Prayer; II. Alms; III. Fasting; IV. The Pilgrimage to Mecca.

Prayer (Es-saleh) the prophet called "the pillar of religion" and "the key of Paradise"; and to those who begged a dispensation from the numerous prayers he said, "There could be no good Prayer. in that religion wherein was no prayer." At first he held it as indifferent in what direction they should turn when they prayed; then, to propitiate the Jews, he made it Jerusalem, but at last fixed upon Mecca; and this direction, called the *Kiblah*, has been ever

[1] Korán, ch. lxxvii.

since retained : the mosques were built on such radiating lines, and in the principal houses niches were constructed, and prayer-carpets laid in the prescribed direction.

The Moslem was enjoined to pray five times in every twenty-four hours, — at Azohbi, before sunrise ; Adokar, just after the sun passed the meridian ; Almagreb, just before sunset; Alaksa, in the evening after sunset, and just before the first watch of the night. No prayer should be offered without a precedent purification. This was an ablution with water, when it could be had ; but, in regions where water was scarce, fine sand or dust might be used. The extent of the purification depended upon the extent of the pollution ; but generally the head, hands, and feet only were washed.[1] In praying, the Moslem prostrated himself, a part of the time touching the ground with his face.

There were congregational prayers, with lessons from the Korán, in the mosque on Friday, and prayers prescribed for special occasions. The Khotbeh, which was at first a general exhortation and prayer, was afterwards made to include the prayer for the Khalif. Certain shrines gave peculiar efficacy to the petitions, and where the prayers were numerous they were told off upon strings of beads or rosaries.

Alms-giving was also enjoined upon all believers. The Zekáh was an annual tribute for the poor, paid

---

[1] "O true believers, when ye prepare yourselves to pray, wash your faces and your hands unto the elbows, and rub your heads, and your feet unto the ankles, and if ye be polluted by having lain with a woman, wash yourselves all over." — *Korán,* ch. v.

either in kind, as of sheep, camels, horses, etc., or in money equivalent, and it varied at different times and in different countries. *Alms.*

Fasting (Es-siyám) was imposed at least during every day of the month Ramadán — the Mohammedan Lent — from daybreak to sunset, and at other special times throughout the year. It has *Fasting.* been supposed that this was based as well upon hygiene as upon religious grounds. These fasts have always been kept with great rigor.

The Pilgrimage (El-hajj) to Mecca and Mount Arafat was to be made annually by those who were able, and they acquired greater sanctity thereby. If possible, it should take place in the month *Pilgrimage.* Dulhagia, and ended with a great festival. There were many exemptions, for obvious reasons, such as the infirmities of age, the tenderness of childhood, and the conditions attending maternity. And when the Moslems had conquered remote lands, the distance made it impossible for the masses of people to perform it. Difficulties were removed, in many cases, by the permission given to pilgrims to trade on their journey.[1] Thus the Hájj combined his devotion and interest, and commerce received an annual impulsion, which no doubt the prophet had in view.

In the list of things forbidden to the believer by the Korán we may also observe the prophet's sagacity. He forbade the use of wine, for he knew its *Things* ill-effects upon health, especially in that *forbidden.* warm region. The temptations to excess were so great,

---

[1] "It shall be no crime to you if ye seek an increase from your Lord, by trading during the pilgrimage." — *Korán,* ch. ii.

however, that, while the Korán prohibited its use, their
epicurean poets dared to sing, " Wine is as the body,
music as the soul, and joy is their offspring." [1]   The
casting of lots and divining by arrows were also
denounced; customs which may yet be observed in
Mohammedan countries, practised by conjurers and
resorted to by the idle and credulous.   Of this lottery
system Mohammed declared, " It is an impiety." [2]
The use of swine's flesh and blood was forbidden, as
was also the eating of an animal strangled or horned
by another, or sacrificed to idols.   Circumcision, long
practised among Eastern nations, and by the Arabians
themselves before Mohammed, — and more recently
discovered among the Indians of South America
and the South Sea Islanders, — was prescribed in the
Korán, but does not seem to have been absolutely
obligatory.

Such, in prominent outline, was the scheme of
religion and government presented by a man intel-
lectually and morally towering above his fellows,
to a receptive and waiting people worthy of it, and
of a better one, grand as it was.   What should be
its fate ?

The chances of his success were greatly increased
at the outset by the schisms in the Christian Church
Prospects of and the petty quarrels among Christians.
success.   Sects had sprung up in great numbers.   A
modern writer has considered the great question of
creed to be narrowed down to a contest between
Mohammedanism and Christianity, and has of course

---

[1] Lane's Arabian Nights, I. 200.
[2] Korán, ch. v.

made the latter bear off the palm of victory.[1] I have noted this, because at that day it was thus that the question presented itself to the more enlightened Arabian minds, and they decided it in favor of Islám. The worship of images, which had by insensible degrees stolen into the Christian Church, gave to Islám a superiority in their eyes, in that it rejécted idolatry in its subtlest approaches, — a superiority over that corruption of Christianity which inflamed the zeal of the iconoclasts, and which even now, in a more enlightened age, may be duly commended. This worship of images in the church catholic was "the incessant charge [against the Christians] of the Jews and Mohammedans, who derived from the Law and the Korán an immortal hatred to graven images and all relative worship."[2] They judged the practice and condemned the doctrines from which such an enormity could spring.

The ignorant and inactive Arab of the town and the wandering and restless Arab of the desert and mountain had alike needed a teacher to reclaim them from idolatry and to give them religious coherence ; a statesman who could unite the scattered tribes into one nation, and show them that in such union alone lay a people's strength ; a military genius who could forecast those schemes of conquest, the only limit to which was the subjugation and conversion of the world. All these characters they found combined in Mohammed, and all these possibilities in his creed,

[1] Bishop Hopkins, of Vermont, in his "Christianity Vindicated." 1833.

[2] Gibbon, Decline and Fall, ch. xlix.

—a creed which they were to carry with them and maintain unimpaired, in the then unknown peninsula of Andalus.

It appealed to their lively intelligence; it modulated and fixed their ancient and beautiful language, rendered sacred by its use in the Korán, which I may, perhaps for the first time, call one of the great epics in the world's literature, of which the prophet is the hero; it utilized their mobility, their endurance, and their skill in the use of weapons, by banding them together for conquest; it made all believers equal in the sight of Allah; it controlled without shackling their independence. It made them a nation of enlightened men and ardent warriors.

It further subsidized what they had so long been accomplishing in the breeding and training of horses; for it must not be forgotten that, from the moment they were marshalled for conquest, they were the best mounted and most dexterous cavalry in the world. It is of course a fable, but they preserve the tradition with great fondness, that their best stock (Bint el ahwaj) is from a mare taken by their progenitor, Ishmael, from a herd of wild horses, and that King Solomon purchased five mares, descendants of this one, from the Ishmaelites. It is accepted as true that the most famous of the breeds, the Kochlani (or Kehilaus) was in existence and well known in the days of the prophet. The Arabian horse from which the English get their thoroughbred stock rarely reaches fifteen hands in height, but, in proportion, he is stronger and fleeter than the English horse, and exceeds him in endurance. To the Arabian, his horse, living near him, sharing his meal of dates and camel's milk, fondled by his children, was his friend, his child, his constant companion, and was, at that day, to be one instrument of his wonderful successes.[1]

Awakened from their ignorance and torpor by the new cry, literally "the voice of one crying in the wilderness," they sprang into marshalled ranks, shoulder to shoulder, and were ready to do deeds of personal daring and of national triumph which should soon fit them to undertake more difficult and distant conquests.

At the age of twenty-five, Mohammed had married a rich widow of forty named Kadijah, of the family of the Koreish, whose commercial factor he had been. He thus became possessed of *The marriage of Mohammed.* fortune to aid his plans. His creed, when he proclaimed it, was at once despised and resisted; it seemed that it must fail for want of adherents. But it found favor in the eyes of his wife, who became his first convert, and, what was better, in the eyes of his cousin Ali, who afterwards married his daughter Fatima, and who, when Mohammed assembled his kinsmen to hear the new revelation, and all were silent, proclaimed with wild excitement, " I will [be your champion], and I will beat out the teeth, pull out the eyes, rip up the bellies, and break the legs of all that oppose you." [2]

[1] In Lady Anne Blunt's work entitled "Bedouin Tribes of the Euphrates" (Harper, 1879), the reader will find an interesting and instructive chapter on horses, written by her husband. He gives a table of descent from the Bint el ahwaj, and traces the pedigree in the male line, through different channels, of the *Darley* and *Godolphin* Arabians, so famous in England.

[2] Abulfeda, Annales Moslemici, I. 11.

This first announcement was made just after the Lenten fast of Ramadán, which he had observed in *His religion announced* seclusion, and with great rigor, and when he was forty years old. The scheme fell flat: for three years he made but little progress; but they were three years of questioning and considering, and over-coming the astonishment and repugnance to so great an innovation. His chief opponents were among the Koreish, who first derided and then violently attacked those pretensions, which restricted their powers and belittled their functions as guardians of the Kaaba. Many times he was obliged to conceal himself from their wrath, and at last, when compelled to flee, he was aided by a stratagem of Ali. Mohammed put his green vest upon his cousin, and ordered him to lie down in his place. His enemies, who wished to pre-vent his flight, peeped through the door, and seeing the pretender, thought themselves sure of the prophet: they were only undeceived when Ali came out in the morning.[1]

Thus he made that Hijra or flight from Mecca to Medina, which ensured his safety, and which, divest-*The Hijra, A. D. 622.* ing his creed of its local character, divulged it to the Arabian world.[1] The Hijra has a varied significance; it was that incipient motion of a mighty pendulum which should increase in mo-mentum and scope, until it should describe a wide arc of oscillation over the East and over the West.

At the time of the flight, Mohammed was about fifty-four years old.

On the death of Khadijah, to whom he was ten-

[1] Abulfeda, Annales Moslemici, I. 22.

derly attached, he married Ayesha, a girl only nine years old, who was to play a prominent part in the fortunes of his creed. She was the daughter of Abdullah Athic, one of his earliest and most influential converts, who, by reason of the elevation of his daughter, has lost his own name in the subsequent history, and is known as *Abu Bekr*, "the father of the girl." [1]

At the first, Mohammed seems to have hoped that he could propagate his faith without resort to violence; but he soon found that he must take up arms in self-defence, and in the thirteenth year of his mission, he announced that God permitted him not only to fight in self-defence, but to propagate his religion by the sword. The revelation came with trumpet tone: "War is enjoined you against the infidel;" "Fight for the religion of God." [2] This announcement raised the spirits and increased the numbers of his adherents: they fought for Islám and received the spoils. They plundered the caravans of idolaters; the hostile Meccans and their wealth were fair prey. The first act of hostility was the capture of a caravan going to Mecca. Soon after this, a caravan under Abu Sufyan, his kinsman and mortal foe, was returning from Syria, and, when near a well called Bedr,[3] the prophet in person attacked it, notwithstanding great disparity of numbers, and captured it. Taking for God and for himself one-fifth of the spoils, he distributed the remaining four-fifths

Permission to use the sword.

---

[1] Ockley, History of the Saracens, p. 376.

[2] Korán, ch. ii. See passim, ch. viii. and ix.

[3] Abulfeda, Annales Moslemici, I. 24.

among his men. When not long after he was defeated by Abu Sufyan at Mount Ohud, where he was thrice wounded, in the year 623, he cunningly attributed his want of success to the disobedience and sins of his followers, in order to dispel the doubts which began to be murmured, as to whether he really enjoyed the Divine favor which he claimed.

In the fifth year of the Hijra, he placed a trench around Medina, and when it was attacked by ten thousand Meccans, he repelled them in the famous " war of the ditch," by the help of a miracle, which he has recorded in the Korán, — "God sent a storm and legions of angels which ye did not see."[1]   His fortitude and valor received at last their reward; the hostile Koreish became disheartened; the increasing forces of the prophet followed their retreating steps to Mecca; he attacked and took it, and thus the city of his humiliation became the Kiblah of the Moslem world: the prophet had honor in his own home.[2]

Medina was, however, his chief residence, and there, in the eleventh year of the Hijra, on Monday, the 12th of First Rebic (June 8, A. D. 632), being then in the sixty-second year of his age, he commended his creed, his people, and his soul to Allah, and waited for the angel of death. The summons came; the angel asked permission to enter. " I give him leave," said Mohammed, and the angel entered

His death.

---

[1] Korán, ch. xxxiii.

[2] Some writers, according to Abulfeda, number all the engagements in which Mohammed took part at thirty-five; others say forty-eight. Annales Moslemici, I. 59.

and complimented the prophet, telling him God was very desirous to have him, but had commanded that he should take his soul or leave it, just as he himself should please to order. Mohammed replied, "Take it then," and expired in the arms of Ayesha.[1] Many refused to believe that he was dead; many entreated that he should not be buried; others thought he still lived in his tomb; and a wild fancy gained favor that relays of angels upheld his coffin as if suspended in the air.

His departure was not untimely: his mission was accomplished; his work done. Considered as a great historic achievement, his scheme of religion and government was a success; his people had both motive and organization for conquest. He had prepared the way for their extension by sending letters, bearing the seal of " Mohammed, the Apostle of God," to the surrounding princes, inviting them to accept Islâm: to the king of Persia, who first scorned his message; to the kings of Ethiopia and Bahrain, and to the governor of Egypt. His message to Heraclius, the emperor of Eastern Rome, whose dominions lay temptingly contiguous to his own, was received with a respect prompted in part by admiration and in part by fear.

Few men, dying, have left their affairs in a more prosperous condition. He had laid out what was to be done, with directions how to do it; but the task was to fall very heavily upon those who were his testamentary trustees. Who was capable and worthy

---

[1] Abulfeda, Annales Moslemici, I. 55, 56.

to succeed the mighty prophet? Who could realize the grandeur of his plans, and carry out his ambitious schemes?

But the creed of Mohammed, in a great degree irrespective of the men who were to succeed him, was, from its very origin, the strong motive power which was to urge the warlike Arabian to the East and West, and to find its most practical result in the conquest of Spain.

CHAPTER III.

THE FIRST KHALIFS.

MOHAMMED, whether by intention or because death overtook him before he expected it, had made no provision for a successor; the Korán contained no mode of appointing or electing one. Rival claims were at once presented, and threatened discord and even disunion among his followers. Among them were two much stronger than all the rest: that of Ali, the cousin and son-in-law of the prophet, the son of the eldest son of his grandfather; and that of Abu Bekr, the father of his favorite wife. Both were among the earliest converts and the most enthusiastic champions of the Faith, and each had a woman's influence to aid him. As a first means, the principal Moslems chose six electors, to whom the matter was committed. When they met, the discussion was long and excited. The friends of Ali were enthusiastic in his behalf; while Ayesha and her party worked hard for Abu Bekr. Omar, an early convert, was another candidate.

But, besides this, there was a strong rivalry between the people of Mecca and those of Medina. Ayesha's influence might not have been strong enough to turn the scale, but the complication was Abu Bekr. most easily relieved, and the people of both cities satisfied, by the election of Abu Bekr as the first Khalifah or *successor* of Mohammed. Ayesha was exultant and Fatima disappointed.

Without attempting to investigate the rival claims, where, to say truth, no claims had any legal value, it is of importance to note that the pretensions of Ali and Abu Bekr, from that very day, divide the Moslem world, and have since not only affected the orthodoxy, but have influenced the politics and even caused the disruption of Mohammedan nations.

The hereditary claim, if there were any, would be with the sons of Ali and Fatima, the daughter of Mohammed; but it was some time before that claim was first advanced by Muawiyah, the son of Abu Sufyan, in order to establish the dynasty in the family of his ancestor, Ummeyah, or the Ommyades of Damascus.

In point of judgment and capacity, however, Abu Bekr was by no means an unworthy choice. The venerable chief entered at once and with ardor upon the plans proposed by Mohammed. He summoned the nation to arms, and, after some desultory, or rather experimental, efforts, he despatched a large force to wrest Syria from the weak grasp of Heraclius. His troops were full of ardor; the new war which was undertaken to propagate the faith would also enrich the faithful, by securing, as the result of victory, the costly spoils of the Lower Empire, of which the marvellous accounts hardly exceeded the marvellous reality. Dusky swarms in white turbans flocked to the standard, as if to a festival, from every district of the land, and from all the tribes of their nation; the towns, as well as the country, sending their proportions; an innumerable host encamped around Medina.[1] Inadequate arms and scanty clothing were more than counterbalanced by zeal and hope. The first victories would at once equip and reward them. The camp grew in dimensions, and Yezid, another son of that Abu Sufyan who had defeated the prophet at Ohud, was appointed to lead the eager force to Damascus, the oldest and most beautiful city in the world.

The instructions of the Khalif were explicit, prudent, and not wanting in humanity. On the commander he enjoined great care of his troops, who were all, the humblest of them, *Moslemah*, children of Islám, like himself, and were not to be treated with harshness or haughtiness. He was to take counsel of the many prudent and brave captains in his company, and act with wariness and prudence: it was victory, and not individual fame, for which all were fighting. To the troops he dictated implicit obedience, and that they should never turn their backs, for they were fighting in the cause of God. To fight was honorable; to conquer was the reward direct from God's hand; to die for the Faith was the greatest glory, for it was written: "If ye be slain or die in defence of the religion of God, verily, pardon from God and mercy are better than what they heap together of worldly riches; and if ye die or be slain, verily, unto God shall ye be gathered."[2] This was the strong point of the exhortation: whatever the result, their reward was great and sure.

His instructions to the army.

---

[1] Condé, Dominacion de los Arabes, ch. iii.

[2] Korán, ch. iii. Condé, Dominacion de los Arabes, vol. I., pp. 36, 37.

The Khalif further commanded moderation and humanity to the conquered. As these instructions were designed to be of permanent application, I give them at length : —

"If God should give you the victory, do not abuse your advantages ; and beware how you stain your swords in the blood of him who yields ; neither touch ye the children, the women, nor the infirm old men, whom ye may find among your enemies. In your progress through the enemy's land, cut down no palms,[1] or rather fruit-trees ; destroy not the products of the earth ; ravage no fields ; burn no dwellings ; from the stores of your enemy, take only what you need for your own wants. Let no destruction be made without necessity, but occupy the cities of the enemy, and if there be any that may serve as an asylum to your adversaries, them do you destroy. Treat the prisoner, and him who renders himself to your mercy, with pity, as God shall do to you in your need, but trample down the proud and rebellious ; nor fail to crush all who have broken the conditions imposed on them. Let there be no perfidy or falsehood in your treaties with your enemies ; be faithful in all things, proving yourselves ever upright and noble, and maintaining your word and promise truly. Do not disturb the quiet of the monk or hermit, and destroy not their abodes, but inflict the rigors of death

---

[1] Pococke (Specimen Historiæ Arabum) says that of the palm-tree they make mattresses, all sorts of basket and wicker ware, flexible lithes and brooms, twine and girths. The kernel of the fruit is an astringent which counteracts the effects of bad water and laxative fruits.

on all who shall refuse the conditions you would
impose on them." [1] The conditions imposed on the
conquered were, to embrace the Faith, to pay tribute,
or to die by the sword. Apostasy, the worst of
crimes, was punished with death.

Such were the moderate instructions of the first
Khalif to his armies; such the spirit with which
Islám began its conquering march. It will be seen
that, in after time, their conduct deviated from this
benevolent rule: but this was due to the demoralizing
effect of war, the fierceness of enemies, which they
imitated or requited; and occasionally they acted
too under the irresistible influence of the *certaminis
gaudia* of the Romans, the wild Berserker fury of the
Northmen, which transforms men everywhere into
lions and tigers.

The unity of Islám, so much vaunted at first, was,
like that of Christianity, soon compromised, and
the Faithful were divided into numerous
sects. The first great division sprang di- Mohammedan sects.
rectly from the claims of rival parties to secure the
Khalifate, and thus has a large political bearing, as
well as a doctrinal interpretation. Thus the party
which accepted Abu Bekr and his two successors,
Omar and Othman, and who claimed to be orthodox,
was opposed by the people who rejected the first

[1] Condé, Dominacion de los Arabes, p. 37. Ockley, History of the
Saracens, p. 94. These instructions, in slightly different language,
are recorded by all historians of the events, and were repeated in
whole or part to Moslem forces in their later history, and on new
theatres of action. Accepting the substance of them, we cannot
but be struck with the humane spirit with which they began their
career.

three Khalifs, and were the champions of Ali; some ranking him as equal to Mohammed, and others making him even the superior of the prophet, as he was the elder in lineage, the son of the oldest son of his grandfather. The orthodox sects had the generic name of Sonnites (Sunnees), be-

Sonnites.

cause they acknowledged the Sunna as a traditional supplement to the Koran, and guided themselves by its precepts. The Sunna may be compared to the *Mishna* and *Gemara* of the Jewish Talmud, and contains the traditional sayings and doings of the Prophets. Of the Sonnites there were afterwards four principal divisions, each following the teachings of a learned doctor: 1. Abu Hanifa; 2. Malik Ibn Ans; 3. Mohammed Al Shâfei; 4. Ahmed Ibn Hanbal. With slight differences of opinion these subdivisions acknowledged each other's orthodoxy,[1] and accepted the succession of Ali as the fourth Khalif, but as not equal to his predecessors in sanctity.

The heretical sects, under the general appellation of Shiites (Shiy a ées), became very numerous. Among these the sectaries of Ali were called by the orthodox party, Shiites, from the term, *Shiyah*, scandalous and reprobate; and although they named themselves *Adaliyah*, those of the right religion, the opprobrious epithet has clung to them in history[2] until the present day. They upheld Ali as the rightful claimant from the time of Mohammed's death,

Shiites.

---

[1] Sale, Preliminary Discourse, sect. viii.

[2] Ockley, History of the Saracens, p. 334. At this time the Turks are *Sonnites* and the Persians *Shiites*.

rejecting the intermediate Khalifs as usurpers. Out of the Korán and the Sunna, the orthodox publicists, or chief Imáms, drew the great body of their The civil civil law, which is to be found in volumi- law. nous digests, each tinctured with the sectarian views of its compiler. I shall reserve for a later chapter the consideration of the doctrines and practices adopted in Spain, when it fell into the hands of the Moslems.

When the army first set out for the conquest of Syria, it was commanded, as we have seen, by Yezid, while another force under a noble Arabian, Kaled Ibn Al Walid, had been sent to Irak and the confines of Persia. The success of this latter general in that field caused him to be recalled and placed in command of the Syrian army, whose task was far more important and difficult. His rapid Kaled, The advance and dashing valor won for him the Sword of proud title, "The Sword of God." Loving God. and tender towards his troops, he was cruel and unrelenting to the enemy. Under his efficient command the army found no obstacle which they could not surmount.

Ever since the palmy days of Constantine the Great, the power of Eastern Rome had been declining; it was attacked by Goths at the north-west, and by Persians and Huns at the east;[1] and the conquest of Damascus was not so difficult a task to the fiery Moslemah as had been anticipated. It was Damascus taken, taken, after a vigorous siege, on the 23d A. D. 634. of August, A. D. 634, and its fugitive inhabitants

[1] Sale, Preliminary Discourse, 26.

were overtaken and many of them destroyed. Damascus was soon to become the seat of the Khalifate. Persia, long weakened by intestine wars, the quarrels of conflicting sects, and a wide-spread profligacy, was the next field of victory for the Moslem arms and Faith. Persia was soon overrun, and then they turned their armies westward.

After a reign of a little more than two years, Abu Bekr died, as some thought from the effects of poison, but really, according to his daughter Ayesha, of a fever taken after bathing in cold water; he was suc-

Omar,
Khalif.
A. D. 634.

ceeded by Omar, in the year 634. This chief, one of the strongest adherents of the prophet, had been among the prominent candidates at the first election, and the disappointed adherents of Ali found themselves too weak at the second election to prevent his succession, but they concealed their hatred and wrath for the time, still hoping for success.

Under Omar, the Moslem arms advanced upon Egypt; his lieutenant in command of the troops, was Amru Ibn Al-As. Near the ancient pyramids, was the city of Memphis, with its fortress of Misrah; this the intrepid Amru stormed, and his camp was the site upon which arose a new city, called, in later days, when it became the capital of the Fatimite Khalifs of Egypt, *El Kahira*, (the city of victory), a name which has been corrupted and modernized into Cairo.[1] With the aid of reinforcements, after four-

---

[1] Ancient Memphis, at the time of Amru's attack, was called *Misr* or *Misrah*. Its modern name was conferred by the conquerors, —*Masr el Kahira*. Its real growth began about the year 970,

teen months of siege, and the loss of twenty-three thousand men, on the 20th of December, 640, they captured Alexandria, a city of ancient renown, and of great existing wealth and splendor. There they found, it is said, — though allowance may be made for the exaggeration of a commander who would magnify his conquests, — four thousand palaces, four thousand baths, four thousand theatres, and forty thousand tributary Jews.[1] In prosecuting their advance, they availed themselves of the line marked by the ancient canal of the kings, between the Red Sea and the Nile, and, in six months, in the years 643–44, reopened it, so that in the seventh month vessels passed from the river to the sea.[2] Starting about a mile and a half from Suez, it extended thirteen miles north-westerly to the Bitter Lake, where there were twenty-seven miles of open navigation; thence, from the northern extremity, it passed through a valley in the land of Goshen, and at last from Abaceh to the Pelusiac arm of the Nile. It was ninety-two miles in entire

The canal between the Nile and the Red Sea.

when it became the capital of the Fatimite Khalifs of Egypt. Cairo became thoroughly Arabian. Poole says, "Since the downfall of the Arab Empire of Baghdad, Cairo has been the chief of Arabian cities, . . . the city in which Arabian manners now exist in the most refined state. The name *Misr* seems to have been frequently used to indicate a large, or capital city." — LANE's *Arabian Nights*, edited by Poole, Preface, x. ; also I. 274.

[1] I shall have occasion to notice the singular fact that to a poet or narrator the Arabians *allow a license of exaggeration*, and the reader of the same kidney knows how to make the due allowance. The Spaniards have a proverb — no doubt Oriental in origin — that the proper measure of belief is *la mitad de la mitad*.

[2] M. Hendy, in Chambers's Papers for the People, art. "The Isthmus of Suez."

length, of which sixty were dug by hand; "and half
of that artificial construction is now so perfect, or so
little damaged, as to require little more than clearing
to render it again navigable."[1] The great achievement of De Lesseps had thus been successfully anticipated twelve hundred years ago.

In Egypt they found six millions of Copts, who
voluntarily submitted to the tributary yoke.[2] They
were the best types of the ancient Egyptian race, and
the most eccentric of Christian sectaries, whose strong
repugnance to both the Greek and Latin communions,
— the Patriarch of Constantinople and the Pope, —
and whose oriental customs made their submission easy
and unresisting. They have in later times dwindled
in numbers, but, retaining their dislike of European
hierarchs, they have their patriarchs in Alexandria.

Yet in ignorance of the value of books, these children of the sword and the Faith consigned the mag-
Destruction nificent library of Alexandria to the fire.
of the Alex- When John Philoponus, the Grammarian,
andrian Li-
brary. begged for its preservation, Amru, who liked
the man, and would have been glad to gratify him,
and indeed saw no reason himself for refusing to
grant his request, still felt obliged to refer to the
Khalif for a decision. The answer was prompt. "If,"
said Omar, "these writings of the Greeks agree with
the Korán they are useless, and need not be preserved; if they disagree, they are pernicious, and
ought to be destroyed;"[3] and so they went to feed

[1] Mr. Maclaren, in the same article.

[2] Condé, ch. iii. ; Ockley, History of the Saracens, 259.

[3] Abul Faraj, quoted by Gibbon, Decline and Fall, ch. ii. and
by Ockley, p. 263.

ovens of the four thousand baths of the city. The story has been doubted by Renaudot, Gibbon, and others; but, besides the *prima facie* appearance of its truth, many Mohammedan authorities unknown to Gibbon confirm the fact.[1] The historian has survived the loss; many of the same authors were elsewhere preserved: but it is our ignorance of others that causes the chief regret; we can hardly overestimate the value of the works there collected, — the manifold annals of the ancient world.

Allah had foreordained a short reign to Omar of nine years. In 643, through the intrigues of the hostile faction, he was stabbed by a Persian in the mosque, and died in three days.[2] Again Ali was expectant, but was again doomed to disappointment. Gloomy and sensitive, he stood apart in the dignity of his claims, while others were scheming and working; and thus it happened that Othman of the house Othman Khalif. of Ummeyah, the brother of Abu Sufyan, A. D. 643. became Khalif by the vote of the commissioners. With a prudence which partook of irresolution and inaction, he greatly retarded the progress of the Moslem armies in the West, by deposing Amru from the command, and, for a brief space, Alexandria fell again into the hands of the Greek emperors. There were, besides, personal reasons for this step; for, in the days when Mohammed and Abu Sufyan were enemies, Amru had been sent to assassinate the latter, and

---

[1] See Milman's note to Gibbon's account, in the same chapter, in which the authorities are given, and a similar destruction mentioned.

[2] Ockley, History of the Saracens, p. 266. *Fica in iliis et infra umbilicum.* — ABULFEDA, *Annales Moslennici,* I. 74.

thus was noxious to Othman, who had also a foster brother whom he wished to put in Amru's place.

Less a warrior than a student, Othman set forth an authentic version of the Korán, a work of the very first importance to the Mohammedan world. There was already great danger that portions of that essential volume would be lost. In the time of the prophet it existed in the form of detached leaves and scraps. Some of these Abu Bekr had gathered into a volume, and the rest existed in the memory of men who had been trained to repeat the revelations as the rhapsodists recited Homer. These from time to time were written down, but different readings had grown into the text. It was due to Othman that the book Hafsa[1] was copied, and promulgated as the only authentic version, and all others abolished and destroyed. After a reign of twelve years, Othman met his fate at the hand of an assassin. It was the reverse of poetic justice that he should have been assassinated while sitting with the Korán in his lap, and that the holy volume should have been sprinkled and stained with his life-blood. It should have been potent to preserve his life.[2] It was curiously claimed that that blood-stained copy of the Korán found its way to the mosque of Cordova. And now, in despite of his few implacable enemies who had no strong man to propose as successor, the party of Ali

Ali succeeds.

---

[1] So called because the more perfect copy — Al Korán Exemplar — had been deposited with Hafsa, one of the prophet's wives. — ABUL-FEDA, *Annales Moslemici*, I. 78.

[2] To the superstitious Moslemah, the loss by Othman of the prophet's silver signet-ring was an omen of his violent death. — ABULFEDA, *Annales Moslemici*, I. 79.

had become so strong as to secure his election. Personally a great favorite, he was the husband of Mohammed's daughter, and, as the prophet had left no son, her claims were magnified, and represented by her husband. The Arabians saw in him the probable father of a succession of Khalifs of Mohammed's blood ; but this was by no means the end of trouble. If he was in the regular succession as fourth Khalif, it was acceptable. But, according to his claims, the election of Ali declared the former Khalifs usurpers, and, with the political imbroglio, there began that conflict of religious opinions which afterwards produced the *Sonnites* and *Shiites*, — the former called by D'Herbelot, "the catholics of Moslemism," and the latter "a Protestant sect, whose green slippers were an abomination to their enemies." Both claimed to find their doctrines in the Korán; both buttressed their dogmas upon a political fact. The strength, system, and wariness of the factions combined to retard the westward movement of the Moslem armies for nearly ten years. Ali, enveloped by suspicion and contention, was obliged to check the career of his troops into Africa proper, in order to protect and consolidate his power at home. Thus the prestige of foreign conquest was lost to his reign ; and the effect was obvious in the degeneracy of his army.

Ayesha, at once the favorite wife of Mohammed and the daughter of the first Khalif, was still living, greatly respected by a strong party, and she denied his claims. She even raised an army to oppose him. Muawiyah, the general of Othman, and in command of the troops, when that Khalif died, refused to recognize

the validity of the election : the army was in opposition
to the government. And so it came to pass that Ali
having vindicated his pretensions, and having tasted
the sweets and the bitter of authority for six turbulent years, fell like his two predecessors under the
knife of the assassin, sincerely mourned by his admiring adherents. He was indeed a notable man, —
soldier, statesman, and philosopher. When at the
first, Mohammed had met his kinsman at a banquet at
the house of Ali to divulge his religion, to offer them
" the good both of this world and of the other life,"
and all were silent, Ali proclaimed his own adherence,
and said, " I will beat out the teeth, pull out the
eyes, rip up the bellies, and break the legs of all that
oppose you." [1] Valiant in every action, he was an
example and a rallying point for the Moslem soldiers,
who named him *Esed Allah Algalib*, the victorious
lion of God, and the *sentences* of Ali [2] are full of
devotion, philosophy, and true wit, proverbs, many
of which would sound well in the mouths of Christian men.

His followers called him *Wasi*, " the executor," or
legatee of Mohammed ; *Mortada*, acceptable to God ;
and among the Shiites of later days he evidently dis-
puted the supremacy of the prophet himself, and was
adored as *Faid Alanwar*, the distributer of lights or
graces. To the Persian sectaries he was *Shak mord-
man*, the king of men, and *Shir Khoda*, the lion of

---

[1] Ockley, History of the Saracens, 15.

[2] The *Centiloquium*, or hundred sentences, is one collection
which has been translated into many languages. Ockley gives a
collection numbering one hundred and sixty-nine. — *Ib.* 339.

God.[1] I have dwelt upon the personality of this man, because his claims operated long after his death in the dethronement and elevation of rival dynasties, and still divide the Mohammedan world to-day into its great religious sects. Next to Mohammed he was the most notable of the earlier Khalifs. With the assassination of Ali, the choice of Khalifs by election came to an end; the office became hereditary with occasional exceptions. Ummeyah, whose name was to be adopted by a powerful dynasty, was of the tribe of the Koreish, co-ordinate with Abd-al-Motaleb, the grandfather of Mohammed. Othman was one of his descendants, and Abi Sufyan was another, who had been made generalissimo by Mohammed himself. Muawiyah, the general of Othman, who had opposed Ali, was the son of this Abi Sufyan, and thus the claimant for the house of Ummeyah. Before the death of Ali, and disregarding the claims of Hassan, his eldest, and of Hosein, the youngest son, Muawiyah, strong in the support of the army, had proclaimed himself Khalif. The nominal reign of Hassan was so short that he was only by title the sixth Khalif,[2] and now Muawiyah determined not only to reign, but to found that hereditary dynasty under which the western conquest was resumed and the Moslems advanced along the northern coast of

Muawiyah.
A. D. 661.

---

[1] Ockley, History of the Saracens, 331.

[2] There are few more touching stories, in this very emotional narrative, than the account of the death of Hosein at the hand of his enemies. This is given in detail by Major David Price in his "Chronological Retrospect; or, Memoirs of the principal Events in Mohammedan History, from the Death of the Arabian Legislator to the Accession of the Emperor Akbar, &c." London, 1811-21.

Africa and into Spain. Thus far the successors of the prophet, simply elected chiefs, had imitated the simplicity and frugality of their founder; but, with the establishment of the Ummeyah dynasty, the Khalif was to become an oriental monarch who would seek to add dignity to his claims and to his person, by the insignia and splendors of a royal court.

He sought a nobler and more convenient site than the sterility of Mecca and Medina could afford, and while he left to those cities all their sanc-tity and their historic renown, he re-membered the charms of Damascus, and determined to make that his royal seat. For many reasons, this was a wise judgment: it gave a new impulse to the Arabians, it broke up local factions, and it was a better point of departure for government and conquest.

Removal of the Khalif- ate to Da- mascus.

One of the oldest towns in the world,[1] it was beau-tiful for situation; so beautiful that Mohammed called it an earthly paradise, and is said to have refused to enter it when he beheld it from the mountain of Saleyeh, because, only one paradise being allotted to man, he preferred that which awaited the faithful in the life to come. It presented peculiar attractions to the inhabitants of the rocks and sands and water-less *wadis* of Arabia; its towers have been compared to " a fleet sailing through a sea of verdure." Abana and Pharpar, the Scripture " rivers of Damascus," — the modern Barada and Phege — " water it with never-

---

[1] It is mentioned in the fourteenth and fifteenth chapters of Gen-esis, as a town existing in the time of Abraham.

failing flow, furrowing it with seven branches and
innumerable rivulets." The enthusiastic description
of Lamartine presents to us its natural features and
much of its ancient architecture as it appeared to the
eyes of the Arabians. They saw, as he did, from a
fissure in the rocky summit, "le plus magnifique et
la plus étrange horizon qui ait jamais étonné un
regard d'homme." The vision loses itself in a laby-
rinth of flower-gardens, fruit-trees, and sycamores.[1]
Ever since its conquest, it must have tempted the
Khalifs as a more fitting royal residence than any in
Arabia. Damascus was also more central than Mecca
or Medina, and of far easier access. It had a good
Mediterranean port at Beirut, fifty-eight miles distant, and another at Acre, giving ready communication with Egypt or Northern Africa; caravans con-
verged to it with the trade of Baghdad, Mecca, and
Aleppo. It had been won in fair fight from the
Greeks; and, for these combined reasons, the founder
of the Ummeyades chose it as the cradle of his
royalty. Here Walid built a magnificent mosque;
here, also, he established himself in the year 673;
and here his dynasty ruled until its overthrow and
the accession of the house of Al Abbas in 746.

The establishment of this family in their new
seat settled or silenced the rival claims, united the
Moslem interests, and permitted new schemes of
conquest.

We may here leave behind us the chronicle of the
Khalifs, except as a matter for occasional reference.
We shall not find it germane to our history to follow

[1] Voyage en Orient.

their fortunes.[1] As we proceed rapidly westward with
_{Western movements.} their victorious generals, their own names and deeds grow dim, while those of their viceroys and amírs who were conquering and coloniz-ing under their orders absorb all our interest. The Moslem armies advanced step by step, fighting hard for what they earned; subduing, proselyting, found-ing, or rebuilding cities, erecting mosques, and with every mosque establishing a school. While at the north, they were daring enough, under Yezid, the son of Mumemyah, to besiege Constantinople; in Africa, they advanced to the ruins of Carthage. They founded or improved the town of Kairuan, only thirty-three leagues north-east of Carthage, and but twelve from the Mediterranean. Under Obah, it _{Obah in Africa.} became a flourishing city, secure, by its inland situation, from the incursions of the Roman and Sicilian navies, the stronghold of a gar-rison to keep the surrounding people in subjection, and a magazine and point of departure for new con-quests at the west.[2] Obah was appointed governor of Africa, and such was his zeal, that he pushed for-ward to the point where the river Sus rolls its tribute into the Atlantic; and, spurring his steed into the ocean until the waves reached his saddle-girths, he exclaimed, "O Allah, if these deep waters did not restrain me, I would yet proceed still further to carry

---

[1] On the other hand, in the general annals, very little is said of the movements at the west. The only reference which Abulfeda makes to Andalusia is in speaking of western progress. "Subactæ tam fuerunt, exempli causa, Andalusia et Chorasana." — *Annales Moslemici.* I. 123.

[2] Ockley, History of the Saracens, p. 367.

onward the knowledge of thy sacred name and of thy holy law." [1] He is even said to have marched to the neighborhood of Tangiers, and held a parley with the governor.[2] But the people of Barbary revolted behind him, and other commanders were to enter upon his labors and to eclipse his fame.[3] Under his successor, Hassan, the inhabitants of Barbary maintained, for many years, a conflict for life and death, led by Queen Cahina, a woman whose masculine valor and womanly fortitude extort our admiration and demand our sympathy. She fought at the head of her troops, and when at last taken prisoner, she refused to redeem her life at the expense of her conscience or her pride. Obedience and tribute were the conditions, but she preferred to give her head to the sword, and it was sent, packed in camphor, as an acceptable tribute, to the Khalif 'Abdu-l-Málek, the fourth of the Ummeyades.[4]

The northern coast of Africa, still retained its Roman names and divisions, — consular Africa and Africa proper, in which were the ruins of Carthage; consular Numidia, Bizacene, and the two Mauritanias, of which one was called Cæsariensis, — containing Algiers and Tlemcen, — and the other known as Tingitania, in which were to spring the populous cities of Morocco and

[1] Condé, Dominacion de los Arabes, I. ch. v.; Ockley, History of the Saracens, 366 note; Cardonne, Histoire de l'Afrique, etc. I. 37.

[2] Ib. I. 35.

[3] Okbah invaded Africa twice; first, when Muawiyah was Khalif, A. H. 46, and again when Yezid had succeeded, in the year '62, when he had the parley with Ilyan; the same Ilyan who, thirty years later, led the Arabs into Spain.

[4] Condé, I. ch. v. The story of Cahina may be read in Cardonne, I. 46–49.

Fez.[1] The plans and prospects of Hassan, as general of the western army, who had conquered the Berbers under Queen Cahina, were now set aside by reason of the appointment of Abdu-l-'aziz, the Khalif's brother, to the vice-royalty of Africa, with his seat in Egypt. He deposed Hassan from the command, and despoiled him of his hard-won treasures. But, whoever was leader, the tide of battle and of progress continued to flow; there was no step taken backward; the revolts of the subjected natives became less frequent and less dangerous. Everywhere the startling cry, *Allah il Allah!* God is God, found an answering echo of unabated sound, *Allah Achbar!* God is victorious; and now, to make further conquests, and to transform the conquered enemies into valiant soldiers of the Faith; to move, with these zealous auxiliaries, to the rock of Abyla; to inscribe *plus ultra* on the opposite pillars of Hercules, where *ne plus ultra* had been blazoned before,[2] and to plant the standard of the prophet in Spain, were to be the work of another commander, upon the consideration of whose labors and successes we now enter. The conquest of Andalus was at hand.

[1] Cardonne, Histoire de l'Afrique, etc. I. 3.

[2] On the royal coin of the Spanish monarchs, to the present time, the columns of Hercules are placed with the motto "plus ultra." The columns and words are also found upon the arms of Granada.

CHAPTER IV.

MUSA IBN NOSSEYR.

THE victorious general whose proud fortune it was to carry the arms and the Faith of the prophet into Spain, and thus to lay the foundations of an empire which was to last for nearly eight hundred years, was Musa, or Moses, the son of Nosseyr. His father, Nosseyr, was a mauli of Abdu-l-'aziz, the brother of the Khalif Abdu-l-málek. This word, *mauli*, which is of frequent use in this history, is somewhat difficult to define: it has no exact equivalent in English. It is applied equally to one who puts himself under the protection of a superior, and to a slave who, after receiving manumission at the hands of his master, still remains under a certain control.[1] In one part of its signification, it is similar to the Roman client in his relation to the patron; in another, it is not unlike the Saxon churl protected by his lord.[2]

Musa's origin.

[1] As there were differences in the character of this clientry, it is manifest that there would be a great distinction also in the grade of the *mauli*. So, too, the position of the lord or master would operate in the position of the *mauli*. Those who were the clients of the Khalif or his brothers might and did occupy very important commands; as in the feudal system the vassal might be himself a great lord or a very honorable individual. Musa was a *mauli* in the more exalted application of the term.

[2] " In the first wars of Islám it was customary for the Arabian

Musa, the son of a mauli, and himself a mauli, probably owed therefore little to birth and family position; but in his early youth he began to display those high qualities which attracted the attention of the Khalif and his brothers, and promised achievements worthy of future preferment. When Abdu-l-málek appointed his younger brother, Besher, to the government of Bosrah, it was Musa who was chosen for his boldness and sagacity to accompany him as Wizir and counsellor, and when, upon the death of Besher, the Khalif was displeased with Musa for a defalcation in the revenue, and would have seized him, the crafty Wizir fled to Damascus, and put himself under the protection of Abdu-l-'aziz, another brother of the Khalif, who thought so well of him that he paid the fine and saved his life.[1]

This Abdu-l-'aziz was appointed viceroy of Africa, with his residence in Egypt; and thither Musa accompanied him as a trusted servant and favorite until he could find a position. He had not long to wait. The new viceroy was either suspicious or jealous of the military commander, Hassan-an-no-man, who had conquered Cahina and her Berbers, and determined to depose him.

On the arrival of Hassan in Egypt he set forth his meritorious actions, and exhibited to the viceroy the Khalif's commission to him as governor of Barca.

generals to grant freedom to all those captives who embraced the Mohammedan religion." — GAYANGOS (AL MAKKARI), *Mohammedan Dynasties*, I. 519, note 21.

[1] From an anonymous history, improperly ascribed to Ibn Koteybah, given in Al Makkari, vol. i. append. liii. liv.

His successes against the Berbers had inflamed the
zeal and the curiosity of the Moslems, and had vindicated his skill as a commander, and the commission
was regular and valid; but Abdu-l-'aziz, in ignorance of the Khalif's action, had already bestowed
the government of Barca upon one of his *maulis*, and,
with high-handed temerity, he tore Hassan's diploma
in pieces, and, exercising at once a bold discretion
and a rare sagacity in reading character, he appointed Musa to the military command in Eastern Africa, in Hassan's place.[1] *Musa appointed to the command in Africa.*

He wrote to the Khalif ardent letters to justify his
action, but the complaint of Hassan at the foot of
the throne found temporary favor in the Khalif's
eyes. The commander of the Faithful was angry
with just cause, and would have reversed the action.
It was manifest that nothing could sustain Musa but
immediate and brilliant success. His appointment
had been made in April or May, A.D. 698, and he lost
no time in assuming his command, bearing with him,
not a commission from the Khalif, but a letter of
appointment from his protector, Abdu-l-'aziz. He
was at the head of a very popular service. Surrounded by a large and effective staff, he numbered
among them, according to Ibn Halib, several *Tabis*,
or followers of the companions of the prophet, — men
who had seen and conversed with those who had
known the prophet face to face.[2] There were also in
his train learned theologians who went to evangelize
the nations whom the sword should reduce to sub-

[1] Ib. liv. lv.

[2] Al Makkari, Mohammedan Dynasties, vol. i. p. 1.

mission;[1] and they proclaimed the traditional saying of the prophet: "Whoever is content to have Allah for his master, Islám for a religion, and Mohammed for a prophet, I will be a warrant to him that I will lead him by the hand into Paradise."[2]   Musa himself has been thought to be one of the *Tabis*, but this can hardly be true, and is probably an invention of those who would heap honors upon him proportionate to his successes.

In a few words, we may trace the lineaments of this distinguished chieftain.   His portrait has been

His person-   painted by the friendly hands of those whom
ality.
                 he led to victory, and by the hostile pencil
of the Spanish historian.   Eliminating the prejudices of both, he was truly a remarkable man, — an accomplished general, a valiant soldier, an enthusiast in religion, instant in prayer, and an eloquent preacher; and if he was, according to Mariana, "a ferocious man," he is also allowed to have been prudent in his counsels and ready in execution.[3]   To his soldiers he

His enthu-   said, "I am a soldier like any of you; when-
siasm.
                 ever you see me do a good deed, thank God
for it, and let every one of you try to imitate it; if, on the contrary, I commit a bad action, let any one of you reprove it and show his dislike, that I may

---

[1] Al Makkari, Mohammedan Dynasties, vol. i. p. 2.

[2] These words were treasured and repeated by Al-Muneydhir, one of the *Ashab* or companions of the prophet, who is said to have reached Spain with Musa at a very advanced age, and who heard them from Mohammed's lips. — *Ib.* I. 3.

[3] To the Spanish historian and Moslem-hater he was, — "Hombre feroz, en sus consejos prudente, y en la ejecucion pronto." — MARI-ANA, *Historia de España*, II. 283.

amend myself." [1] "You may safely rely on me as your commander, for I shall seize every opportunity of leading you on to victory, and, by Allah! I will not cease making incursions into yonder high mountains, and attacking the strong passes leading into them, until God has depressed their elevated summits, reduced their strength, and granted the Moslems the victory. I shall lead you on until God Almighty makes us masters of all or part of the territories lying beyond them, . . . which His immutable decrees have already allotted us; for He is the best of decreers." [2]

It gave new enthusiasm to his faithful soldiery that his petitions to Allah seemed to prevail mightily. Once, in a season of great drought, he prayed fervently for rain, and the answer was immediate; refreshing torrents fell to cheer the hearts of his host, and to strengthen their confidence in him whom Allah was so ready to hear. So earnest was he in his petition that he either forgot or purposely neglected to incorporate in it the Khotbah or usual prayer for the Khalif. One of the congregation rose, and remarked the omission. He was ready with his answer: "This is neither the moment nor the place to invoke any one but Allah. (May His name be exalted.)" [3] So eloquent was that prayer that it was afterwards generally used on similar occasions, and was found among the Moriscoes of Spain nine centuries later.

---

[1] Al Makkari, Mohammedan Dynasties, I. app. lvi.

[2] Ibid. lvii.

[3] It was the custom to read the Khotbah every Friday in the mosques. — AL MAKKARI, I. 395, note 11 ; Ib. 252.

Nor were other and more remarkable supernatural auguries of his success wanting to inspire his credulous troops. On his arrival to take command of the army, one of these had been manifested. While he was reviewing the first division, a sparrow flew to him and nestled in the folds of his robe, upon his breast. He caught it, and, cutting its jugular vein, he smeared his garments with the blood, and plucking its feathers scattered them in the air, exclaiming, "Victory! victory! my friends. By the Master of the Kaaba, victory is ours, if" — he reverently interpolated — "such be the will of Allah, the Almighty!"[1]

Omens of success.

He reorganized the army, and gave them, by the order of the viceroy, three times the arrears of pay due them; and then put them in motion, on the traces of Okbah, towards the regions watered by the Sus, inspired with an ardor which should carry them far beyond any yet attained limit.

The River Sus, as it flows through the western part of Africa, gives two distinct names to the surrounding territory — Sus al-Adani, that towards the east, and Sus al-Aksa, the farthest or western portion. These names have been retained to modern times, and are applied to the country lying along the coast. Sus al-Aksa, the southern portion, stretches inland to the desert of Sahara; and Sus al-Adani, northward and westward into Mauritania; the boundaries have never been well defined. The town of Sus lies in Al Aksa.

---

[1] It was the practice to cut the throat of every animal that was eaten or sacrificed. — JACKSON's *Morocco*, p. 21.

To the Atlantic limit, Musa led his army with uninterrupted movement. The incursions of Okbah
had only stirred up without subduing the Reaches the
people of Sus. The task of reducing those Atlantic.
in the southwest to submission Musa intrusted to
his son Abdullah [1] with an adequate force, while he
himself moved cautiously but steadily towards the
Pillars of Hercules. It is impossible now to define
the exact localities and the family characteristics of
the various tribes mentioned by the Arabian chroniclers. We are told that the Zenetes, the people of
Zab and Dehrar, of Sahra and Mazamuda, were
brought into subjection; all agreeing to pay tribute,
and great numbers embracing Islám.

The tribute and the offerings were large, and many
slaves were taken. In order to appease the Khalif,
and to vindicate his fitness for the appointment to
the command, which, it will be remembered, was as
yet unconfirmed by the sovereign; and at the same
time to retain the favor of the Governor of Egypt, who
had placed him in command, Musa sent large presents
of money and many slaves to both, and thus purchased the sanction of his mercenary and jealous
superiors. The number of slaves mentioned as the
Khalif's share, after two successful expeditions, was
very large. Musa wrote to Abdu-l-'aziz, the viceroy
of Africa, — thirty thousand; and when the astonished viceroy returned the letter, saying there must
be some mistake, Musa adroitly answered that the

---

[1] Al Makkari, I. 258. Condé gives this expedition to Abdu-l-
'aziz, another of Musa's sons, with ten thousand horse. The difference is unimportant. — *Dominacion de los Arabes*, I. ch. vii.

secretary had made a blunder, it was not thirty thousand, but sixty thousand ! [1]

And his skill in dealing with the vanquished was equal to his diplomacy and his soldiership. He had

His skill in conciliating conquered tribes.

first awed them and punished their resistance, and when they had succumbed to the power of his sword, and were ready to receive his conditions, expecting them to be rigorous, they were amazed by a display of clemency. He taxed his eloquence to win them. He told them that strife between him and them was an unnatural strife ; that they were all *Aulad Arabi*, sons of the Arabs, men of the same ancient race, and destined to have a glorious share in the victorious fortunes of their brethren from the east.[2] The promise caused them to accept without question the asserted unity of origin.

Ethnology has thus far afforded us but little exact information concerning the tribes inhabiting what

Berbers and Moors.

we now call the Barbary States, that territory lying north of the Great Desert, of which Morocco and Tripoli are the extreme countries. The inquiry is still going on, and much may be yet learned; but the name of these states is adopted from a single well-defined tribe or clan called the Berbers, — the word Berber means *noble*, — who seem to have retained their individuality, while surrounded by a strange, heterogeneous, and fluctuating mixture of peoples.[3] Their traditions vaguely point to a resi-

---

[1] Al Makkari, I. app. lviii.

[2] Condé, Dominacion de los Arabes, I. ch. vi. Al Makkari, I. 511, note 15.

[3] The slaves were principally negroes from the Soudan.

dence, in a remote period, in the land of Canaan, from which their progenitors fled before the Heaven-directed vengeance of Joshua the son of Nun, with the invading host of the Israelites. Whatever may have been their origin, Musa saw at a glance that, in tastes and habits, they were like the Arabians. Like the "tent-people," they wandered in roving bands; they had the same love of war and plunder. They were similar in physical and mental characteristics, and these points of congeniality might well be exaggerated by reason of the evident advantage which must spring from a union between them for purposes of conquest. They had been partially conquered again and again, and were accustomed to a change of temporary masters. Brought at an early period under the dominion of Carthage, which consisted of incursions and retreats, when the power of Carthage was broken, they had come under the nominal sway of Rome. The insecure grasp of the Romans was relaxed when the Vandals poured furiously down across the strait. The Vandal kingdom had been shattered by Belisarius and the forces of the Eastern Empire.

With these conquerors there had been no affinity or union, but now they found the rationale of the present conquest to be a union with the Arabs, under the most attractive and exhilarating conditions.

The number and strange mixture of religious creeds among them presented no obstacle to the solution of the problem: Islám was better, and far more remunerative. Some few had adopted a nominal Christianity from the Roman empire, but it was a bare form without spirit. There were many Jews, whose belief did less indignity to the creed of the prophet, in that it rejected the Messiah, whose Christian claims interfered with Islám. Besides, the Jews could honor Mohammed for his adoption of their theogonal and historical books; and they found a common origin in the loins of Abraham, a common bond in the semi-brotherhood of Isaac and Ishmael. Some of the tribes, or many among them, had been already somewhat Moslemized by contact with the earlier invaders; but far the greater number were ignorant idolators, and, like the Arabs in the "days of ignorance," steeped in superstition. Thus most of them were ready to acknowledge the superior claims of Mohammed, and to accept the rich promises held out by him to all the faithful.

Islám, as when first presented to the Arabians, suited their tastes, and promised to develop their powers; it exalted them in the scale of humanity; it gave them coherence, it seemed to insure success.

Thus, on the part of Musa, after a quick comprehension of the situation, the wholesale conversion of these western tribes was a master-stroke of policy, without which, indeed, his military projects would have had slow and painful progress, or would perhaps have failed entirely. We may give him credit as a propagandist, but the general wanted troops, and thus he secured them.

Wholesale conversions.

He preached to them, he prayed with them, he consorted with them; and the results of his policy were immediately manifest and cheering. From the south the people of Gadames, and along the northern line of the Great Desert, came flocking to his standard;

at one time to the number of twelve thousand sea-
soned and valiant warriors.[1]

The war of the Moslemah in Africa was at an end;
the army of Musa was largely recruited, and combinations for unlimited conquest were formed.

The inhabitants of the country, long known to the
Romans as Mauritania, were called by the generic
name of Mauri, or Moors; and when this The Arab-
combination was formed, the host that was Moors.
now ready to invade Spain, under the enthusiastic
leadership of Musa, appeared in history as the *Arab-
Moors*, who combined the native force and original
momentum of the Arabians with the endurance and
numbers of the people of Western Africa.

In Egypt and in Damascus, all tongues were loud
in encomiums of a commander who could convert
whole nations to the Faith, with but little shedding of
blood, and turn them at once into valuable auxiliaries
and allies. Thus, what had seemed a wild and impossible notion, of invading Western Europe, became
a glorious and feasible purpose.

It has been already seen that, while the military
ambition of Musa never flagged, the interests of the
Faith never suffered at his hands. In every The piety of
town and in every permanent camp — in Musa.
many cases soon to become a town — a mosque arose;
at one end the Kiblah, directing the prayers of believers towards the holy city of Mecca; at the other a

---

[1] Later, the Berbers revolted from time to time; it was not
against Islám, but either against oppressive local governors or in the
hope of founding native kingdoms independent of the Khalifs and
their government.

square tower, called a minaret, surmounted by the flag-staff, which attracted the constant regards of the Moslemah. Within, was the *minbar*, or high pulpit, sacred to the prophet, from the steps of which — not from the desk at the top [1] — one of the Imaums, on every Friday, recited the prayers, expounded the Korán, and preached hortatory and war-inspiring sermons.

From the minaret (mád'neh) [2] the muezzin, in his green robe, called the faithful to prayer five times a day, with a solemn power in his living voice, which neither flag, trumpet, bell, nor fire could simulate or rival: "Come to prayer, come to prayer! come to the temple of salvation! Great God! Great God! there is no God except God!" In the early morning he added and reiterated, "Prayer is to be preferred to sleep!" And throughout the vast camp, those who were hindered from going to the "temple of salvation" spread their carpets and, kneeling towards the kiblah, raised their hearts and voices to Allah.

When the houses of officers and soldiers were built of reeds and clay, the mosques were constructed of wood and stone. To such as were too distant to hear the muezzin's invocation to prayer, a white flag was displayed, called *El Alem*, the signal.

The Khalif Abdu-l-malek died at his royal seat in

---

[1] At this early period, the pulpit was left empty in honor of the prophet, the Imaums preaching to the people from one of the steps. At a later day, the Khalifs made no scruple of addressing the people from the pulpit itself.

[2] The exact date of the introduction of the minaret is not known: in the earliest days, the prayer-time was proclaimed from the roof of the mosque.

Damascus, in the year 705, and was succeeded by his son, Al Walid, whose good fortune it Khalif Abdu-l-malek dies. Al Walid succeeds. A. D. 705. was to be to declare with truth that in his reign the religion of Mohammed had been proclaimed and triumphantly established from the banks of the Ganges to the surges of the Atlantic.

We have now reached the year of the Hijra 88 (A.D. 706). The appointment of Musa had been made by Abdu-l-'aziz Ibn Meruan, the Viceroy of Egypt, ten years before, by a stretch of authority unusual among the officials of the Khalif, whose word was law, with all the force of religious sanction. The confirmation, as far as is known, seems to have been held in abeyance; at least there is no record of the explicit sanction of the Khalif. It may be that Musa was held in a state of probation.

But Abdu-l-'aziz, the viceroy, died in the year 86 and, when his brother Abdullah acceded to the government of Egypt, it is probable that Musa renewed his oath of allegiance to him.

On the accession of the new Khalif, Al Walid, the great successes of Musa had commended him to the whole Moslem world, and Al Walid lost no Confirms Musa. time in confirming his appointment, and enlarging the scope of his commission.[1] He was named Supreme Commander of the Moslemah in the west, and Amir of Africa. His jurisdiction promised

---

[1] Al Makkari, I. 510, note 7. Condé says that the Khalif appointed him to the command in the year 83. If this were true, Al Walid only reconfirmed what had been already done by Abdu-l-malek. Condé also mentions the latter confirmation, Dominacion de los Arabes, I. ch. vii.

to excel in importance that of Egypt itself; and consequently he was to receive orders, not from the viceroy, but directly from the Khalif at Damascus.

To give additional weight to his expedition, as one of special interest to the Commander of the Faithful, large reinforcements were sent him from the east, representing the principal tribes of Arabia and Syria. Men of the most distinguished families joined him eagerly; and thus, with Africa and Mauritania converted to the Faith and brought under subjection to the Khalif, he set at work to prepare for the greatest, and apparently the most difficult, exploit yet proposed to the Moslem arms; one which was to be of immediate concern to the Christianity and nascent civilization of Europe, to consolidate the former, and give a new impulsion to the latter, and thus to present one of the most striking chapters in history, ancient or modern.

To aid him in this colossal undertaking, Musa was fortunate in having six valiant sons, four of whom

Musa's sons. figure largely in the annals. They were Abdullah, Abdu-l-'aziz, Meruan, Abdu-l-'ala, Abdu-l-malek, and Abdu-r-rahmán.[1] Of these, the eldest, Abdullah, had, as early as the year 704, conducted the first Moslem fleet from Eastern Africa, and had ravaged the coasts of Sicily. He was now placed in command of the frontier of Kairwan, to

---

[1] Al Makkari mentions Abdu-l-malek but once, as governor of Maghreb, I. 292. Abdu-r-rahman is a somewhat conjectural person, whose existence is gathered from the fact that Musa has been named Abú Abdi-r-rahmán, the father of Abdu-r-rahmán. I. 547, note 19.

keep open communication with the East. Upon
Abdu-l-'azis was conferred the charge of the southern
boundary of Sus, to keep in subjection the country of
Dara and Tafilet and the border of Sahara; while to
Meruan was confided the more glorious service of
marching to Tangiers, on the strait of Gibraltar, the
ancient capital of Mauritania Tingitana, called in
the narrative of Al Makkari, " the citadel of their
country and the mother of their cities." [1] From Tangiers the landscape of southern Spain opens in most
attractive loveliness.

It is a question of little moment, and cannot easily
be answered, to which of the Arabian generals Tangiers surrendered. Meruan marched upon it The capture
by his father's order. Al Makkari says of Tangiers.
Musa took it himself, but this may mean by the
hands of his son; and he allows that other historians
attribute the conquest to Tarik el Tuerto, a splendid
hero, who will soon appear upon the scene. The
city resisted the first attacks, but at last succumbed
to one or more of these warriors, and the banner
of Islám floated on all its towers, flaunting porten-
tous defiance to the anxious inhabitants of the Andalusian coast.

As seen from the water, Tangiers rises in a gentle
amphitheatre on the slopes of two hills, of which the
citadel occupied the northern eminence, and the city
itself the southern slope. It looks directly across

---

[1] Al Makkari, I. 252. In view of the repeated conquests of
Africa in earlier times, I am at a loss to understand how he could
add, "They say that Tangiers had never been taken by an enemy before the days of Musa." The Arab-Moors altered its ancient name,
Tingis, into *Tanjah*, " Protected by the Lord."

from the centre of its broad-armed but shallow bay, upon the bluffs of Spain, and has properly been called the African key to the strait. To the Arab-Moors, it was to prove a valuable watch-tower, and an admirable port in which to make preparation for the invasion of Spain.

As soon as it surrendered, the command of the garrison was given to Tarik Ibn Zeyad Ibn Abdillah, a warrior who now first appears prominently in the history, but who had doubtless proved himself a valiant and tireless chieftain in the van of Moslem progress, and who was soon to win a greater glory than any others engaged in the conquest. His later fame is assured, but his original obscurity makes it difficult to ascertain his birth and nationality. The most generally received account is that he was a native of Hamdan in Persia, who became in his early youth a *mauli* of Musa. It is probable that his enthusiasm, as a proselyte, interested him particularly in the conversion of the Berbers; he became closely allied with them, and was greatly honored by them, and this may account for his being called by many writers a Berber.[1] He is described as a tall man, having red hair and a white complexion, who had lost one of his eyes, and had a mole on his hand. In the Spanish histories he is called Tarik el Tuerto, an ambiguous expression, which may mean either " one-eyed " or " squint-eyed."[2]

The restless energy of Tarik did not permit him to

[1] Al Makkari, I. 266. See also app. lxx.
[2] Tuerto from *torcer*, *to twist*, would seem to mean the latter; but the prevailing opinion seems to be that he had lost an eye.

remain long inactive in his new command. Separated by a mountainous promontory from Tangiers was another stronghold on the strait, nearer to the opposite coast of Spain: this was Ceuta or Septa, which was held for the King of Spain by a Gothic general named Julian by the Spaniards, and Ilyan by the Arabians.[1] Against this fortress Tarik directed his arms, but without immediate success. Such were the valor and energy of Ilyan, displayed in effective sallies against his assailants, that Tarik was driven back to his quarters in Tangiers.

What had been thus far accomplished may be regarded as the prologue to the magnificent drama now opening of the Conquest of Spain by the Arab-Moors. The invaders had secured their *point d'appui.* They were in large numbers, well-equipped and inured to war. For more than three-quarters of a century they had been conquerors; they were burning for greater conquests. They had evangelized and transformed the world that lay behind them, actually converting the western nations into *Aulad-Arabi,* sons and brothers of the Arabians in religious faith and practice, while under the influence of a new enthusiasm, from Arabia and Syria, a tide of reinforcements was beginning to pour, to cement their conquests, and give new strength to their authority.

In readiness to invade Spain.

Nor was there ever better material with which to

[1] Septa, so called from its seven hills or hillocks, had been captured by Belisarius from the Vandals, but was recaptured by the Goths from the Byzantine empire after several attempts. For the most striking of these, see La Fuente, Historia de España II. 337.

undertake such an invasion. The eastern contingent
was formed of soldiers and the sons of soldiers for
three or four generations: every man was reduced to
muscle, and was in the best fighting condition. To
power of endurance and experience in war, their long
succession of victories had added prestige and wealth.
As warriors of God and His prophet, the meanest of
them could aspire to the highest earthly honors as
the reward of constancy and valor; and, if he fell in
battle, he was sure of the immortal joys of Paradise.
These qualities, acquirements, and hopes, they had
imparted to their new allies.

Their long and arduous campaigns in countries,
differing greatly in topography, had taught them the
principles of strategy, — the military grasp of the
nature and resources of an extended territory, —
while in continual battle, they had acquired with
their skill in arms the simple tactics suited to their
needs, the first principle of which was to attack the
enemy wherever he presented himself.

They had a large contingent of cavalry, which they
increased whenever they could procure or capture
horses. They kept up the Arabian breeds as far as
they could, especially that of the Kochlani, which
had a lineage of more than fifteen centuries, and
which were to be the progenitors of the famous Barbary horses. Thus to overrun a country, retire unbroken from unexpected resistance, and return speedily
to the attack, the Arab-Moors, now about to enter
Spain, were the finest and readiest light troops in the
world.

And then the prospect of success was no vague or

visionary dream. Their *tabis* repeated, and the tradition has all the appearance of truth, the Prophetic
declaration. saying of Mohammed, as his fervent imagination reached into the future: "I have seen before my eyes the East and the West, and every one of the regions comprised in them shall be subdued to my people." In fulfilment of this prophetic declaration, they had reached the columns of Hercules, and could see, as in a magic mirror, the green land of the opposite shore. The last stronghold of the Goths was Ceuta; that captured, the next step was to cross the strait and conquer Andalus.

Here, and in this happy frame of mind, we leave the Arab-Moors for a brief space to devise their plans for the new campaign, in order that we may cast a glance across the strait, and see in what condition the Gothic kingdom was to receive the threatened incursion. This inquiry must be brief, but it is necessary thus to array the combatants against each other in a clear light, in order that we may discover the philosophy of the great events which followed immediately after the shock of battle.

BOOK II.

THE DOMINION OF THE GOTHS.

———•———

CHAPTER I.

THE GOTHS: OF THEIR ENTRANCE INTO SPAIN.

IT was said in the beginning of this history that in writing of a conquest it is first necessary to present in outline a history of the origin, characteristics, and motive of the conquerors. This I have endeavored to do with sufficient detail in the preceding chapters.

It is also true that, to attain fully to the value and conditions of the conquest, we must consider the origin and character of the people, and the state of the kingdom upon which the invasion is to be made. We are thus required to turn aside, for a brief space, to see who the occupants of the Peninsula were, in person and institutions, and how they were prepared to meet the impending incursion of the Arab-Moors. I shall therefore present a brief sketch of the well-known history of the Goths, and of their dominion of three centuries in Spain, dwelling here and there more particularly upon those facts and events which are strong links in the

The Goths. They occupy Spain for three centuries.

chain of causation, and conspire to present the philosophy of the great event.

This brief inquiry will involve a consideration of the condition of the Peninsula before the Gothic period, the circumstances of their coming, the motive and purpose of their settlement, their attainments in civilization; their relations to the Christian religion, the enervation which crept upon them in their new seats, the fruit of idleness, luxury, and sin; their political and social decline, and their consequent inability to cope with the coming invaders.

If we go back to the dominion of Rome in the Peninsula, in her palmy and vigorous days under the later commonwealth and the earlier empire, we shall find her power more absolute and less questioned in Spain than in any other of her provinces. Spain as a Roman province. It was the boast of the Roman Cæsars that, for four centuries, Spain was in a permanent state of tranquillity. In the reign of Tiberius, with a population of between seven and eight millions of people, — larger than that of Gaul, — only three legions, from fifteen to twenty thousand men, — were stationed within her borders, and these more for free quarters than for active service.

Rich in agricultural products, abounding in cattle, yielding the fruits both of the tropics and the temperate zone, with mines of gold, silver, quicksilver, and precious stones, with quarries of the finest marbles and other building material, Spain sent food and treasures to Italy, and was one of the brightest and most valuable jewels in the Imperial diadem. With clear, reflected light, Spain shared in the glories of the

Augustan age. For two years (25 and 26 B.C.) Augustus took up his residence there, reducing a few of the still wild and refractory tribes — the *guerrilleros* of that time — to submission, after a battle in the broken country around Velleia, among the sources of the Ebro, and guarding the northwest by a naval force of triremes on the Bay of Biscay, from the mouths of the Garonne to the Adour. He gave the people wise and clement laws. He founded or enlarged military colonies, bearing Roman names: these were at strategic points, and some of them had been already occupied from an early period as native towns. Such was the Roman origin of Saragossa, (Cæsarea Augusta), which was to play such an important part in all later periods of Spanish history; of Braga in Portugal (Braccara); of Lugo (Lucus); of Merida (Emerita); of Pampeluna (Pompeiopolis), and many others.

His policy in Spain, maintained after his departure by Agrippa, conduced greatly to that long period of tranquillity which seems marvellous when compared with the constant ebullitions in other parts of the empire.

But Rome was at last to yield to the incursions of those northern barbarians whom she had at first despised, and to whom, in incessant warfare, she had taught the military arts by which they were to compass her dismemberment and final overthrow. They came with constantly increasing numbers and momentum : at first in successive shocks, now here, now there ; and then, as it were, in a concerted movement along their whole line upon the

The Northern Barbarians.

fainting, reeling, supine giant. One strong element of their power was motion, incessant motion. In their earlier movements upon Rome, their purpose seems to have been to invade, despoil, destroy what they could not carry away, and then retire to prepare for a new incursion upon such points as promised victory and new spoils. They were still in principle nomadic peoples; they had not risen to the idea of a bounded and settled nationality; what they called their country at any time had no bounds and no permanence; it was simply the territory they could conquer, and which became in turn a point of departure for new lands and richer spoils. " Ibi mihi patria, non ubi nascor, sed ubi pascor."

The occupants of the lands which tempted their invasion were enemies, to be driven out, or treated as slaves, or annihilated. The geographical limits of their western and southern marches were the shores of the Atlantic and of the Mediterranean; and even this latter boundary ceased for many of them to present a permanent barrier; they crossed it in wild career, and poured upon Africa.

What has been said may be considered as applicable to most of the northern tribes of Scythia and Germany who invaded the Roman Empire of the West. When they reached middle Europe they found the more attractive seats of the west and south occupied by earlier races from the east, and consolidated into a vast empire, which they were not at first strong and compact enough to destroy.

Thus some of them wandered or were driven into the inhospitable north; but, moved by cupidity and a restless ambition, they were not satisfied to remain in those sterile and inclement regions, while they heard exaggerated accounts of the luxurious delights and accumulated treasures of the south. They marched southward, to be defeated again and again, to receive tribute-money, to have lands assigned for their residence, never abandoning hope of the coming day when their victorious hosts should wrest these treasures and delights from the enervate grasp of the Roman empire.

For a long period the Danube and the Rhine, — the former rising within the re-entering or bend of the latter, — flowing in different directions, formed a natural fosse between the Roman dominion and its northern assailants. Schooled but untamed by disaster, the barbarians at length forced these outworks, and then for a long period it was rather the prestige of the imperial name than the power of the imperial arm which postponed the conquest and subversion of the empire. They made fierce and swift incursions, and retreated with their booty. They came again: they asked for territory for settlement, and obtained it; they joined the Roman armies as auxiliaries. They laughed when they received land as a *beneficium*, subject to tribute; their campaigns were reduced to system; they were consolidated into confederations and so-called nations; and thus they seemed in readiness to sweep down upon Rome as a submerging torrent. What should give initial velocity to their marshalled forces? The impetus was an extraneous one; it came as a propelling force from behind.

The Huns, a furious horde, impelled by the same

nomadic principle, but moving with a greater momentum, came galloping from the shores The Huns; of the Caspian, where they had become liar mission. compacted after leaving Tartary; charging, without respect of persons, upon all men and all things appearing in their path, destroying what resisted them, scattering what could not withstand them in all directions, and giving to the denser masses which they found in middle Europe a thrust forward, pushing them westward and southward, and forcing them upon the territory of Rome, that they might lessen the severity of the shock from behind.

I pass now to a brief notice of those races or confederacies which, obeying the laws to which I have thus generally referred, were precipitated upon the western provinces of the Roman empire, and were carried by impetus and ambition into Spain, and some of them even beyond its southern limits.

First in order of these northern peoples came the Alans, the Suevi, and the Vandals. These were soon driven forward and unseated by the Visigoths.

The Alans may be easily traced back to their earlier seats between the Euxine and the Caspian. Thence, impelled by the Huns, they had moved into Pannonia, proceeding with but The Alans. little organization, under the new impulse of self-preservation. When the Huns appeared, unheralded and frightful to behold, the Alans were struck with panic: a part of them were overthrown; the main body fled westward, first towards the shores of the Baltic, and then, deflected by the current, to the southwest.

They were emphatically men of the sword. Wild and intractable, they shrunk from the bonds and discipline of confederation. They were Pagans of a bloody type; a part of their ritual of worship was to mutter incantations around a sabre stuck in the ground; and, when arrayed for conflict, they hung the skulls of their enemies slain in battle at the pommels of their saddles. With the momentum they had received, after the furious surge of the Huns had spent its force, and was finding its ebb, the Alans passed through Gaul into Spain in the beginning of the fifth century. In northern Spain they found a halting-place. They foraged in the river valleys of Portugal, and their roving bands spread all over the Peninsula, with little consistence, and consequently with little power. It is therefore difficult to trace their influence in the later periods of history. They appear as a distinct people for only about eight years, —from 409 to 417.

Over the same track came the Suevi, and nearly at the same time. They were a compact tribe, with far more coherence. They had occupied and left

The Suevi.

settlers in a hundred cantons between the Oder and the Danube, and had impressed their name upon a portion of the region since known as Suabia (Schwaben), one of the ten *circles* into which Germany was divided previous to 1806. By the requirements of their military government, each canton was bound to furnish one thousand men annually to do battle in the interests of all. They too were Pagans. Every year, at the opening of their campaign, they sacrificed a man to propitiate their god of war. As a sign of nobility, they brought with them from the east the custom of wearing their hair at its full length; but in preparing for battle they gathered it up in a bag, that it might not impede their activity nor interfere with the use of their weapons. Following the Alans into Spain, they retained their compact order, and, instead of spreading to the south, they settled chiefly in northern Portugal and Galicia. So remarkably have they retained their distinctive character, that, while there are no geographic reasons for the separation of Portugal from the rest of Spain, we find them to-day, although they have had foreign masters, a distinct nation in the west of the Peninsula, with a language of their own.[1]

But the fiercest irruption yet experienced by the west was that of the Vandals, — so fierce that, like a man running down hill, they could not stop themselves as long as the course was clear in their front. When first known to history, they occupied the shores of the Baltic between the Vistula and the Elbe. This tribe was stronger in physical type, and more united in purpose even than the Suevi. Ishmaelites of the north, their hand was against every man. Not only did they continue their progress against the Roman dominion, but they fiercely attacked all the combinations of men who stood in their way. Cruelty and destruction were their tutelar divinities. What they could not put to sordid use,

The Vandals.

---

[1] The author of the "Monarchia Lusitana" says that the Castilians, as late as the seventeenth century, called the Portuguese *Sevosos*, as an opprobrious name, —a corruption of *Suevos*, bearing out the opinion I have expressed.

they mutilated and defaced; they razed churches and palaces; they sacked for treasure; they cut pictures and broke statues to pieces. Fire and sword went hand in hand, in the van of their hosts; and thus they justly earned the monstrous celebrity of leaving their name to the world in all future time as a synonym for ruthless and useless destruction.

In such a spirit they swept down upon Spain, to plunder and scatter the Hispano-Romans, as well as to drive out their Teutonic kinsmen, who had preceded them in the southwest. So great was their momentum, however, that they did not remain long in the peninsula; and they left few tokens of their passage. The southern province, where they halted for a space, bears their name. They were there called Vandalocii, and the territory Vandalitia. The convenient dropping of the initial letter has made it Andalusia.[1]

All the tribes or nations thus far mentioned may be considered as only the advanced skirmishers of a more solid and serious invasion, — one which was to result in a permanent occupancy of the Peninsula, and to present a very important constituent in the later history: this was the invasion of Gaul and Spain by the Goths. One of the two grand divisions of the Gothic confederacy was coming more slowly and more ponderously upon the Roman empire of the west. Their move-

The Goths: a more serious invasion.

---

[1] It was a wild fancy which assayed to derive the name from Andalos, the son of Tubal, the son of Yafeth, the son of Núh. Ibn Hayyan, Ibn Khaldun, and others, agree that it is from "Andalosh," a nation of barbarians, who settled there. Gayaugos says the sound of *v* cannot be made without the *hamsch*.

ments were directed by a concerted plan, and conducted with greater system, for that wonderful people
had for some time contemplated the founding of
stable kingdoms upon the ruins of Rome, and were to
display their eminent ability in Italy, Gaul, and Spain,
to transform the tributary provinces of the Roman
empire into distinct and independent nationalities.

Thus in numbers, in concert, in military system,
in enduring valor, in historic prestige, and in pride
of race, the Goths were superior to Alans, Suevi, and
Vandals, — the foremost among the nations coming
out of the north, which Jornandes, their historian,
calls "the forge of mankind." [1]

Springing like them from the generatrix of peoples
in Asia, they were already at or just before the beginning of the Christian era, divided, according to
the territory occupied, into two great nationalities ;
one lying along the shores of the Baltic, and the
other between the Don and the Danube. A large
number had penetrated into Scandinavia, whence
they were to return southward, with increased vigor.
Without an exact definition of their geographical
limits, those occupying the eastern seats were called
Eastern or Ostro-Goths, and those to the west,
Western or Visigoths. [2]

They had long caused the Romans to fear and con-

---

[1] Jornandes made an abridgment of the History of the Goths,
from the great work of Cassiodorus, which has been lost, — "De
Getarum sive Gothorum origine et rebus gestis."

[2] It is difficult to state the time and circumstances of this division.
Gibbon says it was made when they emerged from Scandinavia.
Guizot corrects him, and says it was after their irruption into and
partial settlement of Dacia.

tend against their power along the line of the Danube.
They had presented a petition, which was virtually a
demand for lands within the Roman territory. They,
like the other northern nations, had yielded to the
pressure of the advancing Huns, and at last they
had marched down, with serried hosts and determined purpose, upon the western empire; the Ostro-
goths making the imperial capital their objective
point, and the Visigoths forcing their way into Gaul
and Spain to establish a permanent dominion.

We must not fail to notice one important fact
They were which enters as a valuable factor in the
Arian
Christians. problem of their later history. Unlike their
northern predecessors, they were not Pagans, but
Arian Christians.

About the year 360 A.D., Ulphilas, the bishop of
Mœsia and Thrace, himself a Goth, who had adopted
the tenets of Arius in that memorable controversy, —
which was not entirely set at rest by the promulgation
and imperial enforcement of the Nicene creed, — made
a translation of the New Testament in that dialect,
which, from the designation of one of his provinces,
received the name of Mœso-Gothic. It was thus
that, a man of mark and influence, a leader of men,
Ulphilas caused all the Gothic people to adopt Arian
Christianity. It gave coherence and concert to these
fierce northern tribes; it incited them to loftier deeds;
it partially introduced a theocratic element into their
government. It tempered, without enfeebling, their
valor, and was, beyond a doubt, the chief cause of
their superiority to the Pagan nations which had
already penetrated into Spain.

It is not pertinent to our present inquiries to consider that large intermediate page in the Gothic Annals which tells of their exploits during their movements to the southwest, and which is so full of romance. In it are contained the convulsive struggles of expiring Rome ; the shouts of embattled hosts, and the clangor of horns ; the torch and sword of a northern Nemesis ; the mighty deeds and striking personality of Alarik ; his storm and plunder of the imperial city ; his secret burial beneath the walls of Consentia, with the spoils and treasures of Rome, in the bed of the river Busento, the waters of which had been diverted from their course, and then allowed to flow again ; a burial designed to be kept so secret, that the prisoners who dammed the stream and dug his grave were put to death, that they might not disclose the spot. These stories may be found in Jornandes, and present strongly the character of this remarkable people.[1]

Their prestige was equal to their energy ; they were feared by all. The infantry, compact and tireless ; a large contingent of cavalry, all clothed in skins and partially protected by defensive armor ; their weapons of offence were javelins, swords, and battle-axes. They wore their hair unshorn, and considered a cropping or tonsure as rendering a person unfit for political or civil offices.[2] As crests to their rude

---

[1] De rebus Getarum, &c., ch. xxx.

[2] This continued during their Spanish dominion. " Asi," says La Fuente, "la décalvacion y la tonsura eran penas infamantes, y llevaban, consigo, la inhibicion de ejercer cargos politicos y civiles ; el monarca ó principe decalvado ó tonsurado no tenia ya otra carrera que la de la iglesia." — *Historia de España,* ii. 401.

helmets, they placed the heads of beasts of prey. Their
very presence struck terror into the hearts of their
enemies, and caused many battles to be substantially
won before the first blow was struck.

After continual battles and sieges, in most of which
they experienced no check, the Visigoths made their
Make their way into Aquitania. way into Aquitania, and thence into Spain.
Into the latter territory their first concerted
entrance was under a chief named Ataulpho, in the
year 414.   And now their progress was sensibly
slackened by the numbers of the original population
who still occupied the soil, — Celtiberians and Hispano-Romans, — and by the singular mélange of the
northern tribes which had preceded them.   The confusion was great; the Alans were chiefly in central
and southern Lusitania, the Suevi in the northwest,
in northern Portugal and Galicia, the Vandals resting
in Andalusia.   The roving bands of each were striking out in every direction, while all over the territory,
but more thickly in Bætica and Tarraconensis, were
the thrice-encrusted people, — Iberians, Celtiberians,
Romans, long known, in a compound designation, as
Hispano-Romans.[1]

I shall only touch upon the more important points
in the successive reigns.   After the death of Ataulpho,
Ataulpho, Sigerico, Walia. and a few months of nominal rule by Sigerico,
the leadership was assumed in the year 417
A. D. 417. by Walia. As yet the Roman idea of a king,
or even a supreme *imperator*, had not been adopted

---

[1] The Basques, or inhabitants of Biscay, are supposed to represent
the old Iberian race, and were never dispossessed of their territories
by any of these invaders.

by the Goths; their chief was not a political *rex*, but a military leader, elected for his great merits.

And besides, in Spain, the Romans were at this period, and for years afterwards, the nominal masters. The Gothic chief found in the embroglio of titular governors, tenants, and serfs, and previous invaders, that it was his best policy to temporize with the Roman claims, and, under the shadowy auspices of the Empire, to turn his arms against the nations who had preceded him. It is said that, discouraged by the condition of affairs in Spain, and with the instinct of movement still unabated, they were at first inclined to march through Spain and cross the strait into Africa; but, to an inland people, the winds and waves of the Mediterranean and want of transportation presented a serious obstacle.

When he had determined to remain in Gaul and Spain, Walia kept his troops busy: he exterminated the Silingi, one of the indigenous tribes; he routed the Alans in battle, and killed their leader; he turned his arms against the Vandals, assailing them with such vigor as to mass them upon the sea-coast, scattering a few to seek refuge with the Alans and the Suevi.

It pleased the Roman emperor, Honorius, to regard the Goths as the allies and instruments of the empire. When he found that he could not control them, he assumed the character of protector and friend: he celebrated their triumphs at Rome, and rewarded their chief with the gift of what he had already grasped, half of the immense territory lying between the Loire and the Garonne. It was no longer a tributary province,

Allies of the Roman emperor.

but a nominally tributary, and really independent, kingdom.

Such was the imperial recognition, when it was quite unnecessary, of that vast Visigothic dominion which, in the fifth century, claimed the larger portion of Gaul and almost all of Spain. It extended from the Loire to the Strait of Gibraltar, and only lacked in the Peninsula the northwestern triangle still in the hands of the Suevi, and a few sheltered spots on the Biscay coast, then and later occupied by the Basques. The headquarters and embryo court of the Gothic chief were at Toulouse, on the Garonne, which continued to be the Visigothic capital from 413 to 507, until its destruction by Clovis, after the battle of Vouillé, near Poitiers.

The Vandals found themselves unable to cope with the greater numbers and superior system of the Goths, and therefore determined to leave the field without further contest. True to their cruel nature and well-earned reputation, as they moved to embark upon the Mediterranean, they committed all kinds of outrages: they sacked and burned the towns and villages of the unresisting inhabitants; they completely devastated the country around Valencia and Cartagena. Then one large band took boats and crossed over to the Balearic islands, which they fearfully ravaged; while the main body concerted to abandon Spain, and, crossing the strait, to move the entire force into Mauritania, except such stragglers as were disposed to join the other nationalities already represented in the Peninsula.

The uncertain condition of the Roman sway in

Africa conspired to give new vigor to their purpose. Just at this juncture, the weak and wicked emperor of the west, Honorius, died, and his sister Placidia, who became regent during the minority of her son, gave a new impetus to the decline of the Roman power, and rendered its enemies more powerful to destroy it. She had at first nominated to the prefecture of Africa Count Boniface; but it was just at this time that Boniface, the imperial prefect, was, at the instigation of Ætius, removed and recalled. To gratify his revenge, he excited the mixed population over which he had ruled to revolt against the imperial authority. This accomplished, he sent a secret messenger across the strait to Genserik, the chief of the Vandals, inviting him to invade Africa, and strike another blow at the Roman dominion.

The pressure of the Goths, and the invitation of Boniface, conspired to transport the Vandal host to a wider field and an untrammelled scope of destruction, and by a better if a longer road to the city of Rome. In May, 429, they crossed the narrow sea, and Genserik the Terrible passed in review, on the African shore, an array of more than fifty thousand warriors, leaving Spain, without reluctance, to the strongest and the bravest who should come after him.[1] The Vandals soon spread over the whole of Mauritania

---

[1] La Fuente (Historia de España, II. 303) makes the Vandal army eighty thousand strong. The error arises in this way: adopting the imperial divisions of one thousand, Genserik appointed, before leaving Spain, eighty chiliarchs, but by the reduction, through desertion and battle, each did not command a thousand men. An average of about seven hundred to each would be nearer the truth.

conquering and forming alliances with the fierce inhabitants, and laying the foundation of an empire which lasted until the time when Belisarius should shatter its power. Nor was it only an empire in possession; it was a new base of operations, from which to assail other portions of the Roman empire and even the imperial city itself. They soon had a considerable fleet in the Mediterranean.

When the Vandals thus left Spain, some of the Alans accompanied them. Others were absorbed by the Goths; many were destroyed, and they

With a few of the Alans. ceased to be a dangerous element in the medley of northern nations collected in the Peninsula.

The Suevi, as we have seen, retained their identity in the west and northwest. The Goths were the chief representatives of the Teutonic power; but the original Celtiberian population, accustomed to servitude, was still in a large preponderance; and there were also in the south, and in arms, numbers of the imperio-Romans, still claiming the prestige of Roman supremacy, especially in that territory later known

The Rûm. as the Algarbe, on the borders of Lusitania and Betica. To all but the northern invaders, the Arabian historians give the generic name of Rûm (Romanos), which they retained after the shadow of the empire had disappeared.

The settlement of the Suevi in northern Portugal and Galicia gave rise to a distinct monarchy, inde-

The Suevi in Portugal. pendent of Rome and the Goths, under Hermanrik, in the year 409; and his long tenure of royal power, until 441, combined with the topography of their residence to strengthen their kingdom. It has been seen that on their entrance into Spain they were Pagans, but they soon found that Christianity in some form was to be a necessary condition of their national existence. It was beaten into them by the Goths in numerous battles; it was in the very atmosphere; and no later than the reign of Recciario, the grandson of their first monarch, who ascended the throne in 448, actuated perhaps in some degree by conscience, more certainly by self-interest, they embraced Arian Christianity; and the bond between them and the Goths was further strengthened by the marriage of this king of the Suevi with the daughter of the reigning Gothic monarch.

Thus we have a clear view of the stage and actors upon which and with whom the Goths were to enact their important and interesting drama. In presenting these preliminary details of well-known historic facts, I have intended simply to refresh the mind of the reader, and to prepare the way for an outline of the Gothic dominion, so strong, and apparently so permanent that it seemed to defy the hand of time; and yet so subtly corrupted, even in the periods of its patent strength, that it was to crumble to dust in a single day, like the fall of theatrical machinery at the prompter's nod.

CHAPTER II.

THE GOTHIC KINGDOM ESTABLISHED.

I PROCEED now to consider briefly — mentioning only the necessary persons and events — the progress of the Goths from this period until the coming of the Arab-Moors.

From their most populous seats in Tarraconensis, with their rapidly developing purpose of national settlement, they spread southward into Andalusia, and northward into Aquitania, establishing military posts upon already fortified sites, and laying the strong foundations of that vast Visigothic empire which was for a brief period to claim the whole territory from the Loire to the Mediterranean.

The Gothic empire in Gaul and Spain.

The stones of the imposing structure were cemented with blood. This first portion of their peninsular history presents to the historical student a wild confusion, a chaos of fighting, obscuring clouds of battle dust, the noise of the captains, and the shouting, garments rolled in blood, from the rising to the setting sun. There were no well-defined frontier limits, no treaties, no faith with enemies, might took the place of right, relics of civilization were spurned by the foot of barbarism; Rome striking impotent and frantic blows, beating the air with averted eyes; the semi-barbarians fighting, on any and every pretext, against each other in Spain; against Ætius, the Catholic and Roman, and against Litorius, the Pagan and Roman, in Gaul. It was an age in which the Spanish historian pithily says, "there were many chiefs, but not a single hero."[1]

It seemed that Providence had abandoned humanity to its fate, and the end must be chaos and universal destruction; but it is cheering as we advance in the history to observe again the hand of the All-Good; to mark the progress, as described by the Grecian poet, from Erebus to night, and from night to æther and the brilliant day.

Barbarism triumphant.

When the light begins to break upon the contending masses, and the situation is more clearly defined, it appears that the fierce movement of the Huns had accomplished its work, undesigned by them; and although, under Attila, they were still hovering about northern Gaul, they were to make no further progress. The fierceness of the leader and the fury of his troops, as unconscious instruments of Providence, have been recognized and retained in memory by the cognomen, which history has given him in all the languages of Europe,—the *Scourge of God; Godegiesel; Azote de Dios.*[2]

His power was at last broken, when Ætius, the Roman general, and Theodoredo, the king of the

---

[1] Muchos caudillos y ningun héroe. — La Fuente, *Historia de España*, II. 319.

[2] He first assumed the title: as he was retreating to Chalons, he said he was "the scourge of God for the chastisement of the Christians."

Visigoths, — showing the combination of Roman name and Gothic power, — confronted him on the plains of Chalons-sur-Marne, in one of the bloodiest battles known in history.[1] The conflict was for a long time doubtful; the Visigothic king was slain: but the Romans and their allies retained possession of the field, while the hosts of Attila reeled back in final retreat, to give their name and somewhat of their ethnic type to a small portion of central Europe.

Attila defeated.

The persistent successive attacks upon the city of Rome, by Vandal and Ostrogoth, so crippled the Roman power, that they aided the Visigoths in confirming their dominion in Gaul and Spain.

For Genseric, the Vandal, did not remain long contented in his new African seats: he crossed the sea to Italy, and marched upon Rome. He stormed the city, and captured it, and there his troops fully vindicated the reputation they had already acquired: for fourteen days that world-renowned capital was abandoned to sack and destruction. Ancient statues and relics of art were broken in pieces and scattered in every direction; public buildings, forum, palaces, temples, containing "the treasures of the world and Jerusalem," which even Alaric had spared, now crackled before the torch or fell beneath the axe, while the ornaments of gold and silver and precious stones were heavily laden upon the backs of tottering horses, and carried to the sea-shore. With their booty they retraced their path

The Vandals from Africa pillage Rome.

---

[1] La mas sangriente que vieron los siglos. — LA FUENTE, *Historia de España,* II. 313.

across the Mediterranean to Carthage. The whole
world, and even the Goths, were amazed at such
Vandalism.

When Theodoredo, the king of the Visigoths, fell
in the battle in the plains of Chalons, his son Toris-
mund enjoyed a very brief period of power, and his
son Theodorik came to the throne of the Goths in the
year 453, not by the right of lineage alone, but by
the election of the Gothic nobles. It soon became
manifest that the Gothic dominion had little to fear
from opposition in Spain, where the very disorder
rendered the conquest easy: the greatest concern was
to secure the possessions in Aquitanian Gaul. The
northern hordes of many names were still marching
down to the Loire, and the Gothic king might well
fear to experience in Gaul the adverse fortune which
had driven the Vandals from Spain into Africa.

It is greatly to our advantage, in seeking to realize
the men and the circumstances of this remote and
confused history, that we have a full-length   Theodorik.
portrait of Theodorik, amid his domestic A. D. 453.
surroundings, from the pen of Sidonius Apollinaris, a
contemporary writer, and an eye-witness of the personality he has so graphically described.[1]

A few personal characteristics apart, we may consider it the description of the habitudes and court-
life of the Gothic monarchs of this period.

[1] Sidonius was a man of rank, and son-in-law of the Emperor
Avitus ; he was born in Lyons, in 431, and died in 483. He lived
for many years in his native city, and during the latter part of his
life was Bishop of Clermont, in Auvergne. He was a Catholic, and
strenuously opposed to Arianism, — the royal creed. His "letters"
present the "time spirit" in an effective manner.

Of Theodorik, he says: His head was round; his hair long, thick, and curly; his eye-brows were heavy, and when he lowered his lids, they reached to the middle of his cheeks. His ears were, according to the national custom, covered by the curls of his flowing locks; his nose was formed in a graceful curve. Luxuriant whiskers grew beneath his temples, but every day he shaved the beard from under his nose and on the lower part of his face. His neck was thick, and his complexion, of a milky whiteness, was sometimes tinted with the bloom of youth.

His portrait.

His daily life was systematic and orderly: the hours of the day were divided between duty and pleasure in due proportion. He rose before daylight, to take part, with a small retinue, in the prayers conducted by his chaplains. Although this was done with proper respect, "it is easily seen," says our author, "that it is a tribute paid rather to custom than to conviction."

Division of time.

The morning hours, until eight o'clock, he devoted to the concerns of his government; the count who held the office of armor-bearer stood near the throne. Guards, clothed in skins, — the corslet of iron being laid aside, — and enjoining silence upon all, stood around, at a certain distance, either outside the apartment or concealed from view by rude screens.

Thus surrounded and guarded, he received foreign ambassadors, and made laconic answers to their diffuse and flattering orations. At eight o'clock, he rose from his throne and took a frugal meal, and then set out to visit his treasures and his stables, — money and cavalry being the chief instruments of his authority.

When he went out to the chase, he would have thought it beneath the royal dignity to carry his own bow. When the hunted animal was about to appear in view, he stretched back his hand, and a slave presented his bow, the string of which was never tightened beforehand; that would have been considered an effeminacy unworthy of a man. He strung the bow himself, and asking, as a matter of form, the direction in which he should shoot, he hit the game with unerring certainty.

His table, in ordinary, was frugal like that of a private person: the most valued part of the meal was conversation, for the most part serious and formal. The artistic skill, and not the price of what he used, constituted its value. The wine-cup circulated only a few times, and his guests had reason to complain of him on that score. It was only on Sundays, in his ceremonious banquets, that there was a grand display, — "the elegance of Greece, the abundance of Gaul, and the ready skill of Italy." His dinner hour was high noon. *Habits of life.*

He rarely slept after dinner; but soon the dice table was set before him. He gladly invoked good fortune, but was patient in hope when it was adverse. If he won, he said nothing; if he lost, he smiled. He was accustomed to set aside, when gaming, the reserve of a monarch, and to induce in those around him a spirit of frankness and familiarity. It gave him pleasure to observe the emotions of those who lost; and he seemed to think that the winner could not enjoy his triumph to the full unless the loser displayed his vexation.

Not unfrequently that pleasure of the king, the cause of which seems so frivolous, was not without its influence on other and graver business. "I myself," says Sidonius, "when I have a favor to ask him, bring about a happy defeat, losing the game to gain my purpose."

At three in the afternoon he returned to the cares of public business: petitioners reappeared; and an importunate court bustled around him until nightfall and the summons to supper caused them to disperse, and leave him to a season of refreshment and rest. Sometimes, during the evening meal, court jesters were introduced, but it was understood that in their buffoonery they must respect the feelings of the guests. No music, vocal or instrumental, was admitted to these feasts. Music was the concomitant of war; the only airs which pleased the king were those which inspired valor.

"Sonorous metal blowing martial sounds."

Finally, when he retired to rest for the night, armed sentinels were placed at every door of the palace.

Such is the detailed description of the person and life of a Gothic chief in the intervals of peace, in that rude age, before luxury had introduced effeminacy. It has, of course, a pendent of a lowering and lurid character. When on the war path, with his fierce northern warriors, such etiquette, simple as it was, was sternly set aside for the rigors of camp life; but it must be noted that the court life thus described was a great departure from their earlier customs, and exhibits a decided progress towards those more refined social customs which they were soon to establish in Spain.

The reign of Theodorik lasted for thirteen years. When he died, in 466, he was succeeded by his brother Eurik.   Up to this time the Visigothic   Eurik. chiefs had seen their interest in a nominal   A. D. 466. subordination to Rome; but now the farce of Roman supremacy was suddenly transformed into the tragedy of her complete overthrow.   That "umbra imperii" which had claimed a show of respect, long after the substantial power had departed, was fast losing its definition, and melting away in a lurid light.   The idea of the Goths, already in process of fulfilment, of establishing an independent dominion on the donation of Honorius, was modified by the fact that the donation of Honorius had no value as a title.   It was upon this modified basis that Eurik was called to act. The day of tribute was gone; the "mouth honor," which was all that had remained to Rome in her latter days, was at an end.   He set to work to conquer his nominal kingdom for himself from titular Roman governors and northern warriors who had preceded the Goths.   He captured Arles, Marseilles, and Clermont; and then he traversed the country from the Mediterranean to the Atlantic.   At Bordeaux he received the forced congratulations of the neighboring princes.   The whole of Gaul bowed before his irresistible arms.

Turning southward, he conducted his army in two corps — one of which he commanded in person —

to all parts of the Peninsula, and in less than three years he held undisputed sway throughout Spain, except in the little shire where the Suevi still lived, less as free tenants than as fugitives who had taken sanctuary with protecting nature.

Thus, cut loose from all connection with Roman affairs, he established the greatest monarchy which was to arise upon the ruins of the western empire. Its territory comprised really all of Spain, except the mountains of Galicia, and the whole of Gaul south of the Loire, from the Durance to the Ligurian Alps.

It is a curious and interesting fact that the "shadow" of the Roman supremacy may be traced from the year 420 to 466 in the names of the Gothic chiefs who bore sway, or had high rank during that period; they were Romanized Greek names; among them are Theodored and Theodorik. Before that we have purely Gothic appellations, — Ataulpho (Adolphus), Sigerik, Walia; and after Theodorik, when the Roman sway was thrown off, we return to Eurik (Ew-Rik, rich in laws), Alarik, Gesarik, Amalarik, Teudis, Agila, and other northern names.

Roman names.

And now the crowning events of the great catastrophe appear. The doomed capital of the world had seen its days of capture and storm and its days of relief. Goth and Vandal had entered it, and retired; but the final conquest, the fall from which there was no rising, was at hand. On the twenty-third of October, 476, it succumbed to Odoacer, king of the Heruli, a sept of the Ostro-Goths. The city founded by Romulus, and the empire first estab-

Odoacer subverts Rome.

lished by Augustus, passed from the weak hand of one who bore both names with a significant diminutive, — Romulus Augustulus. Odoacer became king of Italy, and established in that peninsula the dominion of the Ostro-Goths, just as the Visigoths had been settled in Spain and Gaul. To put a good face on the disaster, Odoacer was nominally a lieutenant of the emperor of the east, the Roman senate having decreed that a western emperor was no longer necessary!

At this juncture, the Gothic power seemed able to stand against the world; but two unforeseen circumstances occurred to impair its fortunes, just when it appeared to be most unassailable. The first was the sudden death of Eurik at Arles, in the year 484, during the infancy of his son Alarik. History continually repeats the lesson that a throne _{Alarik II, A. D. 484.} left to a child, who can only act through counsellors, is greatly injured by this very fact; and, although the Gothic monarchy was still elective, royal lineage was already strong, and the election was but a form of adopting the king's son.

While thus the plans of Eurik were frustrated by his death, and there was no one left to carry them forward, there appeared in Northern Gaul a warlike hero of another confederacy, actuated by the same ambition and proclaiming the same rights of conquest. This was Chlodowig or Clovis, the chief of the Salian Franks. The people were confederated Germans, who had reached that point of progress which finds strength in union. Many small tribes had banded together to form a nation. It was not a wild horde which was marching down upon the Visigoths, but a nation in arms; and their chief was worthy to lead them to victory and conquest. An exponent of his race, he was a man of great gifts and rare individuality. Like Amadis, he was a "love child," the natural son of Childerik by Basina, a queen who had deserted her husband to follow the fortunes of her lover, and who had gained thereby a nobler destiny.

From his little Batavian kingdom, including Tournay and Arras, too small to confine such powers, Clovis marched down with but five thousand men, and extended his territory against all opposition to the bank of the Loire. Behind that natural entrenchment he consolidated his power; but not content with this he constantly organized detachments to the south to devastate and pillage Aquitania. Cruel and inflexible, he was feared by his own troops as much as by his foes; but if they suffered from his tyranny they were content to grow rich by the spoils to which he led them.

Clovis and the Franks.

The young successor of Eurik, Alarik the Second, was no match for such a chief: prudence prompted him to negotiate rather than fight. He met the king of the Franks on an island in the Loire near Amboise, and concluded a treaty which made the Rhone and the Loire the frontiers of their respective kingdoms. But Clovis was only temporizing, and soon found good reasons for breaking the stipulations. Originally a pagan he had become an Orthodox Christian entirely from self-interest, and was ready to do battle against heresy, especially when the heretics had possessions which he coveted. He had married, while yet a pagan,

Clothilde, a Catholic princess, who had endeavored in vain to convert him to her faith ; but, at the desperate battle of Tolbiac against the neighboring Allemani, a struggle of life and death, in the moment of imminent danger he had declared that if he should gain the victory he would espouse the religion of his wife. He had been successful and had kept his promise,[1] not, however, without some immediate but temporary loss of popularity. The superstition of the pagan was transferred to Christianity, and was to work wonders in this new connection.

And now a dissembled zeal gave him a just cause for breaking his treaty with Alarik and the Goths. They were Arians, and no Arians should remain in Catholic Gaul. He had besides a secret ally in the Gothic territory. The Gallo-Romans were not altogether satisfied with the Gothic rule, and a powerful faction among them sent secret messengers to Clovis asking his assistance, which he was only too ready to give. Thus religion, avarice, and an apparent sympathy for the oppressed, conspired to give cause for the invasion.

[1] Henri Martin, quoting from Gregory of Tours (Gesta Regum Francorum), and from the " Lives of the Saints," gives the invocation of Clovis on the field in the following words : " J'ai appelé mes dieux, et ils ne m'assistent point dans ma détresse ; ils ne peuvent donc rien, puisqu'ils ne secourent pas ceux qui les servent. Christ, qui Chlothilde assure être le fils du Dieu vivant, j'invoque avec foi ton assistance. Si tu m'accorde la victoire sur mes ennemis, et que je fasse l'épreuve de cette *vertu* que t'attribue le peuple qui t'est consacré, je croirai en toi, et je me ferai baptiser en ton nom." The Chronicle adds : " Comme il parlait de la sorte, voici que les Allemans tournèrent le dos et commencèrent à prendre la fuite, et quand ils virent leur roi tué, ils se soumirent au pouvoir de Chlodowig." — *Histoire de France,* I. 421.

The anger of Alarik when he discovered the treachery of the Frankish chief knew no bounds. Contrary to the advice of his father-in-law, Theodorik,[1] he determined to fight. The contending forces met at Voulon, on the left bank of the Auzance, nearly opposite Quinçai, about four miles west of Poitiers, in the year 507.[2] On this ground, memorable in the history of wars, the Franks made their irresistible advance.

The battle of Voulon. A. D. 507.

The Gothic army was entirely defeated; Alarik was slain; and the kingdom of Clovis was only limited by the river Garonne, because Theodorik, the Ostro-Goth, interposed to stay the further progress of the Franks. The dismayed Visigoths began to fear that safety and permanence could only be assured south of the barrier of the Pyrenees; and abandoned their capital of Toulouse for a safer stronghold in the peninsula. The conquering Franks already dreamed of following them thither, and were making preparations to advance. But five years later the Frankish progress received a severe check by the death of Clovis, and the short-sighted policy which left his territory to be divided among his sons. These unnatural brothers were soon so occupied in robbing each other that the Goths found a respite even in Aquitania, which they could not have secured by their own power of resistance, and

Alarik defeated and slain.

Death of Clovis.

---

[1] Theodorik advised him not to " venture his destiny upon a cast of dice " with troops for some time past inexperienced in war.—H. MARTIN, I. 438.

[2] There may still be seen the remains of entrenchments and heaps of stones, defending the foot of a mound, which is covered on the other side by the Auzance.—*Ib.* 447.

were thus able to consolidate their strength in Spain.

The death of Theodorik, the Ostro-Gothic king of Italy, in 526, left that dominion to his young grandson, Athalarik, and the removal of his pow- Death of erful hand made it necessary to define the Theodorik. A. D. 526. limits of the two great Gothic kingdoms of Spain and Italy, including portions of Gaul, in order to keep the peace and strengthen the alliance between the two youthful monarchs who occupied the respective thrones.

Amalarik, the grandson of Alarik II., was now upon the Visigothic throne. The division was thus established : To the kingdom of Italy was decreed all the country from the left bank Amalarik, the grandson of the Rhone to the Alps, including Arles of Alarik. and Marseilles ; to that of Spain appertained all the rest of Gothic Gaul, nominally limited, as we have seen, by the river-courses of the Rhone and the Loire, but in· reality a dangerous .debatable ground, constantly exposed to Frankish raids and devastations, and really more under Frankish than Gothic rule. Various were the modes in which it was attempted to secure the peace of Aquitania,—battle, truce, treaty, and intermarriage ; but the history moves in a series of dissolving views, leaving the student little time to study one phase before another appears.

The son of King Amalarik espoused Clothilde, the daughter of the Frankish king; but she was a Catholic and he an Arian, and the conflict of creeds again disturbed the peace of their union. She resisted all his efforts to convert her to his views. He treated

her with great harshness, and thus what was meant
to be a means of pacification became an additional
cause of strife. The two nations flew to arms upon
this new quarrel, and the conflict of creeds fanned the
flame into a brighter blaze, which was never quenched
until the conversion of the Goths from Arianism to
Catholic Christianity at a later period. It is thus
curious to see the holy conflicts of Nice and Constantinople reproduced, amid the clash of barbarian arms
in the west.

The aggressive policy of the Franks was manifested
in the year 533, by the subversion and occupancy of
Burgundy, which was a new blow to the
Gothic power in Gaul. From this newly
acquired territory the adventurous Franks organized
new incursions into Aquitania. In the year 542
Childebert, king of Paris, and Clothaire, king of
Soissons, formed a league to make a formidable invasion. Sweeping away all opposition they crossed the
Pyrenees, ravaging the country as they advanced, and
entered Pampeluna, Calahorra, and many other towns.
Undaunted, they pressed forward, meeting little resistance, to the siege of Saragossa. Here, too, in the
opinion of the monkish chronicler, they might have
been successful, had Heaven not been propitiated by
the rigorous fasting and penance of the besieged, and
by the gracious and powerful intercession of the
glorious martyr, St. Vincent. The pious Childebert
moderated his battle fury and forgot his ambition
when he saw the long religious procession of men in
sackcloth, and women in garments of mourning, bearing the stole of the saint. He not only relented from

his purpose, but petitioned that he might have, instead of spoils, the precious relic of the martyr. Raising the siege he marched back into Gaul, with rich booty from other towns, and the stole of St. Vincent from Saragossa.

Once more marriage was resorted to in order to patch up the quarrel, and to present a new expedient for gratifying the ambition of the Frankish monarch.

Athanagild, a rich and powerful count, had usurped the throne, and strengthened his power by a nominal alliance with Justinian, the emperor of the east. He had two daughters, Galesuinda and Brunehilda, whose reputation for excellence and beauty had extended to Paris and Soissons. Turning in temporary disgust from the rude, violent, and lustful scenes enacted at their courts, the Frankish monarchs, Sighebert and Hilperik — grandsons of the great Clovis — rested their hopes upon these royal beauties of the south. The former ruled in Austrasia, and the latter in Neustria. The romantic story of their marriages with the daughters of Athanagild may be found in the "History of the Franks," written by a contemporary and eye-witness, Bishop Gregory of Tours, and, while it is of great interest as a narrative, it is of special value as presenting a picture of the relative civilization of the Goths and Franks, greatly to the advantage of the former.[1]

Royal marriages.

---

[1] The story is very vividly reproduced and expanded by Augustin Thierry in his interesting pictures of Frankish history, entitled, "Récits des Temps mérovingiens," which combine the profound research of the philosopher, the simplicity of the chronicle, and the high strain of the epic. The work is more interesting than romantic fiction.

Sighebert, the younger, a just and continent prince, disgusted with the polygamy and concubinage practised by his brothers, resolved to have but one wife, and she must be of royal lineage. With this purpose he solicited from Athanagild the hand of his younger daughter, Brunehilda. The Gothic king saw in such a union political advantage, and assented readily. A numerous and splendid train traversed the space from Metz to Toledo, where Athanagild had established his court, to receive and take back the beautiful bride.

The marriage was celebrated with great pomp at Metz, in the year 566, and good angels hovered over Sighebert the happy pair. The royal Frank was and Brune- hilda. heartily in love, not for a brief honeymoon; for the princely lady had those gifts of beauty, elegance, honesty, and prudence in happy combination, which retained and strengthened her husband's ardent affection during his whole life.[1]

The contemporary prelate enlarges with evident pleasure upon the magnificence of the marriage festivities, the banquet, the Latin epithalamium by Venantius Fortunatus, the service of gold and silver, the deep drinking, the rude merriment and wild revels in honor of the great event. But the historic significance was of far greater importance, and of this the participants were not aware.

The auspicious character of this happy union, however, produced its most important immediate effect upon Hilperik, who, led by the example and incited

---

[1] Erat enim puella elegans opere, venusta adspectu, honesta moribus atque decora, prudens consilio et blanda conloquio. — GREGOR. TURON, *Hist. Franc.* LIV.

by the apparent good fortune of his brother, determined to go and do likewise. He also sent an embassy to Athanagild, to ask the hand of his daughter Galesuinda, but not with a like immediate success. His debaucheries had been so excessive that her father, and more especially her mother, feared to abandon their chaste and lovely daughter to his polluting arms. The maiden herself was reluctant; but Hilperik, eager to obtain the object of his new desire, promised to give up all his wives and concubines, to lead a virtuous life, and to present his bride, as a *morgane ghiba* or morning-gift, with large portions of territory, including the towns of Limoges, Cahors, Bordeaux, Bearn and Bigorre. To the Gothic monarch this offer was very tempting, as it increased his power in the north, and strongly cemented the political union between the two nations.

So, in spite of the reluctance of the maiden and the prophetic fears of her mother, Galesuinda was borne, with a splendid retinue, — her mother bearing her company as far as the mountain barrier — into Neustria. The marriage was celebrated at Rouen, with as great splendor as the nuptials of her sister.

For a time all promised well; the king really abandoned his former wives and mistresses, and seemed heartily enamored of his bride. But the youngest and most cunning of his favorites, Fredegonda, appearing to accept most humbly her changed fortunes, only entreated that she might be permitted to remain in the palace as a servant of the new queen. With great want of foresight, and perhaps with a lingering fondness for her person, Hilperik permitted this.

For some months the union was peaceful and happy; but at last the savagery of the imbruted Frank burst forth. He grew tired of his wife and of monogamy: the Christian institution of marriage trammelled his wild passions. He dissembled with Galesuinda, took the expectant Fredegonda back to his embraces, as a concubine; and one night, by his order, a servant entered the chamber of his queen and strangled her while she was sleeping. Fredegonda was restored to her station as his wife; and the gentle and virtuous Galesuinda disappeared, as she had come, "amidst Merovingian barbarism, like an apparition of another age." [1]

Fredegonda's wiles.

This episode is as instructive as it is pathetic. The Franks, instead of advancing in the morals and refinements of civilization, had been retrograding. In the comparison naturally presented, the Goths had accomplished much more than their northern neighbors, but the barbarous power of the north was not impaired, while the softer influences of the south had already robbed the Goth of some of his robust manhood. Not yet able, in default of numbers, to occupy Aquitania entirely and permanently, the Franks were making steady progress in controlling it. The five towns given to Galesuinda as a morning-gift had been and were, in some degree, to remain a debatable ground. Clovis had entered and abandoned them, and his successors had made furious raids, ending only in their nominal supremacy. They belonged in

[1] A. Thierry, Récits des Temps mérovingiens, premier Récit.

reality to the chief, who could hold them, and as long as he could hold them.   Thus most of the time they were in a condition of military sequestration, actually pertaining to neither nation.   It was thus manifestly a stroke of state policy in the Gothic king to require them to be secured to his daughter, because " the confused notion which existed among the Germanic nations respecting the difference between territorial possession and the right of government might some day free these towns from the Frankish rule; but the king of Neustria did not perceive this." [1]

To those who read this history more in detail, it will be further manifest, that the constant struggle between the two conquering races, the Goths and the Franks, in this very territory, and the rival claims of many chiefs, were beginning to establish two distinct aristocracies in southern Gaul, which were to take permanent consistence in the later history, and to influence that history in all future periods even to the present age, — the Frankish aristocracy of the north, with the preponderance of the Teutonic element; and the Gothic aristocracy of the south, with a large infusion of the Gallo-Roman element.   It must be observed that apart from this twofold nobility the *Gallo-Romans* remained as the *people*, in both sections.   By this phrase I mean the Romanized Gauls, who were more modified by historical circumstances in the north than in the south; but who, all over Gaul and in all periods since, have opposed the high claims and rigorous exactions of French aris-

---

[1] A. Thierry, *Récits des Temps* mérovingiens, premier *Récit.*

tocracy. If France became afterwards an absolute monarchy, the peasants and *bourgeoisie* have suffered most, not from royal edicts, but from the grinding *corvées* of their feudal nobility; absolute monarchy sustaining and depending upon an aristocracy which, as far as the lower orders were concerned, was absolute also.

CHAPTER III.

GOTHIC KINGS FROM LEOVIGILD TO WITIZA.

IN the list of Gothic monarchs, many of whom are not worthy of extended notice, we have now reached the name of Leovigild, who ascended the throne in the year 572. Upon the death of Athanagild, there had been an interregnum, variously estimated at from five months to five years, at the end of which Liuva, one of the counts of the empire, had been raised to the throne by the nobles. But being of a modest and retiring disposition, he requested that his brother Leovigild should be made his partner in the monarchy. This done, he preferred to remain in Narbonne, and to give up the dominion in Spain to Leovigild, who, by the death of Liuva, in less than a year, became the sole monarch of the Goths throughout their entire domain.

This king was well informed, energetic, and firm of purpose, a statesman who seemed to take in at a glance the defects and needs in the existing order, political and religious, with a purpose to repair and correct them.

It has been seen that the monarchy, which, from the old elective principle, had become virtually hereditary until the extinction of the family of Theodoredo, had returned to its normal elective modus. Counts and generals figure in the list of kings. To increase his power, Leovigild persuaded the nobles to associate with him in the royal dignity his two sons, Hermengild and Recaredo, as "princes of the blood" and heirs to the throne. With this accession of power he began to form an imperial court.

Up to this time to speak of the insignia of royalty was to speak somewhat figuratively, but henceforth the phrase has real meaning. Leovigild, to add to

Imperial aspirations. his dignity, erected a throne and put on the purple mantle :— his family were to be *porphyrogeniti.* He received foreign ambassadors, and all petitioners among his own people, with a crown on his head and a sceptre in his hand. Other monarchs had possessed wealth and received tributes for themselves; he was the first to establish a national treasury, with a system of vouchers for disbursements and receipts.

While thus strengthening the monarchy, there was another subject of great concern which required to be handled with great caution and prudence. It had been manifest for many preceding reigns that the theological element was one of the chief causes of discord among his people. There were orthodox Catholic bishops, and a large proportion of the people, chiefly the Hispano-Romans, were Catholics, while most of the Goths were Arians, and their views were supported by the crown. But it was asserted that Athanagild had become a Catholic just before his death. To abandon the Arian dogma would be to come into harmony with Papal Rome, to the great political advantage of the Spanish kingdom. And yet, in this condition of unstable equilibrium, it was necessary to proceed with great deliberation.

His first measure was tentative, and yet looking towards the end, rather than definitely proposing it. He convened a council of the bishops at Toledo, and proposed to them the prepara- Arianism arraigned. tion of a new formulary of the initiatory rite of baptism, which should be acceptable to both Catholics and Arians. His request gave rise to warm controversy. The Arians were ready to accept such a compromise; but the Catholics were alarmed; a few of the Catholic bishops expressed themselves favorably, and the project was carried out; but when the work was done, it was found, as the king had probably anticipated, unsatisfactory to the majority, and was rejected.

But, as far as the king's scheme was concerned the attempt was by no means a failure: he had accomplished his secret purpose. The Arian dogma, without being abandoned, was greatly impaired, and the next step towards its speedy and final expulsion was rendered easy. That next step was to be taken ankle-deep in blood. This controversy was to figure, surrounded by the painful details of a public tragedy and a parricidal crime.

It happened thus: Theodosia, the first wife of Leovigild, was a Catholic, the daughter of one of the last and nominal Byzantine governors of Carthagena, and she had borne him his first-born son, Hermengild. As this boy grew up under his mother's nurture, he embraced her faith, and his choice was strengthened when he arrived at man's estate, by his marriage with a Frankish princess of the same creed. Thus the chief heir was a pronounced Catholic.

All this would have given but little concern to the king, who was already planning to return to the Catholic faith, had it not been that, on the death of Theodosia, he had married Gosuinda, a zealous Arian, zealous to persecution of all opposers, and not staid by the fact that the chief opposer was her husband's son; rather, perhaps, strengthened in her zeal by this fact.

What had been before a controversy, conducted with deliberation, now became a quarrel, angry and vindictive. Ties of blood were forgotten, or rendered the strife more bitter. The prince raised a party with arms in their hands, and soon the father and son — sovereign and subject — were arrayed against each other in the field. Thus the religious element was merged into political treason. After numerous The martyr, conflicts, sieges, and truces, Hermengild fell St. Her- mengild. into his father's hands; was judged and condemned; was proof against all inducements to recant, and was beheaded in prison, — not for being a Catholic, but for being a traitor and a contuma- cious rebel; but Catholicism had scored a point in the game.

The people were confounded and shocked at such a spectacle; they did not denounce the rebellion, and, from sympathy with the sufferings and the fortitude of the undaunted prince, they began to sympathize with the dogma for which he had suffered. There are many saints in Spanish history; but the most notable work achieved by any — more potent than any recorded miracles — was that of the royal martyr, St. Hermengild ; the Catholic faith was watered by his blood ; nothing could now impede its growth.

Leovigild did not survive his martyred son more than one year, and when he found himself dying at Toledo, in 586, he embraced — it was currently believed — the creed of Rome, through the earnest and eloquent persuasion of Bishop Leander of Seville. His conduct no longer seems strange with regard to the doctrine of Arianism ; to explain it we have but to collate these facts : It was still the Gothic creed ; Hermengild was in seditious revolt against him as a son against his father, as a heretic against the Arian faith, and, worst of all, as a subject against his king. His Arian wife influenced him in his belief and in his cruelty ; but when death was about to come, his eyes were opened ; earthly incitements lost their power ; he decided according to his conscience, and thus farther paved the way for the abandonment of Arianism in the next reign. It should also be recorded, to the credit his statecraft, that he succeeded in incorporating the kingdom of the Suevi with the Gothic dominions, and thus reigned without a rival in the Peninsula.

His son Recaredo determined, as soon as he ascended the throne (586), to carry out his father's plans ; but, before he could accost the theological question, he found other and more immediate demands upon his energy. To show, however, at once his judgment of his father's cruelty, he gave over to torture the warrior Sisberto, who had

Recaredo.

beheaded his brother, and this act was greatly to the satisfaction of the people.

While thus vindicating Hermengild, he was called upon to resist the influence which Hermengild had excited. The Frankish monarch Gouthram, nominally in the interests of the party in the kingdom raised by Hermengild, but really for his own aggrandizement, had advanced with a large army to drive the Goths out of Septimania.[1] With Recaredo seemed to come back for a time the pristine vigor and valor of the Goths; he imparted his spirit to his generals. The commander of the Gothic army, small in comparison with the forces of Gonthram, was commanded by Duke Claudius, the Governor of Lusitania. The victory of the Goths was complete; the Frankish army was entirely overthrown in a single battle, which, according to Isidor of Seville, was without a rival among the actions which had been fought in Spain;[2] and the monkish chroniclers, followed by later historians, with their usual credulity have ascribed it to a miraculous intervention of Heaven in the cause of a monarch who was about to restore the Catholic faith in the Peninsula. Thus, with the blessing of Heaven, Recaredo returned to this new task.

Defends his northern frontier.

[1] Septimania, in the Merovingian times, was that narrow irregular strip on the Mediterranean coast, from the extremity of the Pyrenees to the mouths of the Rhone. It includes Montpelier, Narbonne, Cette, and Perpignan. It was of great value to the Goths as a northern march.

[2] Nulla unquam in Hispaniis Gothorum major vel similis extitit. Something like this, however, is asserted of most of the victories which receive the eulogium of the ecclesiastical chroniclers.

In his handling of the religious problem, Recaredo acted with great discretion. Like his brother, but secretly, he had embraced the Catholic creed, with commendable prudence. He did not, *His prudence.* however, announce this to his kingdom until ten months after his accession. Then he exhorted, but did not attempt to coerce, his people to follow his example.

Little by little the Gothic people had become ready for the change, and at last eager for it. Three years after his father's death, and four after his brother's martyrdom, he convoked the Third Council of Toledo, and presented to that body his *The Third Council of Toledo.* abjuration of Arianism. It was an august national council, composed of sixty-two prelates, — the largest but one of all the Hispano-Gothic councils.[1] The archbishops of Toledo, Merida, Braga, Seville, and Narbonne, were represented by their procurators. Leander, Bishop of Seville, was the Pope's legate. The king was in attendance, and presented his *tomo,* or royal memorial, for himself and his Queen, Badda, and with this his act of conversion to the Catholic faith, which was registered and sanctioned by the council. The time and the mode were admirably chosen.

Thus the great change was accomplished at last

---

[1] The former councils had consisted of from six to ten bishops. "Concilium Toletanum III. (omnium Hispaniensium celeberrinum, quod in eo gens Gothorum abjurata hæresi Ariana ad Catholicam fidem est conversa) habitum anno IV. Reccaredi regis." Era 627 ; A.D. 589. — *España Sagrada,* vol. ii. The most numerous council was the Fourth of Toledo. convened by Sisenando in 633 : sixty-six bishops were present.

without tumult or blood, and the first "Catholic"
The first "Catholic" monarch of Spain. monarch of Spain was anointed with holy oil by the metropolitan at Toledo. If the kings of Spain, in the later history, are distinguished by the title of "Catholic Majesty," it is not that they have been holier than other monarchs, nor that they have been the chief protectors of Catholic truth, although, as a rule, they have been zealous defenders of papal claims. History teaches us that we must go back to find the origin of this title in the conversion and coronation of Recaredo.[1] The imprudence of Hermengild and the hypocrisy of Leovigild had paved the way for the grand and popular success of Recaredo.

To the ecclesiastical historians the monarch who had consummated this grand work appears in the most brilliant light, — "the most glorious, Catholic, and orthodox Recaredo."[2]

Let us recur for a moment to the scene, which is certainly among the most notable in the history of
The scene of the conversion. Christianity. The bishops, in their eagerness to hear the king, almost anticipated his decision with their tumultuous acclamations. He announced that the nation was converted from the Arian heresy, and that he had called them together, not to deliberate, but to ratify and to give glory to God.

Three days of fasting and prayer were proclaimed,

---

[1] "Si los monarcas españoles se decoran hoy con el titulo de magestades catolicas, la historia nos enseña su origen, y nos lleva a buscarle en Recaredo."—La Fuente, *Historia de España*, II. 364.

[2] España Sagrada, VI. ch. iv.

and then a paper is drawn up, setting forth their new confession in accordance with the decisions of the four general councils, — of Nicæa, Constantinople, Ephesus, and Chalcedon.[1] They seem pervaded with new joy, which finds its vent in bursts of praise. They ascribe "Glory to God, the Father, the Son, and the Holy Ghost, who has deigned to give peace and unity to this church! Glory to our Lord Jesus Christ, — God! — who has united to the true faith the illustrious nation of the Goths, making of all one fold under one Shepherd." And then pausing to give due praise and thanks to Recaredo, as the pious and august human instrument, they return to the elevated burden of the chaunt, — "Glory to our Lord Jesus Christ, who liveth and reigneth with God the Father in the unity of the Holy Ghost, world without end."[2] Thus the farthest west was echoing back, after the lapse of two centuries and a half, to the memory of the mighty Athanasius, saint and exile, the antiphonal cry that Jesus Christ was "God of God, Light of Light, Very God of Very God." Arianism had fled howling from Spain into perpetual exile.

The Nicene Creed was accepted in its integrity and something more. With the zeal of new converts they were eager, if possible, to strengthen the claims of Him whose divinity they had so long denied; they gave a dangerous emphasis to their doctrine by add-

---

[1] "Pliego en que manifesto la fé que profesaba, autorizada con las decisiones de los quatro concilios generales, — niceno, constantinopolitano, ephesino y calcedonena." — *España Sagrada*, VI. app. viii.

[2] *España Sagrada*, vol. vi. ch. iv.

ing to their belief in the Holy Ghost, "the Lord and
Giver of Life," — *spiritum sanctum, Dominum et vivi-
ficantem*, that He proceeded not only from the Father,
but also from the Son — *Patre Filioque*.   These are
not the words of the Nicene Creed or of the Eastern
Church, nor until a later period of the Roman Catholic Church.   The account of its adoption by the Pope
is a history of gradual introduction.   First, it was
rejected at Rome; then it was tolerated as a special
chaunt.   When Charlemagne, two centuries later, became angry with the weak emperors of the East, he

Filioque. found in this little phrase, *Filioque*, a means
of retort, a manifesto of the Latin church
against the Greek church; and thus what was designed for the neophytes of Spain, as a new tribute
of honor to the God-man, became one cause of division between the Latin and Greek communions, and
has been a bone of contention for snarling dogmatic
theologians from that day to this.   The question is
raised to-day in councils and conventions, when its
historic consequence at least has departed.

Great indeed was the joy in Rome and throughout
the wide extent of the Latin church, when the tidings

The joy of came that the Catholic faith had been estab-
Gregory the
Great. lished as the national religion in Spain.
Pope Gregory the First, well named the Great, like a
commander in some high fortress, had been directing
the energies and watching the fortunes of the Latin
church in Europe.   It was already claiming nothing
less than universal supremacy.   He had been casting
eager glances into Saxon England, and was about to
form a strong establishment there; he had sent ardent

missionaries into Germany. He had been praying earnestly for the conversion of Arian Spain, a more difficult task than the reclamation of heathen nations, especially since the Arian dogma was a time-honored and political element of the Gothic system, — a religion of the conquerors as in conflict with that of the conquered races. And now, as it were in a moment, his prayers were answered, and he was ready to sing *Nunc dimittis.*

The letter of Recaredo, announcing the change to the Pope, was reverent, joyful, and enthusiastic;[1] and the answer of the Holy Father was full of fervent gratitude and almost unbounded praise. He was equally loud in his praises of Leander of Seville, to whose constant labors the conversion was in part due. All that he himself had done for the church was small in comparison; slackness in contrast with their zeal. In the final judgment the difference would be manifest, as he could come with empty hands, and the king should appear, followed by crowds of the faithful, whose souls had been won to the faith by his persuasion.[2]

The king's letter and the Pope's answer.

In return for the presents transmitted to him by the king, and in acknowledgment of his piety, the delighted pontiff sent a piece of the true cross,[3] some

---

[1] The letter is given in full in "España Sagrada," VI. app. viii.

[2] "Que diré, en el juicio final, cuando me presente con las manos vacias, y vos vayais seguido de rebaños de fieles cuyas almas habeis ganado á la fé con solo el imperio de la persuasion." — GREGORIUS MAGNUS, L. VIII. epist. 128 ; quoted by La Fuente, *Historia de España*, II. 364.

[3] The discovery of the identical cross upon which our Saviour suffered, offered a large field for poetry. See, among others, the poem

of John the Baptist's hair, and two keys which had
been in the possession of St. Peter, in the opening of
one of which were filings from the chain which the
apostle had worn in prison. In that credulous age
these gifts were the noblest reward for the conversion
of a kingdom. They were significant and symbolic,
and the people believed in them.

Recaredo died in the year 601, leaving behind him
the reputation — besides his great missionary work —
of having accomplished more for the consolidation of
the Gothic authority than all who had reigned before
him. He had united all the tribal elements
into a political and religious whole, — Suevi,
Gauls, Hispano-Romans, and conquering Goths — and
they were, as never before, one nation. And this
union, upon an equality of interests, had greatly advanced the claims of individual liberty, by operating
a fusion, more or less complete in different sections, of
the heterogeneous elements of race, custom, and belief.
Conquerors and conquered met upon common ground,
and the spirit of patriotism began to diffuse itself into
all classes. There might be, and there was to be,
royal oppression ; but it was hereafter to be felt by
the Goths and the Hispano-Romans alike, and a common burden is patiently borne.

Recaredo had enlarged and improved the Breviary
of Alarik II. He had restored the Latin language to
public documents, to the services of the Church, to
the conservation of the national annals, and in some
degree to social conventions. To the illiterate people

Recaredo's great work.

of Francisco Lopez de Zarate, fragments of which are given by Ochoa,
in his "Tesoro de los Poemas españoles," p. 427.

this may have seemed an evil; but to Spain it was a benefit. He thus preserved an element, otherwise in danger of being lost, which was to enter largely into the modern Spanish, and which was to give refinement to that melodious tongue; and in their Latin garb he kept for history materials which became the common property of every scholar, and which if only retained in the rude and corrupt Gothic of that day, would be now almost as difficult to decipher as the hierographs of the East.

One word more as to the mental and moral personality of this distinguished monarch, which is vividly set forth by Isidor of Seville. He was attractive in manners, and generous in disposition. If he imitated the Byzantine emperors, his father had set him the example; and he found his accession of dignity of value not only in strengthening the Gothic throne, but in increasing the national power. His wealth was freely bestowed upon the poor as well as upon the court; and he used his authority for the general good, "that he might merit a happy end by reason of his good works." [1]

The reign of Recaredo may be regarded, like that of Alfred in England, as the highest and culminating point of Gothic prosperity; and its close may be taken as a proper point of pause to consider the true character of that dominion. We are at once led to acknowledge with pleasure that these wild northern people, who had precipitated themselves Gothic civilheadlong into Gaul and Spain, with no ap- ization. parent motive but that of conquest, and who had

[1] La Fuente, Historia de España, II. 369.

been commonly regarded as the enemies of mankind, had been, in the age of which we are speaking, transformed into generous protectors of humanity. Upon the ruins of a shattered and dismembered Rome, a new society had been founded in Spain, stronger, more influential, and, on the whole, more humane, than that of provincial Rome itself. The slavish torpor produced by four centuries of imperial despotism, and which had made the inhabitants of Spain an easy conquest to their Northern invaders, was shaken off, and the vanquished had now risen to something like an equality with the conquerors. It is true that in the gradual process, there was at first cruelty and oppression, but, with the settlement of the Goths, gentler counsels prevailed. The common opinion, formed in ignorance of the facts, has long been that the Goths were only brutal marauders, rivalling in cruelty and inhumanity the Vandals who preceded them, and the Franks who were treading upon their heels. Our brief summary thus far must show that the historical facts do not warrant such an adverse judgment : the most careful and philosophic historians do not share it.[1]

"The conquest of the southern and eastern provinces of Gaul by the Visigoths and Burgundians," in The opinion of Augustin Thierry, "was very of Augustin Thierry. far from being as violent as that of the North by the Franks. At their entrance into Gaul they showed themselves generally tolerant. They united to a spirit of justice more intelligence and a greater taste for civilization. . . . They soon ac-

---

[1] This view is corroborated by the accounts of Tacitus, Sidonius Apolinaris, Salvian, and Orosius.

quired the love of repose; they daily became more like the natives, and tended to become their neighbors and friends. . . . Thus the wounds of the invasion became gradually healed; the cities raised up their walls; industry and science revived once more; Roman genius reappeared in that country where the conquerors themselves seemed to abjure their conquest." [1]

Had it been possible to continue this progress without external resistance and loss of power within the realm; could the Goths have preserved their original vigor, while they cultivated clemency and the refining arts, — the remaining history to be recounted would not have been one of disasters and decline; but, as has been said, their national greatness culminated with its first great national achievement, and the historian has only further to narrate their effeminacy and their gradual downfall,— temporarily stayed by the potent energy of a single arm, and their sheltered position in the Peninsula.

Their decline.

They exchanged their rude frankness and their frugal habits for the polished manners and luxurious customs of Rome, so long naturalized in Spain. Their stationary condition, after centuries of martial movement, affected their military vigor; the softer climate of their new residence impaired their hardihood. They lost by degrees in mental and physical strength

[1] A. Thierry, Dix Ans d'Études Historiques, Ess. 24. Professor Bosworth, in the preface to his Anglo-Saxon Dictionary, speaks of the Goths as among those valiant nations "who left their native climes to destroy tyrants and liberate slaves, and to teach men that, nature having made them equal, no reason could be assigned for their becoming dependent, but their mutual happiness."

more than they gained in refinement and taste. In this lotos-torpor they might have remained, had not a vigorous invader appeared.

Upon the death of Recaredo, the crown descended to his son, Liuva II., a youth of twenty years, who was unable to control the kingdom. The reign of violence again began. A traitor named Vitericus, who had already experienced the clemency of his father, taking advantage of the king's youth, gained over the army and slew the young king in the year 603. Like Julian the Apostate, but without his genius, Vitericus thought to make a grand stroke by restoring Arianism. He failed. He was

Vitericus.

assassinated by his own partisans at a banquet, in the year 610. His successor, Gundemar, reigned but two years; and in 612, to stay the violence, and once more to restore at least partial order, there came to the throne a notable man, whose executive ability was felt everywhere, and whose clemency was to be experienced by all the dwellers in Spain, except the unhappy children of Israel. The name of this prince was Sisebuto.

The story of the persecution of the Jews in all ages since the crucifixion is inextricably connected with the history of every nation in Europe. The Wandering Jew is its allegorical presentation.

Persecution of the Jews.

When in days of peaceful interval, it has seemed that he might take his seat and rest his weary limbs, a trumpet sounds the ringing cry, " Up, and move on ! " Upon the throne of the Eastern empire, at the beginning of the seventh century (610-641), was seated Heraclius, the slothful and superstitious ruler, who saw the origin of Islám in Arabia, and who, in the last years of his reign was to abandon to the Arabians the territory which he had rescued from the Persians. Addicted to astrology, this emperor had read in the celestial combinations that the Roman empire of the east was to be subverted " by a wandering and circumcised people." The distinctive features and the powerful consolidation of the Mohammedans and their converts were not as yet sufficiently manifest to point them out as the coming destroyers. To whom then could the star-prophecy refer but to the Jews ? His determination was at once taken; he would not only expel them from his dominions, and destroy those who refused to depart, but he would prevail upon all nations in alliance with him to do the same. At different periods in their history, and especially incident to the persecution of Vespasian and the destruction of Jerusalem, many of the unfortunate nation had taken refuge in Spain. They were quiet citizens, engaging in no tumults; money-getting, but industrious. Urged by the request and incited by the example of Heraclius, Sisebuto issued an edict in the year 616, that, within a year, the Jews in Spain should either embrace Christianity, or should be shorn, scourged, and expelled from the kingdom, and their property confiscated. The scheme, which seemed formed to extirpate heresy, and might on that ground, in those dark and superstitious days, be palliated, was full of evils. It was a premium on hypocrisy ; for hypocrisy was an instrument of self-preservation. Ninety thousand Jews made a nominal submission ; but Christian sus-

The superstition of Heraclius.

picion saw through the policy. They were subject to espionage, and treated with great contumely. They were compelled to abjure their faith, and despised for abjuring it. It seems like divine retribution that when Sisebuto died in 621 it was supposed that he was poisoned; and the deed was at once, but unjustly, ascribed to the Jews.

I need hardly mention the nominal rule for three months of his son Recaredo II., of whom history has preserved no authentic record. The decline of the Gothic state was now manifest. To stay it, the nobles elected Swintila, a successful general, who, it was hoped, could strengthen the government with the weapons of the army. When the Goths entered Spain they had found a Byzantine colony in the south, which had continued in a languishing condition during the successive reigns, tolerated rather than cherished by some monarchs, and ill-treated by others: whatever may have been the Gothic claim of eminent domain, this colony was in reality a foreign settlement on Spanish soil. Swintila determined to expel or absorb these semi-military representatives of the Eastern empire. He succeeded, and could then boast for the first time, that every foot of Spanish territory was under the Gothic sceptre.[1]

In his own accession the hereditary principle which had been adopted had been set at naught; he desired to re-establish it by associating with him in regal dignity his son Ricimer. But the circumstances were not propitious; the governor of Gothic Gaul, Sise-

---

[1] Sin que un solo rincon de ella dejara de obedecerle. — LA FUENTE, *Historia de España*, II. 409.

nardo, headed the numerous malcontents, and invited
the Frankish king Dagobert to join him in an invasion of Spain, which meant the dethronement of the
king. The allied forces crossed the Pyrenees and
marched to Saragossa. Swintila advanced to meet it,
but before they could join battle his army became
disaffected, and proclaimed the rebellious governor
king. Swintila could only save himself by flight
and concealment. Of the usurper who ruled for five
years, and of his successor Chintila and his son Tulga,
nothing need be said. In the year 642, the Chindasu-
into,
chief men of the kingdom met, and elected as A. D. 642.
king an old but distinguished chief named Chindasuinto, whose name (*Kind suinth*, strong in children) has
a peculiar significance, in that his heirs, at some remove, were to play a prominent part in the remainder
of the Gothic drama.[1] With regard to the burden of
his years and his popularity, no objection was made to
the elevation of his son Recesuinto as joint-occupant
of the throne. This was done in 649, and the young
man became the real monarch during the remaining
three years of his father's life. The rational and mild
rule of the Goths and the laws of Recaredo had intended to make, as I have said, all the people equal ;
but the claims of blood assert themselves in spite of
the enactments of kings and councils.

One important distinction remained : thus far the

---

[1] It is curious to observe the meanings of names among the Goths,
as indicating or predicting character. Witikind, wise child ; Recaredo, *rede, reke*, word of vengeance ; Luiva, *lewo*, a lion ; Leovigild, *lewo-gild*. And also among the Franks ; Gouthram, strong
in battle ; Hildebert, wonderful in fight.

Goths and the Hispano-Romans were forbidden to
Intermar-
riages.
intermarry, and this prohibition constituted
virtually a system of caste; it kept up in
families the old rivalries of race. This Recesuinto
determined to abolish. By annulling the law, he gave
vent to the long-cherished desire for more intimate
union: many such marriages were celebrated and the
fusion was far more complete. No step so favorable to
the consolidation of the Gothic dominion had yet been
taken, since the promulgation of the unity of faith.

We have now reached in the chronology another
period of prominent importance in the Gothic history;
one in which we find the immediate origin of that
political condition in which the ruling dynasty was
found, when the Arab-Moors crossed the strait to
invade Spain. Strange to say, while the preceding
history stands out in clear light, and that directly
following may be studied in true detail, this middle
ground of the landscape is somewhat cloudy and difficult of definition. The king who stands as the vague
Good King
Wamba.
usher of this new order is Wamba; his reign
is referred to as a time of Arcadian rule, a
golden age of the declining dominion. The sentiment
with which the days of Wamba are still mentioned
in Spain is of mingled reality and fancy, a combination of what leads the Englishman to speak of the
time of "Good Queen Anne," and the Frenchman to
drain his *vin du pays* in honor of *le roi d'Yvetôt*.[1]

---

[1] On sait que Béranger dans la première chanson de son recueil fait
du roi d'Yvetôt le modèle des potentats, bon petit roi peu connu dans
l'histoire, mais plus heureux qu'aucun monarque ayant pris le plai-
sir pour code. — BESCHERELLE, *Dictionnaire National* voce *Yvetôt*.

Noble things are supposed to have been done, and great happiness secured to the people in the time of good King Wamba; but the time and the events are so vague that "the phrase *en el tiempo del Rey Wamba* proverbially denotes a date beyond legal memory — 'as old as the hills.'"[1]

It was the custom among the Goths to hold the election for a new king in the place where the late king had died. Recesuinto had breathed his last in a little hamlet then called Gerticos, about eight miles from Valladolid, whither he had repaired with the hope of recruiting his failing strength. He left no son to aspire to the succession. There the electors, now distinctly discerned as the higher nobility, the bishops, and the generals, met, and fixed their choice upon a venerable Goth, named Wamba, chief among whose many claims to their suffrage was the fact that he had constantly declined to accept station and authority. According to Ambrosio de Morales, in his "Coronica General," their decision was determined by miraculous intervention. St. Leo, inspired by Heaven, directed them to seek in the west a husbandman named Wamba. Soldiers were sent out on this search, and found him, like Cincinnatus, at the plough. They announced to him his good fortune, which, to their astonishment, he at once declined to receive. In answer to their urgency, he told them he would accept the crown when the dry rod which he held in his hand should grow green again. To his great astonishment, as well as to theirs, he had scarcely

[1] Richard Ford, Handbook for Spain. Original edition. II. 776.

uttered the words before the dry wood was covered with green leaves. Similar stories have been told of other kings unexpectedly raised to the throne; but, whether the account be true or not, its spirit is quite consistent with the later life of the reluctant monarch.

The vote in his favor was unanimous, but he still shrank from the weighty responsibility, and again

Compelled to accept the throne. firmly refused. Whereupon one of the military chiefs in the electoral college rose, and, drawing his sword, advanced towards him, crying out, " If thou be still obstinate in refusing the crown we offer thee, I will this moment cut off thy head with this sword." [1]

Thus threatened, what could Wamba do but reluctantly accept the dangerous trust? He was escorted more like a prisoner than a monarch-elect by the electors and the army to Toledo, where he was anointed and crowned.

His conduct satisfied their most ardent hopes. If a just and incorruptible rule could have given new life to the sinking government, and averted the coming catastrophe, the reign of Wamba would have accomplished this. But it was not in the power of man to do more than arrest for a time the downward progress. With the vigor of Recaredo, he crushed a revolt among the Gascons. Quick to detect and prompt to defeat conspiracies, he was clement to the discomfited conspirators. One illustration may suffice. A demagogue, named Paul, who became an

---

[1] Nisi consensurum te nobis promittas, gladii hujus mucrone modo truncatum te scias. —JULIAN OF TOLEDO, *Historia Regis Wambæ*, cited by La Fuente, *Historia de España*, II. 427.

impudent pretender to the throne, thought it would be an easy task to depose an old man, unused to the exercise of power, and one upon whose head the crown sat so lightly, by reason of his reluctance to assume it. He had mistaken his man. The king at once marched against him, and overthrew him in battle. But when he held him as a prisoner, instead of enforcing against him the penalty of death, in accordance with the decree of a former council, he was satisfied to sentence him to the tonsure, in order to ensure his perpetual seclusion.

Wamba fortified Toledo by building an additional wall around it, and in grateful memory of this and other improvements to the city, there may still be read over the great gate the inscription, *Erexit fautore Deo rex inclytus urbem, Wamba.*

He was so just, and his just deeds are so much left — as to their details — to conjecture, that the historians have nothing to say of him, except what is laudatory. The fact seems to be that he was far too good for such an evil and perverse generation, and so his reign came to a sudden and untoward end.

Ervigio, a youth who had in his veins the ever self-asserting blood of Chindasuinto, and who had been so specially favored by Wamba that he had gained great authority in the government, aspired to the sovereign rule. The old king had "borne his faculties so meekly," and "been so clear in his great office," that he would not, like Macbeth, murder him to gain the throne. He secretly determined to render him incapacitated to reign. He drugged him with a potion, and while Wamba was

The stratagem of Ervigio.

under the influence of the anodyne, he had him tonsured, proclaiming afterwards that it was by the king's desire. The law was superstitious and strict, that no person who had received the tonsure should ever sit upon the Gothic throne. Whatever might be thought of the mode and motive of the deed, there was no question as to the incapacity which it produced.

Fortunately for the claims of Ervigio, when the
Wamba's good old king returned to consciousness, he
seclusion. was not disposed to question the treacherous act; he cheerfully retired from a throne which he had never wanted, and entered upon a seclusion the more grateful on account of his arduous labors; and Ervigio was proclaimed in his stead.

The people, however, were not satisfied with the declaration of Ervigio: they loved Wamba, and would have assurance that he had not been wronged. To satisfy them the new king convened the twelfth council of Toledo, in the year 681. It was composed of thirty-five bishops, three vicars, four abbots, and fifteen palatines. The king entered the hall with a feigned humility, and presented to the council the testimony of certain of the higher nobles that Wamba, when in peril of death, had received the tonsure and put on the habit of a monk. This part of the story may be questioned, but what remains to be told is probably true. There were then produced one document containing the voluntary abdication of Wamba, and signed by his own hand, and another in which he recommends that Ervigio should be anointed and crowned as his successor. Upon these the council acted, and eight days after their decision the metropolitan of Toledo poured the holy oil upon his unholy head.

The seven remaining years of Wamba's existence corresponded with the tenor of his whole life. A gentle and consistent monk, he lived happily, apart from the world which he had never loved ; and the distracted realm was left under the control of a suspicious and self-seeking monarch, who accomplished little for the amelioration of its condition, but rather accelerated its decline.

With the desire of continuing his dynasty, Ervigio had effected a marriage between his daughter Cixilona, and Egica, a relation of Wamba; and when he approached the end of his life, having obtained the consent of the bishops and grandees, whom he summoned in haste to his dying bed, he released them from their oath of fealty, and abdicated in favor of his son-in-law. This completion of his worldly policy being effected, that he might depart in the odor of sanctity, he caused himself to be tonsured, and yielded his last breath in the cowl of a monk.

The first act of the new king, like many who had gone before him, was to convene a council, — the fifteenth of Toledo. The principal business of this council was to settle a curious question of casuistry. It was this: As a condition of his succession, he had promised the dying Ervigio, with an oath, that he would always protect the rights of his daughter's family, and especially those of her mother and brothers.

<small>Egica succeeds Ervigio.</small>

But when he was anointed as king, he had also

taken the customary oath to do equal justice to all
his subjects. Now, among the acts which

A question of casuistry. had made the fame of Ervigio *ni agradable
ni honrosa*, he had despoiled many of the nobles of
their lands and treasures, and bestowed them upon
his daughter, and other members of his family. On
the accession of Egica, those who had been thus dispossessed were clamorous for restitution; and thus
the two oaths seemed to be brought into antagonism.
Which should he keep? which was the stronger?
could they be harmonized? Such were the questions proposed to the council.

It is to the enduring honor of this august body that
they upheld, with no dissenting voice, even when a
monarch might have desired it, the great principle,
that " even-handed justice " is the first duty of kings.
Their decision was, " that the first oath, that of protecting the family of his predecessor, was only obligatory so far as it was not in contravention of the
justice which he owed to all his subjects." It is unfortunate, for it leaves room for a suspicion of collu-
sion, which it may be hoped is groundless, that this
noble declaration chimed in with the tortuous policy
of the king. He took advantage of it to oppress,
instead of to protect, the family of Ervigio; and thus,
while consulting his own interests, he avenged, if
vengeance was due, the dethronement of his kinsman
Wamba.

To his son Witiza, he gave an important post in
Galicia with rich revenues, and at last elevated him
to royal dignity, not as prince of the blood, but as
joint monarch, as is certified by the coin which he

issued, bearing the superscription, *Egica rex*, *Witiza rex : concordia regni.*   In the court of Witiza, at Tuy in Galicia, the royal residence at Toledo was imitated, and the young prince was rehearsing the part which he was soon to be called upon to play.   It is doubtful how long this joint reign continued ; some writers fix its end in the year 699, but the most authentic date is that given by Isidorus Pacensis, who places the death of Egica in 701.   He left to his son a kingdom to all appearance no less strong and valuable than it had been for many years ; in reality rushing, with increasing momentum, to hideous ruin, and the king himself the presiding demon of its destruction. Of the remaining period of the Gothic dominion, it is necessary to speak more in detail, and with more careful examination of authorities.

CHAPTER IV.

WITIZA AND RODERIK.

W HEN the Gothic king Egica died, in November, 701, his son Witiza, who had been for some time provincial governor in the northwest, and who had conducted the affairs of his department wisely and well, hastened to Toledo, and was proclaimed sole monarch on the fifteenth of the same month. The first years of his reign were full of promise. His private life was exemplary. His generosity was singularly conspicuous. He caused the registers of criminal processes, and all papers which could prejudice the person, honor, or estate of any of his subjects, to be burnt; all overdue taxes were remitted. He thus began to rule with a general amnesty and a *tabula rasa* of financial impositions.[1]

From good to evil.

Great was the joy of his people, and with it their respect for a monarch who seemed to set so noble an example to his court, of a regular life, a generous sympathy, and a determination to encourage good and repress evil.[2] All persons who had been un-

---

[1] Ambrosio de Morales, De la coronica general de España (Alcalá de Henares, MDLXXVII.), lib. xii. 197.

[2] Ambrosio de Morales, xii. 198. "Witiza florentissime regnum retemptat, atque omnis Hispania gaudio, nimium freta alacriter lætatur." — *Isidorus Pacensis*, c. 30. "Verdad," says Mariana,

justly exiled by his father, says Morales, he recalled to their homes and rights.

But these first acts and this display of virtue were but the refinement of hypocrisy, a means of securing power. It was like the early promise of Nero, and the popular manifesto of Henry VIII. Such, at least, is the accepted judgment of Spanish history. He was soon to plunge into a career of private vice, which was to lead to public crimes, and hasten the destruction which was already threatening the Gothic dominion in Spain.

To satisfy his vanity, he surrounded himself with flatterers instead of honest men; to gratify his lusts, he took to himself numerous concubines; and not to appear as the chief sinner, he encouraged his courtiers to do the same. Never, if the earlier chroniclers are to be believed, was there a filthier condition of society than that which he inaugurated. No wife or daughter, whether of noble or humble family, was safe from the lascivious king and the corrupt court.[1]

Impiety kept pace with impurity. He permitted the priests to marry and keep mistresses, and human frailty even under the ecclesiastical frock, with such august example, was but too glad to obey the abominable law.[2]

"es, que al principio Witiza dio muestra de buen principe de querer volver por la innocencia, y reprimir la maldad." — *Historia General de España,* II. 369.

[1] La Fuente, Historia de España, II. 455.

[2] Ley abominable y feà, pero que a muchos, y *a los mas* dió gusto. — MARIANA, *Historia General de España* II., 370. "Que mando en publico que los señores de su casa y corte, y los obispos y clerigos pudiesen tener todas las mugeres y mancébas que a cada uno pluguiesse." — AMBROSIO DE MORALES, XII. c. 65.

Another of his edicts gave great dissatisfaction, for
what would be in our day regarded as a liberal enact-
ment was in that day a great scandal in
Christian eyes.   He ordered that the exiled
Jews should be permitted to return to Spain, and should
have almost equal privileges with the other races.[1]

Recalls the
Jews.

But the greatest crime of all, in the judgment of
the chroniclers, is that, when reproved by the pope, he
bade the Holy Father open defiance.   When
an envoy was sent from Rome, threatening to
deprive him of his kingdom if these offensive edicts
were not at once repealed, he replied with a counter
threat that he would march an army to Rome and
unseat. the pope.   He then issued a new edict, that
under pain of death no ecclesiastic should obey any
direction from the pope.[2]

Defies the
pope.

But while thus defying the Pontiff, he endeavored
to secure the sanction of the church in Spain to his
iniquitous decrees.   The metropolitan at Toledo was
Archbishop Gunderik, a pious but feeble primate, who
could not restrain the license of the king, or punish
the irregular life of the nobles and clergy.   His weak
efforts were resented.   He was deposed, and Sinderedo, a more pliable prelate, appointed in his stead.[3]

---

[1] Haber dado licencia a los Judios para volver á España y mora
en ella libremente. — LA FUENTE. *Historia de España*, II. 457.

[2] "So pena de muerte que ningun ecclesiastico obedeciesse al
Romano pontifice.—MORALES, *Coronica General*, lib. xii. ch. 65.
In these statements we have the concurrence of San Sebastian,
Isidorus, Pacensies, Lucas de Tuy, and the Archbishop Rodrigo.

[3] The character of Sinderedo is presented in a clearer light, from
the fact that, after the Arab-Moors had penetrated into Spain, he
deserted his post and took refuge in Rome.   Isidorus Pacensis says:
"Qui et post modicum incursus expavescens, non ut pastor sed ut

But this was not enough. To crush all opposition, he issued an impious edict that the church should have " two husbands," and to effect this, in contravention of ecclesiastical canons, he appointed Oppas, his brother in blood and sin, who was already Archbishop of Seville, to be joint Archbishop of Toledo and Metropolitan of Spain, without giving up the Archprelacy of Seville. This was with the ready concurrence of Sinderedo. Thus, under " two husbands," the refractory bride of Christ was reduced to a sordid and servile submission.[1]

But the court and people, although greatly contaminated by the evil communications of Witiza, became disgusted at last with his disorders and debaucheries, and especially with his impiety. *Popular discontent.* In the midst of their folly, they scorned the royal fool. Intrigues and conspiracies against the throne became the order of the day ; and the majority began to cast their eyes toward the lineage of a former and a better king, Chindasuinto, with the purpose of bringing it in for the purification of Spain. Witiza was not slow to divine their intentions, and he took prompt measures to defeat them.

mercenarius (not as shepherd but as hireling) Christi oves contra decreta majorum descrens, Romanæ patriæ sese adventat." — *España Sagrada*, 8, 298.

[1] "Este arçobispo Sinderedo contra Dios y justicia consintio que el rey metiesse por fuerça en la silla y dignidad de Toledo á Oppas su hermano, arçobispo que era en Sevilla, con retencion de ambas iglesias.—MORALES, *Coronica General*, LXII. ch. 65. This author makes a summary of the situation in these words: "La nobleza de los Godos, la religion de los sacerdotes, la honestad y limpieza de las mugeres, todo se voluio *en una horrible fealdad.*"—*Ib.*

Royal names and family relations in this and the preceding periods are exceedingly confused, but the most probable story, as we gather it from the chroniclers, is this: Recesuinto, the son of Chindasuinto, had died, leaving no heir, and had been succeeded, as has been seen, by the good king Wamba in the year 672. In that stormy time, the reigns were short; and there were still living two other sons of Chindasuinto, — Theodofredo, Duke of Cordova, and Favila, duke of Cantabria and Biscay.[1] To these the people now turned for help in their sore emergency, and these Witiza determined to destroy root and branch. Theodofredo, forewarned, wisely kept out of the king's reach, although one of the legends asserts that he was afterwards taken and his eyes put out. Favila, less prudent, was captured and put to death; and Witiza is accused, perhaps with a partisan malignity, of the monstrous crime of seizing and outraging his widow, upon whom his lustful eyes had before been fixed.[2] But, like Fleance escaping from Banquo's fate, the success of this scheme was defeated by the escape of a son of Favila, named Pelayo, a valiant youth, who disappears for a brief season from the annals, to emerge

---

[1] La Fuente, however, says in a note (Historia de España, III. p. 456) : " En cuanto á Teodofredo, el arzobispo Don Rodrigo le hace higo de Recesuinto, no de Chindasuinto, y esto podia ser muy bien." The word *son* is frequently used in a generic sense, and these sons of Chindasuinto may have been his *grand-sons*.

[2] This story is told by Mariana : La Fuente thinks it improbable because the age of Favila — sixty years — would hardly warrant his having a wife for whom Witiza would have an illicit love. " Edad no muy á proposito para tener una muger á quien Witiza amase torpemente."—*Ib.* A decided *non-sequitur.*

again into historic light as the chief of that little band which was to begin in feebleness and sorrow the reconquest of Spain.   Pelayo was to be the father of a long line of kings, who were to recover step by step from a foe as yet unheard of, the dominion which the Goths were about to lose.

When the Gothic monarch could no longer fail to see how odious he had become to all his people, whom even his cruelties could not torture into ab- Witiza dis-
ject submission, he determined to secure mantles
Spain.
immunity by rendering the nation impotent.   He issued orders to dismantle the fortresses, and to throw down the walls of the cities in the disaffected districts, that treason might no longer shelter itself and plot in citadels.

A few places were exempted, in which to secure his power.   Among these were certainly Toledo, the residence of his court, and the centre of his operations ; Leon and Astorga, distant posts in the north, where he had large garrisons for putting down disaffection[1] in that region.

Further to secure, as he said, the tranquillity of the realm, endangered by the quarrels of factions, he proceeded to disarm all the people, and thus while, in the words of the chronicle, " Witiza, the wicked, had

---

[1] Most historians assert that this demolition was quite general. It is easy to see, however, that the unwalling of a few towns would be greatly exaggerated and multiplied.   La Fuente says : " Esto esta en manifesta contradiccion con lo que sabe ocurrio en la invasion sarracena, puesto que los Arabes hallaron muchas ciudades con sus murallas, y muchos demolieron en castigo de su resistencia. — Historia de España, II. 456, note.   See also Ambrosio de Morales, Coronica General, LXII. ch. 65.

taught all Spain to sin," he left the sinners helpless, victims to his own tyranny, and incapable of resisting foreign invasion, inviting that invasion indeed, from the warlike and encroaching nations which lay around the Peninsula.

But, at last, the measure of his iniquity was full. In the year 709, he suddenly disappears from the scene. What became of him? *Dios sabe.* Some say he came to a tragical end, having been killed by a body of conspirators, headed by Roderik. Others assert that he died of a natural illness at Toledo.[1] The annals of the period are rich in food for poetry, but very untrustworthy as to historical details. It seems, however, established that in the eighth year of his reign his plans were thwarted by death; and that he left an odium upon his name and family, which, when combined with the aspirations of nobles and the conflict of factions, excluded his sons Eba and Sisebuto from the succession.[2]

Witiza disappears or dies.

But all other claimants and aspirants were doomed to disappointment, when Roderik seized the vacant throne, and became, by the superior strength of one of the factions, the King of the Goths in February, 709.[3] So great is the obscurity created by contradictory annals and confusing legends, that it is difficult to define the origin and personality of Roderik. Some of the historians assert that he was the

Don Roderik usurps the throne.

[1] Ambrosio de Morales, lib. xii. p. 199.

[2] That he left sons is certain, and they played a prominent part in the succeeding events. Their number and their names differ in the Arabian authorities. Ibun-l-kúttiyyah (quoted by Al Makkari, I. 512) mentions three, — Almond, Romalah, and Artabas.

[3] Gayangos, in Al Makkari, I. 325, note 57.

son of Theodofredo. Mariana states the complicated lineage thus : The daughter of Chindasuinto had married a valiant Greek,[1] named Ardebasto. Their son, Ervigio, who reigned only a few months, left a daughter, who married Egica, the nephew of good king Wamba. From this marriage sprang Witiza and Oppas, and a daughter, who is supposed to have married Count Julian or Ilyan. Theodofredo he supposes to have been the son or grandson of Chindasuinto; and, if Roderik was the son of Theodofredo, this would place him in the male line of succession.[2]

The lineage thus claimed is not certified by adequate proof, and has been rejected by many, after industrious efforts to substantiate it. The matter is of little moment. Ibnu Hayyan, whose *muktabis* was written about the middle of the eleventh century, and who made such a study of the question as was possible at that time, declares that he was not a descendant of the kings who occupied the throne of Andalus, but a powerful and noble lord, much respected for his talents and courage, and that having formed a considerable party *among the people,* he was strong enough to snatch the sceptre from the sons of

---

[1] In most cases where the term Greek is used, it means Hispano-Roman, and the confusion of names grows out of the fact that Greece had become a part of the Roman empire of the east.

[2] It is a curious fact that Roderik is the only Gothic king who is called in history *Don.* This title, a contraction and corruption of *Dominus,* suggests to my mind his *Hispano-Roman* character and partisanship, and also that he bore it as a department commander before his accession, and retained it afterwards. It was frequently given by the church, and Gonzalo de Berceo applies it to our Lord.

En el nomne del Padre que fizo toda coza,
Et de Don Jesu-Christo, fijo de la gloriosa.

Witiza. This would indicate that the Hispano-Romans were still a large factor in the Gothic state; for we are informed by Morales that Roderik was aided by the Romans, who loved his uncle Recesu-into.[1]

That he was a man of uncommon sagacity is certain. Leaving out of consideration many local factions, there were two great parties in the state ; the oppressive monarchy and the suffering people. Roderik succeeded in placing himself at the head of the people's party; and he contrived also to gain the assistance of many persons, who had during the reign of Witiza been promoted to stations of honor and influence, but who, foreseeing the crisis, looked to the overthrow or death of the king for new opportunities of aggrandizement: they cared for parties only as means to personal ends.[2]

The circumstances of the accession of Roderik are somewhat further mystified by the assertion of Isidorus Pacensis, that he invaded the kingdom with tumult at the bidding of the Roman senate.[3] The reference must of course be to the Eastern empire, if a Roman senate gave such advice ; but I prefer to

[1] Coronica General, lib. xii. ch. 66. He also says that Roderik obtained aid from " those of Constantinople ;" but this is not very probable, although it is suggested by Isidorus Pacensis.

[2] This concurrence of office-holders will serve to explain the observation of Mariana, that Roderik was elevated to the throne " por voto, como muchos sienten de los grandes." —*Historia de España,* II. 375. The adherence of the *grandes* and the people was from widely different motives.

[3] Rodericus tumultuose regnum, hortante Senatu Romano, invadit. The words have a clear meaning, and are not easily set aside, but I know of no strong corroboration of the fact.

think the Roman advice and assistance relate to the Hispano-Roman element, as opposed to the Gothic dominion from the first. The house was divided against itself; the government was oppressive, and had become weak. The people, who had been kept down for three hundred years, were beginning, when it was too late, to assert themselves. In former reigns, attempts at amalgamation and fusion had been made. Recesuinto, within half a century before, had permitted and encouraged intermarriages; but Witiza was strong in his opposition to such a fusion, and did all in his power to maintain the distinction between the conquerors and the conquered. Explain these things as we may, the historic fact remains. The opportunity was presented to Roderik; he seized it; the so-called rebellion set up its standard in Cordova, and grew by rapid accretion. He marched to the capital, Toledo, where, after tumult, ensued inaction : crowds stood gaping by as he placed the Gothic crown upon his own head.[1] It was a crisis in the affairs of Spain, a reaction from much that was evil.

Indeed, to a distracted realm and a despairing people, it seemed to promise a remedy for all existing troubles. Men admired the sagacity, skill, and daring — rare qualities in a Gothic monarch — which he had displayed in achieving his elevation. Although somewhat advanced in years, "his eye was not dim, nor his natural force abated;"

The people hope for amelioration.

---

[1] A careful collocation of events and comparison of authorities have fixed the date of his accession in the year 709. It is curious that both Isidor de Beja and Sebastian of Salamanca make it 711. The determination of the true date is due to Don Pascual de Gayangos.

he presented the judgment of a reformer, and the power of a restorer. Of great physical strength, accustomed to toil, inured to hunger, to extremes of heat and cold and loss of sleep, he was brave enough to dare any adventure.[1] He attached men to him by his liberality, and won them to an admiring confidence by a rare physical magnetism.   But the usurper, or conqueror, had succeeded to an authority, which, subjected to the violence of factions, and threatened by foreign enemies, demanded strength of will, energy in action, and a ceaseless vigilance.   The career of Roderik had given promise of all these in happy combination. These hopes were destined to be grievously disappointed.

There seems to have been a lulling, contagious poison in the crown and mantle of a Gothic monarch.

Roderik's torpor. The king's right hand lost its cunning. The grandees were luxurious and enervated; the people were powerless, most of them without arms, and unused to wielding them.   In the war of factions, and amid the strife of tongues, they had scarcely heard the *techbir* which was. now sounding its wild alarums across the strait; and, in the temporary cessation of internal quarrels, Roderik and his lotus-eating court were dreaming the hours away, careless, if not entirely ignorant, of the simoom which was about to pour its deadly blast upon the beautiful fields of Andalus.

----

[1] Such is the summary of his character given by Mariana, to whom, in his later crimes, he appears as " peste, tison y fuego de España."   I have not referred to the evidently erroneous interpolation of a king *Aconsta* between Witiza and Roderik, which is mentioned by Morales (Coronica General, LXII. c. 66.) His name is not given in the generally accepted list of Gothic monarchs.

The historian Mariana justly characterizes the condition of affairs as *grandemente miserable*. The time of the nobles was passed at the festive board; they were connoisseurs in delicate dishes and wines, but the feasters had lost all skill in arms, all the enthusiasm for war which had ushered their progenitors into this lovely land, and were impotent should they be brought to blows with an alien enemy.[1] And this ignoble luxury of the great was in terrible contrast with the forlorn condition of the masses. Since the time of Egica, the father of Witiza, more than once a pestilence had swept over the land destroying many lives, and hindering labor in the fields, so that just before the invasion of the Arab-Moors, famine had combined with disease to produce a general debility, a torpor of despair.[2]

Miserable condition of the Gothic kingdom.

From all these causes the military energy which had rendered the Goths so successful as conquerors had lost all its pristine vigor. With the establishment of their permanent settlement, the active northern man had become relaxed and effeminate: renovation or destruction formed the only alternatives of his future. Was renovation possible? Scarcely so, under the best conditions and with herculean efforts; in the actual conditions and in view of the

---

[1] "Todo era convites, manjares delicados y vino, . . . pero muy inhábiles para acudir á las armas, y venir á las puñadas con los enemigos : . . . gente mas curiosa en buscar todo genero de regalo." — MARIANA, *Historia de España*, II. 375.

[2] Morales says (Coronica General XII. 69, 5), "Habia habido continua hambre, y pestilencia en España, con que se habian debilitado mucho los cuerpos, sin lo que el ocio los habia enflaquecido."

already portending invasion, absolutely impossible. Of this assertion the proof will now be laid before the reader, and he shall judge for himself.

One romantic feature in the history of Roderik must not be omitted. If the testimony is not very strong, some of the earlier historians have asserted, Exilona, the and there is no counter-proof, that, some time wife of Don Roderik. before his accession, he had married, under curious and interesting circumstances, a lady called in the chronicles *Elyata*. The story is that a vessel, storm-tossed on the Mediterranean, had been so fortunate as to find refuge in the port of Denia, a fortress on the Mediterranean coast of Spain, within the limits of Roderik's command. As it came in, the Spanish soldiers, impelled by curiosity, crowded the shore. They feared at first that it might be the leading vessel of the long-talked-of but never-credited invasion from Africa; it proved instead to be a helpless bark, in a shattered condition, hardly escaping from the perils of the sea, and containing the person and suite of a Moorish princess. She was of course detained, but hospitably entreated; and, when her first unavailing sorrow for her untoward fate was appeased, she found in her new situation much to make her contented and cheerful. She suffered no loss of consideration in becoming the willing bride of such a noble lord as Don Roderik. She forgot her country and her father's house, embraced Christianity without reluctance, and was baptized with the Christian name of Exilona. With him she was raised to the Gothic throne, and was destined after his disappearance to play a prominent and no less romantic part in the later history.[1]

As the successful revolution which raised Roderik to the throne had begun in Cordova, a more populous centre of the Hispano-Romans than Toledo, he transferred his court to the former city, making it his capital; he enlarged and adorned the palace, which the Arab-Moors afterwards called by his name, — *Balatt Rudherik;* [2] but, as we have seen, he did little to put the kingdom and the people in a proper condition of defence against the coming invasion.

In reparation of the injustice of Witiza, he recalled Pelayo from his concealment, and made him his *protospatorio,*[3] — first swordsman, or commander of the guard.

The sons of Witiza had fled at Roderik's accession into Mauritania, and were to take part in the treason against him. It is said that he sent them friendly messages, and that they returned to give him apparent aid in his fast-increasing troubles. It is not improbable that they returned. We have the authority of Al Makkari that they collected troops to repel the coming invasion; but it is manifest that they were playing a double part. The king promised the restoration of their estates. If the king was success-

---

[1] We shall see that the Queen of Roderik became the wife of Abdul-l-'azis, the son of Musa. This at least is historic truth. The story of her former fortunes is not of much importance. It will be found, with romantic coloring, in one of Irving's charming "Spanish papers." — *The Loves of Roderik and Exilona.*

[2] Al Makkari, I. 208.

[3] La Fuente makes him *Condé de los espatarios ;* i. e. commander of the royal guard, III. 60 ; also Morales, XXI. c. 69.

ful, they would receive them; if not, they would bargain with the invaders, and get back their property from either hand. That was a game in which, with due caution, they could not lose, whatever the result should be; and such games as this have been frequently reproduced in the history which constantly "repeats itself."

I have thus briefly traced in outline the progress of affairs in Gothic Spain, down to the period in which we left the Arab-Moors ready to make their daring invasion. Roderik had ascended the throne in 709. We have now reached the autumn of the year 710. It remains to call the attention of the reader once more to the political and military situation at this juncture, and also to the geographical and topographical elements which were to form a prominent feature of the coming campaign.

The only stronghold remaining to the Goths in Africa was Ceuta, with its limited *comarca*. The fortress was strongly garrisoned, and commanded, as we have seen, by a general, called by the Spanish historians Julian, and by the Arabians Ilyan.

Jutting out into the Mediterranean from the African shore, just west of Ceuta, and covering it like an The geography of the Strait. enormous military *traverse*, is a rocky promontory, three miles in length, and connected with the main land by a narrow isthmus, on which the town is built. This peninsula, known to the earliest navigators as *Mons Abyla*, seems to beckon across to *Mons Calpe* on the Spanish shore, since known as the Rock of Gibraltar. The citadel of Ceuta was upon the Mons Abyla, which bears the modern name, *El monte del Hacho.* The two promontories were called, in classic times, *Columnœ Herculis,* — the pillars of Hercules; and upon them, as a comment on the timid navigation of the ancient world, were inscribed the words, — *Ne plus ultra.*

It might well have been claimed by the inhabitants of Spain that the African shore was in reality Spanish territory. The geological formation of the Spanish headlands differs entirely from the Spanish inland. The Phœnicians had a tradition that the continents had been united by an isthmus, through which a canal had been cut, which by its gradual widening had become the strait.[1]

Be that as it may, the strait between Spain and Africa had been more probably opened in some primeval convulsion of the globe, before national rivalry could be concerned about its command.[2] The strait is about twelve miles in length, from Cape Spartel to Ceuta on the African side, and from Trafalgar to Europa Point along the Spanish shore. The narrowest point is at Tarifa, where the distance across is about thirteen miles. A constant current setting eastward from the Atlantic, of about two miles an hour, supplies the losses of the Mediterranean by evaporation, and renders western navigation difficult when western gales occur.

---

[1] For the legend of the canal, see Al Makkari, I. 27, 28. Alexander the Great is the hero ! The author says : "If we are to believe ancient traditions, *he must also have resided in Andalus.*" The fable had its origin among the Christians of Spain. It was borrowed from them by all the later Arabian geographers.

[2] "Ceuta should belong, as it once did, to the owners of Gibraltar, and then the command of the straits would be complete, except in fogs." — FORD, *Handbook for Spain,* I. 280.

The Rock of Gibraltar forms a promontory about three miles in length.   East of it the sea grows sud-
The Rock of Gibraltar. denly wider; on the west is the Bay of Gibraltar, enclosed by the Rock, and Cabrita Point.   This bay is five or six miles wide, by about eight in length; and, although somewhat exposed to the sudden fury of a storm-wind called the "Levanter," — "the tyrant of Gibraltar," — it is a tolerable harbor, which in modern times has been rendered secure by moles built out from the Rock.   Opposite Gibraltar, on the western shore of the bay, is Algeciras.[1]   It was called by the Arabians *Jeziratu-l-Khadra*, or the Green Island, a name now transferred in Spanish form to the small island lying in front of it, which bears the name, *Isla Verde*.

I have repeated these well-known details to assist the fancy of the reader in realizing the circumstances of the eventful crossing, soon to be made, which was to change the complexion of Spanish history for all coming time.   It had been long in coming; fortuitous events had seemed to hasten or delay it; but the day of doubt and preparation had reached an end.   Nothing on earth could now avert it.   The enthusiastic Moslemah had conquered northern Africa; there was nothing in northern Africa to tempt the moving mass of fanaticism and valor.   The helpless condition of Spain invited their attack : the words of their prophet

---

[1] Algeciras is called by Strabo, Ιουλια 'Ανοικία; by Pliny, *Julia Transducta*; and by other Latin writers, *Portus Albus*.   *White* to the Romans, it was *green* to the Moors.   For a detailed description of the Rock and its historic fortunes, the reader is referred to " A History of Gibraltar and its sieges," with photographic illustrations by J. H. Mann, London, 1870.

urged them to carry the holy faith into all benighted lands, until they should come to the point, *ubi defuit orbem*. They were eager for the rich Gothic spoils; and Musa was already counselling with his valiant lieutenant, Tarik, as to the final preparations for the invasion, when an unexpected event occurred, which, anticipating their fondest hopes, and opening the gates of Andalus, ushered them upon all that they asked, — "a fair field and no favor" on Spanish soil.

Note. — THE DEFENCE OF WITIZA.

After careful consideration of the subject, I have found myself compelled to accept the general verdict pronounced by both Spanish and Arabian historians upon the conduct and character of King Witiza. Justice, however, requires that I should notice the attempts that have been made to mitigate the severity of this judgment, and to palliate — on the part of some to justify — his conduct. He reigned less than eight years, and there were certainly, before his accession, causes in operation tending to the destruction of the Gothic monarchy. The latest occupants of a falling throne under such circumstances become, by common consent, the scape-goats.

The Gothic church had always displayed great independence of Rome ; and, while it recognized the successor of St. Peter, doctrines were fiercely discussed between the pope and the Spanish prelates ; and, when Rome appears as a censor in history, allowance must be made for the vigor and temper of the anathema.

Then there was the conflict between the Gothic people and the Hispano-Romans, in which the latter had slowly been gaining ground, and Witiza was the representative of the former : the history has been written in the interests of the latter.

Many of the acts called crimes by the monkish chroniclers would in this day be considered the signs of liberal progress, had such been his intention.   Such are his clemency towards the Jews, his impatience of the pope's dictation, and even his permission to the ecclesiastics to marry.   The further allegation that he allowed them to keep mistresses might well be an exaggeration of the permission to marry, or mark the general demoralization, like that in some of the South American republics.   It is further stated that Isidor de Beja, the contemporary historian, even while mentioning some of his offensive public acts, does not portray him as the cruel and dissolute prince presented by the later historian.   But this proves nothing, as the chief value of a contemporary historian consists in telling the truth, but scarcely ever "the whole truth;" and, like Falstaff's lion, his instinct would prompt him to spare the prince.

The first writer to whom we owe this dark picture of Witiza is the author of the "Chronique de Moissac," a Frenchman, who wrote a century after his death, when Catholic Europe was deploring the infidel dominion in Spain, and arraigning all men and all things that had conduced to it.   The abuse of Witiza grew apace ; crime after crime was added to his account, until Mariana gathered together the scattered charges into an avalanche of monkish fury, which still crushes his bleeding remains.

The subject remained without alteration and without interest, until the latter part of the eighteenth century, when Witiza found a champion in Don Gregorio de Mayans y Ciscar, spoken of by La Fuente as a very celebrated and elegant writer.   In his "Defensa del Rey Witiza" he has, with much patience and erudition, attempted to show that this king was really an excellent man, and as a monarch remarkably just and beneficent ; and Masdeu, in his "Historia Critica de España," has followed in the same path ; referring to the account of Padre Mariana in these words : "All this narration must be taken as fabulous."

With these suggestions, the reader will be prepared to consider the subject, if he finds it of compensating interest.

Isidorus Pacensis (Isidoro de Beja) was Bishop of Badajos.

He wrote a chronicle of the most memorable events in his own time, and placed it as a continuation to the chronicle of his distinguished namesake, Isidor of Seville. The title is, " Isidori Pacensis Episcopi Chronicon : Incipit epitome Imperatorum vel Arabum Ephemerides atque Hispaniæ Chronographia sub uno volumine collecta." This work is found in full in " La España Sagrada " of Flores.

CHAPTER V.

THE ASPECT OF THE GOTHIC DOMINION.

IT would be interesting to trace, in this connection, the progress of Gothic civilization, and especially the growth of those institutions of society and government which, notwithstanding the downfall of the Gothic monarchy, have survived and made themselves felt in the subsequent Spanish history. But the scope of this work compels me to limit myself to a few observations concerning the structure as it presented itself to the assaults of the Mohammedan invaders.

Even while Witiza was opposing the pope, the church in Spain was the strongest element of national power. The throne rested upon the altar, and the church strengthened itself by thus supporting the throne; but the chief source of influence was the church. In the thirty-three great councils which were convened during the Visigothic dominion, from that of Tarragona in 516 to that of Toledo in 700 or 701, the king was at least the nominal head; but they were primarily ecclesiastical councils, in which, while affairs of state were also discussed, the learning and piety of the bishops, and their official influence with the people, were almost supreme. The superiority of the church to the state was at first easily maintained: but they played into

each other's hands; and in the more modern history
of Spain this combination may be clearly discerned
as an heirloom from the Gothic period, when the Inquisition accused and condemned men, and then
released them for punishment " to the secular arm."

These councils secured the inviolability of the mon
arch, with the threat of ecclesiastical punishment
against seditious persons, in whatever way — by succession or usurpation— that monarch may have come
to the throne.   As a return, the monarch was bound,
by decrees of the early councils, to guard the inviolability of the Catholic faith.   Thus church and state
were in close bonds.   In virtue of this compact, the
king, as secular head and protector of the church,
exercised the right of nominating and translating
the bishops, a right, which, as we have seen in the
case of the translation of Oppas, was productive of
great evil.

If we look for the origin of secular representative government among the Goths, we find it
thus inextricably connected with the ecclesiastical.
Were these councils the sole origin of the states-
general or *cortes* of the nation ?   The question has
been discussed by learned Spanish civilians, Its connec-
with contrariety of opinions.   But whether ular affairs.
they were the only civil conventions or not, we may
accept the opinion of the learned Marina in his
"Teoría de las Cortes," when he claims that the national councils of Toledo were political congresses,
with all the conditions of such bodies.   "Who does
not see here," he says, " the whole nation, united, and
legitimately represented by the most distinguished

persons, and by its principal members, and displaying
its energy and authority upon subjects of the greatest
interest, and which bear upon the temporal prosperity
of the republic ? " [1]

In view of this assertion, let us look at the composition and some of the proceedings of these councils.
The first of the nineteen councils, so called ecclesiastical, which deliberated upon distinct points of the
civil government, was the third council of Toledo,
which convened in the year 589. It was composed
entirely of bishops ; the only secular representative
being the king, who presided, and who guarded secular interests. It was not until the eighth council of
Toledo that nobles took part in these deliberations, —
nobles not in our present understanding of the
word, as those who held hereditary family dignities
— but those who held their titles as names of official service — a few dukes and counts (*duces et
comites*) and some officers of the palace named by
the king.

The composition of that body was as follows :
Fifty-two bishops, eleven vicars, eleven abbots, one
arch-priest,[2] one precentor (*primicerio*),[3] and seventeen
nobles and palatines.

Some of the later councils, held in other cities, and

[1] This opinion of Marina has been combated by Sempere y Guar-
nios in his " Historia del Derecho."

[2] The arch-priest, or chief presbyter in a district, had charge of
the churches where there was no bishop.

[3] The choir-master in a cathedral church. As the service was
choral, the office was laborious and important. As this is the only
council in which a precentor sat, it may be believed that he was
conductor of the choral services.

convoked no doubt only for the settlement of ecclesiastical questions, were composed of bishops The councils partake of both characters. alone; but in most of the other councils of Toledo the secular element is found, although the ecclesiastical largely predominated. In the eighth council the king, Recaredo, in his opening address, enjoined upon the bishops to "judge all causes presented them with the rigor of justice, but tempered with mercy." "I give my consent *to the laws you ordain*, in which you will omit what is superfluous, and explain obscure or doubtful canons." "And to you, illustrious barons, chiefs of the palatine office, distinguished for your nobility, rectors of the people by your experience and equity, my loyal companions *in the government* by *whose hands justice is administered*, . . . I charge you by the faith which I have avowed to the venerable congregation of these holy fathers, that you do not oppose (*que no os separeis*) what they enact, knowing that if you comply with these my wholesome desires, you will please God, and *I, approving your decisions*, shall likewise obey the divine will."

Coming with almost their primitive rudeness into Spain, which was yet under the influence of Roman institutions and customs, the Goths soon began to accept and assimilate this higher civilization of the conquered people, and then, in turn, to become their teachers. In the laws issued by Eurik and Alarik, there was one code for the Goths and another for the Hispano-Romans. As there grew a more intimate association among these several peoples, attempts were made to frame codes which should govern both alike.

Such were the partial efforts of Recaredo, Chindasuinto and Recesuinto. At last all these
codes were digested into one called "Codex
Wisi-Gothorum" and "Forum Judicum;" or by the
later Spaniards, "Fuero Juzgo," and "Libro de los
Jueces," (Book of the Judges). This excellent code,
which grew by accretion and combination, at different
periods, took its form and name during the joint reign
of Egica and Witiza; and it is probable that the final
compilation was set forth, at the desire and with the
sanction of Egica, by the sixteenth council of Toledo,
in the year 693, only eighteen years before its suppression or sequestration by the invading Arab-
Moors. It was issued, in the semi-barbarous Latin of
the time, for the Hispano-Romans; and in that more
barbarous dialect, mixed German and Latin, for the
Goths.[1] It remained in these tongues until the
reconquest of Cordova by Fernando III., in the thirteenth century, when it was translated by his direction into the Spanish idiom of that period (*de aquel
tiempo*); a new dialect in the process of formation,
which differs essentially from the later Spanish of
the charter of Aviles and the Poem of the Cid. The
process of codification was analogous to that by which
Justinian produced the "Corpus Juris Civilis." There
were first the *laws of the kings*, corresponding to the
royal laws of the early Roman state, and partaking

Codes of
civil law.

---

[1] Mas que lenguage, que idioma era este? Ciertamente ni los
Godos del Tajo pudieron, ni quisieron acaso, conservar la palabra
bárbara de los Godos del Danubio, ni el pueblo hispano-romano
podia hablar el culto Latin de Ciceron y de Vergilio. — LA FUENTE,
Historia de España, II. 504.

also of the edicts, epistles, and rescripts of the emperors. Then there were the *acts of councils*, which may be compared to the *acta* and *consulta senatus*. These were inserted in the code, with notes to that effect. Thirdly, we have laws, unnamed as to their origin or authority; and, fourthly, others, which bear from their earliest appearance, the note, *Antiqua*, or, *Antiqua nova emendata*, the antiquity of which relegates them to the Roman codes, and the emendations of which mark their application to the Gothic system. Thus, in the "Fuero Juzgo" we have an epitome of the sources of Gothic dominion — Roman culture, Teutonic independence, and the ubiquitous and powerful influence of the Latin church, through the provincial councils, which gives a theocratic element to the Gothic government.

This famous code has been differently estimated according to the country and prejudice of the critics. To one it is the best of all the *barbarous* "Fuero codes. To Montesquieu, in his learned and Juzgo." elegant research after an abstract perfection, in his famous work "De l'Esprit des Lois," the laws are puerile, overcharged with rhetoric, disgusting by reason of their superstition, and not arriving at the object aimed at; "frivolous in matter, and gigantic in form;" but, nevertheless, displaying a condition of society more cultured and refined than that of the Burgundians and the Lombards.

To the clear and impartial judgment of Guizot, the Visigothic code presents in its *ensemble* an erudite, systematic, and social character; and, according to Romey, in his History of Spain, "no body of laws, digested in the middle ages, has so nearly approximated the object of legislation, none has better or more nobly defined the law." It is by the collation and combination of such diverse opinions that we may strike the mean of truth, and do unbiased justice to the Gothic, legislation.

In the title which treats of the election of princes, the clear trumpet note of that Gothic freedom which
Fosters civil liberty. was nourished in the forests of Germany, and maintained among the winter rigors of the Baltic, rings out. "If," it declares to the monarch elect, "if thou doest the right thou shalt be king; and if thou doest not the right thou shalt not be king." Thus the monarch, first of all, was subject to law, and the people judged him. But the Goths, satisfied with the assertion, unfortunately gave it no adequate sanction. The only remedy for tyranny was in revolution, which, if successful, received the concurrence of a church council. Thus we find the deposition of Suintila in 631, sanctioned by the fourth council of Toledo, "on account of the extreme tyranny he exercised over the people."[1] Civil liberty was only endangered or restrained by the church.

The *Fuero Juzgo* is comprised in twelve books, arranged according to titles, and to the laws are prefixed the name of the king to whom they owe their origin. The first five relate to civil and private cases; the next three, to criminal laws and penalties. The two following to public order and commerce, and the twelfth to the extinction of Judaism and heresy. Everywhere is asserted the equality of all before the

---

[1] Propter crudelissimam potestatem quam in populo exercuerat.

law. The responsibility of judges is gravely dwelt upon in terms which might serve as a model in our own days. The penalties are severe against those who do wrong for importunity, through ignorance, through fear, and even at the command of the king.

Capital punishment, according to the code, is of rare application, and only for "enormous crimes." Even in such cases a commutation was fre- Punish-
quently made from death to putting out the ments.
eyes. Symbolic punishments were greatly dreaded. — to shave the head rendered a man infamous; and the greatest shame was to be compelled to ride through the streets on an ass. Public whippings were common, as were also private ones, before the judge and a witness. These were for low and degrading offences. Among a people accustomed to violence and the law of the sword, insults, wounds, contusions, and homicide in all its forms, were looked upon and legislated upon with greater leniency. Like the Saxons, and from the same original source, the Goths established a tariff of money valuation for all these, which was known in the Heptarchy as the *wer-gild* or *man-money*.

The Gothic law protected the rights of the family, — the rights of marriage and dower; and the limitation of the exercise of paternal power, in happy modification of the absolute and cruel control given to the father by the Roman code.

The Gothic code gives us some idea of the condition of agriculture by the many laws which it contains for the protection of landed estates and cattle-farms. The punishments for violations of rights of this character are detailed and severe.

We see in this part of the legislation the steady transition in the Gothic economy from arms and
The protection of agriculture and the useful arts. spoils to the more peaceful and settled condition in which arts and agriculture, the production of articles, — the growth of the soil, and the work of the artisan, — for exportation as well as home consumption, transformed these nomadic warriors into a nation and their camp leader into a king.

Navigation was guarded by wise laws for the purposes of commerce as well as of war. It is recorded that in the time of Wamba (672–680), when the coast was threatened by a Saracen flotilla of about three hundred vessels, he was able to provide for the encounter an equal number of Spanish galleys.

With the Salic spirit, the law of entail by male inheritance was made absolute; and the abstract principle of Feudalism obtained, but it was not of the binding force which it acquired in France, and later, under the Conqueror, in England. It was a northern, German feudalism, not unlike the clientry of the Roman law. Men of lower ranks were glad to place themselves under the protection of the rich and noble, but they could leave this association or change it when they pleased.

Thus, in a word, the "Fuero Juzgo" seems to unite the old and the new; and it was kept by the little band of Gothic Spaniards, who were driven by the Arab-Moors into the northwest, as a germ of jurisprudence which was to expand and grow with the slow but unremitted reconquest. It bound them firmly together, in the protracted strife of centuries, with the infidel.

When we seek to discover the signs of intellectual development, under the Gothic dominion, we find the result what we should naturally expect under der existing conditions. There is no record of elegant literature like the epic poems, dramas, satires, and finished odes of Greece and Rome, which are only produced in a high and long-continued civilization, when the writer is sure of an audience.

Intellectual development.

The best Gothic scholars gave their attention to what, in their view, were the more important subjects of theology, ethics, and jurisprudence. "When Chindasuinto," says La Fuente, " sent Bishop Tajon to Rome, he did not send him to find the poetical works of Horace or Lucan, but the moral treatises of St. Gregory the Great, which were commentated and amplified afterwards by that illustrious prelate of Saragossa." [1]

They were not without careful historians, or rather chroniclers, first among whom may be mentioned Paulus Orosius, a priest of Tarragona, the friend of St. Augustine, the Bishop of Hippo, whose "History of the World from the Creation to the year 416," closes with the capture and sack of Rome by Alarik in 410. Its reputation was great, and an Anglo-Saxon version, by King Alfred, caused it to be well known in the north. From his day to that of Isidor de Beja, a contemporary of the conquest, we have a list of learned writers of great value

History.

1 Historia de España, II. 515.

to the student of history : among these may be mentioned Idacio, and Juan, abbot of Viclara ; and Julian
of Toledo, who wrote an account of the expedition of
Wamba against the pretender, Paul Maximus, and a
History of Spain under the Goths, which has unfortunately been lost. Greatest of all to the Spaniards
— "præclarum et venerabile nomen " — is St. Isidore
of Seville (*Isidorus Hispalensis*), the restorer of letters
in Spain, the last writer of classic Latin, called by
the eighth council of Toledo, — " excellent doctor,
glory of the catholic church, the most learned man of
the time, who was to throw a lustre upon the last
centuries." He wrote on many subjects, and adorned
them all. Among his works are a chronicle, a history, lives of illustrious men, commentaries on the
Holy Scripture, books of sentences, offices of the
church ; treatises on the nature of things, on gram-
mar and logic (*de controversia*), on ethics, on the lives
of saints of both testaments ; a collection of old
canons of the church in Spain, and a famous work on
etymologies. I might go on with the list, to include
works on almost every subject, even upon tactics and
nautical affairs, painting and architecture.

The medical art in Gothic Spain had little scope,
and almost no development. This too was due to the
prejudices of a fierce people, who depended greatly
upon nature to repair the inroads of disease.
Medicine. Certainly the art held out few attractions
to practitioners. If a patient was weakened by the
medicine administered, or by bleeding, the physician
was fined. If the patient died, he was held guilty of
homicide, or rather was considered in the light of an

assassin, whose life was at the pleasure of the victim's family. No free woman could be bled or receive medicine at the hands of the physician, except in the presence of some of her male relations. There was no pay unless the cure was complete. It may be readily imagined that with such conditions the medical art could make little progress, and that epidemics would sweep over the land without impediment, except what the prayers of the Church could offer.

The progress of the Gothic Spaniards in art was more marked. They excelled in the manufactures of flax and wool; they made colored glasses, especially for the adornment of places of worship. Art and manufactures. In imitation of Roman remains they built and enlarged cities, and erected numerous churches; but the peculiar school of architecture known as the Gothic, with the wedge-shaped roof, the lancet windows, and the pointed arch formed of two arcs intersecting in an angle of sixty degrees, was not introduced into Spain until the thirteenth century, long after this Gothic power had disappeared.

The Goths coined money of various denominations, and specimens remain of the eighteen Gothic kings from Liuva to Roderik (571–711). These were of gold or of silver gilt, and bore the head of the monarch in effigy on one side.

There are numerous lapidary inscriptions in Latin, some of which are of value in the settlement of dates.

This very brief notice of the progress of the Goths in Spain will suffice to satisfy the reader, that their sway from the fifth to the eighth century, was, on the whole, a grand and powerful dominion; in its day

the most powerful and progressive, erected by any
Northern nation upon the ruins of the Roman empire
of the West.   They had conquered the Romans; they
had arrested and driven back the Huns in their wild
career; they had subjugated and paralyzed the Suevi
and the Alans; they had forced the Vandals into
Africa; they had made good their claims to the immense territory lying between the Garonne and the
columns of Hercules; they had established the church,
and made it not only the ally but the august monitor
and guardian of the state; and to crown all, they had
digested a body of laws, powerful to govern, and, on
the whole, remarkable for its liberality, to bind the
people of the country and all their interests together
as a great nation.   What could imperil, what could
overthrow, such a consolidation of progress and
power?   Effeminacy, inaction, and vice.

CHAPTER VI.

ILYAN AND THE MOTIVES OF HIS TREASON.

WHAT may be called the great historic causes having been already given, if we now endeavor to discover and to place in logical combination the immediate causes of the Conquest of Spain, we shall find them to be connected with two important considerations. The first in order is based upon the sound judgment and determined purpose of Causes of the Moslem general, Musa Ibn Nosseyr, quest. combined with the enthusiastic valor of the troops under his command. After unparalleled successes in Northern Africa, where martial strength and moral influence had transformed the conquered nations into soldiers of Islám, Musa had now confronted, Musa Ibn on the opposite side of a narrow channel, Nosseyr. an effete government, an enervated and disunited people, an undefended coast-line, with the purpose of conquering the Peninsula, and of giving his eager soldiers the rich accumulated spoils of which they had heard so much. This cause of the conquest will illustrate itself fully as we proceed; it was always present and always potent, and must be accorded the greatest weight in the historic problem.

The second and still more immediate cause is presented to us in a story, in which we think we find

glimpses of real history, combined with much that
has been considered purely legendary. It
is certainly doubtful in its details, if not in
its very conception, and yet it contains somewhat of
philosophic truth. And here let it be observed that
in no part of the domain of history can a writer less
afford to neglect legends, which, although acknowledged to be in some degree fabulous, contain often
the most valuable and brilliant materials for a true
record; the fiction is the modus in which the wonder-
eyes of the time reflected the fact; the allegory gives
other names and magnifies the *res gestæ*, but the real
men existed and the deeds were done.

In the legend now to be considered, the dark hero
appears in historic personality, and the purpose
ascribed to him was really accomplished. He is called
in the Spanish chronicles Count Illan and Don Illan.[1]
The unfortunate heroine, his daughter, figures as Florinda in her days of innocence, and after her undoing
is known by the contemptuous epithet *la Cava.* I
shall have occasion later to consider the personality
of these characters more at length, and shall only
add that so many respectable historians, both Spanish
and Arabian, have presented the story, that an outline of it at least could not be omitted in these
pages, even were the doubt of its reality far stronger
than it is. Count Ilyan appears as the Lord or
Sahib of Ceuta and Tangiers. Ambrosio Morales
referring to the account of Roderik of Toledo, speaks
of a certain Count Requila as commanding on the
African Coast, and of Ilyan as stationed at Alge-

The story of Ilyan.

---

[1] The liquid sound of the *ll* would make it sound *Ilyan.*

ciras on the Spanish shore.[1]   This offers no difficulty,
as we may readily suppose that a change in the command, quite usual, had transferred Ilyan to Ceuta.
After an examination of the records, we are satisfied
as to the personality and the titular authority of the
man; but the nature of his relation to the Gothic
government of Spain cannot be so readily determined.
That he owed some sort of allegiance to that government, and was commanding under its orders, there
seems no doubt; but Ceuta and Tangiers were distant
strongholds separated from Spain by a wide and often
stormy strait, without ready and regular communications.   The Gothic monarchs, who succeeded each
other rapidly, were indolent, and, when roused from
their inaction, principally concerned with the factions
of the realm.

Under these circumstances, the Lord of Ceuta
became bold and formidable to the surrounding Africans on his own account; and when the Arabs arrived
in Mauritania he appeared to them, as he was in
reality, not as a general of the Gothic king, but as a
tributary prince, who was but little, if at all, controlled
by the monarch at Toledo.

If, during the reigns of Egica and Witiza, generals
thus situated had been keeping the districts in subjection, and fortifying themselves against the advancing Arab-Moors, in the name of the king, it was
because he had been sending them troops and munitions of war, and had thus really maintained them as
the outlying picket of the Gothic kingdom.   Even
then the modus of their defence and resistance was
left to themselves.

[1] Coronica General, LXII. c. 65.

But now there was a great revolution of interests;
with the accession of Roderik, there were two royal

Ilyan, the man of a party. parties in the State. To this tributary
prince, as I have ventured to call him, who
had borne the commission of Witiza, Roderik might
seem a usurper; and, in the interests of the family of
the deposed or dead monarch, Ilyan might consider
the new reign as a fair mark for hostile action. And,
with this slackening or entire rupture of allegiance,
his local power became more valuable in his eyes
than even the safety of the realm.

Such being the general condition of affairs, and in
those days of darkness when might made right, why
should not a powerful baron in Africa do just what
Roderik had done in Spain, — usurp the supreme
power? Certainly there were many other precedents
for such a course, and the moral inhibition was
entirely without force. If, to add to these cogent inducements, there were held out to him hopes of unusual reward or preferment, or if there was awakened
a strong feeling of revenge, he might go farther and
join with an alien enemy to destroy the monarch,
who was not a simple usurper, but a wicked and
oppressive usurper.

What has been thus stated in general terms probably took place. Ilyan had been the brother-in-law
and friend of Witiza. Ilyan had cause of quarrel
with Roderik, and had no doubt dissembled his sentiments while watching the course of events. The
Arab-Moors had come upon him, taken Tangiers, and
assaulted his stronghold of Ceuta. What should
he do, — resist them to the uttermost, or make terms

with them, and let them conquer Spain if they could?

No doubt there was a conflict of opinions in his mind; but the temptation was great to secure his power and guard his Spanish possessions by preliminary treaty, and then to usher the Arabian arms into Spain, especially as he was not in condition to impede their progress, and thus unseat the usurper, with the vague hope, if not with specific agreement, that when the power of Roderik should be destroyed, and a large booty secured, the invaders, seating a son of Witiza upon the throne, should return to Africa, and be content to found a grand empire there,[1] leaving him secure in his power.

Having given thus a preliminary view of the circumstances, and a statement of the "divided duty," as it may have appeared to him, it becomes necessary to present to the reader what is really known of the man who plays such a prominent and repulsive part in the annals of that eventful period. This is due on general principles to the interests of historic truth, always in such danger of perversion, and also to the claims of a man, however remote from our age and sympathies, who, in legend and poem, and in history — in Arabic, Latin, and more

What is known of his personality.

---

[1] This opinion, which appears in many of the earlier writers, is thus echoed by La Fuente (Historia de España II. 479) : Creerian y *acaso lo concertaron asi,* que destronado Rodrigo, su principal objeto, habrian de contentarse aquellos ó con tributo, ó cuando mas con la posesion de alguna parte del territorio español, como en tiempo de Atanagildo habia acontecido con los Griegos imperiales buscados como estos, por auxiliares para destronar un rey. — *Historia de España*, II. 479.

modern Spanish, has been branded as one of the most
wicked among historic characters — a Christian governor who opened the gates of his country to the invasion and occupancy of an alien race, impelled by an
infidel creed; a traitor to his king, his country, and his
faith.

He appears to us in many and vague shapes, and we
cannot do better than to consult the most respectable
authorities, and fashion our man after a combination of
these. The Ilyan of history is the resultant of many
Ilyans, as presented by the reason or fancy of the
writers who have undertaken to present his likeness.

Isidorus Pacensis, and the continuator of the chronicon Biclarense (de Viclara), who are contemporary
The Ilyan of historians, make no mention of him at all.
the chroni-
cles. This silence would be fatal to his claims,
were it not that the notice of the conquest by both
these writers is exceedingly brief: the facts at that
time were not well known; and their chief concern
was absorbed in the great event itself, and not in the
mode and accessories of it. Nor is Ilyan mentioned
by the monk of Abelda, who wrote of these affairs in
the latter half of the ninth century; but his authority
is chiefly the earlier chronicles to which I have referred.

As with regard to the chronicles of other nations,
a time came long after these events had happened,
when scholars began to examine them more criti-
cally, to search for and collate all the information
possible. So we are not astonished to find the first
mention of the story of Ilyan in the important work
of the monk of Silos *(chronicon silense)*, who wrote

in the beginning of the twelfth century.[1]   The writer
is clear in his details, and it is evident he is not in-
venting the story.   He appears rather to be   Arabian
translating from an earlier *Arabian* historian;   accounts.
for we know that the narrative of Ilyan's treason on
account of the rape of his daughter, is to be found
in an anonymous Arabian geographer of the ninth
century, in many Arabian histories of the tenth, and in
that of Al Bekri, who wrote in the eleventh century.

His first appearance on the historic stage, in the
Latin *chronicon silense*, is under the name of *Julianus.*
The former Arabian writers call him *Balyán* and *Al
Ilyan.*   Ibnu Khaldun, who wrote in the latter half
of the fourteenth century, and who stands pre-emi-
nent among the Arabian historians for truth and industrious research, calls him *Elyano.*   In the history
of the king Don Alfonso he appears as *Illan.*

Condé's Arabian authority does not mention him
by name, but says, "At this time certain Christians
of Gesira Andalus, offended by their king Ru-
derik, . . . came to Musa Ben Noseir and invited him
to pass into Spain." [2]

There seems also to be some vagueness as to the
nationality of his birth.   The Spanish historians declare him to have been a Goth, or at least a native of
Spanish soil.   They assert that he married the sister

----

[1] This chronicle may be found in Flores, " España Sagrada," vol.
xvii.

[2] Condé adds, in a note : " The affront here alluded to is without
doubt that caused by the amours of the king, Don Rodrigo, with
the daughter of Count Julian."— *Historia de la Dominacion*, I., ch.
viii.   He too carelessly dismisses the story as a Moorish fiction, as
the Spanish historians would be glad to consider it.

of Witiza, and had large possessions in Spain, while
he held for a time the lucrative and important command in Africa.   If of an Hispano-Roman family he
would still be a Goth by allegiance and official duty.
The Arabians who found him in Africa, and who knew
little of Gothic affairs, might well be mistaken in
Was he a considering him, as they did, the king of
Berber mer-
chant? the Moorish tribe of Ghomarah, Sahib of
Ceuta, and by inference a Moor or a Berber.   He
was besides a " Berber merchant," who had increased
his wealth by a brisk trade between Spain and Africa.
His importance may be further estimated by the fact
that Al Bekri, writing in detail of the Mauritanian
coast, notices a river which bears the name Nahr
Ilyan, a palace then standing as Kasr Ilyan, and an
aqueduct as Ayn Ilyan.

It will be remembered that the region called Mauritania had been successfully overrun by Numidians,
Romans, Vandals, and Greeks of the lower empire, all
of whom had left stragglers or colonists among the
original inhabitants.   Thus, at the time of which I
write, it was occupied by a heterogeneous population,
with great diversities of origin and characteristics,
with comparatively little local attachment, and less
of what is now called patriotism.   The descendants
of the Roman and Byzantine conquerors were called
by the Arabs *Rúm* or Romans.   To them Ilyan was
one of their people, and we find a palliation of his
after conduct in the words of the chronicle of Don
Rodrigo, that " Don Julian did not come of the lineage of the Goths, but of the lineage of the Cæsars,
and therefore was not grieved that the good lineage

(the Gothic) should be destroyed." That he is declared to have been a *comes Spathariorum* to Roderik, is quite consistent with this view; for this was a title of actual military authority, and not of noble dignity,[1] or of race distinction.

Thus the personality of Ilyan seems to be the resultant of many forces and interests, — and not a Goth, of any faction, although up to the time of his treason ostensibly desirous to preserve the Gothic power in Spain. As to his creed, both Spaniards and Arabians agree that he was a Christian, and indeed there is nothing in his history to show that he was at any time an apostate from the Christian faith.

I have already spoken of his probable relation to the Gothic government, as that of a nominal tributary, and in reality a very independent viceroy. The weakness of the Goths in Africa. Incident to the internal troubles in the Peninsula, the Gothic power, beyond its limits, may mean anything, from a vigorous rule to a mere shadow of control. The Goths had taken Ceuta in the time of Sisebuto (612-21), but beyond Ceuta and Tangiers, and the adjacent strip of coast, the control was uncertain and variable. One element of its weakness is found in the fact that, often in those troublous times, it was rather from the desire of the rulers in Africa than from any urgency at Toledo that the connection was maintained. The lieutenant across

---

[1] It is also easily explained that the Arabians call him *al mukaddam*, or governor of the outposts, — a word which has been corrupted in Spanish into Almocaden, and which has been supplanted by another title used in the Spanish conquests in America, —*Adelantado*, one who goes forward, *adelante*.

the strait might often have asserted his independence, had it not been that he looked for help and countenance to the Gothic government of Spain, against the incursions of the mountain tribes of Atlas, and later against the rumored irruptions of the advancing Arabs.

So, on the other hand, it was not until they found themselves threatened by the terrible inundation which had already poured its waters from Syria to Barbary that the Gothic kings began to regard their lieutenants and garrisons at Tangiers and Ceuta as an important barrier against these invaders from the east. The apprehensions were not, however, great even to the latest moment. It had been like the cry of "wolf" in the fable; they had been coming, coming for more than three-quarters of a century. The doubt was natural whether they would ever come. There were therefore surprise and sad misgivings when the intelligence came that they had really captured Tangiers and assaulted Ceuta; but even then the hope was strong that the strait and a strengthened *garda costa* would keep them off or drive them back.

We are entirely in ignorance how long Ilyan held the command at Ceuta. The Arabian chronicle informs us that when at a much earlier period (A. H. 62) Okbah, on his second incursion, had appeared before the walls of Tangiers, Ilyan came out to meet him, and even accompanied him into Sus-al-Aksa, no doubt satisfied that he should subdue the native tribes and keep them in subjection. But Okbah had been obliged to retrace his steps and abandon his conquests, and the Berbers had successfully opposed his successor Hassan. Thirty years

Ilyan in command at Ceuta.

had now elapsed; and when we are told that Ilyan, now dreading the new tide of Mohammedan invasion, had strengthened his fortifications, and resisted the advance of Musa and his lieutenants, we are further corroborated in the view that his command had been of a permanent and almost uncontrolled character, and that he was primarily concerned as to his own interests and the security of his principality. Thirty additional years had made him more sagacious. The ally of Okbah was the enemy of Musa, at least for a time.

We have seen that Musa had captured Tangiers and been repulsed at Ceuta. It was just at the time of these later movements that Roderik had usurped the throne; and we are led logically to the conclusion that Ilyan, who, though never caring much for the Gothic government of Spain, had still resisted the Moslem advance, would be ready to secure his own interests, if he could do so, by making a treaty with the Arabs; and if necessary, while making the best terms for himself, he would even aid them in what he would have been powerless to avert, the invasion of Spain; thus bringing — who could tell? — relief and comfort to the suffering people, upon whom the hand of the usurper was as heavy, without lineal claim, as the hand of Witiza had ever been. The historian finds himself encircled by many conjectures, which the reader must share and solve with him.

From what has been said, it will appear, as the most satisfactory judgment, that Ilyan was a Hispano-Roman; that he was a nominal rather than real dependant of the Gothic king; that he cared little for

Gothic Spain; that he held undisputed sway on the Mauritanian coast; that he was the secret enemy of the usurper Roderik; that his troops were not Goths, or even Hispano-Romans, but chiefly Africans of mixed races; that he was the chief of "foreign merchants," as well as the "Sahib of Ceuta," where everybody who could be was a trader; that his principal wealth was due to his energy in this trade; that he consulted his own interests in dealing with the Arab-Moors; and that he undertook to aid what he could not prevent. Such seems to me the political view of the situation, and of the man who was confronted by the vanguard of the Moslemah.

But he was a Christian, and we are at first inclined to think he should have had some "compunctious visitings of Nature," which would obstruct the path into which his steps were tempted, and demand Ilyan a Christian. some striking excuse to be presented at the bar of history, for the unpardonable sin against the Holy Spirit of Christianity. Even here I am inclined to look for some palliation of his conduct. He neither knew nor understood the true doctrines or full value of the Christian religion, which under Witiza was but the shield of hypocrisy and cruelty; he was ignorant of the tenets of Islám, but he recognized it as a widely conquering faith. He probably regarded the religious element as but of slight importance in the transaction, and did not let it stand in the way of making the best bargain for himself, while punishing the crimes of the Gothic monarch.

Whether it be true that he had married the sister of Witiza, and thus had a claim to redress the wrongs

of his wife's nephews, it seems certain that the sons
of Witiza did, upon the accession of Rod-   The sons of
erik, go over to Africa to present their griev-   Witiza.
ances and ask his aid.   They told him how the injustice of Roderik had still further weakened the
slack allegiance of the people.   Many in Spain were
ready for a new revolt; many asked, without thinking of the means, an amelioration of their condition,
but the sons of Witiza, dissembling their wrath, were
concerting for vengeance against Roderik, and for a
recovery of the royal power, or at least of the estates
of their father.   They found in Ilyan an interested
ally; here was a new motive: he had thus far resisted
the advance of the Arab-Moors; he would resist no
longer.   And yet he sought in every direction for a
still more potent and satisfactory reason than any or
all that had yet been presented.   And here the history seeks for assistance from the somewhat legendary story of Florinda, which, if it were true, would
present a crowning motive for his treason; one which
transcends and absorbs all the others, and transforms
the traitor prompted by sordid self-interest into the
stern and implacable avenger of his daughter's ruined
honor.   This story must be examined with the
respect due to its importance and its unrivalled
pathos.

CHAPTER VII.

THE STORY OF FLORINDA, COUNT ILYAN'S DAUGHTER. THE JEWS.

WOMAN'S wrongs have asserted themselves far more powerfully in history than woman's rights. The sacredness of woman's chastity has been defended by the most unchaste of peoples. Among the most important epochs in the annals of several nations have been those which are marked by the redress of violence to woman's honor. The siege of Troy in the immortal poem of Homer, so vivid in its delineations of human character that it did not need to be reclaimed, as it has been by the recent explorations of Schliemann, from poetry to sober history, was undertaken to punish the abduction of Helen by Paris the son of Priam.[1] The final crash of the tottering Roman kingdom was due to the violation of the chaste Lucretia by Sextus, the son of Tarquin the Proud, and the very name of king was thenceforth abhorred throughout the land. The sacrifice of the young Virginia by a father's hand, as preserved for us in the pages of Livy, trammelled the authority of the degenerate consuls, brought back the tribunes, and gave new protection to the liberties of

Woman's wrongs in history.

---

[1] Bleda observed the parallel in speaking of Florinda : — "Fué la hermosura desta dama, no menos dañosa á España que la de Elena á Troya." — *Coronica de los Moros*, p. 146.

the Roman people. It is unnecessary to multiply illustrations from history; in our own modern society the same story is often repeated; the letter of the law is impotent against bloody redress, in token that woman's honor is the holiest thing on earth.

And so, according to legend and chronicle, which have passed into history, the seduction of Count Ilyan's daughter by Roderik gave final cause and decent shape to the nascent treason, and led to historic results, even more remarkable and fatal than those recorded in the Grecian and Roman story. Ilyan, who, as we have seen, had already made up his mind to treat with the Arabs, had found, if not a justification of his purpose, at least a salve for his conscience, in the demand for swift and complete retribution.

It was the custom in Gothic Spain, as in many other of the new European monarchies, for the children of the principal grandees to be brought up at the royal court. This custom answered a double purpose; there they received the best and noblest training of the time, fitting them for their exalted stations; and they also served as hostages for the good conduct and loyalty of their parents.

The boys, as pages of the household, were exercised in the use of arms, and became acquainted with knightly duties and functions. The king's pages became squires and men-at-arms; the squire only waited for opportunities, which were not long wanted, to win the spurs of a knight. To the ambition and valor of a knight there was no limit. The girls were in attendance upon the queen and her noble companions, performing such conventional service as befitted their station without making them menials. They were taught to sing, to dance, and to embroider; in short, to prepare themselves by that ornamental education which has been the bane of woman in all ages, not excepting our own, for such brilliant and well-dowered marriages as the king should provide for his wards.[1]

For generals on distant and unsettled service, this custom had peculiar advantages. They were glad to leave their children where, so far from being neglected during their absence, they would be nourished and trained in the best conventional manner without concern and expense to them.

Thus it seems not improbable that during the reign of Witiza, who is supposed to have been Ilyan's brother-in-law, and while Ilyan and his wife were living at Ceuta, their young and beautiful daughter Florinda was left at the court of Toledo, as maid of honor to the queen. It would appear that after the accession of Roderik — accepted at first with dissimulation — and before Ilyan had time or reason to remove her, she remained in the same position. Ilyan would plan to reclaim her; it was to the interest of the new king to retain her.

Florinda a maid of honor.

The story which follows is decked in the garments of romantic fiction by El Rasis; but it contains a body of truth, from which these robes of fable may be withdrawn, and which has been accepted by numerous historians, both Spanish and Arabian.[2]

---

[1] Al Makkari, I., 256 and 513, note 30.

[2] The work, which bears the name of El Rasis, claims to be a

It is related that the old and dissolute king, Roderik, first saw Florinda, as the old and lecherous judges saw Susanna, in the bath. From a concealed position he beheld her disporting with her companions, and unconsciously revealing her beautiful form, secure in her innocence and seclusion. The demon of lust, almost expelled by age and satiety, was aroused to new life.[1] He assailed her chastity, by daily importunity, and with all the prestige of his royal power; and, at last, either overcame her scruples, or resorted to violence to effect her ruin.[2] Appalled by the prospect of consequences, after his success, he tried to prevail upon the unhappy girl to conceal her undoing from her parents. She feigned to obey him; but when his suspicions were allayed, she succeeded in despatching by a trusty messenger a letter and a token to her father at Ceuta: if one failed, the other would tell the story. Al Kortobi, in his history of the Spanish khalifs, rejects the letter, and says that notwithstanding the precautions of Roderik "she contrived to acquaint her father with her situation by sending him a splendid present, and among the articles composing it a rotten egg:"[3] this

Her ruin.

translation by a priest, Gil Perez, from the Arabic. It is in reality not so; but, as Condé says, "a wretched compilation from barbarous old chronicles;" it has no value except for some geographical details. From it Irving drew largely in his "Legend of Don Roderik."

[1] "Avino que jugando con sus iguales, descubrio gran parte de su cuerpo. — MARIANA, *Historia de España*, II. 469.

[2] Cardonne, who writes from Arabian authorities, asserts the latter. "La resistance qu'il éprouva ne fit qu'irriter sa passion; et il dut à la violence un bonheur que l'amour lui réfusoit." — *Histoire de l'Afrique et de l'Espagne*, I. 65.

[3] Al Makkari, I., appendix, xliv.

was the token. The letter of which others speak is
certainly well conceived. " O my father," she wrote,
" would that the earth had swallowed me up, before I
found myself in condition to write these lines to
thee ! " [1]

Spanish poets in all later times have made much
of this pathetic appeal; [2] but among the historians,
patriotism, or rather pride of race, has prevailed over
sympathy. They are almost unanimous in making
Florinda share the blame; and the name is now
never given to children, but only to dogs.

A square tower on the bank of the Tagus, and at
the foot of the rocky steep upon which the palace
stood, was long pointed out as the place where the
maiden was bathing — *el baño de la cava;* but recent
examination has dispelled the interesting illusion,
and the discovery of the ruins of two piers, rising to
just below the water-level shows the supposed bath-
house to have been the covered entrance of a bridge.[3]

Nor is there much better foundation for the name

[1] Lope de Vega, who works up the story in his epic poem " La Jerusalen Conquistada," pithily expresses the effect of Florinda's letter, —
    " Breve proceso escrive aunque el sucesso
      Significar quejosa determina,
    Pero en tal breve causa, en tal processo
      La perdicion de España se fulmina."
                    Lib. VI.

[2] Mascarenhas, a Portuguese poet, lends her some sympathy in his
" Viriato Tragico," —
      Filha que á honra mais que um Rey presava,
      Hispanha culpe a força sem desculpa,
      Nam culpe a bella, que nam teve culpa.
                  II., 118.

[3] N. A. Wells, Picturesque Antiquities of Spain, p. 113.

of a gate at Malaga, — *la puerta de la cava* ; so named, says Morales, because Florinda passed through it with her father to embark for Africa.[1] It is not without significance that tradition thus traces the ill-fated Florinda to the seashore, where, having played her tragic part in the story of the conquest, she disappears from our vision. She rises like a ghastly apparition to invoke the conquest, and sinks into the earth when the invocation has been heard and heeded.[2]

When the news reached Ilyan, his anger against Roderik was ungovernable. "By the faith of the Messiah," he exclaimed, says Ibn Khaldún, *Ilyan's anger and his action.* "I will undermine his throne, and disturb his kingdom, until the whole is overturned and annihilated." But it was necessary to dissemble in order to recover his daughter, who was still in the king's power. Without delay he crossed the stormy strait, — it was in January, — and appeared unbidden and unexpected at Toledo. It had been his custom and his duty to report to the king in person on the duties of his post and the condition of the province, once every year, but not in the stormy season ; and when he came he was in the habit of bringing to the king, with his tribute, presents of the various productions of

[1] " En Malaga hé visto la puerta en el muro, que llaman *de la cava*, y dicen le quedo aquel nombre, habiendo salido esta vez ella por embarcarse." — *Coronica General*, LXII. ch. 47, sec. 4. Mariana says, what may be said of many such traditions, " Cosa recibida de padres á hijos." — *Historia de España*, II. 380.

[2] " Præterea furor violatæ filiæ adhoc facinus peragendum, Julianum, incitabat, quam Rodericus Rex, non pro uxore eo quod sibi pulchra pro concubina videbatur, eidem callide surripuerat." — *Chronicon Silense*, apud Flores, *España Sagrada*, XVII. 270.

Africa. When he thus suddenly appeared at court, unheralded and without gifts, the king upbraided him with this unusual visit, contrary to standing orders. "What brought thee here?" said the guilty king. "Thou knowest very well this is neither the time nor the occasion for thy coming to court." Ilyan answered that his wife was very ill, and greatly desired to see their daughter. Neither the king nor Ilyan was deceived, but both dissembled. The former, with secret reluctance and misgivings, consented to Florinda's departure; and, as Ilyan was leaving his presence, he said: "O Ilyan, I hope I shall soon hear of thee, and that thou wilt endeavor to procure for me some of those very swift *shadhankah* (hawks), which are a source of pleasure and amusement to me, since they chase and hunt the birds, and bring them to me." Ilyan almost betrayed himself, as he replied, " Doubt not, O king, but that I will soon be back, and by the faith of the Messiah, I will never feel satisfied until I bring thee such *shadhankah*, as thou never sawest in thy life." "But Roderik," says the simple Arabian chronicler, "did not understand the meaning of his words;"[1] or, if he did, he could not then resent them.

Ilyan hurried home with his daughter, embarking, as has been suggested, from Malaga, through the " gate of Cava," a name which has perpetuated for her the blazon of dishonor. Her guilt has been accepted by the Spaniards, because Spain was lost when she was deflowered, and they vainly think to remove the stain in some degree from their national honor by fix-

[1] This conversation is given by Ibn Khaldún, — quoted by Al Makkari, I. 256, 257.

ing it upon her reputation. Had she resisted and preserved her chastity, Ilyan, they believe, would have lacked the motive for his treason, and would have not introduced the Moslems. She has been more honestly held responsible by the Arabians, who guard their women with .gratings and locks and eunuchs ; and to them it seems impossible that she should have lost her virtue, even at the will of a monarch, without her own complicity in the deed.[1]

Such is the story: if it be true, and if the lust of Roderik gave immediate and crowning motive to the treason of Ilyan, it must not be forgotten that there were other springs of action and sources of influence which conspired with the conduct of Ilyan, and without which his purpose could not have been achieved. These he determined to combine and use. He knew that many persons of high station were disaffected to Roderik, but not ready to move until they saw a prospect of success. He saw that to the oppressed people a change of masters promised a chance of amelioration. He was in constant communication with the despised but sagacious

Other causes for the invasion.

---

[1] Although veritable history preserves no farther notice of Florinda, the reader will find in the *romance*, which is miscalled *La verdadera historia del Rey Don Rodrigo*, which Miguel de Luna pretended to translate from the Arabic, a dramatic account of the return of *Illan* and his family to Spain, and the suicide of his daughter, who threw herself from the top of a high tower.—Ch. xviii. 81. Of Miguel de Luna's work La Fuente says, " Si es que no invento su historia, que nos la dió por traduccion." He at least was able to translate ; for we are told in *Biblis. Hispan. Nova* (vol. ii., voce *Michael de Luna*), that he was sprung from Arabian converts, and was regius professor of Arabic, —" Granatensis, ex Arabibus conversis oriundus, hujus linguæ interpres Regius."

Jews in Africa, who were thoroughly allied with their brethren in the Peninsula. He lost no time in gaining the control of all these interests, to combine them in a party which should acquiesce in his schemes. He wrote letters and sought interviews; he appealed to each class, and to many individuals according to their foibles; to some he promised revenge; to others gold; to the ambitious he showed the prospect of place and power in the new order of things; to all he offered a new Spain, an Arcadian country, from which the old evils and oppressions should disappear.

> "— Si qua manent sceleris vestigia nostri,
> In rita perpetua solvent formidine terras." [1]

And yet, when on the very verge of ruin, Gothic Spain still presented a formidable front to the coming invasion: a dominion of three hundred years without even partial overthrow, was not to be shaken by the rape of a girl, whatever her rank, the rancor of factions, or the disaffection of a single general. [2]

---

[1] The Pollio of Virgil, Ecl. iv. 13, 14.

[2] I have honestly endeavored to present the principal features of this romantic story, because, after careful consideration, I am inclined to think that it is founded on fact. It has at least a *prima facie* air of truth. I have already said that the argument against it, from the fact that it is not noticed by the earliest historians, is a weak one. They were very brief, and did not present the details, but were chiefly concerned about the terrible consequences. The Marquis of Mondejar in his "Advertencias," makes much of this failure, and regards the story, as Condé does, as a " Moorish fiction." San Pedro Pascual confuses us still more, by declaring that Roderik was not elected until after the Arab-Moors had entered Spain, and ventures the opinion that Witiza was the guilty king (*vide* Mariana, Historia de España, II. 382). As for the " Moorish fiction," it may be believed that the Arab-Moors, who bargained with Ilyan,

I have already spoken of one important constituent in the combinations of Ilyan, upon which, as it has asserted itself in all periods of Spanish his- The attitude tory, it seems proper to dwell a little more of the Jews. at length : I refer to the Jews. Nothing is sadder, while nothing is more unique, more entirely *sui gene-ris*, in the history of the world than the separate and peculiar existence of this injured and everywhere persecuted people, who have been — especially since the Christian era, which their blind and cruel act of unbelief inaugurated — despised, trodden down, hunted, exiled, tortured, and killed. And yet quite as striking is the moral power which they have wielded over their persecutors. While the Christians were slothful in business, slack in industry, and wasted what they had, the Jew gained and hoarded; "accommodated" the spendthrifts with usurious loans, and appealed for precedent to Jacob's stratagem, —

> "This was the way to thrive, and *he* was blessed ;
> And thrift is blessing, if men steal it not." [1]

It was only thus that they could revenge themselves on their oppressors. They were thus brought into relations, which must now be considered, at once with the Christians in Spain and with the Arab-Moors in Africa, and out of a combination of these relations

knew most about it. They profited by it, and would hardly have invented it, as it would derogate from their merits in conquering Spain. The details are only to be expected in a later age, of greater research, and more emulous historians, not too far removed from the reach of valuable tradition.

[1] Merchant of Venice, Act I. scene iii.

they emerge to view as a potent element in the Arabian conquest and after dominion in the Peninsula.

Of their first coming thither there is no certain record. We may believe that when the fleets of Solomon made their voyages to Tharshish, — "for the king had at sea a navy of Tharshish with the navy of Hiram: once in three years came the navy of Tharshish, bringing gold and silver, ivory, and apes and peacocks," — a few of the adventurous Israelites remained in the Peninsula, and formed a nucleus for others who, when Judea was overrun by hostile armies from time to time, left their country, and wandering along the northern coast of Africa, and hearing tidings of their brethren in Spain, joined them there. We know that when the Romans conquered the Peninsula they found a considerable number of Israelites domiciled there. When, after the terrible siege of Jerusalem, by Vespasian and Titus, "one stone was not left upon another" of the city of their love and pride, crowds of exiles wandered westward to swell these numbers. Spain was a quiet Roman province, and there by their industry, frugality, and skill in business, the Jews made themselves useful members of society.

There were many who remained in northern Africa, and who were in constant and cordial intercourse with their brethren in Spain. There they might have fondly hoped that their wanderings were at an end: not so; fierce persecutions were in store for them there as elsewhere.

When Heraclius became emperor of the East, and

How and when they came to Spain.

determined to punish the Jews in his dominion, his ambassadors made a treaty with the Gothic monarch, Sisebuto, one of the articles of Their persecution in Spain. which required that all recusant Jews should be driven out of Spain. This article was also embodied in the Visigothic Code.[1] By its terms one year was given to them in which to decide whether they would confess Christ and be baptized, or be shaved and scourged, their property confiscated, and themselves forced to leave the country.[2] In such a fearful contingency the majority became hypocrites. Ninety thousand are said to have submitted to baptism; but the enforced Christian rite was but a mask for the circumcision which was still secretly active, and they were thus transformed from quiet and orderly subjects into concealed and intriguing foes. But even those who patiently submitted were not, as we have seen, secure from humiliation and new indignity; they were despised for their apostasy, which was but a new proof to their tormentors of their sordid character.

The fourth council of Toledo, held in the year 633, indeed revoked the former decree requiring them to be baptized; but this apparent clemency was neutralized by the cruel requirements that the children of those who had accepted Christianity should be taken from their parents to be more fully educated in the Christian faith, and that those Jews who had married

---

[1] Codex Wisigothorum, XII. tit. iii.

[2] Confesar la religion cristiana y bautizarse, ó ser decalvados, azotados, lanzados del reino y confiscados sus bienes. — LA FUENTE, *Historia de España*, II. 406.

Christian women should either embrace the religion of their wives, or be separated from them. It was further decreed by the council that, in a judicial trial, no Jew could give evidence against a Christian.[1]

This placed the Jews at a fearful disadvantage. The rigor increased. The sixth Toledan council, *The sixth council of Toledo.* in 638, was more outspoken, and not much more cruel when it enacted "that Judaism would not be tolerated in the realm;" the eighth council prescribed new rigors against them. These enactments produced in part the desired effect; large numbers banished themselves, taking refuge in Africa from Christian baptism and persecution; there too they were ready to join any respectable conspiracy against the government and the people who had so constantly oppressed them. For this scarcely concealed purpose at least they received full credit; and when Egica ascended the throne in the year 687, they were under special *surveillance*, as it was averred that the Jews in Spain and Africa had entered into a special agreement to aid in the destruction of the Gothic monarchy. Thus, while to hate and persecute the Jews was considered an undoubted part of Christian duty in the abstract, their reported conspiracy added fuel to the flame. We may therefore fancy the astonishment of the Gothic nation and of the Christian world when Witiza, to serve his own ends as it was believed, removed the anathema and disabilities, and restored them partially at least to a condition of security and ease. This apparent clemency

---

[1] La Fuente, Historia de España, II. 415.

disgusted his subjects, not so much because he set aside ecclesiastical canons and secular laws as because he dared to run counter to the universal and unrelenting prejudice which ignorantly based itself upon the claims of Him who had forgiven His enemies upon the cross.[1]

Let us turn for a moment to see how they were regarded by the Arab-Moors. Their early relations to the creed of Mohammed have already been presented. We have seen that they had been powerful in Arabia before the advent of the prophet. Princes had embraced the Law of Moses, and the efforts of Mohammed were strenuous to convert them. When he found this a very difficult task, by the general claims of Islám, he asked for, and received, special revelations denouncing them: in numerous passages of the Korán their unbelief is rebuked and their fate declared. Notwithstanding this, they do not seem to have been regarded with the same disfavor as other unbelievers : they were among the first people allowed to compound for tribute ; and, if still despised, were permitted to live in peace. But now, in northwestern Africa, they had risen in importance. What rendered them dangerous to the Gothic Christians gave them new value in the eyes of the Arab-Moors, who were making ready to invade the Peninsula. These disaffected and confederate Jews

The Jews and the Arab-Moors.

---

[1] This prejudice is clearly expressed by comparison, in the words of Julian, the historian of Wamba. In his terrible denunciation of the Franks, he says : — " Perfidiæ signum, obscenitas operum, fraus negotiorum, venale judicium ;" and adds, "et quod pejus his omnibus est, contra ipsum salvatorem nostrum et Dominum, Judæorum blasphemantium prostibulum habebatur."— *España Sagrada*, VI. 544.

formed a band of intelligent and useful auxiliaries in
the scheme of the Moslem conquest. The martial
sounds of the Moslem hosts made pleasant music in
their ears. National allegiance they had none. They
had the warrant of history that the change of masters
would ameliorate their condition : they would aid and
serve the kindest. Mohammedan Spain would be
better than Christian Spain, because it would be more
tolerant. For the Christian Messiah and for the
prophet of Islám they had equal disregard; and thus
the readers of later Spanish history will find that, in
troublous times, they often, like soldiers of fortune,
changed sides, and not unfrequently held the balance
of power through the influence of their unity and
their wealth. As a single illustration : When the
Moslems began to persecute them for their money they
turned to the Christians and brought to the throne
Alfonso VI., of Castile and Leon, in the year 1085.

As we read of their checkered fortunes, we are
struck with the fact that the important part they
have played has been purposely ignored or belittled
by both parties to the struggle; but it is not difficult
to discover the truth, in spite of the reluctant
mention or intentional silence of both Spanish and
Arabian historians, — the former prompted by religious rancor, and the latter by a pride of conquest
which would not share the glory with such humble
agents. It seems certain that, in concerting his plans
for the conquest, Musa had early taken the Jews into
his counsels: he received valuable information and
gained important statistics from them which they had
learned in the way of trade.

It is also asserted that after Count Ilyan had been in communication with certain disaffected Goths in Spain, he also sought the aid of the Jews, as an important element in carrying out his purpose. They gladly listened to both commanders, and probably supplied money, which their sagacity assured them was as safe and profitable an investment as in those turbulent times they could make.

We may now return for a moment to Roderik and the impending invasion as it actually took shape before his eyes. His newly acquired power *The plans and views of Roderik.* seemed well established; his kingdom was a fair show. He could still defy " malice domestic " and " foreign levy." He had indeed his suspicions of Gothic disaffection, and every day brought stronger corroboration of the presumptuous purpose of the Arab-Moors; he knew that the children of Israel were secretly leagued against him, but thus far he had no doubt of his ability to withstand all these united enemies, and place the Gothic power upon an eminence of authority and glory which it had never yet attained. If he had entertained misgivings as to the fidelity of Ilyan, he seems to have dismissed them.

This general, when he had first contemplated his treason, had represented to Roderik, or had engaged others to do so, that, as his throne was sufficiently secure against internal danger, he should *The insidious advice of Ilyan.* employ his troops chiefly on the two frontiers, — at the north, against the constant outbreaks of Cantabrians and Gascons, and also to watch the Franks who made frequent irruptions south of the

Pyrenees; and at the south, especially in Northern Africa, where the Berbers and Moors had made common cause with the Arabians. Following this counsel, at least in part, the king sent most of his cavalry and infantry to the north. It does not appear whether he strengthened the coast-guard on the Mediterranean, or sent additional troops to Ilyan. If he did, this aided Ilyan's purpose, for they became partakers of the treason. We shall see hereafter that when the news of the invasion reached the king, he had left Toledo and was in person at the north, putting down a revolt which had broken out at Pampeluna.

This preliminary having been thus skilfully arranged, Ilyan entered into negotiations with Musa for the delivery of Spain into his hands. Of the persons, place, and mode of communication, there are several accounts. According to Al Makkari, "no sooner did the Lord of Ceuta arrive safely in his dominions, than he went to see the Amír Musa Ibn Nosseyr, and proposed to him the conquest of Andalus."[1] Al-Kortobi says that the place of the interview was Kairwan.[2] Others say that he chaffered, not with Musa, but with Tarik el Tuerto, at Tangiers. It seems probable, as suggested in the *Reyhám-l-Albab* of Mohammed Ibn Ibrahim,[3] that he had an interview with Tarik as the nearest commander, but wrote an eloquent and urgent letter to Musa the General-in-Chief, soliciting him to make the invasion, and alluring him by the value of the

Ilyan's secret alliance with Musa.

---

[1] Al Makkari, I. 264.
[2] Ib. I. appendix, xlv.
[3] Ib. I. 516.

prize, and the ease of its attainment. The spirit of this letter may be accepted if we doubt that the words have been preserved. "Hasten," he wrote, "to that country where the palaces are filled with gold and silver, and those who dwell in them are like women, owing to the exuberance of their comforts and the abundance of their riches."[1] He told him of the unprotected condition of the kingdom, the cities without fortifications, the citizens without arms, a large number of the nobles disaffected towards Roderik; the sons of Witiza at the head of a secret faction, ready to declare for the Arab-Moors, on condition of the restoration, not of the crown to their family, but of the estates of which they had been despoiled. He promised to show Musa the way, and to give up to him, with the sovereignty of Ceuta, all the places under his control in Spain;[2] on what terms of compensation we are not informed. Doubtless he claimed much more than the gratification of his revenge.

Such were the overtures to Musa; to consummate the project required only his acceptance, but that, tempting as was the prospect, could not be given without the consent of the Khalif at Damascus. Musa was loyal to his sovereign, and would adventure nothing, least of all such a momentous campaign as this, without the assurance of the Khalif's sanction.

[1] Al Makkari, I. 516.

[2] Cardonne, Histoire de l'Afrique et de l'Espagne, I. 68. He says, but without specifying his authority, — "Il (Ilyan) possédait aussi en propre plusieurs villes dans la Castille, et étoit le seigneur le plus puissant et le plus riche de l'Espagne."

CHAPTER VIII.

SOME ALLEGORICAL LEGENDS.

L EAVING for a brief space the veritable, or rather generally accepted, history of men and events, I think it proper to mention a few of the romantic legends, which, under the fantastic garb of allegorical fiction, are not without valuable historical meaning. Framed after the facts, they are based upon the facts, and we cannot afford to neglect them. Such legends of this critical and transition period abound, and like gorgeous clouds sailing before the breeze, clearly indicate the current of history and represent the age and its actors.

A Grecian king of Cadiz, says one of these — for by a singular fancy the Greeks are the nation of many of these myths and Alexander the Great a popular hero — had a daughter of peerless beauty, whose hand was eagerly sought by many of the other kings of Andalus, "for that country was then ruled by several kings, each having estates not extending over more than one or two cities." [1]

The Grecian king and his wise daughter.

---

[1] Al Makkari, I. 259. If we are to interpret this as referring to the Gothic dominion, these kings were the counts, dukes, and wardens who held provincial authority under the king.

The father was in a quandary, but the damsel who was as wise as she was beautiful, soon limited the number of aspirants, by declaring that she would have no husband but a "sage king." Wisdom, in her use of the word, was a difficult fashion even among kings; as she used it, it implied supernatural agency. Many at once relinquished their pretensions upon this announcement. Only two of her admirers were willing to subject their wisdom to the test, and to these two she proposed the following tasks : The two tasks to prove the "sage king." Of the first she demanded the construction of a water-wheel on the main land, connected with an aqueduct to take the water into Cadiz. To the other she proposed the invention and construction of a talisman which should preserve the island from the invasion of the Berbers or any other enemies from Africa. "Whichsoever of the two," said the princess, " executes his task best, shall be my husband." [1]

Both kings set to work with great alacrity. The labors of the first were successful, and here the story is only semi-legendary. He erected an hydraulic machine on the mainland, just opposite to the long narrow peninsula upon which Cadiz stands, and receiving the water by pipes or canals from springs in a neighboring mountain, caused it to pour upon a wheel, and thus sent its refreshing streams by an aqueduct across the bay into Cadiz. This is the traditionary account of an aqueduct, traces of which were still visible in the eighteenth century, built by some enterprising person unknown to the real record,

[1] Al Makkari, I. 515, note 39.

by means of which pure water was carried into the city. "It consisted," says Al Makkari, "of a long line of arches, and the way it was done was this: whenever they came to high ground or to a mountain, they cut a passage through it; when the ground was lower, they built a bridge over arches; if they met with a porous soil, they laid on a bed of gravel for the passage of the water; when the building reached the seashore, the water was made to pass under ground, and in this way it reached Cadiz. That part of the aqueduct nearest to the sea, Ibnu Sa'id tells us was visible at the time he wrote."[1] The exact modus is not clear in this description; but the fact remains, and truly the builder is entitled to be called a "sage king." The person of the princess melts into thin air, and the fair spirit of progress usurps her place.

The task imposed upon the other aspirant was far more difficult, for the aid of magic was necessary. It was, however, to appeal through the influence of superstition to the self-interest and the fears of the people. It is asserted that there was an old-time prophecy, deduced from a consultation of the stars, that "by two nations only were the Goths to be disturbed in their enjoyments, and to be hated on account of them, and these were represented to them as people unaccustomed to the luxuries of life, hardened by privation and fatigue; in short, the Arabs and the

---

[1] Al Makkari, I. 77. Salazar, a Spanish antiquarian, believes that the water was brought from streams quite near the town of Xeres. This would magnify the genius and labor of the constructor, as Xeres is thirty-three miles distant. This rivals the modern water-supplies, of which our civilization boasts so much.

Berbers." [1] How should this second king prove his sageness, and secure Spain against such invaders ?

He would build a lofty column upon the border of the strait. Upon a solid foundation the square white shaft rose high in air, visible from all parts of the sea as vessels approached. On its summit he placed a colossal statue, fashioned of iron and copper melted together, representing in feature and costume a Berber. The beard was full and flowing, and a tuft of hair hung over its forehead. The right arm was extended, pointing towards the sea and the opposite coast: in the hand were a padlock and keys; and it seemed to say, " No one is to pass this way." [2] It was as if a Berber prisoner was thus pinnacled to warn his brethren of their fate if, like him, they should venture into Spain.

The two kings worked rapidly to anticipate each the other in the completion of his task; but the constructor of the aqueduct was first successful. Large numbers of the people came together to see this new wonder, which promised so much happiness. The water began to flow and the wheel to move, amid the loud acclamations of the assembled multitude.

The successful builder of the aqueduct.

Meanwhile, the constructor of the statue was just putting the finishing-touch to his colossal talisman, when this news reached him. His heart sank, and, in his profound chagrin, he threw himself from the top of the column, " by which means the other prince, freed from his rival, became the master of the lady, of the wheel, and of the charm." [3]

[1] Al Makkari, I. 258.　　[2] Ib. I. 261.　　[3] Ib. I. 261.

Entirely fictional as seems this story of the talisman, it is not without a moral, which lends somewhat to the historic philosophy. It tells of the declining vigor of the Goths, which would protect itself by playing upon the superstition of the Africans; it is an acknowledgment of the fears of a Berber invasion, even before the Arabians had begun to move from their native seats. It threatened with shackle-bolts and fetter-locks, instead of with the sword of a vanguard. The talisman was a watchtower, like the signal tower of Gibraltar, from which the news of active movement in Africa could be telegraphed through Andalusia; and the catastrophe to the builder, who leaped to death from its top, is, to my mind, significant that, after all the labor, the spell was to prove impotent to quell the terror of the people, or give strength to their opposition, as the rumors increased in numbers and in volume that the Arabs had come and were uniting with the Berbers and Moors in Northern Africa.

But of all the legends which bear upon this history, the most remarkable and significant remains

The legend of Don Roderik and the enchanted cavern. to be mentioned. It has had a much larger circulation than the rest merely as a romantic fiction. The local historians of Toledo, among whom are Rojas, Francisco, Pisa, Roman de la Higuera, and Lozano,[1] have fondled and enriched it with jewels of romance, which so bedizen the honest legend as almost to disguise its real allegorical mean-

---

[1] Pisa wrote "Descripcion de la Imperial Ciudad de Toledo," &c., 1617. C. Lozano's work is, "Los Reyes nuevos de Toledo, 1674." Another Lozano (Pablo) wrote "Antigüedades Arabes de España."

ing. To the poets it has been a never-failing source
of inspiration. In his poem, "De la Jerusalen Conquistada," [1] Lope de Vega makes a Spanish pilgrim narrate to Saladin the ruin of Spain, the details of which
he can hardly tell without tears, even after so long an
interval : —

> "Apenas puedo
> Sin lagrimas nombrar le ——.
> La portentosa cueva de Toledo
> Que hoy vive en tantas lenguas de fama." [2]

Upon it are founded the learned and ponderous
epic of Southey, and the graceful romaunt of Walter
Scott ; it figures, with simple and pathetic interest for
the reader, in a charming Spanish paper of Washington Irving, a poem except in form.

According to Gayangos, it is not, like so many
other stories, a fiction of the pious chroniclers of the
Middle Ages ; its origin is unknown ; but, recited by
the improvisatores in the principal cities, — Cordova,
Seville, and Toledo, — it always found entranced
listeners ; it circulated among the Jews, Muzarabs,
and Arab-Moors, in the *patois* of commingled dialects
called *Aljamia*. Thus it passed and repassed, like
current coin, between the Christian and Mohammedan
story-tellers, until at last it became assimilated in a
history, unhappily too much already pervaded by the
imaginative and romantic. All this does not seem to
me due solely to its interest as a story : it has a
meaning, and an important one ; and thus we accept
these legends as containing valuable contributions to
the true history.

[1] First published in 1609.   [2] Lib. vi.

In or near Toledo was an ancient palace, or, as some of the legendists say, a spacious cave, further excavated and fashioned into many rooms. In one of these a wise Gothic king, knowing the prophecy that Spain was threatened with invasion by people from Africa, had placed a secret spell, which, so long as it remained secret, would protect the country from such an incursion. Prudence as well as superstition had guarded the talisman. Each Gothic monarch since had, upon his accession, placed another padlock upon the massive gate, so that when Roderik came to the throne there were many such padlocks. Al Kortobi says twenty; Al Makkari, twenty-seven.[1] Some say the keys had been intentionally lost; others, that they were hanging to the locks. In either case no one had been disposed to use them; the secret was inviolable until, in an evil hour, curiosity, unrest, and avarice prompted Roderik to discover it. He loudly declared that the whole matter was an ancient jest, having its origin in a superstitious age, and that it was high time to expose it. He hoped to find the dark recesses of the palace gleaming with gold and silver and precious stones, which might be put to use in supplying his exhausted treasury.

It was in vain that his bishops and counts endeavored to dissuade him from the rash purpose.

Roderik insists on opening it.

"Do not innovate, O king," they said, "upon a custom which thy predecessors have hitherto kept most religiously."[2] "Give us thy estimation of the sums of money and jewels thou thinkest this

---

[1] Al Kortobi, App. to Al Makkari, I. xliv.   [2] Ibid.

palace contains, name even as many as thy fancy
can represent; and we shall collect them among us,
and bring them to thee without fail, rather than thou
shouldst thus innovate and violate a custom which
our kings thy predecessors kept as sacred, since they
who knew well what they did commanded that none
should after them presume to investigate the mystery."[1]
Roderik steeled himself against all entreaties. The
rusty locks were opened or forced; the doors grated
upon their hinges, and he entered with his train. In
vain he passed with rapid steps from room to room;
he found no treasures except the jewelled temple of
Solomon, which we shall find presenting itself in the
veritable history of the conquest. But in another apartment the portents of the insulted spell were displayed,
and the forebodings of the courtiers verified. On the
wall was a rude painting in which were represented a
number of horsemen, some with turbans, some bareheaded, with locks of coarse black hair hanging over
their foreheads. They were dressed in skins. Their
horses were of Arabian breed; the arms were scimitars and lances, with fluttering pennons. In the
centre of the apartment was a marble urn, in which
was a parchment scroll; on this was written: "Whenever this asylum is violated, and the spell contained
in this urn broken, the people represented in the
picture shall invade and overturn the throne of its
kings, and subdue the whole country."[2] The turbaned people in the painting were Arabians; the

---

[1] Al Kortobi, Al Makkari, I., App. lxxiv.

[2] The details of this story are variously related by different
writers. I have adopted the version given by Al Makkari, I. 263.

bareheaded barbarians were Moors or Berbers; the time for the fulfilment of the prophecy was at hand.[1]

The rash monarch, struck with sudden terror and repentance, escaped with his train into the open air, and ordered the gate of the palace to be closed, but it was too late; his destiny had been revealed to him, and was now borne by rumor all over his kingdom : in the eyes of the multitude he was a doomed man.

"Some," says Mariana, with refreshing simplicity, "regard all this as a fable."[2] A fable it certainly is, worthy the palmiest days of necromancy. It seems at the first glance a fable without any basis of historic reality. Washington Irving indulged his antiquarian fancy by inquiring and searching, when at Toledo, for the locality of the story, which he did not expect to find. So, in point of fact, the story, as such, must share the fate of the thousands which cluster around the cradle of every new dominion, even when its progeny are fancied to descend from heaven. But like many such, by its first framers, accustomed to

[1] Latinas letras á la margen puestas
   Decian : — "Cuando aquesta puerta y arca
   Fueran abiertas, gentes como estas
   Pondrán por tierra cuanto España abarca."
                          LOPE DE VEGA,
                   La Jerusalen Conquistada, Lib. vi.

The poet conceives an echo : —

   Sonaba el eco : " Pocos años vivas
   Y en otras partes ; Infeliz Rodrigo,
   Ya se te acerca el barbaro castigo."
                                          Ibid.

[2] Algunos tienen todo esto por fabula. — *Historia de España*, II. 381.

the illustrative forms of apologue and parable, it was
meant to convey some of the grand features of the
age, the country and its people.

In it who fails to see the condition of affairs in
Spain ? We behold a rash chieftain breaking, by his
usurpation, the established order of the The inter-
Gothic rule, at a time when such conduct the legend.
would not be tolerated. The discontent of the nobles, and the patient grief of the bishops, appear in
their entreaties that he would not force the spell.
The fable displays the truth that he was, at once,
fearful of the punishment, which he was conscious of
deserving; and bold enough to wish to know the full
extent of the coming retribution, that he might prepare to resist it. To the cursory reader of fairy tales
it may be, as Gayangos has styled it, an "amusing
legend;"[1] to the historian it is a very sad one. The
parchment prophecy was but the clear announcement
of what had so often been rumored in Spain; that the
Arabs and Moors had formed an alliance to invade it.
The ruthless opening of the enchanted palace repre-
sents the bitter conflict of hope and fear in the mind
of the king; the writing, fabled to have been found
in the urn, and corresponding to the figures on the
wall, was already displayed in letters of fire, to all
who had eyes to see, upon the gates of the ancient and
"imperial city of Toledo."

Before closing this chapter and proceeding to the
stirring events which are soon to follow, I feel disposed, even at the risk of some repetition, to give

[1] Al Makkari, I. 516, note 46.

some further consideration to the alleged conduct
Further con-
sideration of
Ilyan's con-
duct. of Count Ilyan, which, by the general consent of the Spanish historians, has been stigmatized as the basest of treasons. The subject has been already brought to the reader's notice. Looking at it, as we do, not only after the fact, but in view of its terrible results, it seems totally unjustifiable. His intention was to subvert the realm, to gratify chiefly personal anger and private revenge. The consequence was, the destruction of a dominion which had the prescriptive rights of three centuries. He gave up the country to immediate pillage and universal desolation. He introduced into a nominally Christian realm an infidel horde, whose false creed threatened to destroy not only the progress but the very tenure of Christianity.

This was all evil, and unqualified evil, as measured by our standards; but, in making up her cases, history must judge the delinquents in her high court according to the law which governed them, the education and temper of the people, and the spirit of the age, — the *zeit-geist* of the German philosopher.

It was still fresh in the minds of the inhabitants — I refer particularly to the Hispano-Romans, who were still in a large majority — that the quiet occupancy of the Peninsula by the Romans had given way to the fierce and oppressive conquest of the Goths. It has been seen that among the Goths there had been no principle of succession to the throne established by law. Indeed the monarchy was elective from the first, and this plan of election was naturally combined with hereditary succession when the heir presumptive was a proper person. If, on the one hand, and in the opinion of a large party, Roderik was fairly elected, he had the best of all rights to the throne; but if, on the other, he had used deceptive arts and violent measures to secure his election, he might well be looked upon as a usurper, to dethrone whom would be a righteous act. Besides, "The people," says the chronicle of Don Rodrigo, "never bore much love to the Goths, who were strangers and conquerors; and when they came had no right there, for the whole belonged to the Roman empire." [1]

This condition of things, therefore, leaving Ilyan for a moment out of the question, partook somewhat of the nature of a civil war; and we are quite ready to understand the assertion that "the monarchy was divided into two factions, of which the (more numerous but) least powerful availed itself of the Arabs as auxiliaries, and that these auxiliaries made themselves masters, and easily effected their intent by means of the divisions of the country." [2]

This destroys much of the romance of the history, but we must be satisfied with the truth. It has been charged that those in Spain who aided to subvert the

---

[1] Ch. 248. Ticknor calls this chronicle chiefly fabulous; but says, with truth: "These old Spanish chronicles, whether they have their foundation in truth or fable, always strike farther down than those of any other nation into the deep soil of the popular feeling and character."—*History of Spanish Literature*, I. 215. The *Spanish* chronicler is a Hispano-Roman — not a Goth — in spirit. The re-conquest was as opposed to the Gothic dominion as the Moors of the conquest were.

[2] Memorias de Braga, III. 273.

Gothic monarchy were unpatriotic. Here again we must refer to the moral and political standards of the time. Loyalty to the wicked and degenerate Gothic kings was not patriotism in the eyes of the Hispano-Romans. In the present day we speak of patriotism as the highest virtue of honest and enlightened citizenship, and we denounce the hypocrites who wear its semblance as a cloak for selfishness. Usually, too, in strong and well-ordered states, the integrity of the country implies obedience to the government. But it was not so in the turbulent periods of European history. There could be little or no patriotism, because there was distinction of classes with disparity of rights. To the favored classes, the good of the country was one thing; to the oppressed orders, quite another. There was no education of the masses, and but little reflection and reasoning. Anger, revenge, and self-interest were paramount as motives of conduct. Governors, instead of maintaining the rights of the people, heaped indignities upon them.

In such a state of affairs, in the history of any people, patriotism is an empty name: desertions of men and masses from one side to the other for real or fancied insults have been common, and have not been regarded as disgraceful.

Measured by such a standard, what terms were the people of Spain, Hispano-Romans, and Goths alike bound to keep with such a government as that of Witiza or of Roderik — men who, to secure themselves in luxurious lust, had pulled down the strong walls of cities, and disarmed the citizens that they might not rise against them ; who had perverted the church and prostituted female honor ?

When it became evident to the more thoughtful among the people that the wicked dynasty of the Goths could only be overthrown by the aid of foreign enemies, the prophecies concerning the Arab-Moors suggested a plan which, whatever its other consequences might be, would at least secure this most desired result.

One word more concerning the probable effects on the Christian religion. The Christianity of Spain was hardly more than a nominal Christianity. Like the faith of Sardis, it had only a name to live, but was dead or ready to die. Certainly Witiza and Roderik, and the magnates who surrounded the throne, felt its vital power no more than had the Catos and Ciceros and Cæsars the spiritual power of the pantheistic pontificate of heathen Rome.

Its doctrines were practically disbelieved ; its holy rule of living despised. The pope was set at naught. Thus, as far as any practical value could attach to Christianity, it was little better than Islám, in the eyes of those who were given over to the indulgence of their own brutal passions. In this part of the treason Ilyan does not stand alone. If he concocted the treason in Africa, it was Oppas, an archbishop, who, according to the chronicle, prepared the way for it in Spain.

Let me call attention finally to the mists that envelop the personality and the authority of Ilyan himself. We can only dimly discern him as a historic character, and the poetry of later days which has adopted him as a dark hero gives us not assistance but additional obscurity. To one poet, Juan de Mena, the gravity of the treason obliterates the gravity of its cause, and he consigns Ilyan and Oppas to the deepest pit of hell.[1] To the Portuguese poet Mascarenhas, the natural right to punish the seducer of his daughter justifies his act; and the bold justice of his conduct reflects upon the degeneracy of later ages, in which such a heroic deed could meet with reprobation instead of praise.[2] The historian, Rodericus Toletanus, who wrote in the thirteenth century, bestows his malediction in true ecclesiastical style of " bell, book, and candle," and consigns his putrescent name to an eternity of infamy and agony.[3]

With the dim lights I have been able to offer, the reader may form his own judgment, which will be, not a justification by any means, but a milder verdict probably than that usually rendered by the Spanish historians, against the man who is believed to have first applied the torch,— when other torches would not have been long wanting, — and set the Peninsula in a blaze of fire, the embers of which have never yet been wholly trampled out.

[1] Cop. 91.

[2] André da Silva Mascarenhas, Destruiçam de Espanha, p. 9.

[3] The archbishop has been speaking of the doubt resting upon the disappearance of Roderik after the battle, and the story that his grave was found at Viseo. He proceeds to say: " Maledictus furor impius Juliani, quia pertinax ; et indignatio quia dura ; animosus indignatione, impetuosus furore, oblitus fidelitatis, immemor religionis, contemptor divinitatis, crudélis in se, homicida in dominum, hostis in domesticos, vastator in patriam, reus in omnes memoria ejus in omni ore, et nomen ejus in æternum putrescet." Rodericus Toletanus, f. 3, g. 19.

BOOK III.

THE ARABIAN INVASION OF SPAIN.

———•———

CHAPTER I.

THE GREAT EXPEDITION OF TARIK EL TUERTO.

WE may now fancy Musa awaiting with intense interest the progress of affairs in Spain. From the windows of his palace at Tangiers,[1] whither he had come in person, he was casting covetous glances upon Gesira-Andalus, the verdant and picturesque land across the narrow sea, upon the conquest of which he had long determined, with a steady faith that Allah and his own sagacity would reveal the best mode of accomplishing his purpose. *Musa's patient waiting.* The proposal of Ilyan had come like a miraculous answer to his prayers, and now quickened his purpose. It made that an easy task which he had expected to find a difficult undertaking. He was glad to be assured that the resistance, if at first strong, would not be long maintained. He would find, besides the powerful aid of Ilyan, confederates in the injured sons of Witiza in whose interests a large party

[1] Desde las ventanas de su palacio de Tanger podia dirigir una mirada ambiciosa hácia las costas de la Peninsula separadas por el estrecho. — LA FUENTE, *Historia de España*, II. 473.

already existed, ready for co-operative action, and
who asked, not to be restored to the throne, but only to
receive again their confiscated estates. A few vigorous
blows, Ilyan said, and said truly, would place him in
undisputed possession of the coveted land of Andalus.
Delighted as he was, the wily Arabian restrained
the exhibition of his joy, while he made haste to test
the honesty of the proposal and the reality of the
His recep- information. He secretly sent spies and
tion of Ilyan. scouts across the strait to find out the political condition of affairs, and to procure such statistics
of topography and supplies as were essential for the
movements and maintenance of his army.

From one of the principal Christians of Tangiers he
gained valuable information,[1] always corroborating
the assertions of Ilyan, and even exceeding them, in
displaying the degeneracy of the crown, the turbulence
of the nobles, and the impotence of the people. In
portraying the attractions of the country itself, simil-
itudes were exhausted. In richness of soil it was
equal to Syria, in climate it was like Araby the blest;
in mineral treasures and gems it rivalled the far-
famed but little-known Cathay; in its harbors and
coast-facilities it was equal to Aden. It was full of
ancient monuments, among which were the great
statue of Hercules at Cadiz, the idol of Galicia, the
vast ruins of Merida and Tarragona.[2] It was a land
" plentiful in waters, renowned for their sweetness
and clearness," [3] the lordly rivers of Andalusia. The
mountain ranges were beautiful to behold, and they

---

[1] Condé, Dominacion de los Arabes, I. ch. viii.
[2] Condé I. ch. viii.   [3] Al Makkarí, I. 264.

enclosed *vegas* of inexhaustible fertility. Truly there would be great glory in conquering such a land for God and his prophet, and the conqueror would be the greatest subject in the empire.

But the very grandeur of the project rendered it so momentous and exceptional that it seemed to exceed the discretionary powers of Musa; and even, in his opinion, those of the viceroy of Egypt. Applies to the Khalif. He deemed it necessary to secure the Khalif's personal permission to undertake it. Swift couriers, on relays and in reliefs, bore to Damascus despatches from Musa, in which with the enthusiasm of a soldier, and the eloquent importunity of a preacher, he pictured to the successor of Mohammed the immense value of the prize, and the miraculous facilities for its attainment. He ventured to refer to his own astonishing progress as an earnest of brilliant success; he repeated how he had subdued and converted the tribes of Barbary, " and raised the banners of Islám on all the towers of Tanja."[1] The strait, he told him, was not an ocean, but only a narrow channel, whose shores were everywhere distinct to the eye.[2]

Al Walid lost no time in sending his sanction, but prudently added, " Let the country be first explored by light troops to overrun it, and bring the news of what it contains; be prudent, and The sanction of Al Walid. do not allow the Moslems to be lost in an ocean of dangers and horrors."[3]

[1] Condé, Dominacion de los Arabes, I. ch. viii.
[2] Al Makkari, I. 265.
[3] In quoting the words of despatches or addresses from the Arabian historians, I have thought it the best way of conveying their information, of setting forth in this dramatic form the real facts of the case.

And now for the first time a Mohammedan army was to enter Spain, for the purpose of conquest and occupancy. There had been former landings by isolated piratical bands. As early as the year 648, an incursion of African troops took place, which was soon dissipated.[1] Again, thirty years later, in the time of Wamba, a Mohammedan fleet of two hundred and seventy small barks was cruising in the Mediterranean, and ravaged the coast here and there;[2] they were said to receive encouragement from Ervigio, who was endeavoring to supplant Wamba. Mariana also speaks of some similar attempts which were made during the reigns of Egica and Witiza, in one of which a general named Theodomir "had triumphed over those who came, in a naval engagement."[3]

But all these incursions were for spoils, ravage, and hasty retreat. They had none of them penetrated far into the interior, but were content with desultory pillage along the shore. Very different was that now organized. The invasion was to be made by an army; men in nations; men of similar races amalgamated into one great host by the cohesion of a creed; elements in all respects diametrically opposed to those in Spain. Japhet and Shem had come from Ararat by diverse routes to confront each other at the pillars of Hercules.

In order to test his sincerity, Musa required of Ilyan that he should first make a hostile incursion into

---

[1] Al Makkari, I. 383, note 17.

[2] Sebastian Salmanticensis, ch. 3. This is corroborated also by Isidor Pacensis, España Sagrada, vol. viii.

[3] Historia de España, II. 381, note.

Andalus. This he did ; embarking in two vessels with a small force, he crossed, and after overrun- Ilyan's re-connoissance. ning the country, and killing many of the inhabitants, he returned to Africa with captives and large booty.[1] This was in December, 709.[2]

It was now the summer of 710 (A. H. Rhamadan 91). Musa commissioned a mauli, who was a Berber,[3] named Tarif Abú Zar'ah, to make a more important reconnoissance. He embarked, in four large boats, one hundred horse and four hundred foot,[4] and, guided by Ilyan, he set sail from Tangiers, and running directly across the strait, landed at " an island opposite to another island close to Andalus." The place of landing they called, as they did many other places, without distinction, *Jezirah-al-Khadhrá*, which means " the green island ;" but it afterwards received, and has since retained, the name of the leader of the expedition, being called *Tarifa* to the present time.[5] Re-

---

[1] Al Makkari, I. 264. This expedition of Ilyan may be properly considered in the light of a preliminary reconnoissance to find the best place for landing troops. It is not mentioned by the Chronicon Biclarense, or by Isidor de Beja, but is so strictly in accordance with the proper prudence of Musa, and the rules for the movement of armies, that it cannot well be doubted. See Ib. I., 516, note 3.

[2] Ib. I. 250.   [3] Ib. I., 517 note 4.

[4] Condé, who ignores Tarif, and makes Tarik the commander of this expedition, says : " Five hundred horses in four large barks." Dominacion de los Arabes, I. ch. ix. Al Kortobi says, "About three thousand Berbers, collected under the orders of Abú Zar-'ah Tarif, crossed the sea," &c. Al Makkari (I. app. xlvi.). Al Makkari seems to have sifted the authorities in giving the numbers I have taken.

[5] Besides the promontory of Tarifa, there is a rocky island projecting into and commanding the sea. In so far, the name was not a misnomer.

maining there only a day, Tarif led his troops over the beautiful mountain path, which, soon coming in view of the magnificent rock, *Mons Calpe*, and its charming bay, finds its terminus at Algeciras. He burned the churches and the crops, captured stores

Tarif's expedition.

and cattle, and took back as many prisoners of higher rank as he was able to guard. Then he retraced his steps, re-embarked, and soon presented himself with his captives to Musa. This was in the latter days of August or early in September, 710.[1]

Doubtless, other small expeditions of a reconnoitring character were made, but there is confusion in accounting for them, and they were only important as preliminary to the great invasion which could not be prepared in a day. The winter was to be spent in organizing for that. But what had been already done made the conquest exceedingly popular in the Moslem ranks. Large numbers of Moors and Berbers flocked to the standards of Musa and Ilyan. The number of believers rapidly increased ; and every believer burned to be a conqueror.[2] To them, no less than to the Arabians, the country was a prospective paradise, far more attractive than any land on the slopes of the Atlas, or in the valleys by the sea. To the latter Jezirah-Andalus was the successful rival of *Jezirah-l-Arabi*, the crown of all their hopes and martial labors.

[1] Al Makkari slightly contradicts himself, although the mistake is of no importance. In one place he speaks of Tarif's return in July, and in another he makes it in August or September. I. 251, I. 265. I have adopted the opinion of Gayangos.

[2] Condé, Dominacion de los Arabes, I. ch. ix.

The returning party of Tarif announced that they had met with no opposition. The troops of Roderik were on the northern frontier of Spain. Many of the nobles in the south were malcontents, already in the councils of Ilyan, and did not dissemble their satisfaction. As for the simple natives, they exhibited a consternation mingled with imbecility; to them this rude incursion promised only a change of masters; already grievously oppressed, they had little to hope from new forms of oppression.

And now all was eager activity in the Moslem host. Never since the the swarms of Abu Bekr had marched to besiege Damascus, just after the death of Mohammed, had so grand a prospect opened before them. Armorers were busy in the camp; horses were collected from all quarters; troops were mustered and drilled; the army was reorganized. Boat-wrights were set at work to prepare a flotilla, capable of transporting an army with its horses, baggage, and munitions of war.[1] From all the information that had been collected, a plan of campaign was digested, and the conduct of the invasion was confided to Tarik Ibn Zeyud Ibn Abdillah, the valiant and tireless chieftain, who had won his reputation in the subjection of the Barbary tribes, who had already been placed in command at Tangiers, and who had been among the more urgent among those who counselled Musa to undertake the conquest.

The appointment of Tarik was a happy one. Whether he was an Arabian, a Persian, or a Berber,

---

[1] Condé, Dominacion de los Arabes, I. ch. ix.

a manumitted slave, or a free-born man,[1] he had been
The appoint-
ment of
Tarik to
command. so distinguished by his exploits, that when
he was named as leader the enthusiasm of
the troops was greatly increased, so that
numbers were obliged to remain behind who were
eager to go. To the Spanish historians Tarik appears
as a person of great consideration.[2] At last, all things
were in readiness: it was now the early spring of the
year 711.[3] Eight months had elapsed since the return of Tarif's expedition. The force now about to
embark consisted of seven thousand selected men, the
greater part cavalry; of whom the most were Moors,
Berbers, and slaves, but all ardent Moslemah. With
them were only three hundred Arabians of pure blood,
most of whom were officers.

To transport this force, a fleet of merchant vessels
crossed and recrossed the Bahr-z-zok-hak,[4] or narrow
sea. Of these a few set out directly from Ceuta, and
a portion crossed from Tangiers, but the main body
marched or sailed from Tangiers to Ceuta, whence they
passed over to *Mons Calpe.* By direction of Musa,

[1] If he had been of a distinguished Arabian family, it would have
been vaunted. His name indicates a grandfather, —Abdullah, — but
no patronymic or tribal connection.

[2] Persona de gran cuento, dado que faltaba un ojo. — MARIANA,
Historia de España, II. 386.

[3] In his corrected chronological list, Gayangos fixes the landing of
Tarik in April 30, 711. Al Makkari makes it August, and, even when
we correct his error, it comes out May or June. Al Makkari, I. 266.

[4] Literally, "the sea of narrowness." Mariana says merchant
vessels were used to avoid suspicion. They were the best for the
transportation of troops. There can be no doubt that the intended
crossing was well known in Spain. The kind of ship was unimportant : the number would excite astonishment.

and for reasons already indicated, Ilyan accompanied the expedition. Tarik superintended the embarkation of the troops, and was the last man to leave the shore.

When the army was about to embark, the devout spirit of Musa found utterance : in the presence of the troops he fell on his knees and prayed most fervently, and with tears, for the help of Allah in this new undertaking.[1] And he was not to be blamed if, with the glory which would accrue to Allah, he saw the honor and fame of his servant Musa. History gives us other notable proofs that religious fervor is the sharpest spur to personal ambition, — also the converse. Musa's prayers.

Whether dreams are ever prophetic may be left as a mystery to the curious psychologist. It is certainly true that, by a happy collocation of past and present, they encourage the spirits and vivify the hopes of men. As the bark which carried Tarik was crossing the strait, fatigued by his labors, he fell asleep, and saw in a dream the prophet of God standing surrounded by the faithful few who had accompanied him in his flight from Mecca to Medina,[2] and by those who had received and protected him in Medina.[3] The warriors of the vision stood with drawn swords of great brightness, and with bent bows pointing towards Andalus ; and Mohammed, in a loud voice, exclaimed, "Take courage, O Tarik, and accomplish what thou art destined to perform !" When

[1] Al Makhari, I. app. xlvii.

[2] Muhajirín, or companions.

[3] Ansares, or assistants. The Spanish Arabs call the former *Ashâb*, and the latter *Tabis*.

the vision began to fade, the prophet and his companions seemed to be pressing forward towards Spain.[1] This was a presage of success ; and when he related it
And Tarik's dreams. to his followers it inspired them with additional zeal and valor. Whatever credit we may attach to the reality of the vision, the effect of its narration was indisputable.

Attempts have been made to determine the exact spot of Tarik's landing; it is a puzzling, but fortunately an unimportant, question. Al Makkari says: "At the foot of the mountain which afterwards received his name."[2] Condé takes him to Jeziratu-l-Khadhrá, which, as we have seen, is the generic name of any green island or peninsula, but which has been supposed to be a small island in the bay of Gibraltar, immediately opposite the town of Algeciras. Captain Drinkwater, apparently without having made careful investigation of the matter, thinks that he landed[3] on the isthmus between Mons Calpe and the continent ; "that is, on the plain just behind the Rock, now called *the neutral ground*," exempt at present from either English or Spanish occupancy.

It is probable that so large a force landed at several points, and at intervals of time. If the weather was bad and the sea rough, they would naturally seek at once the shelter of the bay ; but, in moderate weather

[1] This story, which is found in Al Makkari (I. 267), is, with slight modifications, related by Cardonne (Histoire de l'Afrique, etc., I. 72), and has been eagerly caught up by many other writers to whom dreamland is a most inviting country. But Cardonne used a number of the historians quoted by Al Makkari.

[2] I. 266.

[3] Siege of Gibraltar, I. ch. ix.

and with ordinary precautions, they would seek the nearest points, and so it is probable that most of the troops went on shore at and between Europa and little Europa Point, and first deployed in what is now called the Alameda. These are conjectures; but on a small elevated flat, just above these points, may still be seen the ruins of a Moorish tower. Very lately a portion of it was pulled down, and on one of its stones was found an inscription, disclosing the year 725 as the date of its completion. This seems to have been a small citadel in case of a retreat, and a lookout for boats crossing from Africa.

Al Kortobi, striving to be more explicit, is more obscure. He informs us that Tarik " cast anchor close to a mountain which received his name. When he was about to land he found some of the *Rum* posted on a commodious part of the coast where he intended to disembark, who made some show of resistance. But Tarik, giving up that spot, sailed off from it at night, and went towards another part of the coast, which he contrived to render flat by means of oars, and by throwing over them the saddles of the horses, and in this way he managed to effect a landing unobserved by his enemies, and before they were aware of it." [1]

The omen of the dream had succeeded so well with the troops that another was not wanting. If Mohammed could point the way to Spain in a vision, they were not unwilling to have cor- The old woman's prophecy.

[1] " A narrative of the principal events attending the conquest, &c.," quoted by Gayangos. I have made this quotation because it indicates that there was some show of resistance offered to the land-

roborative testimony as to the fitness and fortune of their leader.   While Tarik was advancing inland from his place of landing, he was met by an old woman of Algeciras, who had been for a long time a widow.   Her husband, she said, had been skilful in predicting future events.   She had often heard him say, when as yet there were no signs of a conquest, that Spain would be subjugated by a tall man, with a prominent forehead, and having upon his left shoulder a black hairy mole—among the Orientals a sign of good fortune.   Tarik at once uncovered his person, and in the middle of his left shoulder was displayed the lucky protuberance.[1]

There is, perhaps, no locality in the world where war scenes so remote in history may be so readily

The famous strait of Gibraltar.

reproduced to the imagination as the strait of Gibraltar and its bounding shores.   The traveller of to-day finds the peculiar and well-defined natural features exactly the same as when the Arab-Moors landed upon the now-famous Rock.   But the illusion is more perfect still.   Let him take the steamer from Cadiz to Tangiers, and in a few hours he reaches the offing, whence, from the shallowness of the water, he must go ashore in the rude boats manned by Berbers.   Just such boats and such boatmen plied

ing, and to present the device, certainly not very clear, for the unobserved landing.

[1] Al Makkari, I. 267. Cardonne, Histoire, &c., I. 74. Moles, among the Arabs, were considered marks of beauty. "The Arabs, indeed, are particularly extravagant in their admiration of this natural beauty-spot, which, according to its place, is likened to a globule of ambergris upon a dish of alabaster, or upon the surface of a ruby." — LANE's *Arabian Nights*, Introduction, note 19.

in the harbor in the days of the conquest, and took
Tarik and his army across. But even these boats
cannot quite reach the land, the water is so shoal.
Two stout Moors wade out and carry him, in rather
unstable equilibrium, to the shore.

In the flat, low houses and narrow streets, rising in
ampitheatre from the beach, he will find the same
oriental life, little changed by the vicissitudes of later
history. There are the same little cramped bazaars,
the dirty market-place, with its asses and camels, and
its squatting hucksters. There are Moorish pick-
pockets in turban and haik, against whose skilful
hands his only resource is buttoned pockets and Argus
eyes. There are women shrouded and veiled, cunningly dropping their veils when not watched by
their lords, to display very doubtful and dirty charms,
just as, no doubt, they disclosed them to the impassioned warriors of Musa and Tarik. The traveller's
fancy will be poor indeed if, in the courteous turbaned captain of the port, he cannot find for the time
the lineaments of Musa, son of Nosseyr, superintend-
ing the preparations for the crossing. Some military
Berber, who has lost an eye, and there are many such,
may figure as Tarik el Tuerto, and a lordly *valet de
place*, with large turban, bare legs, and red sandals or
slippers, bearing most probably the name of the false
prophet, will describe to him the same eastern life as
that of a thousand years ago. Islám, unchanged in
drugging doctrine, now no longer powerful to nerve
the arm and fire the heart, dwells in the mosque,
barred against the Christian infidel. In a word, if we
may trust to historic comparisons, in the Tangiers of

to-day, he sees the Tangiers of Musa; if there be a difference it is found not in modern progress, but in modern degeneracy.

And now the traveller may cross with the Arab-Moors. Once more balanced, as were the Moslem chiefs, in the arms of wading Berbers and rocked in their rude boats, he reaches the steamer and sets out on the track of Tarik. In front is the island of Tarif; before him soon rises in elephantine proportions the famous Rock "like a beacon spreading its rays over the seas and rising far above the neighboring mountains: one would say that its face almost reaches the sky, and that its eyes are watching the stars in the celestial tracts." [1] Such it was to the Arabian poet, and since then it has been justly called "a mountain of histories."

He passes Europa Point, and entering the bay soon finds behind the mole a safer harbor than that of Tarik's day. Within the narrow limits of the town at the western base of the mountain, and on the Alameda, he sees the camping ground of a portion of the Moslem army. By zigzag paths he climbs the rock to the signal tower, and from its sharp elevation he looks out upon an exquisite picture of Nature and of History, a complete and living map of the famous strait. Far below at his feet lies Europa Point, with its light-house and batteries, jutting out, at the present day, rather in defiance than in greeting, to its sister promontory on the African shore; on his right is the beautiful bay of Gibraltar; around him are two continents, the Atlantic and the Mediterra-

From Tangiers to "the Rock."

---

[1] Al Makkari quotes an anonymous poet of Granada, I. 60.

nean, and the five historic kingdoms of Andalusia, soon to be devastated and deluged with blood. Opposite, the town of Ceuta gleams white upon its seven hills, and Mons Abyle asserts its kinship with Mons Calpe.

Nor is it only a map, but a beautiful, colored map: the green and gray of the Spanish coast; the deep, deep blue of the midland sea; the lighter perspective blue of Africa in clearly defined outlines; all gently checkered, perhaps by the varying shadows of the fleecy clouds which are scudding under the sun. As his enchanted gaze rests upon this wonderful panorama, it needs no vivid imagination to see the drama of the conquest unfolding: it is there under his very eye. The numerous vessels in bay and sea, crossing each other's track in sunlight and shade, are the fleet of Tarik, plying back and forth between Africa and Spain. The drums and trumpets of the British band playing upon the Alameda, rising fitfully and faintly upon the ear, are pressed into the service of Fancy, as the clanging horns and atabals mustering the dark squadrons of the Arab-Moors. Centuries recede; the traveller stands on the rock of Tarik; he sees the coming of Tarik, and he keeps time, with pulse and foot, to the grand quickstep which is ushering Arabian civilization into degenerate Spain.[1]

[1] I hope I have not transgressed the rules of historical composition, by presenting in this form my personal observations and feelings, as I stood upon the signal tower of Gibraltar. I have considered the scene and the emotions it excited so exceptional, as to warrant me in describing both ; and I am sure of the sympathy of all who, with a taste for that period of Spanish history, have found themselves on the same spot.

CHAPTER II.

THE ARMIES IN ARRAY; THE FIELD OF BATTLE.

THE landing of Tarik's forces was completed on the 30th of April, 711 (8th Regeb. A. H. 92),[1] and his enthusiastic followers at once named the promontory upon which he landed, Dschebel-Tarik,

Dschebel-Tarik.

the rock of Tarik. The name has been retained in the modernized form, Gibraltar. It is also spoken of in the Arabian chronicles as Dschebalu-l-Fata, the portal or mountain of victory.

The Moslem forces were organized into several detachments, to scour the country and to look for the approaching enemy, who was now reported to be mustering in haste to resist the invasion. The vanguard composed of cavalry was confided to Mugheyth Ar Rúmi.

[1] I have, as before said, adopted this date from Gayangos, who has compared the different statements of historians; if there be still a doubt in the mind of the reader, perhaps he will settle it by adopting the devout language of Al Makkari (I. 268) :—" God only knows the truth of the case." The confusion of the calendars is difficult to unravel. Isidor de Beja seems to have been mystified, and the account in the España Sagrada (II. 55) is not more correct : "De aqui se sigue que la perdida de España empesó, segun Isidoro, en el año 713 del Redentor, y escogeron por epocha de la general perdida de España al siguiente 714, porque en este fué el lamento mas deplorable."

The story is found in Xerif Idrisi, the Nubian geographer,[1] and has been repeated by many historians, that Tarik then ordered the boats to be burned, in order to take away all hope of retreat. _{The burning} This device is not new, and in this case is, _{boats (?)} to say the least, very doubtful. It originated probably in the exaggerated account of a Christian spy sent by Roderik into the enemy's camp, who may have been there when most of the boats had gone back to Africa for re-enforcements and stores, and in preparation for the transport of Musa's army. He believed that as they were not still in the Bay of Gibraltar, they had been destroyed, and made up the rest of the story, telling the king on his return, " They have set fire to their vessels to destroy their last hope of escape."[2]

The story has been repeated to magnify the valor and hardihood of the Moslemah.[3] We shall see that re-enforcements were soon sent to Tarik, in large numbers, and it seems certain that the boats were kept plying between the continents, to keep open

[1] Chap. IV. sect. i.

[2] Al Makkari, I. 274.

[3] Condé (Dominacion de los Arabes, I. ch. ix.) mentions this statement. La Fuente has adopted the error : " Habiendo ya hecho quemar Tarik las naves para que no quedara á los suyos ni otra esperanza ni otra eleccion que la victoria ó la muerte." — *Historia de España*, II. 479. Burning transport vessels did good service for the apostate Julian at the Euphrates, but it was done under a strong necessity to prevent the fleet from falling into the hands of the garrison of Ctesiphon. Speaking of a similar act of Cortéz at Vera Cruz, Bernal Diaz tells us that " it was done by the common consent of all to have the assistance of the mariners." — *Verdadera Historia de la Conquista*, pref. iv. Tarik had neither reason for the alleged act.

constant communication. To burn the ships would have been madness; ordinary prudence would have forbidden the deed.

The history of the movements which preceded and brought on the decisive battle is confused and obscure; all that we can certainly know is that they occupied more than two months. The Gothic forces assembling to make head against the invaders were small, and rather watched than resisted them. A valiant Goth, called in most of the chronicles, Theodomir, who seems to have been so long count or governor of south-eastern Andalusia as to cause the country to bear his name, — the land of Tadmir, — appears dimly upon the scene, at the head of a hasty levy of seventeen hundred men, defending, says Condé, the passage from the Green Island to the mainland,[1] skirmishing three days with the enemy, watching his movements and sending despatch after despatch to Roderik. In many of the chronicles the general who thus confronted the advance is called Sancho,[2] and in others he is Iñigo or Ignatius. Sancho is mentioned as a cousin of the king. It may be that three persons answering to these names were at the head of different detachments detailed on the same general service; but, from the fact that in later days the Spaniards give a number of Christian names to the same person, I am inclined to think that these are but

[1] Dominacion de los Arabes, I. ch. ix. La Fuente (Historia de España, II. 459, 479) calls him a general of Witiza who had before driven off the Moslems, who in the reign of that king "infestasen las costas de España, y aun hiciesen en ellas algunos daños."

[2] Cardonne, I. 74. "Il leva à la hâte quelques troupes dont il donna le commandement a Sanche, prince de son sang."

three names for the same person, Theodomir being
the normal Gothic name, and the others being Spanish
names adopted by later historians.

Be this as it may, the danger had become imminent, and it found Roderik unprepared. He should
have been with a large army on the shores Roderik un-
of the Bay of Gibraltar; all that he could prepared.
do instead was to send down in haste one or more
reconnoitring parties, but could only inform the
king of its accomplishment and of the advance.

In the words of a letter conceived by the chronicler, as giving the most exact impression of the real
state of the case, the surprise and the consternation,
Theodomir says to Roderik, "My Lord! there have
come forces adverse to us from parts of Africa.
Whether they have dropped from heaven, or sprung
up through the earth, I know not, having found them
suddenly before me, and encountered them on my
path. I resisted them with all my power, and did
my utmost to maintain the passage, but have been
compelled to yield to their numbers and the impetuosity of their attacks; wherefore they have finally
encamped on our soil in despite of my efforts. And
now, my Lord, since the matter is thus, I entreat you
to succor us with all speed, and with the largest force
you can muster. Come yourself, also, in person, for
that will be better than all." [1]

This despatch handed down by tradition, probably
reached Roderik not at Toledo, but hastening down
from the northern frontier, whither by the crafty

[1] Condé, Dominacion de los Arabes, I. ch. ix.

advice of Ilyan he had sent his troops, to quell the
unquiet Cantabrians and to put down an insurrection
in the territory of Pampeluna[1] incited by the party
of the sons of Witiza.   Whatever his former faults
and errors, as soon as Roderick received the momentous news he exhibited much of his earlier energy
and fire.   He sent in every direction throughout the
kingdom to levy troops.   All who were of age were
required to join his standard.[2]   The rallying place
was Cordova, whither he repaired and took up his
abode in the royal castle.   Here the motley force
was collected, and received by the king.   The character and composition of the army differ greatly
according to the nationality of the chronicler.   To
the Arabian historians it has seemed good to exalt
the equipment and extol the valor of an army which
they were to annihilate : the stronger the enemy, the
greater the glory of the conquest; and so we read
that the force of Roderik "amounted to nearly one
hundred thousand men, provided with all kinds of
weapons and military stores."[3]

The Spanish historians on the other hand, and with
more truth, seek for some consolation in their defeat
by exaggerating their really weak and unprepared
condition.[4]   "What a force!" says Mariana.   "The
army was composed of all sorts of rubbish, gathered

---

[1] Al Makkari, I. 268.

[2] Mariana, Historia de España, II. 389.

[3] Al Makkari, I. 269.

[4] The monk of Silos was not among the underraters ; he says,
"At Rodericus, dum hostis auditur advenisse, collecto Gothorum
robustissimo exercitu, acer et imperterritus primo subiit pugnæ." —
España Sagrada, XVII. 270.

without discrimination, with but little drill : they
had neither strength in their bodies nor valor in their
souls; the squadrons were badly organized ; the arms
eaten with rust; the horses lean or weak, unused to
bear dust, heat, and stormy weather. They were
marvellous cowards, without courage, and even without the physical strength to endure the toils and dis-
comforts of war." [1]

We must add to these disabilities that, in that
army fearful of the invasion, there also existed the
elements of treason. Al Makkari says that, at the
request of the king, the sons of Witiza joined him
at Cordova with a large contingent, but that such
was their distrust of him that they would not bring
their troops into the town, but encamped outside of
the walls. There is no evidence of fact to deny or
disprove the assertion, but I would reject it on the
grounds of improbability.[2] Leaving them out of the
consideration, Roderick perceived, even in the councils of war, his own unpopularity and the lukewarm-
ness of his generals. In the rapid rush of affairs it
was too late to take order with such a spirit, with any
hope of converting or crushing it. All must be cast
upon the hazard of the die. The cast was made, and
he must blindly abide the result.

He sent down a considerable force of cavalry to aid
Theodomir in delaying the enemy's advance, and

---

[1] Mariana. Historia de España, II. 389. "Gente la mayor
parte allegadiza y mal armada, llenaba ya los campos de Andalucía."
— LA FUENTE, *Historia de España*, II. 479.

[2] For a consideration of this improbability, see the note of Gayangos. — AL MAKKARI, I. 527, note 69.

ordered him, while so doing, to fall back slowly on the main body. With great industry he organized his troops as he marched; and, as his force grew in numbers and consistence, his hope revived that, in spite of all portents and defects, he was still strong enough to drive the invaders into the sea. It was the levy of a nation against a handful of rash adventurers.

Thus the two armies approached each other, — the Arab-Moors advancing to the neighborhood of Medina Sidonia, and the army of Roderik to Xeres de la Frontera and the banks of the Guadalete. The advanced parties of cavalry were engaged in numerous skirmishes, in which all historians agree that the advantage was always on the side of the Moslemah.[1]

The armies approach each other.

The detachments into which Tarik had divided his army had been for two months diligently employed in scouring the country, taking all the supplies they needed and could store, and destroying what they could not use; demanding from the natives tribute, or urging apostasy from the Christian faith upon all whom he found and who had dared to remain behind in the general panic. But he kept all his bands within easy rallying distance, in readiness for the great encounter which he knew was at hand, with an army determined to fight, and which, he sent word to Musa, without re-enforcements, "it was not in his power to resist, except it was God Almighty's will that it should be so."[2]

[1] "Tuvieron encuentros y escaramuzas, en que los nuestros llevaron siempre el peor." — MARIANA, *Historia de España*, II. 387.

[2] Al Makkari, I. 270.

At this instance, Musa sent him five thousand additional men; and, even thus recruited, he saw that the conquest of Spain would not be effected without a severe struggle and much bloodshed.

It will be forever impossible to determine the exact spot upon which the great battle was fought, if, indeed, it took place on a single field. As a general rule, historic names for battles only indicate the proximity to some town or stream, without topographical accuracy. It is so in the present case. One accepted name of the battle is that of Xeres de la Frontera, because that is supposed to have been the nearest town to the scene of conflict, and it was already a place of some prominence.

It has been also called the battle of Guadalete.[1] This river flows for seventy-five miles across the plain of Sidonia, and empties by two mouths into the Bay of Cadiz. Its banks have been accepted by the chroniclers as the scene of the encounter. It was a dividing line: a natural trench for the protection of the Gothic army, and an obstacle to the Moslems; and, if not chosen prospectively, the movements of the two armies soon indicated that as the locality on which they were likely to meet. Later explorations give us no assistance. No traces remain

The exact spot unknown.

---

[1] Condé says, "The opposing hosts found themselves face to face in the plain traversed by the Guadalete." — *Dominacion de los Arabes*, I. ch. x. Cardonne, when he places them "on the borders of the Lethe," means the same river. — *Histoire de l'Afrique*, &c., i. 75. The assertion of one Arabian author that the armies met on the banks of the Wáda Bekkeh may refer to a small stream flowing near the town of Bejer, quite near the coast. — GAYANGOS in *Al Makkari*, I. 526, note 67.

to identify the spot; and it is now asserted that the bed of the river has been decidedly changed since the battle was fought, — a thing that is not uncommon in Spain.[1] The general phrase, "On the banks of the Guadalete in the territory of Sidonia"[2] is very vague, since the *comarca* of Sidonia included the towns of Arcos, Xeres, Algeciras, Tarifa, Cadiz, and Bejer. The assertion of Al Makkari that "the two armies engaged near the lake or gulf"[3] indicates, in all probability, the lake of La Janda, near the city of Medina Sidonia. The nearest approach to a settlement of this question may be found in the conjecture of Gayangos, "that the memorable encounter took place near the sea, and close to Medina Sidonia, since the battle having lasted eight days, as is unanimously agreed by Christian and Mohammedan writers, it might have commenced between Bejer and Medina Sidonia, and ended near the Guadalete, the intermediate distance being only about twenty English miles."[4] The end to which this refers would be, not the fierce encounter of the armies, but the after carnage in the

---

[1] I was so informed on the spot in 1870. Mr. Henry Blackburn, speaking of the freshets in the Spanish rivers, says, "In the plains the country is often flooded for miles, and in the mountainous districts the swollen rivers do scarcely less damage, by carrying away bridges and dwellings in their downward course to the sea. Some have forced themselves altogether into new channels, and it is not uncommon to have to ford a river or cross by a ferry-boat within sight of a massive Roman bridge, which is standing high and dry on the bank." — *Travelling in Spain at the Present Day*, p. 100.

[2] Al Makkari, I. 273.

[3] Ib. I. 274.

[4] Ib. I. 527, note 67.

first pursuit near the river bank. This view is quite compatible with placing the depot of the Gothic army at Xeres, and strong guards at the fords or ferries of the river.[1]

But the importance of fixing the exact site sinks into insignificance when we consider the great battle itself, the momentous interests at stake. Here was to be illustrated a principle, afterwards propounded to Queen Elizabeth by Raleigh, when the armada of Philip threatened England, — "the invaders can only lose a battle, the invaded may lose a kingdom." Never, indeed, were greater interests involved. The Goths and the people of Spain were fighting for their homes, for their Christian faith, and in support of a dynasty which had been three hundred years in undisputed possession of Spanish soil. They had rushed at the call of the king in large numbers to the field, but oppression had destroyed the muscles of their arm, the fire of their eye, and the valor of their souls; they were full of melancholy forebodings, as fact and fable, the sad vision and clustering predictions of the chroniclers, indicate; they longed for victory, but they expected disaster. The battle was half lost before it began.

[1] There is still pointed out near the bank of the river a small hill called *El Real de Don Rodrigo*, which may have been occupied by the king as temporary headquarters during the collocation of his forces. No remains of armor or human bones are found. Lope de Vega, in his *Jerusalen Conquistada* (I. vi.), takes a broad poetic license when he writes, —

> "Gran tiempo conservaron sus arenas
> (Y pienso que ha llegado á la edad mia)
> Reliquas del estrago, y piedras echas,
> Armas, hierros de lanza y de flechas."

The Arab-Moors were moving in the flush of a continued conquest, which had constantly extended their dominion, and vindicated the divine inspiration of their prophet. Every victory had strengthened their faith, and every increase of faith nerved their arms for new success. Thus it happened that twelve thousand Moslems dared to assault a force of eight times their number, buttressed by a nation on its own soil, and were sanguine of the result, — the conquest of the earthly paradise of Andalus, or heaven and the houris.

CHAPTER III.

THE BATTLE IN THE PLAINS OF MEDINA SIDONIA, COMMONLY CALLED THE BATTLE OF THE GUADALETE.

THE army which Roderik, hurrying down from Pampeluna, had been able to gather, has been variously estimated. Most of the Arabian historians compute it to have numbered ninety The Gothic army. thousand.[1] A respectable portion of this force, clad in mail, and armed with swords and battle-axes, were posted in front of the centre; while a small number, equally well equipped, were held in reserve for a critical moment. In the second rank he arrayed his main body, which, in the haste of the emergency, he had been unable to supply with defensive armor, and whose weapons of offence were rude and motley in the extreme, — bows, lances, axes, clubs, short scythes, and slings.[2] His cavalry was placed upon the wings, on one of which, if we may credit the chroniclers, was the brother-in-law of the fighting bishop Oppas, Ilyan,

[1] Cardonne says 100,000. Histoire de l'Afrique, &c., I. 75. Ibnu Khaldun is the only Moslem authority which reduces the number as low as 40,000. Others, with a natural exaggeration, report 100,000 cavalry alone.

[2] Los Christianos, vestidos de lorigas, y armados los unos de lanzas y espadas, los otros de hondas, haches, mazas y guadañas cortantas. — LA FUENTE, Historia de España, II. 480.

who had infected the troops under his command with his own treasonable spirit.

There were several elements of weakness in this very superiority of numbers. Beside the contingents of Ilyan and Oppas, there were many officers and men in the main ranks of Roderik whose loyalty or dis-affection would depend on circumstances : they were on the fence. If in the impending battle Roderik should seem to be gaining the day, they would be loyal, and would join him in completing the victory ; on the other hand, they only awaited the slightest prospect of defeat to desert their ranks and leave him to his fate. The men themselves had little stomach for the fight. It seemed to them that they could gain little and lose nothing by a change of masters.

Notwithstanding their numerical superiority, they were far inferior in equipments ; they were unskilled in the use of arms, unaccustomed to serve in large bodies, and therefore lacked coherence, and were fear-ful of the perils of battle. It may well be doubted whether the king himself was competent to command so numerous an army, even if it were perfectly organ-ized,[1] and whether he had generals of skill to aid him ; and it is very certain that there was no bond of union between the officers and the newly recruited men, — one of the strongest elements of success in war.[2]

In the Moslem army everything was different. The

---

[1] When the command of the French army against Germany was given to Moreau in 1800, Napoleon doubted whether there were *two* men in France who could command a hundred thousand men. Napoleon was *one*.

[2] With the tenth legion Cæsar could conquer the world.

troops were united as one man in the fervor of an
all-conquering faith; they were thoroughly The Moslem
disciplined, according to their simple tactics; host.
well armed, obedient, accustomed, for several generations, to move and fight in masses; enthusiastic for
the person and prophetic fortune of their leader, Tarik;
inspired by the prestige of aggressive advance, and
the greatness of the spoils.

The greater number wore mail, the making of which
they traced to King David, to whom God "made iron
soft, and it became in his hands as thread." [1] Some
carried lances, and scimitars or cutlasses of Damascus steel, others were armed with light long bows.
More than half the number were mounted on swift
horses, of Arabian and Barbary breed. The motley
varieties of shade and color; the dark armored figures
interspersed with turbans and burnus of white, red,
and black, presented a picturesque but confusing front
to the doubting army of the Gothic king.[2]

The seven thousand men who had crossed the strait
with Tarik had been re-enforced by Musa Its re-en-
with five thousand, so that the Moslem general forcements.
advanced to the field with twelve thousand Moslemah,
most of them cavalry. He had also been joined by

[1] The complete mail was of two kinds: the *sirgh*, which fell like
a mantle to the knees, and the *kembaz*, which extended only to the
waist; the arms were enclosed in plates of steel, and an iron cap,
tás, completed the suit. The troops of Tarik were, perhaps, not so
completely armed.

[2] "Their breasts were covered with mail armor, they wore white
turbans on their heads, the Arabian bow slung across their backs,
their swords suspended to their girdles, and their long spears firmly
grasped in their hands." — AL MAKKARI, I. 273.

Ilyan with a considerable contingent, which Al Makkari says was intended " to guide the forces of Tarik through the passes in the country, and gather intelligence for them." The number of this contingent is not known.[1]

As soon as Tarik had certain intelligence of the numbers and near approach of the Gothic forces, he collected his scattered detachments, and went to meet the enemy on the ground which Roderik had already chosen : here the two armies encamped within sight of each other.

In those early days, before the invention and discovery of gunpowder, the field of battle was far more contracted, and the actual fighting much more compact, and, it may be added, far more heroic. The distance of an arrow's flight marked the farthest point of uncertain contact, and the battle must be decided either by a hand-to-hand conflict, or by an unusual panic in one of the armies, which conquered without blows. In that period of warfare generalship consisted principally in personal valor and the power to organize and inspire men.

The armies of those days did not move without the impedimenta of women and children, although in the hasty levies of Roderik we may believe these were comparatively few on either side ; these, joined with the non-combatants of the immediately surrounding country, formed anxious crowds hovering like mist-wreaths upon the surrounding eminences,

[1] Cardonne, whose numbers cannot be depended on, computes the entire re-enforcements at 7,000, which, however, may include Ilyan's contingent. Histoire de l'Afrique, &c., I. 75.

helpless, but deeply interested spectators of the bloody drama which was about to open, and the like of which had not been seen for many generations.   Writers in both interests agree that the battle lasted eight days;[1] but, as this seems to be the stereotyped period for the battles of that day, we may either discard it entirely, or consider it as meaning several days of severe struggle, or as including the time between the first serious skirmishing and the desistance from the pursuit.

The faint light of the dawn on Sunday, the nineteenth of July, 711 (A. H. 28th Ramadhán, 92), disclosed the advance of both armies, as if animated by one spirit, to the shock of battle. *The battle in array.* It was the morning of a bright, sultry summer day. Spanish clarions sounded the notes of defiance, and were answered by Moorish horns, sustained by the sharp, shrill rolls of kettle-drums.   As they drew nearer Gothic shouts were echoed back by the *lelies*[2] of the Moslemah.   The earth trembled under the tramp of the forces.   The decisive moment was at hand, and it was then that Roderik, as he looked upon the Moslem host, is reported to have exclaimed, " By the faith of the Messiah, these are the very men I saw painted upon the scroll found in the mansion of science at Toledo ! "   The chronicler adds, " And from that moment fear entered his heart."[3]   This attribution of sentiment is proved to be unjust.   His

---

[1] Al Makhari, I. 274.   Condé, Dominacion de los Arabes, I. 56. Cardonne (I. 75, 76), says there were four days of skirmishing and three of actual battle.   This would give *one* to the pursuit.

[2] *Lá ilá-ha illa-lláh* — (there is no deity but God).

[3] Al Makhari, I. 273.

portents were indeed thus far realized; but, with
this partial fulfilment of the prediction, his courage
seems to have risen, and he appears to have done; by
precept and example, all that a man could do to
avert the dreaded issue.

He had brought with him in carts and on sumter
animals his wardrobes and his treasure in jewels and
money, and, according to Al Kortobi, long trains of
mules, whose only load was ropes to pinion the arms
of the captives; "for he did not doubt that he would
soon make every one of the Arabs his prisoner."[1]

He had travelled southward to the field in a litter
or chariot of ivory lined with cloth of gold, and drawn
by three white mules harnessed abreast. The silken
awning of the vehicle was profusely sprinkled with
pearls, rubies, and the richest jewels.[2]

Although past the prime of life, this mode and
splendor of conveyance were not so much to spare
himself the fatigues of the road, as to keep up his
state and dignity, in accordance with the custom of
the Gothic monarchs.[3] The chariot was his throne,
and he sat within it with a golden crown upon his
head. "He was dressed," says Al Kortobi, "in a robe
made of strings of pearls interwoven with silk."

[1] This statement, which may be considered a poetic fancy of Al
Kortobi, is found in his "Book of the Sufficiency on the History of
the Khalifs," translated in part by Gayangos, and placed in the appendix to the work of Al Makkari.

[2] Ib.

[3] Gayangos computes his age at eighty-five; but the elements
of computation are very vague. Mariana says the chariot in which
he rode was, "un carro de marfil, vestido de tela de oro, y reca-
mado conforme a la costumbre que los Reyes godos tenian quando en-
traban en las battallas. — *Historia de España*, II. 291.

Tradition has ventured to preserve the scornful and fiery address which he made to his troops before the engagement commenced. It is not less, but perhaps more, veritable than the speeches in Livy and Sallust, and is at least valuable in presenting the view taken by the earlier chroniclers of his circumstances and the state of his mind. While the historian cannot believe in the transmission of the exact words, he must permit a chastened imagination to lead his judgment, and must be content to relate what the real facts show to be most probable. In this way traditional addresses, when coming to light soon after the event, and generally adopted by the succeeding writers, may be accepted as of historic importance.

From his moving throne of ivory, as he passed through the ranks, he told his men how he rejoiced that the time had come to avenge the in- Roderik's address to his troops. sults offered to a great nation and to the holy faith by this low rabble, abhorred of God and men.[1] Up to this time, and in all their African conquests, they had made war upon eunuchs and barbarians; and now, puffed up by their slight successes in landing, God had blinded their eyes and let them fall into a snare. He had, he told them, himself collected a large army, whose duty was only prompt and valorous action, which would assure them an easy and complete victory. "Remember," he said in conclusion, "your antecedents, the valor of your Gothic ancestors, and the holy Christian faith, under whose

[1] Canalla aborrecible á Dios y á los hombres. The whole address may be read in Mariana (Historia de España, II. 391), and, slightly modified, in most of the Spanish historians.

auspices, and for whose defence, we are fighting."
Then, descending from his chariot, and putting on his
horned helmet,[1] he mounted his war-horse Orelia, and
taking his station upon the field, issued his orders for
the battle, which only awaited the first blow.[2]

[1] Flores, in his " Medallas de España," a work of great value, describes a coin, struck at Egitania, bearing the head of Roderik
crowned with such a helmet.   Lope de Vega fancies the helmet surmounted by a sphere,—

El yelmo coronado de una *esfera*,

Que en luces vence al circulo estrellado.

Jerusalen Conquistada, I. vi.

[2] A word more with regard to the manner in which Roderik
came to the field, that we may not share the injustice of his enemies.   Al Makkari says he arrived in a *litter*, which may be taken
as a general name for easy conveyance.   Condé, probably interpo-
lating his Arabian authorities, makes him come in an *ivory chariot*.
The Chronicle of Don Rodrigo describes in detail the *car*, with a
tent pitched upon it, under which he sat, and which was drawn by
two horses "of great size and gentle."   It seems to me reasonable
that in travelling from the north through tracts of unpeopled country, over roads which, even at this day, are so bad —*meo quodam
dolore* — that the Spaniards call them *caminos abandonados*, he
either rode on mule-back or in a litter, suspended between two horses
or mules, one in front and one in rear, a mode of conveyance common to this day in Spain and Spanish countries.   Every traveller
knows that there mules, for steadiness and endurance, and where
great speed is not in question, are superior to horses for carriage use.
Nearing the towns, and when he reached the encampment of his
forces, he would present himself to his troops in regal dignity, by
mounting his *carro de marfil ;* and, at the moment of action, all
writers mention his appearance on horseback.   This is all conjecture, drawn from my experience of travel in Spain and Mexico ; but
it may tend to show that the man who rode Orelia into the fray was
not an effeminate creature, because he came to the field in a litter or
a chariot.   However, in the words of Gayangos, " When the principal events of that momentous period remain enveloped in darkness
and confusion, how can we expect to dissipate the shades that cover
the minor details ?"

The first movements of the battle on Sunday, the opening day, were experimental; a general trial of stratagem and skirmishing, advances and retreats, partial shocks, with no decisive advantage on either side. Night came to end this desultory fighting, and the opposing forces drew off a space to spend the time in brief repose or in preparation to renew the conflict in the morning. No sooner had the dawn of the next day appeared than the struggle was resumed with increased bitterness and fury. It continued all day long; but the events of the day before were re-enacted, with like indecisive results.

On the whole, however, when the day came to an end, it was found that the Christian Goths had gained somewhat on their enemies. The Berber contingent of Tarik had been driven back,[1] and the disparity in numbers was beginning to tell. Such fighting as that of the first two days, it was manifest, would be greatly detrimental to the Arab-Moors. On the simple principle of continued attrition, it would soon wear them out. They could not afford to lose equal numbers with their enemy, and they had already lost more. The moral effect was great. The Goths had taken fresh heart, and were ready to press them with new vigor, hopeful to crush them with numbers, and drive them back pell-mell into the strait. What would have been the issue had they succeeded is left to conjecture. One result of a decided advantage would have been to kill the treason, confirm the doubting,

---

[1] Gayangos implies a partial defeat from the impassioned speech of Tarik, about to be recorded: "Whither can you fly?" — AL MAKKARI, I. 524, note 52.

and rouse the whole Gothic nation to arms and action.

It was in this despondent condition of the Moslemah, that the bold speech and dashing valor of the one-eyed leader turned the scale. The men spent that night with their arms in their hands, and Tarik was on horseback most of the time, "and they all passed that night in constant watch for fear of the enemy." [1]

On the morning of Tuesday, the third day, after placing his men in position, he rode through the ranks exhorting, reasoning, beseeching, and inspiring. He had need of all his resources of logic, eloquence, and personal magnetism; for it was to be feared that, on the first vigorous onset of the Goths, his African troops, most of them recruits, would give way. He began his fiery harangue by rendering thanks and praise to Allah, "the Compassionate, the Merciful," for what he had already achieved, and then implored His all-powerful assistance in the coming struggle. He rebuked their despondency, and fortified the lesson by representing the horrors of retreat. "O Moslemah, conquerors of Almagreb,[2] whither can you fly? The enemy is in your front; the sea is at your back. By Allah! there is no salvation for you but in your courage and perseverance. Consider your situation. Here you are on this island,[3] like so many orphans cast upon the world; you will soon be met by a powerful enemy,

Tarik's fiery harangue.

---

[1] Al Makkari, I. 272.

[2] Al-maghubu-l-aksa, the extreme west of Africa.

[3] The Arabians considered the Peninsula an island.

surrounding you on all sides, like the infuriated bil-
lows of a tempestuous sea, and sending against you
his countless warriors *drowned in steel*, and provided
with every store and description of arms." He
showed them that their only hope of safety was in
immediate attack; their only means of subsistence
in capturing the enemy's stores.

"Do not think," he procceded, "that I impose upon
you a task from which I shrink myself, or that I try
to conceal from you the dangers attending this our
expedition." He promised to exceed them in self-
devotion and valor; and then he tried to allure them,
by describing the rich rewards which would follow
their victory, — cities and castles filled with treasures
and luxuries. "You must have heard," he said,
"numerous accounts of this island; you must know
how the Grecian [1] maidens, handsome as houris, their
necks glittering with innumerable pearls and jewels,
their bodies clothed with tunics of costly silks, sprinkled with gold, are awaiting your arrival, reclining on
soft couches in the sumptuous palaces of crowned
lords and princes.

He told them — referring especially to the Arabians
— that they were the chosen heroes of the Khalif
'Ab-du-l-malek Ibnu-l-walid, and that God would

---

[1] There is a confusion in the use of the word *Grecian*, which is
thus explained. The Arabians called the Christian Spaniards *Rúm*
or Roman, as being so long under the Roman dominion, and this was
translated into *Grecian*, because the Eastern or Greek empire of
Rome alone remained at that time. La Fuente thinks this refers to
the Hispano-Roman population, and not to the pure Goths. "Los
Arabes llamaban *romano* á todo el que no fuese arabe, ó acaso godo
puro." — *Historia de España*, III. 67, note.

reward their endurance and valor, "both in this
world and in the future;" and he ended the impassioned harangue with the shout, "On, warriors and
believers; do as you see me do. Guala! Guala!
Follow me, O men! I shall not stop until I reach
the tyrant in the middle of his steel-clad warriors,
and either kill him or he shall kill me!"[1]

It is not difficult to conjure before the fancy the
tall form of this dark warrior, in gleaming mail, su-
perbly mounted and caparisoned, his one eye blazing
with the light of battle, galloping hither and thither
among his men, stopping for a moment here and
there, and ejaculating, not in one place only, but in
many, and repeating in detached utterances the substance if not the exact words of this traditional address. Then let the imagination reproduce the effect
of his burning words, the answering eyes of the re-
inspired soldiers, the shrill cries of assenting ardor.
" We are ready to follow thee, O Tarik! We shall all, to
one man, stand by thee, and fight for thee, — nor could
we avoid it were we otherwise disposed; victory is our
only hope of salvation!" The address and the response
were the *mot d'ordre*. The Arab-Moors pressed forward
to the attack, and their historians vie with each other
in describing the shock of battle. Again are heard the

---

[1] The word *Guala* means *God to aid*. *Taghiyah*, which is
translated *tyrant*, has the force of the Greek τύραννος. The words
of Tarik's address are found in Ibn Kuteybah, — conditions of com-
mandment and government. The versions of Condé, Cardonne, and
Al Makkari differ slightly in words, but the ideas are the same and
the logical sequence. Like the address of Roderik, it is only traditional, but comports perfectly with the man and the situation. I
have adapted the abstract given above from the several versions.

blare of Gothic trumpets and the clangor of atabals and *báz;* so terrible is the meeting that one likens it to the day of judgment, and another compares it to " that of two mountains dashing against each other." [1]

Fancying that he recognizes Roderik, by his resplendent armor and brilliant staff, Tarik cleaves his way through a mass of intervening troops, and rides furiously upon a Gothic general of lower rank, whom he has mistaken for the king, and cleaves him to the ground with a mortal stroke. The Moslem soldiers, deceived like himself, believe that the king is killed, and follow their leader with renewed ardor. The false news spreads through the Christian ranks, and is readily believed; they are appalled at the fury of the new onset, and make faint resistance, where the stoutest might not avail.

Rumor of Roderik's death.

It was just at this critical moment, when the centre of the Gothic line was pierced, that Bishop Oppas, the somewhat legendary brother-in-law of Ilyan, is said to have drawn off, with a strong contingent, to join the Moslem ranks ; and such a defection seems to have hastened, if it did not decide, the issue of the contest. Some chroniclers say that the injured sons of Witiza were also there, placed by Roderik upon the wings, and that they too retired from the battle, and left the king to his fate. But all this is conjectural. Who commanded the treacherous contingent, and what was the exact part it played, cannot really be known.[2]

---

[1] Al Makkari, I. 273.

[2] After careful examination of the authorities, it seems quite improbable that the sons of Witiza were there. They were in deadly

But, with the furious charge of Tarik, the entire aspect of affairs was changed. The elated Moslemah advanced along the whole line. The wings of the

The shock of battle, and the rout of the Chris- . tians. Gothic army gave way before the headlong rush of their cavalry. The weakened main body could no longer resist. The Christian host was struck as with palsy; the palsy gave way to panic; the panic prompted retreat; the retreat became a rout. Bereft of reason, they did not think of a rallying point in their rear, every soldier turned his back in flight, threw away his arms, and sought only for his own safety. Stores and treasures were left behind: the wounded were forgotten. They scattered, like dead leaves in an autumnal gale, in utter confusion throughout the surrounding country. The Moslem advance, systematic and orderly, but rapid and relentless, gave no time for the dissipated mass to coalesce; it became a swift pursuit, and was continued, until, in some directions, the dripping sabres of the cavalry were sheathed "for lack of argument," and, in others, they halted to reform and join the main body.

I have already spoken of the duration of this series

opposition to their father's supplanter, and had crossed over to Africa to secure the aid of Musa in reconquering their rights. They received a promise from him, not to restore them to royal power, but to give each of the three one thousand farms in the conquered territory, for which, no doubt, he claimed their allegiance and aid. But, if they were not on the field in person, they were fully represented "by Oppas and other secret partisans, whom fear or the wish of better accomplishing their treason, still retained under Roderik's orders." This is the opinion of Gayangos. — *Al Makkari*, I. 527, note 68. The fact of the treason is manifest; the names of the traitors and the details may be doubted, but are suggestive.

of actions. There seem to have been three days of severe fighting. If, as is asserted by Ar-rázi,[1] the battle began on Sunday, the 28th of Rhamadan (July 19), and ended on Sunday, the 5th of Shawál (July 26), probably two of the days thus included were spent in the pursuit, the complete dispersion of the Gothic remnants, and the return of the detachments to the moving headquarters of the army.[2]

It is manifestly impossible to arrive at anything like an accurate estimate of the numbers killed, wounded, and missing in the Gothic army. There could have been no attempt at the time to make such an estimate; there were no data for later computation: it was impossible, for to them it was a complete disaster, a hideous ruin. Not only were thousands lying heaped upon the battle-field, but the highways, the by-roads, and the open plain, into the interior, were strewn with corpses; the wounded had dragged themselves into thickets to die, as far as possible from the shouting horsemen who were rushing on like a storm-blast. Up to the moment when the Christian troops were struck with panic, we may consider that the losses were nearly equal on both sides. After that — such was the carnage — we may hazard the conjecture that they lost three times as many men as the Arab-Moors. But the determination of numerical loss, even could we know it exactly, is of little

[1] A historian of Cordova, in the tenth century.

[2] The words of Ar-rázi are, " At the end of which (period) God Almighty was pleased to put the idolaters to flight, and grant the victory to the Moslems." Cardonne says the *eighth* day was that of the final struggle on the field.

importance, when we consider that the Gothic-Span-
iards had lost everything; that this single battle had
despoiled Spain of all her array and her manhood,
and is justly marked in her annals as pre-eminently
unfortunate and tearful.[1] Spain was delivered up
helpless to the Moslem invaders, and their king — the
victim of his own crimes and his generals' treason —
had disappeared, when, culpable as he was, he would
have been at least a rallying centre for national pride,
if there were any remains of such a sentiment among
the degenerate Goths.

Of the Moslem losses we may speak with surer
judgment. The chronicles tell us that the victorious
army found in the camp of Roderik rich and large
spoils. They seized all the money and treasures he
had brought; there were great quantities of victuals
and stores; an immense number of arms were gathered
upon the field; from the dead bodies they stripped
the clothes, and took rings and other ornaments, —
gold from those of the nobles, and silver decorations
from the corpses of the private soldiers. And, better
than all this great booty, they secured a large number
of horses; sufficient, it is said, to supply their losses,
and mount most of their foot-soldiers, and thus greatly

---

[1] A la verdad, esta sola battalla despojó á España de todo su
arreo, y valor. Dia aciago, jornada triste y llorosa. — MARIANA,
Historia de España, II. 393. This is the sonorous echo of a contemporary voice. "Quis enim narrare tanta pericula ? Quis dinumerare
tam importuna naufragia ? Nam si omnia membra verterentur in
linguas, omnino nequaquam Hispaniæ ruinas vel ejus tot tantaque
mala dicere poterit humana natura." — ISIDORUS PACENSIS apud
Flores, *España Sagrada*, VIII. 291.

increase their strength for a vigorous and rapid advance.[1]

All the spoils collected on the field were divided by Tarik, according to the equitable rule of the Korán;[2] one-fifth he set apart to be delivered to Musa for the successor of the Prophet, and the rest was distributed among the troops, to reward their valor and incite them to new deeds of daring. It is distinctly stated that the distribution of the four-fifths was made to *nine thousand* of the Moslemah. This probably excludes the contingent of Ilyan. We may believe that the whole Moslem force was engaged, consisting of the original seven thousand who crossed with Tarik, and the five thousand sent by Musa as a re-enforcement before the battle. Of these twelve thousand he must, therefore, have lost three thousand, — a proof at once of the valor of his troops and of the vigorous resistance made at first by the army of Roderik.[3]

During a brief period of rest, and while organizing for a systematic advance, Tarik had sent an officer to Musa to report in detail what he had accomplished from the day of landing until the consummation of the great victory.[4] Whether he was honestly mistaken in thinking he had slain the king, or whether, knowing he had not, he desired the glory of such an exploit, and the dramatic effect it would

Tarik's despatch to Musa.

[1] Al Makkari, I. 277.

[2] Korán, ch. viii.

[3] The accounts of losses by the earlier chroniclers are not even shrewd guesses. Gibbon has repeated a ludicrous error in saying, "The plain of Xeres was overspread with *sixteen thousand* of their dead bodies."

[4] Condé, Dominacion de los Arabes, I. ch. x.

produce, he sent to Musa, as the king's head, that of the noble knight he had slain with his own hand. And then, certain of the enthusiastic thanks of his commander and the eulogium of the Khalif when the good news should reach Damascus, he set forward without delay to summon and occupy the panic-stricken cities of Spain. But he little understood the ambition and jealousy of Musa. He might have been pardoned for failure: he was to be punished for his success.

And here we may pause for a moment to consider Roderik's the fate of the unfortunate Gothic king. fate. Spanish historians and Arabian chroniclers have borrowed from each other in describing the royal state in which he advanced to the fatal field, and in echoing the proud and scornful words by which he sought to inspire his troops. Gibbon regards his grandeur as a proof of effeminacy, and, in high-sounding phrase, declares that " Alarik would have blushed at the sight of his unworthy successor, sustaining on his head a diadem of pearls, incumbered with a flowing robe of gold and silken embroidery, and reclining on a litter or car drawn by two white mules." [1] The sneering censure seems unjust. As has been already described, Roderik travelled to the field in the manner best calculated to vindicate his dignity and husband his strength. He was king of a great realm, and he came in kingly state, by litter or chariot, fittingly adorned. That he fought on horseback is conceded by every historian. Tarik supposed that he

---

[1] History of the Decline and Fall, V. ch. li.

"recognized the king by his decorations and the horse he rode." [1] The beauty and fleetness of his milk-white steed called " Orelia " [2] have been no less clearly stated in sober history than celebrated in legend and poetry ; and Mariana, who calls him " peste, tison y fuego de España," and, indeed, exhausts his vocabulary in abuse of the man, allows that he fought among the foremost, seeking points of weakness and danger, like a brave soldier. [3]

What became of him ? His fate is uncertain, and he adds another name to the long list of curious stories, like that of King Arthur, which have pleased the fancy while they taxed the credulity of posterity. Few, if any, think that he was the warrior slain and beheaded by Tarik ; but Isidor de Beja, and the continuator [4] of the " Chronicon Biclarense," — the only two contemporary writers, — declare that he fell upon the field. Many of the Mohammedan writers assert that he was killed, but that his body was never found. The most generally accepted account of his disappearance is, that, finding the day lost, he was borne along with his panic-stricken army, and attempted to save himself by flight ; but that, weak from his wounds and exertions, and incumbered by the weight of his

[1] Condé, Dominacion de los Arabes.

[2] Equus qui Orelia dicebatur. — RODERICUS de Rebus Hispaniæ, III. cxxiii.

[3] Historia de España, II. 393. Speaking of the last overwhelming attack of the Arab-Moors, and the desertion of Oppas, La Fuente says (Historia de España, II. 482) : " Rodrigo, sin embargo, no desmaya, antes crece su arrojo, y pelea con bravura, — inutil esfuerzo aúnque laudabile."

[4] Juan de Viclara (Viclara is the monastery) lived in the sixth century. The continuator was the contemporary of the conquest.

armor, he reached the maches of the river, and was there either slain by the pursuers, or drowned. It has been asserted that his war-horse, riderless, caparisoned with a golden saddle, richly adorned with rubies, was found in such a spot, and that near him were a royal crown, a purple mantle, and one sandal, embroidered with pearls and emeralds, having the strings still fixed to it.[1]

This account has led to another conjecture, of which the first historic mention is made by Sebastian of Salamanca, in the early part of the tenth century. According to this writer, it is supposed that when Roderik in his flight had reached the river-bank, and found his horse plunging in the mud, he threw off his mantle and crown, and even his sandals, as royal insignia, to escape recognition, and struck off in the western country, away from the tide of pursuit. Then comes the story — which may be "one of the pious frauds of which the tonsured chroniclers of the Middle Ages were often guilty,"[2] — that he was, after painful wanderings, sheltered at last by religious charity, and, during the remainder of his life, expiated his follies and his crimes in the garb and cell of a monk. Alfonso IV. (el Monje), whose accession to the throne of Portugal was in the year 925, — more than two centuries after the disappearance of Roderik, — wrote to Sebastian, Bishop of Salamanca, — who embodied his words in the chronicle: "The path of Roderik's flight is not known. . . . In our modern times, when we ourselves peopled the city of Viseo and its Co-

[1] Al Makkari, I. 274, app. xlviii.
[2] Ib. 528, note 71 ; the words of Gayangos.

marcas, wresting it from the power of the infidels, there was found in a certain hermitage or church, a sepulchral stone on the cover of which was seen an epitaph, ' Hic requiescit Rodericus ultimus Rex Gothorum.'"[1]

I have been thus explicit in presenting the story in the words of various writers, not because it seems to have any foundation in truth, but because it has not been without historical importance. Like the British Celts who long cherished a vague hope of the miraculous return of Arthur, the small remnant of Christian Goths may have believed that their king who did not die upon the field was making atonement for his crimes in some mysterious hiding-place, and would come forth purged from his sins, and favored by Heaven to lead them to victory against the ruthless invaders.[2] The Arabian chroniclers, even

[1] The matter is thus stated by Roderik of Toledo, who wrote in the beginning of the thirteenth century, "Quid de rege Roderico accederit ignorantur; tamen corona, vestes et insignia et calciamenta auro et lapidibus adornata, et equus qui Orelia dicebatur, in loco tremulo juxta fluvium sine corpore sunt inventa. Quid autem de corpore fuerit factum penitus ignoratur, nisi quod modernis temporibus apud Viseum civitatem Portugalliæ inscriptus tumulus invenitur, ' Hic jacet Rodericus ultimus Rex Gothorum.'"

In the "Coronica del Rey Alonso" (segunda parte), we find, "Despues á tiempo en la ciudad de Viseo en tierra de Portogal fué fallado un monumento en que estava escrito — 'Aqui yaze el Rey Rodrigo, el postrimero rey de Godos.'" These versions have all the same traditionary source given above, and the story has been simply repeated by later writers.

[2] The reappearance of Count Ilyan, Roderik, and the milk-white steed Orelia in the Asturias ; the sacrament administered by the hermit king to the penitent traitor, and the part played by Roderik in the battle at Covadonga, as related by Southey in his romantic

those who think he was killed by Tarik, mention the doubt; one of them with effective simplicity concluding the matter by saying: " But God only knows what became of him." [1] With this conclusion the reader will be ready to concur.

All that can be clearly known is that he disappeared, leaving but a doubtful memory and a harmless ghost to haunt the legendary realm. More modest than the young Duke of York or Don Sebastian or the French Dauphin, who have appeared in prosaic personality, the spirit of Roderik has been content with that poetic justice which prescribed death or oblivion as the only fitting end for him who, in one battle, had lost "the fame of the past, the hope of the future, and the dominion which had lasted for three hundred years, all destroyed by (what to the Spanish historian was) this ferocious and cruel race." [2]

It may well be considered that the fate of Roderik was a just retribution for his crimes, but it is curious to observe the conflicting judgments as to the immediate cause. The Arabian historian from whom Condé has drawn his account says, "Such are the misfortunes that may happen to monarchs, when they

poem, show what striking materials these legends offer to the fancy of the poet. It is not astonishing that so little of the true history can be clearly discerned. The historical student has just grounds to accuse the poets in this matter.

[1] Al Makkari, I. 274. "God is all-knowing," or "God only knows," is the convenient refuge of the Arabian writers whenever the subject is obscure or doubtful. The phrase and custom have passed into the Spanish language, and the only answer to *Quien sabe?* which really means "I do not know," is *Dios sabe.*

[2] Mariana, Historia de España, II. 393.

take a conspicuous place in the midst of the battle."[1] Gibbon, who had too readily adopted the severer verdict against Roderik, cites, with sanction, a senseless judgment of Ben Hazil of Granada,[2] "Such is the fate of those kings who withdraw themselves from the field of battle." On which of these grounds shall he be condemned? The reader is in condition to form his own judgment.

It is hardly necessary after these details to pause for a moment to consider their philosophy: it is so manifest. First, we find here the harmony between the apparently conflicting theories of liberty and necessity. It is one of the practical lessons of history that if action is free, results are certain and inexorable, and thus historic philosophy has been able to deduce general laws from the logic of human life, as invariable as those of exact science and organic nature. *The philosophy of the situation.*

The Goths in the fifth century had established an empire in southern Gaul and Spain. Their mastery was due to their race-vigor, cradled in the German forests, and the enthusiasm and impetuosity of their movements. Their dominion in Spain had lasted for three centuries. From Ataulphus to Roderik thirty-two kings of their race had held sway in the Peninsula. The period of their struggle to conquer that domain had been a period of primitive strength: as long as they were active they were powerful. But

[1] Historia de la Dominicion, I. ch xi.

[2] 'Ali Ibn 'Abdi-r-rahmán Ibn Hudheyl, who, in his " Sacred Expeditions " and other works, was by pre-eminence the *military* writer of the Arabs in Spain. Condé calls him Ben Huzeil, and Gibbon Ben Hazil. — *Hispania Vetus.*

when the day of action was over, when they became stationary, they became sluggish. Africa, to which, with their initial velocity, they might have gone, was already occupied by their predecessors, the Vandals; and thus the momentum was checked, which might, without due deliberation, have carried them across the strait. But Africa had no attractions for them compared with those of Spain, where Nature was lavish of her charms, and where the genial climate of their new abode contrasted delightfully with that of their earlier seats. The first delicious experience might have warned them of the consequences. The pristine vigor succumbed; they became enervated and the result speedily followed.

First despoiled of their French possessions, and then sheltered from their fiercer Frankish cousins by the Pyrenees, their feats of arms had degenerated into the suppression of an occasional rebellion, which gave opportunity rather for cruelty than for courage; or a feud of sections easily adjusted by compromise. They had been consolidated into a nation, but every element of consolidation was of the nature of an anodyne. In the place of warlike achievements of which they had lost all usage, they had little taste for mental culture : they had no scientists, and have left no literature. The only other alternative was luxurious living, and the civilization which is nourished by luxury alone is soon drowned in effeminacy. They had enslaved and imbruted, instead of elevating the Hispano-Romans whom they found in Spain. They forgot in their pride of place, what the historian is in danger of forgetting, that when the Romans and the Goths appeared in the Peninsula as the masters, they were only conquerors, representing dynasties of oppressive governors, while the great mass of the people were of those indigenous races, which, although trodden down by successive invasions, did not die under the rod, but actually throve, while their masters succumbed, and remain to this day the principal constituent in the population of Spain. Thus like some imposing edifice, the very massiveness of whose construction renders it unstable unless the foundation be deep and strong, the Gothic dominion being one of a conquest which had not won the hearts of the people, was not able to withstand the whirlwind which had come against it. Like the house in the parable, " it fell, and great was the fall of it."

Look at the other side. The Arabs and their African converts and allies, although not so strong in physical type, were an ardent and mobile *The prestige of the Moslems.* race, inured to hardships, constantly exercised in arms by their constant condition of war, keenly searching for perilous adventure, burning with desire not simply to conquer but to possess. Impetuous in battle, they did not content themselves with organized columns of attack and the shock of masses; in the words of their own historian, " They mixed in with the infidel," every one seeking his own exploit, without losing sight of the order of battle. In their progress through northern Africa they had instructed and assimilated the nations they had conquered; thus their numbers grew by harmonious accretion. Although no longer a distinct race, they were most of them of the same origin, and they were all the faithful children of Islám. Their first zeal grew warmer from day to day for a creed which had so wonderfully vindicated its claims, by carrying its champions eastward to India and westward to the extremity of Africa; which placed no bounds to its extension other than the limits of the known world, and which promised them as spoils of battle the treasures of every kingdom and country.

They had lost no momentum; their celerity increased with their conquests. And so when this furious whirlwind, gathering nations in its train, burst upon the effeminate and irresolute Goths, they fell, or fled before it, and were swept away, — swept in eddying circles into the defiles and valleys of the Asturian mountains, while the turbaned host, unimpeded, occupied their seats, partitioned their lands, and even rushed by to defy the defenders of Christian Europe on the fields of Touraine.

It is not astonishing that history is full of parallels, or rather of repetitions of itself. The defects

Parallel between the conquest of England and that of Spain. and faults of human nature are the same in all ages: the violations of law are similar, and like causes produce like results. The mind of the reader cannot fail to advert, as he reads the curious record of the Moslem conquest, to the series of events so strangely analogous which marks the conquest of England by the Normans in the eleventh century. As we pass through the great gallery of historical pictures, it seems almost as if the latter, with only changes of costume and names, were copied from the former, so close is the reproduction.

Like the Gothic monarchs of Spain, the Saxon

kings of England, once irresistible conquerors, had become stationary, sensual, vicious, and enervate. The people were better than their rulers, but could not fail to be influenced by their vices and rendered impotent by their factions and their oppression. As in Gothic Spain civil dissensions were constant, so in Saxon England there were hostile parties in the court, contests for the crown, and struggles for the great earldoms. Just across the English channel — like the Arab-Moors across the strait of Gibraltar — the Northmen sea-kings had wrested lands from the French, had established a vigorous independent state, and sought to enlarge it by conquest. They had lost nothing of their primitive vigor in the period of a hundred years between Rollo the Marcher and Duke William : the Norman was "the foremost man in Europe."

As the treason of Count Ilyan aided the invasion of the Moslems, so the coalition against Harold, of his brother Tostig and Harold Hardrada, shackled the Saxon strength. The fleet of William landed at Pevensey without opposition, and marched inland to find Harold at Senlac, just as Tarik, crossing the other "narrow sea," landed at Gibraltar, and marched inland to encounter Roderik in the plains of Sidonia.

The analogy continues to the very end. In the Spanish battle the day seemed at first to go against the Moslemah, but the personal valor and inspiration of Tarik turned the tide. So, in the English battle, around the standard of the Fighting Man the Norman army was on the verge of defeat, when William led the charge in person and won the victory. Roderik fell upon the Spanish field, or disappeared forever, and all Spain was at the mercy of the conqueror; so Harold perished at his post, and Saxon England, like Gothic Spain, was lost on the issue of a single battle.

In the details of these events, the reader will find still more curious resemblances, material and ethical, and in the events themselves, the moral lesson for individuals and nations sparkles on the surface of both records.[1]

[1] As there are vague rumors of Roderik's escape and hiding in a hermit's cell, there were not wanting stories that the wounded Harold had not died, but that, borne from the field of Senlac, he had been cured of his wound by a "Saracen woman," and passed the rest of his life in a convent, where "he died at a great age, having only in his last moments revealed to those around him that the lowly anchorite was no other than the native king of conquered England." — E. A. FREEMAN, *The Norman Conquest of England*, III. 344. He quotes from the "Vita Haroldi," given in "Les Chroniques Anglo-Normandes." This last doubtful story is not needed to find in these two events the most striking parallel in all history.

CHAPTER IV.

THE RAPID AND BRILLIANT PROGRESS OF TARIK.

AFTER despatching his report to Musa in Africa, Tarik passed his whole army in review, and then sent forward his detachments to receive or enforce the submission of the towns in the Comarca of Sidonia. He thus occupied without much resistance Xeres, Moron, and Carmona. Xeres submitted after a short siege; Moron and Carmona surren- Tarik occupies the adjacent towns. dered immediately; but the detachment under Zeyd Ibn Kassed which advanced to Eziya was met with a determined opposition. The inhabitants of the latter place, re-enforced by a remnant of Roderik's army, made a desperate defence, causing proportionally greater loss to the Moslems than any they were to sustain in their future encounters. It is said that by a lucky chance Tarik contrived to capture the governor, who had secretly left the city, and released him upon his promise to surrender the town, which he fulfilled.[1] Having thus occupied the immediate territory south of the Guadalquivir, it now became necessary to recruit and to reorganize his army, before placing that river-barrier between himself and the sea. No mention is made of his having occupied

[1] Al Makkari, I. 275.

Seville, nor, as a military precaution, does it seem to have been necessary or proper; it was on the right bank, and the detachments left at Carmona and Moron could watch it while he penetrated into the interior. To Ecija, his headquarters, crowds of Arabs and Berbers came flocking across the strait, with and without orders from Musa, and were gladly received without question into his diminished ranks. Leaving small garrisons in the conquered towns, he collected his detachments and reorganized his forces for an immediate advance. He would lose not a single moment in carrying the conquest to completion.

A few troops of the baser sort, intent only upon spoils, had seized treasures and re-embarked for Africa,[1] regardless of the conquest and the propagation of the Faith; but with these exceptions the ardor and obedience of the men were unabated, and their hopes were high.

It was in this condition of things that Tarik was stunned by the reception of a peremptory letter from Musa, severely reprimanding him for having made the attack without his orders,[2] and enjoining him to remain where he was, and not to move until he should join him with large re-enforcements. Musa supposed Tarik to be still upon the field of battle; the ground of his order Musa stated to be the danger of proceeding into an unknown

Musa orders him to remain where he is.

[1] Al Makkari tells of one band, every soul of which perished in their attempt to cross. They betook themselves to their Koráns and to prayer, but without effect. Above the storm they heard a retributive voice crying out, "O my God! drown them all." — I. 8.

[2] Al Makkari, I. 283.

territory of such extent and resources, with so inadequate a force.   Tarik was further reminded and
warned that the Commander of the Faithful had
enjoined the greatest prudence and constant care for
the safety of the Moslemah.

Thus far it may be allowed that there was no
obliquity of purpose in Musa's action.   His own
caution in preparing the expedition, and the explicit
mandate of the Khalif, are warrant for this view.   It
was a bold and most perilous adventure upon which
he had entered, and, as supreme commander, he had
not only the right, but the responsibility of its
conduct.

From his point of view across the strait, there was
an apparent rashness in what Tarik had dared and
accomplished, which might well call forth the fears
and the caution of the chief: but the after- Musa's
conduct of Musa leads us to observe a tives. mixed mo-
change in his sentiment; it shows that he was
soon actuated more by jealousy than by reasonable
prudence.[1]   Even when he ceased to fear for his
advance, he was angry that his zealous subordinate
had achieved so brilliant a success without his own
presence, and he was further unwilling that Tarik

[1] Condé, Dominacion de los Arabes, I. ch. xi.   Ibnu Hayyán,
and indeed all the Arabian writers agree in imputing this jealousy
to Musa.   It is curious to observe that, while Musa was envious of
Tarik, the Khalif Al-Walid was concerned about the ambitious
projects of Musa : his success was becoming too great for a subject.
The Khalif ordered the Kadi, after prayers in the mosque, to implore the Almighty that He would defeat Musa's plans.   Afterwards
on receiving assurance of Musa's loyalty he was pacified.   MS.
ascribed to Ibn Koteybah, Al Makkari, I. app. lxxii.

should go forward and add to his fame. It was for this reason that he directed the advance to be stayed until he could join his lieutenant with all his available force, and not only reap the laurels that remained, but, while thus achieving the further conquest, appropriate those already won, for Tarik was only carrying out *his* plan.

In furtherance of this purpose, he transmitted at once to the Khalif a glowing account of the crossing which *he* had ordered, and of the terrible battle which had been won under *his* direction by one of his sons. He sent the embalmed head of the Gothic knight, slain by Tarik at the battle in the plain of Medina Sidonia, as that of King Roderik; but he forgot to mention the actions and merits of Tarik, or of any of the commanders.[1] Such unimportant details were lost in the glory and grandeur of the victory. "O Commander of the Faithful!" he wrote, "these are not like conquests; they are more like the meeting of the nations on the last day of judgment."

But Tarik, up to this time as subordinate as he had been valiant, was a warrior of too fiery a temper to brook such restraint at such a moment. He received Musa's commands with astonishment, discussed them with impatience, and determined to disobey them. To make a show of proper caution and prudence, he assembled his chief officers in council, and laid the orders of Musa before them. Fully imbued with his spirit, they were of his opinion.

---

[1] La Fuente echoes the statements of the chronicles : "Calló el nombre de vencedor como si quisiera atribuirse á si mismo el merito de tan venturosa jornada." — *Historia de España,* III. 24.

The opportunity was too precious to be lost; "instant advance" was the unanimous cry. There was no insubordination, no strictures upon Musa's orders, no question as to his motives. It seemed clear that Musa's fears were due to his absence and his ignorance of the true condition of affairs. If he were there, they were sure he would give very different orders; and it was not only the prerogative, but the manifest duty of a wise commander to use his discretion in setting aside orders, where the good of the cause was at stake, and where the orders were based upon ignorance and imperfect knowledge.

Tarik ventures to disobey.

As might be expected, the most clamorous voice in the council for immediate advance was that of Ilyan. Either his vengeance was not yet fully appeased, or he feared, lest, if the Goths should have time to rally, the tables might be turned upon the Moslems, and, with a Gothic restoration, he, the traitor, would receive the retribution due to his crime.

He urged a vigorous advance, without a moment's delay. The destruction of the Spanish army, which had contained all their best warriors, — many of whom had fallen with the king — had struck terror into the Gothic heart. "Since thy enemies are panic-struck," Ilyan said, "and their armies dispersed, proceed to their capital, and destroy them before they have time to collect their forces again. Take expert guides from among my people, divide thy armies into bodies, and send them to different parts of the country, and, if thou wilt follow my advice, thou wilt thyself take a division of it, and march to Toledo, where their great men are by this time assembled to deliberate upon their affairs, and unite under a chief of their own choosing."[1]

The strong purpose of Tarik being thus further fortified by the concurrence of the council of war, and by the practical advice of Ilyan, he at once pro-

His generals ceeded to carry it out. In order further to
in council
concur. appal the enemy, he is said to have resorted to a disgusting stratagem. If we may believe the accounts, he ordered some of the dead bodies of the Spaniards to be cooked in large copper vessels used for preparing the food of the troops. This was done in the sight of the Christian prisoners. They were then cut into joints, as if to make a banquet for his men. When the horrible repast was ready, some of the captives were allowed to escape, that they might spread the report of this revolting cannibalism, and lead the Spaniards to believe that their assailants were brutes, and not men. The stratagem is quite credible: it would add horror to fear.[2]

---

[1] This address of Ilyan, with modifications, may be found in Condé, I. ch. xi. In Roderik of Toledo, III. ch. xxii., and in the exact words given above in Makkari, I. 277. The words of Condé are, "When they have once recovered themselves, it will be easy for them to gather new forces, as well as to reassemble and reanimate the now discouraged troops whom thou hast scattered. Hasten, therefore, to penetrate into the provinces, and occupy the chief cities without delay; for if thou canst make thyself master of them, but more especially of the capital, thou wilt then have nothing to fear." He assumes that the Goths could muster plenty of men. It was spirit that was wanting.

[2] Gayangos says, he has read the story in the history of Ibnu-l-Kuttuyah, a writer of the tenth century, and a descendant in the female line of Witiza. His name was Abu-Bekr-Mohammed. Ibnu-l-Kuttuyah means "the son of the Gothic woman," — AL MAKKARI,

Tarik now held a review of his whole force. He praised his troops for what they had already accomplished, and gave them instructions like those issued at first by Abu Bekr: they were to respect the rites and the customs of the inhabitants, not to molest the peaceable and unarmed; to attack only those who were with weapons in their hands, and to take no plunder except on the battle-field, or in the storming of cities. He divided his army into three detachments, besides the main body. The first he confided to Mugheyth Ar-Rumí, the cavalry commander who had led the advance after the landing. He was instructed to proceed at once with seven hundred horse direct to Cordova, the ancient and rich city on the right bank of the Guadalquivir.[2] He led the van of the invasion. The second division was commanded by Zeyd Ibn Kassed As-Sesekí, a valiant officer of sound judgment, enthusiastic for the faith of Islám, of established family, who had crossed with Tarik in the first reconnoissance, and had doubtless been distinguished in the great battle. He was instructed to proceed eastward to Malaga, and overrun its Comarca, and, after terrifying the inhabitants into submission, to rejoin Tarik on his northward march by way of Jaen. A subdivision of the force of Zeyd, constituting the third detachment, was to branch off to Granada (Gharnattah), the capital of the Comarca of Illiberis (Al-

I. 460. We know that the family of Witiza went over to Islám, and were duly honored by the Khalif. The authorship gives some show of truth to the story.

[1] Condé, Dominacion de los Arabes, I. ch. xi.
[2] The river is navigable as far as Cordova.

Birah), and demand its submission.[1] The main body, commanded by Tarik in person, marched more slowly northward by way of Cordova, upon Toledo, the Gothic capital, the seat of the remaining strength and coalescence of the Spanish Goths.

Let us follow, in this order, the fortunes of these several divisions, as with one purpose they started upon the work of conquest. Mugheyth Ar-Rumí, — the Roman or Greek, — the commander of the first, while a child, had been taken prisoner in an incursion made by the Moslemah into Rúm ; i. e., some parts of the excluded dominion of the Eastern Empire of Rome. He had been carefully educated with the sons of the Khalif in the faith of Islám ; and, when of age, had been liberated from his nominal servitude and promoted in the army. During the conflicts in Africa, he had displayed such valor and daring as preferred him to higher commands; and when the invasion was ordered he ranked next to Tarik among the Moslem generals, and was " celebrated by his prudence and deep acquaintance with all the stratagems of war."[2] " Trained to horsemanship and all manner of military exercises," he was the model and admiration of his soldiers.

The movement in three divisions.

---

[1] Condé, Dominacion de los Arabes, I. chs. x. and xi. ; Al Makkari, I. 530. I have adopted the opinion of Gayangos, — that Tarik, on his way from Ecija to Toledo, would not pass through Jaen, but that, as Jaen lay on the route between Granada and Toledo, it was occupied by Zeyd. Much on such points is left to conjecture, as there is considerable confusion in the statements of writers ; but a glance at the map often helps us to make conjecture probable.

[2] Al Makkari, II. 15.

He advanced with his seven hundred horse upon Cordova. Most of the inhabitants had fled with precipitation, but the town had been entered, and was now held, by a few fugitives from the field of Sidonia, the whole number, including invalids and old soldiers, being about four hundred.[1] As the river lay between him and the city, this impromptu garrison was not disposed to surrender without an effort at resistance. It was rather an impulse than a hope which prompted this determination. The people were in great fear. Many were ignorant and passive; the more intelligent had hoped that when the king was dethroned, and large spoils had been secured from the rich repositories of the principal cities taken, Tarik would be content and return to Africa. But this steady tramp northward showed them their error; it now began to be manifest that he meant complete conquest and permanent occupancy, and they were not in a condition to resist his purpose.

Mugheyth reached the river-bank opposite the city, and encamped in a forest of pines. By means of captives, whom he released and sent into the city, he then summoned the garrison to surrender. These were the alternatives he offered: All who yielded themselves should be subjected only to a moderate tribute; he would give a place in his ranks and a share of the spoils to all who would embrace Islám. But, if the town resisted, and compelled him to attack, he would not attempt to restrain the fury of his troops, but would put all the inhabitants

Mugheyth at Cordova.

---

[1] Condé, Dominacion de los Arabes, I. ch. xi.

to the sword. With his little advanced guard of seven
hundred horse, he could hardly have made good his
words; but it is probable that Tarik on his way to
Toledo with the main body, halted at Cordova for a
few days to give a show of large strength, and it is
certain that when he continued his march he left Mugheyth a sufficient re-enforcement to carry the place.[1]
However, the first impulse of the garrison grew into a
desperate determination to test the power of the Moslem assault, and they might hope, if overpowered,
that they might still escape and fly northward.

From a shepherd, whom he had captured, he learned
the weakness of the garrison and the condition of the
city. Forcing him to act as guide, Mugheyth, taking
advantage of a dark and stormy night, selected a
thousand horsemen, and mounting a man behind each,
en voltigeur, crossed the river by swimming. By the
time they had crossed and formed, the rain had turned
to hail,[2] which by its pattering drowned the trampling
of the horses' hoofs, and enabled them to follow the
guide unobserved to a breach or weak spot in the
wall through which an entrance might be effected. At

The strata-
gem for
obtaining
entrance.
the foot of this partial breach was a tree, by
means of which a nimble soldier, after some
hard climbing, was able to reach the opening.
He carried with him as a rope Mugheyth's turban,

---

[1] One account makes Tarik march from Ecija to Toledo, through
Jaen, which is very improbable, as it was out of his way, and Zeyd,
in marching northward from Malaga, would naturally pass through
Jaen. Alhobi says he went to Cordova, and remained there nine
days, after which, impatient of the delay, he left Mughyeth to pro-
secute the siege. This is the opinion of Gayangos.

[2] Al Makkari, I. 278.

which he had unrolled, and, by its use, in a short time a considerable number were on the top of the wall. The violence of the storm had caused the negligent sentries to leave their posts, and the assailants found no one to contest their entrance. Those who had mounted the breach, leaping down the parapet, entered the city and rushed to open the gates. Mugheyth entered with his whole force. All who resisted were cut down; and before day Cordova was in the hands of Moslemah. Most of the inhabitants fled to the mountains; the few who remained implored the clemency of the conqueror; who, in spite of his former threat, contented himself with punishing their vain resistance by imposing so heavy a tribute that it was called "the tribute of blood," and detaining as hostages a number of their principal men.

But the conquest of Cordova was not yet complete. In the western part of the city was the church of St. George, a strong and large edifice. In this the brave governor with his four hundred men shut himself up, and, with barricades, determined to hold out to the fatal extremity.[1] To this Mugheyth laid siege, expecting to starve them into submission, and especially by cutting off their supply of water. He occupied the palace of Roderik, and employed the remainder of his force in reducing and appalling the surrounding country, while he watched the church-citadel.

The obstinacy of this church-citadel touched his honor and his generalship. The great enigma after they had, in spite of this close siege, *The citadel holds out.*

---

[1] Condé, Dominacion de los Arabes, I. ch. xii. ; Al Makkari, L. 278.

held out for so many days was, how they were supplied
with water.   Provisions they might have collected to
last for some time, but they had no water in the
building.   By means of a Soudan slave of his, who,
after being captured by the Christians, had escaped,
Mugheyth learned that there was an underground communication from the church to a well-spring outside.[1]
By diligent search the spring was found; its waters
were cut off; and the garrison, thus reduced to its last
extremity, was again summoned to surrender.   The
commander refused.   The siege had now lasted for three
months, and Mugheyth, exasperated beyond control,
gave orders that fire should be applied to the church.
Most of the brave defenders were burned up, and the
spot long bore the name of " Kenísatu-l-harakí," —
the church of the burning.   Condé says they perished
to a man;[2] but there is a romantic story, which may
be true, that the governor, who had conducted the
vain defence with so much constancy, with very few
of his companions, contrived at the last moment to
escape; and that, Mugheyth pursued and captured him
with his own hand, and held him as a striking proof
of his prowess as a soldier, and his success as a general.   What gives color to this statement is, that we

---

[1] I omit the fanciful story told by Al Makkari of the astonishment of the Christians at the color of the negro, and their attempt
to wash him white.   It can hardly be believed that "they had
never seen a man of his color before." — AL MAKKARI, I. 279.

[2] I. ch. xi. This fact, if it be a fact, throws light upon the
phrase, "tribute of blood." But the words, "the last man of the
four hundred died fighting," may be reckoned a very slight exaggeration in a story which tells of a citadel devoted to the flames
after obstinate refusal to surrender.

find it related in the after history that Mugheyth considered so brave a man as a fit present to the Khalif, and a living testimony to his personal prowess, and intended, therefore, to send him to Damascus. But we shall see that at first Tarik, and afterwards Musa, contested his possession of so valuable a prisoner, and rather than give him up to the latter, his captor slew him with his own hand, and thus put an end to the controversy.

The final reduction of Cordova left Mugheyth free to employ his troops, in conjunction with those of Tarik, in such a manner as his chief should The final direct. It was now the end of August, 711. submission. He placed, as had been done elsewhere, the local authority in the hands of the Jews of the town, the only people he could trust, and fortified his control by taking hostages from among the principal men. He made the palace his head-quarters, thus inaugurating its future grandeur and power. Retaining around him a sufficient garrison, he then spread the remainder of his troops through the Comarca, awaiting the orders of Tarik. From this time Cordova remained in Moorish hands, continually growing in power and splendor, until, with the Moorish dominion, it began to decline in the early years of the eleventh century.

Meanwhile, the second division under Zeyd Ibn Kassed, had proceeded, without delay, to conquer Malaga and overrun its Comarca. He met with little resistance, and was soon able to send or take a strong detachment to Gharnatta, the *Medina* or Granada capital of the district of Al-Birah. Here opens its gates. they found no opposition; and here, also, they found a large number of Jews, well advised of their coming and their purpose, ready to welcome the invaders, and glad to find in the Berber ranks many of their brethren, who, although converted to Islám, retained the instincts of consanguineous blood.[1] Into their hands, Zeyd gave the government of Gharnattah, assured of their energetic co-operation in the Moslem schemes. The number of Jews in that town and the power reposed in their hands, caused the place to be called, in all its earlier history, *Gharnatta-al-Yahood*, Granada of the Jews.

The work allotted to Zeyd occupied him four months, from early in August until the end of November, at which time he proceeded direct, by way of Jaen, along what is now the high-road, to join that contingent of Tarik's army which had been left at Toledo, according to his former instructions.[2]

We now reach the bolder and more important

---

[1] " There is every reason to believe," says Gayangos, " that their conversion was neither so sudden nor so sincere as to blot out immediately all recollection of their former habits and religious ceremonies, and that they felt great sympathy for their former brethren." — GAYANGOS, AL MAKKARI, I. 531, note 18.

[2] There are conflicting and confusing accounts of the Moslem occupancy in the south-east of the Peninsula. Ibn-l-Khattib, and other historians, ascribe the conquest of Malaga and Granada to the sons of Musa. But Musa and his sons did not arrive in Spain until March or April, 712, a year after the landing of Tarik ; and simple prudence on the part of Tarik demanded these incursions to guard his flank and rear as he advanced. I regard, however, the occupancy by the lieutenants of Tarik as slight and nominal : hostages were taken, and councils of Jews established. When Musa came with a large increase of force, he doubtless placed adequate forces in these towns ; and where, as is probable, some of them had revolted, he reconquered them. This view harmonizes the apparent conflict.

movement of the main body under Tarik.   Although
the exact line of his march is not known, it is most
probable that he had accompanied Mugheyth to Cordova, or joined him there, and, impatient of the protracted siege, had pushed on, after a few days' delay,
to Toledo.   If he marched in a straight line, he would
encounter the high ranges of the Sierra Morena and
the mountains of Toledo.   There is every reason to
believe that he found the easiest route along the valley of the Guadalquivir, through the pass in the
former range near St. Elena, and then, by way of Man-
zanares and Alcazar, to the capital.[1]

The city of Toledo, the ancient Toletum, had been
chosen, for good reasons, by the Gothic monarchs as
the chief seat of their court.[2]   It was cen-   The advance
upon Tole-
tral, salubrious, and naturally strong.   Like   do.
Rome, it stood on seven hills.   In the time of Livy,
although a small place, its strength was notable : he
calls it *urbs parva sed loco munita.*   Julius Cæsar had
made it a fortress, and the Emperor Augustus had
constituted it a seat of chief magistracy.

It could not fail to attract the attention of the
Goths as a stronghold.   Standing on its rocky heights,
it commands the surrounding country in every direc-

---

[1] This is the railroad route to-day.   It kept him in easy communication with Zeyd.   He may, however, have struck northward
through Estremadura to the valley of the Tagus, and followed that
valley through Talavera to Toledo.   There is every reason to believe
that Musa afterwards took the latter route ; but he had no need of
the precautions which it behooved Tarik to take.

[2] Strictly speaking, the Goths had no single capital : they had
many chief cities, where, at different times, the court was assembled.

tion, and presents an impassable fosse in the narrow but rapid flow of the Tagus (Tajo, the rent or fissure in the mountain), which increases in velocity as its channel is contracted, and which more than half surrounds the place in a circular arc.

The walls built by the Romans were adopted and rebuilt by the Goths. In the year 554, Athanagild had made it the seat of his court,[1] and though, in the next reign, Liuva did not reside there, his brother and successor, Leovigild, removed thither from Seville, and gave it new and additional prestige. The good Wamba had increased its strength, by erecting around it a second wall, enclosing the extensive suburbs which had sprung up with the increase of population, in the construction of which he used the stones from the ancient Roman amphitheatre.[2] He had, moreover, extended its influence by enacting a law that all persons, ecclesiastic and secular, should repair under arms to any point, within one hundred miles of the capital, at which there should be menace of danger to the country.[3] From the time of Wamba, it was in reality, if not in name, the Gothic capital of Spain. It was here that Roderik, upon his removal from Cordova, had established his luxurious court in a splendid palace, built by Wamba, and enlarged and embellished by Witiza. Standing on a rocky eminence overlooking the river, it was at once a palace

[1] " . . . fijando ya definitivamente en Toledo la corte, que antes no se había establecido aun en determinado pueblo de España." — LA FUENTE, *Historia de España*, II. 339.

[2] Ib. 437.

[3] This law may be found in the " Fuero Juzgo." — *Lib.* IX. tit. ii. l. 9. The penalty for disobedience was banishment.

and a citadel, called by the Moslems Al-Cazar, a name
which implies the glory and power of the Cæsars,[1]
and vindicates the extension and influence of the
Roman empire.

Such was the Toledo which Roderik had lost, and
such the prize which offered its large attractions to
the eager band of Tarik.   Here, if anywhere, after the
fatal battle, the stand of the Christians should have
been made ; and there had been time for such a stand
to be organized, had they not lost both head and
heart.   The advance of Tarik had been necessarily
slow and cautious ; but the case seemed hopeless.
The fame of his victories had struck terror into all
hearts.   The chief nobles and warriors upon whom
the people might have relied in their extremity had
fallen on the field.   Those who had fled into Toledo
only thought of further flight.   And every day
brought new testimony to the valor and number of
the Moslems, and the ubiquity of their light and fleet
horsemen.   There were in the city no munitions of
war : the paralyzed inhabitants had collected no store
of provisions.   There could be no hope of succor from
without, and while, in the last resort, the Christians

---

[1] The name Al-Cazar, or Al-Kasr, — the Cæsar, — seems to have
been applied by the Arab-Moors to any large and splendid establishment, — a bazaar, a caravansary, as well as a palace.   The site of the
Gothic palace is not now known.   The Al-Cazar, which the Moors built,
was not on the site of Wamba's palace, but, probably, near it.   That
also disappeared, and its site is now occupied by a hospital and two
convents, — of the Concepcion and Santa Fé.   The ruined Al-Cazar
now shown is a comparatively modern structure ; the eastern portion
having been built by Alfonzo VI., and the rest by Philip II.   It was
fired by the French in 1810.   It was of this that the Irish traveller
was made to say that they *built ruins* so beautifully in Spain.

were going in sad procession to invoke the assistance
of St. Leocadia in their great exigency,[1] the vanguard of Tarik appeared before the town. If the
Christians were in despair, the Jews, who had dissembled their joy, scarcely waited for his summons to
counsel an immediate surrender.[2]

The inhabitants only hesitated that they might obtain the most favorable terms, and then opened their
gates. The terms of Tarik were dictated by
his characteristic clemency and generosity.

It makes terms and surrenders.

He required all persons to give up their horses and
arms, in order to destroy the chances of revolt. All
who chose to leave the place might do so unmolested ;
but they must leave all their goods behind. To those
who remained and paid tribute the free exercise of
their religion was allowed. No more churches
should be built without permission ; and there should
be no religious processions,[3] which might, on the one
hand, be a cover for plots and revolts, and, on the
other, perhaps might, in the opinion of the wary commander, by their æsthetic attractions, unsettle the
Moslems in their faith. With a judicious policy,
Tarik conceded that the people should be governed
by their own municipal laws, with the proviso that
they " were not permitted to punish or otherwise impede any who should desire to become Moslemah." [4]
Thus originated the Murzarabic religious services
which were so long conspicuous in Toledo. These

[1] Al Makkari, I. 533, note 25. Gayangos cites Lucas Tudensis.

[2] Gayangos further quotes, " that the Jews opened the gates of
the city to the Moslems." — *Ib.*

[3] Condé, Dominacion de los Arabes, I. ch. xii.   [4] Ib.

terms being accepted, Tarik marched into the city
with a portion of his army on Palm-Sunday of the
year 712, and took up his temporary quarters in the
palace of Wamba ; " [1] but it was only for a brief period
of rest and reorganization.

The easy rendition of Toledo exhibits the entire
loss of hope throughout Christian Spain ; for eight
months had elapsed since the battle near Guadalete,
time enough to have united in and around Toledo a
larger army than that of Roderik, had there been any
spirit for the fight,. or any hope for the future.

The conquerors found the palace of Toledo more
than their fondest fancy had anticipated. The treasures were manifold and curious. There The treas-
                                         ures of
were large urns and vases of gold and sil- Toledo.
ver, filled with jewels, — pearls, emeralds, rubies, and
topazes ; splendidly embroidered tunics, rich robes
and costly hangings, emblazoned armor, rare swords,
and other weapons of every description.

There were found many valuable manuscripts, and,
among twenty-one of special value, containing the
Torah, the Gospels, and the Psalms, there was also
one copy of the " Book of Abraham," and one of the
" Book of Moses." [2] Other books in the collection

---

[1] 11th Jumada, A. H. 93. The history of conquests shows us
that in most cases it is greatly to the advantage of the conquerors
to leave the existing municipal laws and officers in force. The conquered people are thus best governed, while their magistrates are
under general military supervision, and responsible for malfeasance.

[2] Al Makkari, I. app. xlviii. I find no explanation of the two
volumes last mentioned. They were probably portions of the Pentateuch ; that they or their heroes were considered of peculiar value
and sanctity may be inferred from the ejaculation of the chronicler,
"The salutation of the Lord be upon them."

described the talismans and the manner of construct-
ing them. Others still were studies in natural history and materia medica. But of more historic value
than all these, were a number of golden diadems
which had been worn by their monarchs. They were
richly adorned with precious stones; upon each was
the name of the former wearer, with dates of his
accession and decease and the number of his children.
The number of these crowns is variously stated at
from twenty-four to twenty-seven; but as Leovigild is
the first Gothic ruler who is known to have assumed
a crown, it is safer to place the number at seventeen. The question is of little importance, but the
fact of finding these votive crowns is significant of
the nature of the Gothic dominion [1] and the national
value of the diadems.

Notwithstanding the variety and value of the treasures found in the city, it cannot be doubted that
much of the wealth of Toledo had been carried away
by the fugitives northward, much of which the sol-

---

[1] There were thirty-two kings from Ataulpho to Roderik, both
inclusive. Condé says there were twenty-four crowns. Al Makkari
states the number at twenty-seven. The former number is given by
Isidor de Béja. Al Kortobi says, twenty-seven. Among the an-
tique treasures in the Armeria of Madrid, the visitor may now see a
votive crown, probably one of those mentioned, with precious stones
and a cross suspended within, with the inscription : "Svinthilano
Rex offeret. Suintilla was the twenty-third Gothic monarch, and
reigned from 621 to 631." It was the custom among these people
that, after the death of every king who had reigned in the country,
his crown should be deposited in that chamber ; each diadem had
the name of its wearer written thereon, with his age and the number
of years he had borne the same. — CONDE, *Dominacion de los Arabes,*
I. ch. xii.

diers of Tarik might, by the ardor and rapidity of their ceaseless advance, hope to overtake and seize in the pursuit.

Such had been the desertion of the capital that but a small garrison was necessary to hold it. As elsewhere, the general control of the town was left to a council of the Jews; and the tireless chieftain then marched in the track of the flying inhabitants, dispersing or capturing wandering bands, and guarding his rear as he advanced by leaving detachments at strong strategic points.

Of the exact route of Tarik we have confused accounts; and it is not now possible to trace it with accuracy.[1] But much of the apparent con- Tarik marches on, fusion is removed when we remember that leaving a garrison at in such an advance — at once reconnois- Toledo. sance and conquest — Tarik sent detachments in many directions, only requiring that they should not proceed too far from the main force, but, in case of necessity, should easily rally upon it. From Toledo he advanced, by way of Alcalá de Henares, to Guadalajara (Wada-l-hyjráh, the river of stones), between the mountain ranges of Toledo and Castile. From the latter point, we may believe that he sent a detachment of cavalry to Medina Celí, on the high road to Saragossa. There, or elsewhere, in a city afterwards called Medinatu-l-mayidah,[2] he is said to have found that wonderful work of art known as the

---

[1] See Condé, Dominacion de los Arabes, I. ch. xiii.

[2] Most writers suppose the table was found at Medina-Celí. All attempts to fix a place named Medinatu-l-Mayidah have failed, because the name means the city of the table, and only implies the city

table of Solomon. It is most probable that it was
carried away by Bishop Sindaredo, the metropolitan
of Toledo, in his flight [1]), and overtaken by Tarik or
by one of his detachments. It had been brought to
light by Roderik, when he forced the enchanted cave
or palace. Such, at least, is the story.

And what was this wonderful table? The writer, who
essays to describe it, is embarrassed with his riches;
The wonder- its splendors have so dazzled the chroniclers
ful table of
Solomon. that each gives a different account of it,
striving to excel others in exaggerating its beauty
and value. Its origin partakes of the marvellous,
and it had the power of a talisman. The more credulous believed that, when the Romans captured Al-
Kodr (Jerusalem), it was among the rich spoils of the
temple: it was the handiwork of the Djinn for king
Suleyman, the wise son of David, and had been kept
among the holy treasures since his day. It fell to
the lot of a king of Spain, and was thus brought into
the Peninsula. This is, perhaps, a rapid way of
reaching the end of another story, which is, that it
was brought from Jerusalem to Rome; that it fell
into the hands of the Goths when they sacked the
Eternal City, and had come with a portion of that

where the table was found. That the table was found between Guadalajara and Medina-Celí there is no reasonable doubt. For a similar use of the phrase, we may find the *pass of Almeyda* in the vicinity
of Cordova, which name probably came from the shape of the mountain at that point. — AL MAKKARI, III. 396, note 11.

[1] Ib. 533, note 24. For the force of the opinion that the table
was found near Alcalá de Henares (Al-Kal'ahen-Nahu, the castle of
the river), see the note of Gayangos. — AL MAKKARI, I. 534.

race into Spain.[1] These legends go to show that it was held in great reverence: it plays an important part in the veritable history.

The judgment of Ibnu-Hayyán is more sensible. Great lords, and even kings, when dying, often made bequests to the church; and with money and jewels thus obtained, rich furniture was prepared for the altar, — gospel stands, altar-cloths, and credence tables. They vied with each other in such munificence; and chief among the ornaments of the altar, in the church of Toledo, was the table of Solomon, — at once a splendid ornament and a worker of miracles. According to some chroniclers, it was of pure gold, richly set with precious stones. Others describe it as of "pure gold and silver mixed, the color yellow and white; it was ornamented with three rows of inestimable jewels, — one of large pearls, another of rubies, and a third of emerald."[2] Others still say that its top was a single emerald. Most writers concur in giving it three hundred and sixty-five feet, each of a single emerald.

The truth, which may be deduced from these wild descriptions, seems to be that it was a very rich and beautiful work of art, probably of clear, green stone,

[1] La Fuente, in speaking of the sack of Rome by the Vandals, under Genseric from Africa, says: "Entre los tesoros, se encontraron los adornos robados, por los Romanos, al templo de Jerusalem. Estraña mezcla de ruinas! todo va pasando á poder de los barbaros!" — *Historia de España*, II. 316.

[2] Al Makkari, I. app. xxxix. To increase our confusion, although the matter is of slight importance, the author of the MS. ascribed to Ibn-Koteybah writes, "They say that this inestimable jewel was a dining-table without any feet to stand upon."

encircled with gold and silver, richly inlaid with costly woods, and adorned with jewels. Such specimens of ancient workmanship are still found in Spain; but, apart from its intrinsic value, was a superstitious charm, which induced the reverence of priests and people alike, and gave color to the traditions of its miraculous origin. It was made by no human hands; it was among the secret treasures which the rashness of Roderik had disclosed when he visited the enchanted cavern; it was the holiest of the holy treasures in the splendid church of the Gothic capital; and the climax of disaster was capped when it fell into the hands of the ruthless infidel. That lost, all seemed to be lost; for the Lord had abandoned his very altar to the barbarian.

Its capture was, therefore, a great joy to Tarik, and he designed it as a worthy present to the Khalif; his next thought was that, when Musa should see it, he would take it away and present it to Al-Walid as his own, with the claim that he had captured it.

To guard his own claim and right, Tarik had recourse to a simple stratagem. Of its numerous feet, Tarik's stratagem to guard his claim as its finder. four were larger than the rest. One of these Tarik removed and concealed, that he might confront Musa with the proof of his exploit, should the day of inquiry arrive. As we shall see, he did not miscalculate the selfishness and cunning of Musa.

Of the further march of Tarik northward, and then westward, before he considered his preliminary task fairly accomplished, only the general direction can be known. From Alcala, or Guadalajara, he crossed the Guadarrama range at an elevated pass, which was afterwards called *Bab-Tarik*, — the gate of Tarik — corrupted into *Buitrago*, a narrow mountain portal between New and Old Castile. Thence Roderik of Toledo takes him beyond the Asturian range to Gijon, on the Green Sea, — the Bay of Biscay. The only limit to his rapid career was *ubi defuit orbis*.

This account has no foundation in truth. A rapidly moving detachment, probably commanded by himself, reconnoitred the country to the north-west, while the main body remained on the Guadalajara, and a strong guard kept the pass. The limit of their scout was Astorga, for the mountains beyond became tangled and difficult, and the greater part of the Christian fugitives were there collected, waiting for a chief who could give them cohesion, and ready, at least, to dispute the further advance of the Moslems. The detachment returned by the pass of Tarik to the Guadalajara, and the whole force took up the line of march for Toledo, to await the unfolding of Musa's plan for the full conquest and permanent occupation of the Peninsula. It was not without sad misgivings that Tarik turned his face southward. Musa had entered Spain in person, and was marching upon Toledo.

For a whole year he had been nursing his jealous wrath, and Tarik might expect not only a severe scrutiny of his exploits, but also a rigorous reckoning for his disobedience. He could only hope that the brilliancy of the former would atone for the apparent insubordination of the latter. With these feelings he re-entered Toledo.

Musa enters Spain and makes conquests.

CHAPTER V.

MUSA CROSSES THE STRAIT AND CAPTURES MANY CITIES.

WE must now go back to see what Musa had been doing across the strait, thence to accompany him into Spain, and to recount his conquests, until we find him once more face to face with his too successful lieutenant.

After despatching orders to Tarik that he should remain in his encampment in Andalusia, on the ground where his great victory had been achieved, Musa lost no time in arranging his affairs in Africa, that he might cross the strait in person at the head of a large force.   Owing to the unquiet condition of The cause of the Berbers, this was a task requiring time Musa's delay in crossing. and caution.   He must first consolidate his power in Mauritania; he must also keep open his communication with Egypt and Syria, threatened by the intervening tribes; he must select troops which were to guard his lines, and those which were to constitute the new army of invasion. These things he proceeded to do with his characteristic judgment and caution.

To accomplish the first two of these purposes, he appointed his eldest son, Abdullah, his deputy in Africa, and fixed his headquarters at Kairwan.   The immediate command of Al Magreb he gave to his second son, Abdu-l-'aziz, who was to make his residence at Tangiers. Filial affection would secure him against ambition and treason.

He then recruited and organized the army with which he was to cross, most of which was cavalry; while large companies of infantry were left in the towns of Northern Africa, to restrain the turbulence of the natives. Several months were occupied in these important preliminaries, and it was not until March or April, 712, that he effected the crossing, a year after the landing of Tarik at Gibraltar. He sailed from Ceuta, disembarked his army, consisting of eighteen thousand men, — probably ten thousand cavalry and eight thousand foot, — at Algeciras, — "avoiding the mountain where Tarik had landed," — and proceeded by slow marches towards the Guadalquivir. His staff was distinguished and efficient. With him were two of his sons, — Abdu-l-'a'la and Meruan, both worthy of their father.[1] Twenty-five *tabis*[2] were in his suite, and numerous noblemen and gentlemen, many of them of the tribe of the Koreish,[3] who had been attracted from Damascus and from Yemen by the stirring news of the successful invasion, and had come to win worldly wealth and renown, or the bliss of Paradise, in the van of the all-conquering Moslemah.

It was not until his arrival in Spain that he could

[1] Al Makkari says three, including Abdu-l-'aziz; but this is evidently a mistake, growing out of his being so near, at Tangiers.

[2] The *ashab* were companions of the prophet; the *tabis*, followers of these companions. The former had seen Mohammed; the latter had conversed with men who had seen him.

[3] Condé, Dominacion de los Arabes, I. ch. xi.

fully know the extent of Tarik's exploits. Conflicting and exaggerated reports and brief statements had reached him from time to time; but the interior of the Peninsula was an unknown land, and it was only when he saw the splendid and extended geographical features of Andalusia, that the truth burst upon him. His general had accomplished the grand task which he had fondly reserved for himself. The conquest of Spain was a fixed historic fact, and the fame of the conqueror could neither be usurped nor silenced. What remained to be done was to occupy places already won, or to extend the Moslem area where there was no grand battle to be offered or accepted, and but little hope of a gallant resistance. The very

His anger increases as he finds what Tarik has accomplished.
facts of the case made it difficult to determine what course to pursue. He might, indeed, take immediate vengeance upon Tarik; but to depose him from command, or to kill him, was to publish to the world the very exploit for which he was punished, and the true motive of the deed.

It gave him no consolation that he could have done what Tarik had done; he had committed a great mistake, and he was doubly angry with his lieutenant because he was angry with himself. He had meant to send him on a strong reconnoissance, which he had reason to think would meet with a partial check; for he knew the prospect that Roderik would assemble a large army to oppose the invasion. Here was his error; he should have been with the invading force, if only to be sure of the situation. Instead of that, he had confided a considerable army to a popular and dashing leader; as the emergency became more pressing, he increased it by a strong re-enforcement, and had thus put into Tarik's hands a large discretion ; to do what ? Manifestly to do the very best and bravest things that such an army could do ; to march without delay in order to find the enemy and to crush him, and, if such marvellous success might be, to conquer Spain, and destroy the Gothic supremacy with a single blow. That was at least the possibility that he should have arranged for. Tarik had done his work too well for Musa's peace of mind, and the world saw that if he had been disobedient, it was to what now proved to be the ill-judged, ruinous, and jealous orders of his chief.

But Musa was as crafty as he was energetic and skilful. Tarik was his subordinate, and he could assume his exploits and merits as his own. He sent no second message, but observed an ominous silence. On his arrival in Spain, he was told by some of Ilyan's men that they could take him by a shorter road than Tarik's to the conquest of richer and more populous cities than those he had conquered: he employed his troops in securing the towns which Tarik had surprised into submission, and in over-running such portions of the rich territory as were off Tarik's line of march.[1] Thus he reoccupied Medina Sidonia and Xeres. For a month he overran the Comarca of Seville, and at last entered the city, and placed there a strong garrison with a military

[1] Condé, Dominacion de los Arabes, I. ch. xiii. Al Makkari, I. 284, who says that at Algeciras Musa " is said to have expressed his wish not to follow the same route which Tarik had taken."

hospital for the sick Moslemah : many of the inhabitants of Seville fled to Beja. Thence he marched to
Carmona, at that time the strongest city in Andalusia.
Either Tarik had not entered it in his northward
march, or, after a nominal submission, it had revolted,
when he had passed by. Aided by a stratagem of
Ilyan, a body of whose men entered the city in the
disguise of pedlers,[1] Musa stormed it and placed in
it a strong garrison. The flight of the inhabitants
from this new and powerful incursion was into the
territory west of the Guadiana, and this determined
the line of Musa's march. He passed from Andalusia into western Spain and Portugal. By this time
he had drawn largely upon his contingent of infantry
to form garrisons for the conquered towns, but he
had received re-enforcements amounting to about eight
thousand cavalry ; with these, he had about eighteen
thousand mounted men, and he marched rapidly to
the conquest of Sibla, Assonoba, Myrtiles, Beza, and
other towns, meeting and easily dispersing wandering
bands of soldiers and outcasts, and encountering nowhere organized resistance, until he reached Merida.
Here he found a far more determined spirit than any
which had been manifested since the taking of Cordova by Mugheyth Ar Rúmi : he hailed this with
the pleasure of an ambitious soldier.

This city had been built by Augustus, and made

---

[1] Al Makkari, I. 284 and 542, note 2. Al Makkari says, Ilyan's
men entered as friends fleeing from the Moslems. Ar-Hazi says,
"in disguise of pedlers." Ilyan seems to have acted as guide to
Musa, as he had to Tarik. As soon as these disguised pedlers were
admitted, they opened one of the gates to Musa.

a Roman *municipium* under the name of *Emerita Augusta*, which coupled the imperial title with the claims of the veterans (*emeriti*) who were stationed, and afterwards settled there.[1] It contained many well-preserved relics of Roman grandeur, among which were the arch of Trajan, afterwards called the arch of Santiago; the ruined temples of Mars and Diana; the circus of Maximus; the aqueduct four miles in length, and the splendid bridge, twenty-five hundred feet long, and supported on eighty-one arches. It has been called the Rome of Spain. Its walls were six leagues in extent, ninety feet wide, and sixty feet high. It had three thousand and seven hundred towers, and eighty-four gates. It was worthy of defence and of capture.

He besieges Merida, — Emerita Augusta.

The Goths had admired its beauties, and utilized its strength. The repair of the walls and of the bridge was one of the principal acts of Ervigio; and when Musa encamped before it he might well be struck, not only with admiration for its proportions and powers, but also with astonishment that, with such strongholds, the Goths could so easily abandon their dominion. A Moorish historian says, with simple admiration, "No man living can fully count the wonders of Merida;" and Musa is said to have declared, when he saw it, that all men had united their knowledge and power in enriching it, and that

---

[1] The town was built A.D. 23, and the first inhabitants were the Emeriti of the fifth and tenth legions. I mention this to show that, notwithstanding the lapse of centuries, the Meridans came of good martial stock, and showed it in their defence.

he would be proportionally happy who should succeed
in making himself master of it.[1]

To the Moslem summons the inhabitants returned
a haughty negative; and it was manifest that the
defence would be fiercely conducted, for the Meridans
of that day were not only the descendants of the
emeriti, but the fathers of men of whom it was afterwards said by the Mohammedan kings that they were
of a seditious character, " constantly revolting against
their governors or against the Sultans of Cordova."[2]
The riches and the strength of the city which caused
Musa to covet its possession, impelled them to make
a vigorous stand in its defence.

No sooner had the herald who brought the summons of Musa left the gates than a large detachment
of the Meridans issued forth at his heels, and attacked
the Moslem army. They were easily repelled and
driven back within their walls, but they left Musa
in no doubt as to the mettle of the people he was
preparing to besiege. Again and again they attacked
his camp; and he was so impressed by the strength
of the defences, and the vigor of these sorties, that
he spent some time in fortifying his own encampment,
and in driving back the sallying parties. It was
manifest that he would need more men than he had.
He therefore sent messengers to his son Abdullah,
who was in command at Kairwan, to gather all
the troops he could spare, and to his son Abdu-l'-

---

[1] Condé, Dominacion de los Arabes, I. ch. xiii.
[2] Al Makkari, I. 61. The city was destroyed in the reign of
Abdu-r-rahmán, and never afterwards (that is in Arabian times)
restored.

'aziz at Tangiers to bring them in person to his assistance.

The valor and constancy of the Meridans cast a faint gleam upon the dark picture of Gothic degeneracy and Spanish helplessness. They had already caused considerable loss to the besiegers, and had sustained little them-selves. The walls were intact : the Arab-Moors had made no progress, when Musa had recourse to a stratagem, which gave a turn to the condition of affairs, and infused a new spirit in his men, while it dampened the ardor of the besieged. He had found in the rocky bluff of the river bank, at a short distance from the town, a cave or hollow, large enough to contain a considerable force. Here, under cover of the night he concealed a number of his troops, both horse and foot. At early dawn he made an open, but feigned attack, upon the walls with a small force. The gallant Meridans sallied out with great determination to repel it. Musa's men, having received instructions, fell back before them, and at last fled as if struck with panic. The deceived Christians followed impetuously, the Moslemah still flying, until they had passed the place of ambush. Then the concealed troops rushed out from their hiding-place with shrill *lelies;* the retreating Moslemah halted, faced about, and showed a bold front. The Christian force suddenly found itself hemmed in between two hostile bands. The stratagem was complete, but the sallying party fought with sublime valor to cut their way back, and made the besiegers pay dearly for their success. The combat lasted for hours, and the carnage was great, but when the fight ended very few of the sallying force had escaped to the city.[1]

In order to form a practical breach, Musa had now recourse to a series of coverings for working parties of his troops which he sent out to undermine one of the towers. The form of these coverings was like a Roman *musculus*, under shelter of which they could push across the open space up to the very wall, and work with pick and spade, protected from the darts and arrows of the garrison.[2]

The party had already made some progress in removing the stones, but in an interval of rest had laid down their implements, and were collected under the shelters, when a band of the besieged made a sudden sortie, surprised them in their unexpecting state, and put them all to the sword. They lay like slaughtered sheep under their covering, and Musa called the tower *Borju-sh-Shohodá,* — "the tower of the martyrs." Both parties were now more disposed to treat.

Gallant as the Meridans had been, they had reached the term of their resistance. Their provisions had begun to fail, and there were no means of obtaining more. Obeying his father's instructions, Abdu-l-'aziz had crossed the strait with seven thousand African horse and a large force of cross-bow men, and had marched without delay to recruit the besieging force. The last hopes of the be-

But they are forced to capitulate.

---

[1] Condé, Dominacion de los Arabes, I. ch. xiii. Cardonne, Histoire de l'Afrique, etc., I. 87 *et supra.*

[2] Al Makkari, I. 284, 542, note 45. Also, Condé, Dominacion de los Arabes, I. ch. xiii.

sieged were now dashed. Their forces had been daily
diminishing by losses in the field and by secret desertion; famine began to gnaw; and the lower classes
—always more readily influenced by selfish considerations — were clamorous for surrender.

With great sorrow the brave defenders found
themselves compelled to submit, and to this end they
held a parley with Musa, and asked him to grant a
safe conduct for a deputation which they would send
him to negotiate the conditions of surrender.

This obtained, the deputies were conducted to the
splendid pavilion of the Arabian commander, where
they found, in the person of Musa, an old man with
a long white beard and streaming white hair. He
received them with unexpected kindness, and praised
the valor and constancy displayed in their defence
of the city. They had been contumacious in refusing
to surrender, but he would grant to their bravery
terms more favorable than their contumacy should
lead them to expect.[1] This first interview was not, however, conclusive. The deputation returned to the city
to describe their interview and to state the condition
of affairs, after promising to come back the next day
to continue the negotiations for surrender. Now, the
next day was the Mohammedan feast of the Passover
(*Ayd-al-Fitr*), also called *Aydu-s-sa-ghir*, the lesser
festivity, which marks the expiration of the *Lenten*
fast of Ramadhan. On that day, the humiliation of
the fast, the sackcloth and ashes being thrown off, the
faithful were accustomed to put on their costliest
garments, to dress their hair, and to anoint their

---

[1] Al Makkari I. 285 ; Condé, I. ch. xiii.

beards.[1] The July morning dawned brightly in contrast with the sad procession which, filing through the gate, reappeared at the tent of Musa, ready to discuss with him the preliminaries for delivering Merida into his hands. Great was their astonishment when they saw before them, not the venerable chief of yesterday, but a man in the prime of life, his beard of a dark-red color,[2] and his robes resplendent with gold and jewels. Such a transformation seemed miraculous in the eyes of the trembling Christians; it inspired so great a fear, that Musa might have imposed, and they would have humbly accepted, more rigorous terms; but he was true to his word, and the deputies returned to declare to the people, that their enemies were "a nation of prophets who could change their appearance at pleasure, and transform themselves into any shape they like." "We have seen," they said, "their king, who was an old man, become a young one; so our advice is this, that we should go to him and grant him his demands, for people like them we cannot resist."[3] The stratagem, simple as it was, was entirely successful.

[1] Al Makkari, I. 543, note 48. Lent ended with Ramadhan. Ayd-al-Fitr was on the first day of Shawwal.

[2] Al Makkari, I. 285. He speaks of their reappearance on a third day, when, to their great amazement, his hair and beard were no longer red, but entirely black.

[3] The story is also told by Condé (ch. xiii.). It would seem that the practice of dyeing the hair and beard with a decoction of henna, common among the Orientals, was unknown to the inhabitants of Spain. They dyed their horses' manes and tails, and striped their camels. The women blackened their eyelids and reddened their finger-tips. One of the poems of the ante-Mohammedan *Moallakat* (Amriolkais) speaks of a heroine as dispensing gifts "with small, delicate fingers, sweetly glowing at their tips like the white and crimson worm of Dabla, or dentifrices made of esel-wood."

Thus the gates of Merida were opened to the Moslemah, and Musa had found in the vigor of the resistance and the difficulty of the capture some slight solace for the mortification he had experienced at Tarik's success. He could make out his case; Spain was not yet fully conquered, and, while adopting Tarik's work as his own, he could exalt the siege and reduction of Merida by skilful despatches higher than any exploit of his disobedient subordinate.

The following were the terms he made with Merida: The troops and inhabitants should give up all their horses and arms. He claimed the property of all who had fled from the city, or who had fallen during the siege; the public treasures, the riches and ornaments of the churches. One half of the churches he would convert into mosques. All persons who wished to depart might do so, but he would retain as hostages a number of the members of illustrious Gothic families, who had congregated there after the battle in the plains of Sidonia. The most notable among the captives was Queen Exilona, the widow of Roderik, the singular vicissitudes of whose fortune were not yet ended. A captive Moorish maiden, she had become the queen of a Gothic monarch; a captive Gothic queen, she is yet to play a part both brilliant and tragic in this history.

It was on these conditions that Musa entered the grief-stricken city with a small contingent of his army, on the Mohammedan Easter, July 10, 712.[1]

The vigor and duration of the resistance had greatly

[1] As to its being upon this festival there is no doubt; but, as the festival is constantly changing its season on account of the lunar

enhanced the triumph of Musa; and it was with a cheerful spirit that he was preparing to march northward,
when he received the unwelcome tidings that a serious
insurrection had broken out in his rear at Seville.
This city, with its Roman citadels and double walls,
had been, during the Gothic domination, one of the
four principal cities of Spain,[1] and the residence of
the Court during one season of the year.   Near it
were the ruins of Italica;[2] and one of its suburbs —
Triana — was so named from the Emperor Trajan.
Strong in their position and proud of their history,
and hoping, moreover, that fortune, which so sternly
resisted the infidel at Merida, might still desert him,
the populace of Seville, disregarding the more judicious counsels of the higher class, rose upon the
Moslem garrison, which was small, and killed eighty
of them.   Similar outbreaks occurred at Niebla and
Beja; and re-enforcements from these insurgent towns
marched to aid the rising at Seville.   The small remainder of the Moslem garrison barely escaped, and,
travelling with haste, and through by-roads, brought

year, the exact date is difficult to decide.   Al Makkari says, "Al-
Fitr of the year 94 (A. H.), "beginning Oct. 6, 712."   Condé gives
it as "the beginning of the moon Shawal of the year 93."   I have
adopted the most probable date.

[1] The others were, Cordova, Carmona, and Toledo.   Strictly
speaking, there was, during most of the Gothic dominion, no single
capital, although Toledo, in the latter reigns became the favorite
residence of the monarchs.

[2] It is worth inquiry, whether the *Italian* band, mentioned in
the book of the Acts, of which Cornelius was a centurion, would not
be more properly rendered, from the Greek, *Italican* "band," or
troops recruited at and near Italica.   The Greek may be translated
in both ways, — ἐκ σπείρης τῆς καλουμένης Ἰταλικῆς.

to Musa at Merida the painful news of trouble in his rear.

He at once despatched his son Abdu-l-'aziz, with a large force of cavalry to punish the insurgents, and to secure his line of communication thus The revolt of suddenly imperilled. The distance between Seville, and its fate. Merida and Seville, a little more than a hundred miles, was rapidly traversed, and, in less than three days, the now frightened inhabitants saw the Moslem column approaching. Resistance to such a force seemed impossible, and the better class of citizens determined to go out and explain to the Arab chief the true circumstances. The excited rabble closed the gates and refused to let them leave. There, an unorganized and feeble resistance was offered, and soon overpowered. Abdu-l-'aziz stormed the gates, and, in ignorance of the extenuating circumstances, began an indiscriminate slaughter of guilty and innocent alike. The rebellion was at once crushed, and Seville, thus terribly schooled, never again ventured to revolt.[1] After strengthening its garrison, Abdu-l-'aziz, following the instructions of his father, moved westward to punish Niebla, and the other insurgent towns, and then returned to take up his military headquarters at Seville.[2] Southern Spain was placed under his control, and his further brilliant movements will be presently considered. It may be supposed

[1] Al Makkari, I. 285.

[2] A distinction should be observed between his military occupation of Seville at this time, and his adoption of it as his capital afterwards, as Amir of Spain, when his father had been recalled to Damascus.

that he still commanded the strait, and ruled by deputy at Tangiers.

Meanwhile Musa, having arranged his affairs at Merida, moved slowly at the end of Shawwal towards

Musa pro- Toledo. He received the submission of the
ceeds slowly
to Toledo. towns on his route, which offered no resistance, and dealt clemently with them. Although his exact route is nowhere stated, a glance at the map will indicate that he marched directly northward through the broad opening in the Sierra de Toledo, now occupied by Santa Cruz de la Sierrá, and passing through what is now Trujillo, struck the valley of the Tagus at the nearest point, and followed it towards Toledo.

As soon as Tarik heard of his approach he marched down the river to meet him, and found the vanguard of his army near Talavera de la Reyna.[1] It was now the middle of August, 712. Sixteen months had passed since these veterans had met face to face: a period of wonderful events; but one in which the sentiments of Musa, instead of being softened against his skilful lieutenant, had increased in bitterness. We may easily imagine the feelings of these distinguished rivals — for such they had become — as they approached each other.

Musa was still smarting under the insult of Tarik's disobedience: his envy had projected revenge; and he was determined to punish with great severity the subordinate who had disregarded his orders, and

---

[1] There are two other Talaveras— la Vieja, on the left bank of the river, ten leagues lower down ; and la Real, which is near Badajos. The position of la Reyna renders it certain that it is the Hedina Talbera referred to by historians.

robbed him of his renown. Tarik, hardly doubtful of his reception, was neither arrogant nor contrite; neither vaunting his exploits, nor acknowledging any violation of duty. He was ready to stand forth to vindicate himself, and all men who should afterwards be similarly situated in history, and to establish a claim for that discretion which should always be the prerogative of an officer of large and separate command.

CHAPTER VI.

MUSA'S TREATMENT OF TARIK.

TARIK and his escort had now reached the van of Musa's advancing army, and it was not long *Musa and Tarik face to face.* before the rival chieftains stood face to face. The former dismounted, and, with reverential salutation, stood at the stirrup of the latter; but, instead of returning his greeting, the angry Musa struck him with his riding wand,[1] and put the sharp question : "Why didst thou disobey my orders?" "To serve Islám; and because we all believed that, hadst thou known the condition of affairs, thou wouldst have ordered us to do just what we did," was the temperate reply. We have here enunciated a principle of discretionary power, of which history presents many remarkable illustrations. Doubtless the discretion in such cases has been generally measured by the results;[2] but surely in no case has a brilliant success more fully vindicated the claim, if success be allowed as a vindication.

---

[1] Al Makkari, I. 286 and 543, note 56.

[2] Admiral Byng was shot for not relieving Minorca in 1756. Nelson was rewarded for capturing the Danish fleet in 1801, in direct disobedience of Sir Hyde Parker's signal to draw out of the action. Steinmetz was relieved from his command and sent home for presuming to bring on the battle of Gravelotte in 1870, although it issued in a victory. The question is always a special one, and each case must be adjudged by history on its own merits.

Tarik reasserted his allegiance to Musa, and ac-
acknowledged his former indebtedness, and then,
mounting his horse, rode as a subordinate in the train
to the gate of Toledo.   As soon as they arrived at the
palace, Musa demanded a strict account of the spoils.
Most of the treasures were in and around the palace,
and they were all, without reservation, delivered up to
him.   Their great number and value might well have
propitiated his wrath and satisfied his cupidity ; but,
after surveying them in silence, he demanded the Table of Solomon, of which he had heard such marvellous accounts, and which, as Tarik had foreseen, he
designed to make a most acceptable present to the
Khalif, in evidence of his success.   It has already
been said, that Tarik, fearing that Musa would rob
him, not only of the table, but also of the fame of
having captured it, had taken the precaution to remove and secrete one of the four principal feet, which
were of emerald.   Musa examined it with curious
admiration, and, at once observing the loss, asked
where the other foot was.   Tarik replied that it was
just in that condition when he found it.   The unsuspecting Musa ordered its place to be supplied with
one of gold, little thinking that the discrepancy was
to tell against him at a future day, when he and his
rival should stand on equal terms before the Commander of the Faithful at Damascus.

Then, thanking all the other generals and officers
for the zeal and valor they had displayed   *Musa's an-
in his service, Musa again turned fiercely gry conduct
Tarik's atti-
upon their leader, and rated him for his   tude.*
disobedience.   The brave delinquent, though en-

tirely subordinate, was by no means servile. He
replied in words of exculpation and remonstrance, and
even ventured a hint of menace. " My only desire,
O Wali," he replied, " was to serve Allah and the
successor of the Prophet. My conscience absolves
me; and I hope that our sovereign, to whose justice
and protection I shall appeal, will do the same." [1]
He seemed to stand alone to suffer the extremity of
Musa's displeasure. Who would dare to espouse his
cause ?

In the midst of the silent and abashed assemblage
only one brave man, himself not without laudable
ambition, was found ready to say a word in behalf of
the humiliated chief, — that was Mugheyth Ar-
rúmi.[2] He knew well the merits of the case, the brilliant bravery of Tarik, and the envious ambition of
Musa. He declared that the whole army knew and
admired the valor and ability of Tarik, and that they
thought him worthy, not of punishment, but of the
highest honors. But Musa would hearken only to
the inner promptings of envy and anger. The course
he adopted was as impolitic as it was unjust, for it
fomented a division already existing between the
Berbers and the Arabians. The former were in enormous preponderance, and were, in an especial sense,
Tarik's men, and they already resented the arrogant
claims of the Arabians of pure blood, most of whom
were partisans of Musa.

Tarik was deposed from command and placed in

[1] Condé, Dominacion de los Arabes, I. ch. xiv.
[2] Ib. He knew, moreover, that on the suspension of Tarik, he
would succeed to his command.

strict arrest.[1] His post was given to Mugheyth, and
Musa wrote to the Khalif an *ex parte* report,
setting forth, in the strongest light, his dis- Tarik placed in arrest.
obedience and insubordination, and veiling the merit
of his exploits as much as possible. The head of
Tarik was in great peril, but Musa prudently awaited
the mandate of the Khalif before proceeding to that
extremity, feeling sure that his course would be sustained.

The Commander of the Faithful was not in ignorance, however, of the true state of affairs long before
the last report. Former despatches had given him
partial information : couriers and travellers had arrived from the seat of war, some of whom had, in all
probability, borne news from Tarik himself, if not to
the Khalif, at least to his friends at court ; and thus,
anticipating the purpose of Musa, he had already
written to deprecate his rigor, and to order that Tarik
should be retained in his command. It was manifest
to the sovereign, in striking the balance of merit, that
if Tarik had disobeyed the letter of instructions, he
had advanced in the true spirit of Mohammedan conquest, and, in surpassing his instructions, had greatly
extended the empire of the Faith. It was further
evident to him that the Moslem interests in Spain
were becoming imperilled by the contentions of his
generals.

It was to guard against this latter evil, at least,
that the Khalif sent an order to Musa to retain Tarik

---

[1] Condé says, " He cast the general into prison." — *Dominacion
de los Arabes*, I. ch. xiv. ; and, also, " He thought of nothing but
the accomplishment of the ruin and death of Tarik Ibn Zeyad."

in his command, or to restore him if he had been deposed, alleging as a reason, that " he must not render

The Khalif restores Tarik to command. useless one of the best swords of Islám ;"[1]
for, where Islám was concerned, there could
be no respect of persons.

This was a severe blow to the pride and to the
prestige of Musa ; but it does not seem for a moment
to have entered into his thought to resist the power
of the Khalif ; his allegiance did not waver.   He disguised his humiliation; set Tarik at liberty — making a show of cordiality — and invited him to his
table.[2]   After this, he restored him to the command,
to the great joy of the army ; the Africans regarding
him as their leader and representative, and the loyal
Arabians bowing with content to the mandate of the
Khalif.

While these important events were transpiring at
Toledo, Abdu-l-'aziz, who had been appointed to the
command in southern Spain, with his headquarters at
Seville, after subduing and pacifying the Comarca,
determined to conduct a distant expedition into Murcia.   This garden-land of southern Spain, hot but
extremely fertile, had not been entered by the lieutenants of Tarik.[3]   It was called the land of Tadmir,
from its government by the same Theodomir, who had
resisted the advance of Tarik, immediately after his
landing, and had taken refuge, with a handful of

---

[1] Condé, Dominacion de los Arabes, I. ch. xiv.

[2] Ibid.

[3] Al Makkari ascribes its conquest to them, but adds that the
account has been called in question. — I. 281, 282.   I have preferred
the narrative of Condé.

troops, in his own territory, after the disastrous battle in which he had borne a conspicuous part.[1]

Abdu-l-'aziz marched to bring him to submission ; attracted as much by the reported beauty and fertility of the country as by the desire to subdue its lord, who was one of the most renowned of the Gothic warriors. The extent of this territory cannot be exactly stated. It included most of southeastern Spain.

As soon as Theodomir heard of the purpose of the Arabian chief, he went forth with the relics of his force, and not daring to meet the formi- *Theodomir resists Abdu-l-'aziz.* dable Arabian cavalry in the open field, he availed himself dexterously of the mountain defiles and gorges, and thus rendered his approach difficult and dangerous. Sometimes he made a dash at the outlying parties of the Moslems, in the plains, but constantly refused the battle which the Arab commander was anxious to bring on, and thus trained his inadequate forces to deal with a numerous and advancing enemy. Once, however, he was overtaken at Lorca, at the foot of a mountain which descends into the little valley of the Cornera River. The Moslemah were here victorious : the shattered troops of Theodomir were entirely defeated, after a very sanguinary struggle, and put to flight by the fierce Moorish cavalry ; and passing in hot haste through Medina-Murcia, they did not stop until they reached Orihuela, a fortified town of great strength, where, with sufficient numbers, they might have long defied the

---

[1] In speaking of his resistance to Tarik's landing, Al Makkari tells us, " He afterwards gave his name to a province of Andalusia, called Beléd Tudmír, the land of Theodomir." — I. 268.

assaults of their enemies. Close on the steps of their
hasty march, they heard the rapid and unrelenting
tramp of the Moslem horse; and they were hardly
within the walls, when they found themselves beset
by the ardent pursuers.

By this time, however, their losses in battle, and in
the scattering of flight, had been so great, that Theodomir felt powerless to stand a siege.   To
gain the best terms, he had recourse to
a stratagem, which was entirely successful.
He had not troops sufficient to man the walls and
present a bold front, and this Abdu-l-'aziz might well
conjecture.   In order to deceive the enemy, he required all the women in the town to dress like men,
and to tie their long hair under their chins to look
like beards.   He then placed them with casques on
their heads and lances in their hands, on the walls
and in the towers, and thus surprised the Arab chief
with the sight of a warlike array far more numerous
than he had anticipated.   They expected an easy conquest; but it promised now to be a difficult and
bloody task against such numbers.   The *élan* of the
Moslemah was tempered by the caution necessary in
attacking so well-defended a citadel.

While this caution was working its result in a
careful preparation for the siege, the Arabian commander saw a single Gothic chieftain issuing from the
principal gate, and making signals for a parley.   A
safe conduct was granted him, and he was brought to
the tent of the Moslem general.[1]   He came, he said,

Theodomir's
stratagem at
Orihuela to
gain good
terms.

---

[1] Condé, Dominacion de los Arabes, I. xi.; Al Makkari, I. 281.

with power from Theodomir to negotiate a treaty. He
spoke with boldness and assurance. He demanded
peace and security for the province and its inhabitants; and he said his lord would only surrender on
such conditions as a generous enemy should grant,
and a valiant and still capable people would be jus-
tified in receiving. Abdu-l-'aziz was both generous
and wise, and the terms agreed upon were such as
Theodomir, there could be no doubt, would be glad to
accept. It only remained to present them to that
chief; but the Gothic cavalier said that was unnecessary, as he had full power to conclude the matter and
sign the treaty. The terms of the capitulation were
at once drawn up and signed by the Moslem general,
and when the Goth took the pen in hand, his signa-
ture informed the astonished conqueror that it was
Theodomir himself with whom he had been treating.
Equally pleased with the cleverness and the confidence of the Christian commander, Abdu-l-'aziz
entertained him with honorable distinction, and sent
him back in safety to the city.

The movements of this force under Abdu-l-'aziz,
which have been so briefly narrated, occupied the
entire winter, and the guerilla warfare of Theodomir
constantly checked the advance of Moslemah; so that
this convention was not made until April, 713.

The exact words of this treaty have been preserved
to us in the Bibliotheca Arabico-Hispana Escurialen-
sis of Casiri. It was drawn up in Latin and The lan-
in Arabic, and I present it in full, because guage of the
treaty.
it displays, in the liberal and honorable dealing of the
Arab-Moors, a glimpse of the spirit which animated

the earlier Mohammedan conquerors, and which was
indeed the normal animus or principle of their progress.   It brings us nearer, too, to the persons of the
contracting parties than any other event or stipulation of the period.   The imagination, which is constantly on the wing among these vague scenes, here
rests and recruits for new labors.   The diaphanous
veil, which so often confuses the historic outline,
is here for a moment drawn aside, and the compact of Orihuela, and to some extent the whole seat
of war, stand out in a clear gleam of sunlight![1]   It
runs thus: —

"In the name of God, clement and merciful: condition of Abdu-l-'aziz, son of Musa, son of Nosseyr,
to Theodomir, son of the Goths [Tadmir Ibn Gob-
dos]: Peace is ordained, and this shall be for him a
stipulation and a pact of God and of his Prophet; to
wit: That war will not be waged against him or his
people; that he shall not be dispossessed of, or removed

[1] The collection of Casiri was made between 1760 and 1770, and
contains a catalogue of eighteen hundred and fifty Arabic manuscripts in the library of the Escurial.   A fire which broke out
there, in 1671, had done the irreparable injury of destroying three
quarters of the whole collection.   The work of Casiri, which opened
to the world so many of the remaining ones, is therefore invaluable,
notwithstanding the errors and defects which have been pointed out
by Condé in his preface.   The text of this treaty is clear.   Its authenticity has been questioned; but, after some examination, rests upon
the opinion of Gayangos, that "there is no reason to doubt its
authenticity."   Its text settles the question as to which of the
Arabian generals was the conqueror of Theodomir.   Some say Musa
himself; this may be explained, as the work was done under his
instruction; others say his son, Abdu-l-'ala.   The Arabian historian settles these questions with the pious ejaculation, "But God
only knows which of these is the true account!"

from, his kingdom ; that the Faithful shall not slay, nor subjugate, nor separate from the Christians their wives or their children, nor do them violence in what pertains to their law [religion] ; that their temples shall not be burned ; — with no further obligation on their part than those herein stipulated. It is understood that Theodomir will exercise his authority peacefully in the seven following cities, — Orihuela, Valencia, Alicante, Mula, Biscaret, Aspis, and Lorca ; that he will take nothing belonging to us, and will neither aid nor give asylum to our enemies, nor will conceal their projects from us ; that he and his nobles will pay a dinar or gold-piece per head yearly ; also four measures of wheat, four of barley, four of must, four of vinegar, four of honey, and four of oil. Vassals and people liable to tax will pay the half. Agreed to on the fourth of the moon Regeb, in the ninety-fourth year of the Híjra (April, 713). The present writing is signed by Otman Ibn Abi Abdah, Habib Ibn Abi Obeida, Idris Ibn Maicera, and Abu-l-Kasim el Moseli."

The conditions are certainly remarkable for liberality. The supplies demanded by the treaty were less exacting, when we remember that the country was exceedingly fertile, that the delicious valley between Murcia and Orihuela is the garden of Spain, where the growth of vegetable food needs little culture, and where even the rain seems scarcely needed to make the fruits and grains plentiful and secure.[1]

---

[1] O'Shea, in his hand-book, quotes a proverb to this effect, "Llueva ó no llueva, trigo en Orihuela." — "Rain or no rain, in Orihuela grain."

At dawn of the day following the signing of the treaty, the gates of Orihuela were thrown open, and a select force of the Moslems entered to take formal possession. Abdu-l-'aziz was still mystified when he beheld the slenderness of the garrison. "What hast thou done," he asked, "with the troops that manned the walls and towers of thy city?"[1] In answer, Theodomir confessed his stratagem, and received from the Moslem commander new praises for his ready and useful wit. His mortification was overborne by his admiration. The treaty was honorably adhered to; for three days the conqueror remained at Orihuela, not as an enemy, but as a guest. There were banquets and fêtes. The opposing warriors met in friendly communion. Not the slightest injury was inflicted upon the town or the people; and the Moslemah left the province, to add to their conquests the other unoccupied cities of southern Spain. The pleasant circumstances attending this campaign relieved the province of Murcia and its seven cities from the presence of the enemy, except small garrisons; and, combined with its distance from the chief seat of war, secured it for a long period from the evil which attended the conquest in other portions of the Peninsula.[2]

---

[1] Condé, Dominacion de los Arabes, I. ch. xv. p. 323.

[2] When the family of Musa fell, and the head of the unfortunate Abdu-l-'aziz was sent to the Khalif Suleyman, Theodomir sent an embassy to him, to beg that he would respect the stipulations of this treaty; and the Khalif ordered that they should be observed. Among the many temporary truces and perfidious violations of treaty, it stands alone; but certainly some of this immunity is due to the fact that the interest of the Mohammedans led them in other directions. Murcia was somewhat out of the field of war.

It has been said that a detachment of Tarik's army, under the command of Zeyd Ibn Kassed, had received the submission of Granada and Malaga. Abdu-l-'aziz, after his departure from Orihuela, passed through the Comar- cas of the Sierra de Segura, retraced his steps in a general direction, and proceeded to confirm these conquests and to place competent garrisons in the more populous towns. Especially did he strengthen the two cities mentioned. Thus he descended to Baeza, occupied Guadix and Jaen, marched to Granada, and, receiving its submission, strengthened anew the Jewish government. Thence he proceeded to Antiquera, and then, marching southward, proceeded to Malaga, which he saw to be of great value as a seaport. He nowhere met with resistance; but, after this tour of armed inspection, he returned to Seville, having confided the power in the conquered towns chiefly to Arabs and Jews. *(margin: Granada and Malaga strengthened by the Moslems.)*

Meanwhile Tarik, as soon as he was reinstated in his command, lost not a moment in vindicating his claims to the compliments of the Khalif, — "one of the best swords of Islám." He had shown himself to be the very best. He stripped his troops to the lightest marching order. The infantry were without baggage; they had nothing but their arms, through which they were to live upon the enemy. The cavalry equipment was reduced to feed-bags, horse-cloths, and copper kettles. Rations for immediate use were carried upon mules, the *arrieros*, or drivers, of which were chosen from the number of those least capable of bearing arms. For future need, *(margin: Tarik's energy when reinstated in command.)*

his troops would live upon the country. Thus he was ready to lead a compact, light, mobile mass to the untried but eagerly-desired fields of northern adventure; and, with the eyes of the Khalif and the world upon him, he would essay to eclipse his former valiant deeds.

Again were repeated the earlier prohibitions against violence and robbery towards peaceful persons. On a victorious field of battle, unlimited plunder was allowed, and cities taken by storm might be sacked; but in each case special permission must be obtained from the leaders. The penalty for violating these instructions was death: it was rigorously enforced, and thus the justice of Tarik gave vigor to his clemency.[1]

Neither chronicle nor tradition has preserved for us the exact route of his force. While it moved forward, we may still believe that numerous divisions were detached, east and west, to reconnoitre and to hold important points. For obvious reasons, there was a division of territory between Musa and Tarik; but both armies marched within communicating distance, in order to concentrate if either should be imperilled by numbers, or if any stronghold, taking advantage of this division of the army, should make an unusually stubborn resistance.[2]

---

[1] Condé, Dominacion de los Arabes, I. ch. xv.

[2] Al Makkari says, "Musa then gave Tarik orders to march before him with his division, Musa himself following with the main body of the troops. Taking the route of Ath-thagheru-l-a'li (Aragon) they subdued Saragossa and its districts, and continued to penetrate far into the country, *Tarik preceding* him, and not passing a place without reducing it, and getting possession of its wealth. . . . Musa followed the track of Tarik, achieving the conquests begun by him,

In pursuance of his orders, Tarik moved eastward from Toledo along the sources of the Tagus, sent a detachment to Cuenca, and then crossing the jumbled mountains of Molina, he advanced along the tributary valleys of the Ebro, with a portion of his forces at least, as far as Tortosa, a strong place on the left bank of the Ebro and near the coast, twenty miles from its mouth. His objective point was Saragossa, a city of great strength and importance. In the Roman times it had been built by Augustus Cæsar, on the site of the ancient Subduba, and it bore his name, *Cæsarea Augusta*. It commands the passage of the Ebro, lying on both banks; and under the Goths it had asserted its strategic value, and was considered the most important city of northeastern Spain. There several important roads meet; and the fortress at their junction watches the passes of the Pyrenees, controls the river, and thus guards the country south or defies it, according to political circumstances. For these reasons, Tarik was not without expectations that the Christians would rally at Saragossa, and make a vigorous effort to stop the victorious career of the Arab-Moors. That city once taken, there was nothing to keep the Moslem army from seizing the mountain passes and threatening

and confirming to the inhabitants the conditions agreed upon by his lieutenant." — I. 288. This mode of procedure would hardly be in accordance with the selfish and ambitious plans of Musa, and, in discarding it and adopting the account of Condé, I have the sanction of Gayangos (Ib. I. 544, note 1), who says, in speaking of Condé's statement, "This is more probable : a man of Musa's ambition could not well consent to follow the track of his lieutenant, and enter cities already plundered by him."

Christendom on Gaulish soil; and this was, from the first, among the fond fancies of Musa.

The judgment of Tarik was not at fault. He summoned the city; and, as it refused to surrender, he was obliged to lay siege to it. The ardor of the besiegers was maintained by the report that it was full of treasures, and their hopes strengthened by the knowledge that the besieged were in want of provisions.[1]

While Tarik had been thus moving eastward, Musa had no less rapidly crossed the mountains, probably by the road at present passing through Madrid, and had occupied Salamanca; thence he struck the valley of the Duero at Zamara. Crossing the river, he sent a strong expeditionary force northward to Astorga, and the confines of the mountain retreat to which the flying Goths had betaken themselves. He found no resistance at any point. Whether he then contemplated an attack upon their Asturian fortresses is not known, but just at this time he received intelligence that his lieutenant Tarik had met with very obstinate resistance at Saragossa, and he determined to re-enforce him without delay, and to share at once the fame and the spoils of so important a conquest. To this end he recalled his troops to the Duero, and, following its valley, reached the mountain chain, which, at a short dis-

---

[1] Condé, Dominacion de los Arabes, I. ch. xvi. The strategic importance of Saragossa was displayed in the Peninsular war, when, according to Napier, "an army in position there could operate on either bank of the Ebro, intercept the communication between the eastern and western Pyrenees, and block three out of the four great routes to Madrid." — *Peninsular War,* I. 48.

tance, separates its source from the little river Jalon, which empties into the basin of the Ebro, a short distance above Saragossa. His presence was hardly necessary to the result, but contributed to hasten it.

Saragossa was in no condition to withstand an ssault. The siege laid by Tarik was already in successful prosecution. The garrison could The siege of expect no succor, and their slender stock Saragossa by Musa and of provisions was beginning to fail. They Tarik. might still, however, have held out for some time, but the arrival of Musa's large co-operating force caused their hearts to sink, and they sent proposals for surrender, on the terms usually granted. Musa was old and avaricious; he had learned that many of the towns of eastern Spain, regarding Saragossa as a safe and strong depository, had sent thither their treasures so that the spoils would be very large and rich. Straitened by want of supplies, they were now entirely in his power; and so, less generous than Tarik would have been, he imposed unusually rigorous terms, demanding what was called from its alternative of the sword, "the Tribute of Blood."[1] The besieged had no choice. They could no longer resist or hold out. They were compelled to accept the hard conditions, to meet which they were obliged to appropriate the treasures and ornaments of the churches, and utterly to impoverish the wealthy citizens. So

[1] Condé, Dominacion de los Arabes, I. ch. xvi. Condé further says that from this time Tarik no longer communicated his undertakings and their results to Musa, but wrote directly to the Khalif, not unfrequently censuring the covetousness of the Wali, whose avarice had become insatiable.

rigorous were the terms that the capture amounted to pillage without a sack; and the lion's portion fell to Musa, who did not share the spoils with his men.

In the capture of Saragossa a great point had been gained, the true barrier between Spain and France had been surmounted; resistance in all eastern Spain was at an end. Musa took a large number of hostages of the noblest families, and left in the city a competent garrison under Hanak Ibn Abdullah As-senani, a noble Arabian of the tribe of the Koreish, who at once began to build a splendid mosque, which was famous in the after history of Saragossa. Thus Saragossa became the stronghold and capital of eastern Spain, and later a centre of rebellion against the Khalif of Cordova.

Once more the armies separated. Musa's forces without a struggle occupied the country between the Ebro and the Pyrenees; he had no difficulty in reducing the region, but promptly received the submission of Huesca and Lerida, Barcelona and Gerona, in that tangled and picturesque country now known as Catalonia, the northeastern corner of Spain.[1]

Meanwhile Tarik had descended the river Ebro to Tortosa on the left bank, and skirting the coast southward, had occupied Murviedro,[2] Valencia, Xativa,

---

[1] " Cateluña (Gotha Iunia) constitutes the northeastern corner of the Peninsula; in form triangular, with the Mediterranean Sea for its base, it is bounded on the north by the Pyrenees, west by Aragon, and south by Valencia. . . . This barrier between France and Spain is intersected by tangled and picturesque tracts, known to the smuggler." — FORD's *Hand-Book*, I. 39.

[2] Murviedro is the *Muri veteres* of the Romans, but is corrupted from the Spanish translation *Muros viejos*.

and Denia.   In that direction he was limited by the
frontier of the little realm of Tadmir, which had been
securely established by the treaty of Orihuela.   The
contrast between the conduct of Tarik and that of
Musa is very striking; while the latter exacted heavy
tribute, and took everything he could for himself,
the former was everywhere clement to the conquered,
and generous to his own troops, and always reserved
a fifth of all the spoils for the Commander of the
Faithful; this was a strong element of popularity,
and, united to his dashing valor, made him the idol
of his men.

The accounts of Musa's farther progress are variously presented by different authors, and apparently
contradictory.   Some of the incautious and romantic
chroniclers confound the movements and actions of
Musa and Tarik; and others, hearing that he made
incursions into the land of Afranj, have invented
details of his march by way of Perpignan to Narbonne
and Caracasonne, and even to Avignon and Lyons.

I think there is no evidence whatever that he
passed the Pyrenees; the movements of his immediate successors have been accredited to Did Musa
him, and this part of the story is, as La pass the Pyrenees?
Fuente says of another account, of an entirely Oriental
cast.[1]   The Arabian writers would naturally exag-
gerate the conquests of their hero, but the Christian
writers of that day make no mention of his incursion
into France, and have an explanation of the matter
in the fact, that, at the time of the conquest, the name

---

[1] "Es de un genero enteramente oriental." — *Historia de España,*
III. 38.

of Franks (Afranj) was loosely given not only to the inhabitants of Gaul, but to the people in the south-eastern Pyrenees; and that Cataluña bore for centuries afterwards the appellation of Ardhu-l-faranj, the land of the Franks.[1] Thus it was that the mistake passed into history that Musa had invaded Gaul.

If such was his intention it was now arrested by an order from the Khalif. He had reached the term of his arduous and distinguished labors. Every step in the remainder of his career was to trouble, misrepresentation, family disaster, loss of fortune, to end in neglect, poverty, and death; but as yet, the prospect was not so clouded but that he might still hope for honor, reward, and a prosperous old age.

[1] On this subject see the note of Gayangos, Al Makkari, I. 544, note 4. He draws his conclusion in these words : " It is therefore probable, not to say certain, that the authors who assert, like the present, that Musa invaded the French territory had no other foundation for their statement than the name of Ardhu-l-farang, generally given to Catalonia." In their furious incursions southward, even while the safe boundary of their kingdom was the Loire, the Franks had several times passed the Pyrenees, and ravaged parts of Catalonia.

BOOK IV.

THE ADVERSE FORTUNES OF THE MOSLEM CONQUERORS.

———•———

CHAPTER I.

MUSA AND TARIK ORDERED TO DAMASCUS.

CONNECTED with the supposition that Musa had passed into southern Gaul, there is a tradition, doubtfully quoted by Al Makkari,[1] that, on his way into Gaul, Musa found some ancient ruins in a great desert, and among them a colossal monument, on which, in Arabic letters, was the following inscription: "O sons of Isma'íl, hither you will arrive, and hence you must return; . . . for if you go beyond this stone you will return to your country to make war upon one another, and consume your forces by dissensions and civil war." The limit of his advance.

The poetic fancy embodies a truth. Musa felt that he had reached his limit: his troops murmured against a farther advance. They wanted rest and an opportunity to enjoy the spoil they had taken. Besides every step north of the Pyrenees exposed them to great perils by weakening their line of communications, and isolating them in a land, the very ignorance

[1] Al Makkari, I. 289.

of which rendered it appalling. Besides this, the condition of affairs in the Peninsula taxed all his powers. So he turned upon his steps.

It is not improbable that, in accordance with the custom among earlier conquerors, he erected a column himself, and placed an inscription upon it to mark the limit of his conquest, and to form a new point of departure for his successors.

We are informed by Al Kortobi that, after the capture of Toledo, Mugheyth Ar-rumí had been sent to Damascus to announce the continued victories of the Moslemah, and that he had been immediately sent back with an order to both Musa and Tarik to turn over their commands to competent persons, and to repair without delay to give an account of themselves and their conquests to the Khalif. Whether Mugheyth was the bearer or not,[1] such an order was, indeed, sent, and could not have been unexpected by the Arabian commander. Tarik had been hoping for it. The truth seems to be that the Khalif was not in ignorance of the true state of the case in all its details. He had been told that the enterprising ambition of Musa had conceived the far greater project of pushing forward across Europe, crushing all opposition, and reaching Damascus by way of Constantinople.

---

[1] Gayangos says, "If Mugheyth went to Damascus after the taking of Toledo, in order to announce to the Khalif the capture of the Gothic capital, he could hardly be back" (Al Makkari, I. 546, note 13). Condé says that, when Tarik was deposed, his command was given to Mugheyth. It is true that, after that, there is no mention of him until the order requiring Musa to repair to Damascus. If Mugheyth remained in Spain, it is not improbable that the Khalif sent the order *through him*, as it concerned both the others.

Such a magnificent project might well provoke his jealousy, and even his fears for his own supremacy, and he had ordered Musa to abandon it.[1]

There was but one additional step to the removal of the man who, even in Spain, had become so powerful as to eclipse the glories of the Khalifate.   To ripen this purpose immediate arguments were not wanting.   Musa's jealousy and ill-treatment of Tarik had been reported.   Odious comparisons were drawn by the troops between the two men, and always to the detriment of Musa.   These were constantly coming to the ears of the Khalif.   Musa was brave in war, and sagacious in government, but he was greedy of fame and of treasure.   He robbed the troops, and stinted in the sums for the Khalif's coffers.   Tarik was brave, dashing, fonder of battle than of wealth ; he divided the spoils with a generous hand, after religiously setting apart the Khalif's share.

The Khalif orders both Musa and Tarik to repair to Damascus.

There can be no doubt that after the reinstatement of Tarik he communicated directly with Damascus, and thus corrected the egotistical and prejudiced reports of Musa.

Thus criminations and recriminations, from which the truth might be elicited, had been long coming to the ear of Al-Walid, and he determined to put an end to the controversy by relieving both commanders,

---

[1] Ibn-Khaldun says, further, that the Khalif feared that if Musa undertook this project his entire army would follow him, and that thus Spain would be lost.   The plan was entirely chimerical, as, not many years later, the victory of Charles Martel between Tours and Poitiers seems to demonstrate.

and bringing them to the bar of inquiry at the foot of his throne.

Other generals should conquer and rule in Spain without quarrelling: and, besides, these two had accomplished the original purpose; they were no longer necessary men.

It has been said that this order did not take Musa quite by surprise. When Tarik was restored to the command, Musa must have had misgivings; the act itself was a humiliation, and was suggestive of further action.

But he was disposed to temporize; it is said that, when he received the order which left the arrangement of the command and the exact time of departure to his discretion, he offered Mugheyth half of his own share of the spoils to withhold it until he could confirm his conquests and make a more complete incursion into northwestern Spain.

Whether it was thus held in abeyance, or whether he himself put off its immediate application, is not certain; but it seems proved that he advanced to Lugo, and sent detachments into northern Spain, even beyond the Asturian Mountains along "the shore of the Green Sea,"—the Bay of Biscay,—as far as the Sierra de Covadonga and the Cave of Auseva, the hiding-place of the little band of Christians, known afterwards as the Cave of Pelayo, —the stern and rude cradle of the reconquest. In this wild region he left small bands of Arabs and Berbers, soldiers who became settlers,— nuclei for new tides of Arab-Moors, to give permanence to the conquest. We are told that, while he was thus push-

Musa procrastinates.

ing forward into Galicia and Lusitania, a second envoy
appeared from the Khalif, in the person of Abú-Nasr,
who upbraided his delay, and in the name of the
Khalif commanded his immediate obedience.[1]

The terms of the order were, that he should appoint
proper persons to the separate governments and commands within his jurisdiction in Spain and Africa,
and should repair, without further delay, to Damascus.
He does not seem to have thought for a moment of
disobeying the order.   He afterwards wondered that
he did not.   The Arabians in Spain had been too
busy with fighting to think of treason : they held to
their allegiance without question or thought. But obeys a
second
The Khalif was the successor of the Prophet, order.
and the guardian of the Faith : to the spread of the
Faith everything was subservient.

Eminent traitors must have material to work with.
The time had not arrived when even a vigorous and
sagacious commander could have proposed to throw
off the yoke of Damascus, and to declare Moslem
Spain and Africa independent nations ; and, if it
would have been possible to a commander strong in
the love and confidence of his troops, Musa was not
such a man.   Tarik was more popular ; but, had he
been in command, he was too loyal.   Musa had caused
dissensions by his own conduct ; he had alienated an
army by ill-treatment of its beloved commander ; he
represented Arabian pride and aristocracy as arrayed
against Berbers and Moors who were vastly prepon-

---

[1] As *Abu-Nasr* means the " father of victory," it has been considered only another name for Mugheyth, who sent this second
summons to Musa chiding his delay.

derant numbers and rivalry. In the weakness of Musa lay the strength of the Khalif.

Musa delayed no longer, but at once appointed governors and commanders to conduct public affairs after his departure. But here his sagacity was at fault. He was preparing great sorrows for himself and destruction to his family and friends, even when he thought his forecast at its best. The part he had to play was delicate and difficult, and he performed it badly; for he was about to incur the ugly charge of nepotism, by leaving all the power in the hands of his sons.

He leaves the conduct of affairs in the hands of his sons.

Retracing his steps, he crossed the mountains at Buitrago, and, passing through Toledo and Seville, he settled the affairs of Spain before crossing into Africa. It was very natural that he should delegate his authority to his sons, especially as they were clever men, worthy of such preferment, and thoroughly acquainted with his projects, and the mode of carrying them out; but it was by no means judicious. The Khalif was jealous of his power: such family aggrandizement could only be regarded with suspicion.

His second son, Abdu-l-'aziz, a manly and gifted youth, was made governor or Amír of all Spain; and his nephew Ayub was second in authority. The seat of the new Amirate was fixed at Seville, nearer the sea than Toledo or Cordova, on a navigable river; this city, while sufficiently central, was in easy communication with the places occupied by the northern conquest and with Africa.

The army of Tarik was given in charge of Habib Ibn Abi Obeydah, who had been with Abdu-l-'aziz at the capitulation of Orihuela, and who was entirely in his interests. The troops on the northern frontier were placed under the command of Naaman Ibn Ab-dillah, who was afterwards to fall gloriously, attempting the extension of the Faith, at the battle of Toulouse.

The affairs of Spain being thus arranged to his satisfaction, and, as he supposed, in his interests, he embarked at Gibraltar with a large retinue, on one of the latter days of August, 713 (A. H. Dulhagiá 94), and crossed the strait. All western Africa he placed under command of his youngest son, Abdu-l-malek; Arabia proper he confided to his eldest son, Abdullah, with a viceregal authority over the whole African territory.

Before he left Spain, he had packed "the jewels, the gold, the silver, the silks and brocades, and the rest of the spoils of Andalus," in thirty wagons, Journeys which made part of the grand procession with train. which he proposed to astonish the intervening countries, and extort the Khalif's encomiums. He placed himself at the head of his train.[1] Thus he began a triumphal march towards Syria, which has hardly a rival in history, — troops, prisoners, treasures, splendor of equipment, which indeed astonished Barbary and Africa, dazzled Egypt, and, contrary to his hopes, awoke at Damascus new envy and new fears lest he should meditate a new conquest there.

Some historians assert that Tarik marched in the train of Musa;[2] others, that he had received the order separately, and had started at once for Damascus.[3]

[1] Al Makkari, I. app. lxxix.

[2] Al Makkari, I. 292.

[3] Condé, Dominacion de los Arabes, I. ch. xvii. "Tarik obedeció al momento. . . . Tarik habia llegado antes que él [Musa] á

The latter statement accords better with the character of the man. His obedience was immediate: he did not wish to delay. He was, besides, unembarrassed by duties of administration, such as Musa had to perform; and he might hope, by anticipating Musa with the Khalif, to clear himself of all charges before his accuser should appear, and make his merits manifest beyond a chance of perversion. Arrived at the capital of the Khalifate, he found that the sovereign, Al-Walid, who was suffering under the pangs of a mortal disease, was absent, in hopes of recruiting his strength, at the city of Dair Marun. Thither, without delay, Tarik followed him, and prayed for an audience; and, when summoned to the Khalif's presence, he appeared respectful but confident, to plead his cause and assert his rights.

The reception of Al-Walid was entirely kind; the first conqueror of Spain, and the first who returned to court, was, for a time, the most distinguished man at court. He was informed that his splendid services were fully known and appreciated; and that in the conflict of reports and opinions, relating to his actions in the Peninsula, his statements were fully believed. If he wondered why, such being the case, he was deprived of his command, and ordered to report at Damascus, the Khalif assured him that he had two good reasons, in no wise affecting his character or his ability. He had

Tarik arrives first at Damascus, and is kindly received by the Khalif.

Damasco." — LA FUENTE, *Historia de España*, III. 37. As Musa was a long time *en route* for Damascus, it does not accord with our knowledge of Tarik's character, or of the Khalif's plan, to believe that he lingered on the road, in so unenviable a station.

been recalled, first, that his life, so esteemed by the
Khalif for his noble and valiant deeds, and so valuable for future service, might not be endangered by
the jealous machinations of Musa and his sons, whose
power was so great ; and, secondly, that the Khalif
might hear from his own lips a clear narrative of the
great events, in which he had borne so brilliant a
part,[1] and which redounded to the glory of God and
the spread of the Faith.

Tarik seized the opportunity thus presented to give
an account of his actions ; and the concluding words
of his address, as given by Condé, are so well chosen
that they deserve to have been truly preserved. " My
lord, O king," he said, " the honorable Moslemah of
thy hosts, who have known my proceedings in Africa
and Spain, can bear testimony as to what my deeds
have been on all occasions ; nay, even of our enemies,
the Christians, I might safely inquire if they have
ever found me cowardly, cruel, or covetous."

Acquitted of egotism, since the question was of.
self-defence, he could not have chosen better words to
epitomize his character as it was known of all men,
and to present himself as the brightest personage of
that marvellous epic.   He was a valiant warrior, a
just man, a loyal subject, a sympathizing commander,
and a generous enemy.   Al-Walid professed himself
greatly pleased with the man, and his words, and gave
him hopes of new and greater distinction.   Thus far
Tarik might consider himself successful in the controversy.

All this argued ill for Musa; but it promised to

---

[1] Condé, Dominacion de los Arabes, I. ch. xvii.

the ear too much for Tarik, more than the Khalif intended to bestow, even while he was speaking these honeyed words : for the renown of Tarik was already too great for a subject; and, besides, the ordeal was by no means completed, for he was to be confronted with Musa, whose story was yet to be heard, and, without whose presentation of the case, the Khalif could not proceed even with a show of justice.

The rhetorical figure of a tide which leads to fortune would be incomplete without a reference to the ebb which is inevitable. Tarik had reached high-water mark: his conquests and his fortunes were at an end; for there was nothing to employ such an arm as his, comparable with the work he had already done. The invader of Spain would be belittled in any other command, and "there were no more such worlds to conquer."

Leaving Tarik unemployed, to await the issue, which was still distant, we return to Musa. His arrival was long delayed, partly because of the pressing business, in arranging the affairs of the several governments, as he passed eastward; partly by reason of the great pomp with which he chose to travel; and partly, too, we may believe, by some misgivings as to his reception at Damascus, which prompted him to put off, by delay, the evil moment of arrival. Under pretext of strengthening the government, it seems almost incredible that he should have remained nearly a year at Kairwan. Well might the caravan with which he moved in eastern Africa astonish the natives by the lavish display of splendor and treasure. With him were his two sons, Meruan and Abdu-l-'ala.

the General Mugheyth Ar-rumí, and one hundred
of the principal officers of his army. To represent the western blood to the expectant Khalif, he
had one hundred Berbers, the sons of the highest
chiefs; kings of the region of Sus-al-Aksa; and native
kings of the Balearic islands; with such surroundings
as marked their ethnic customs and stations. But, more
to his glory than these, behind him rode four hundred
nobles, the sons of Gothic and Frankish kings, each
of whom wore a crown and a girdle of gold; and thirty
thousand captives of lower rank followed in rear. In
front, and at intervals in the train, were wagons and
camels, laden with money and jewels. He carried
with him the novelties of the west, to astonish and
gratify the east. There were hawks, and mules, and
Barbary horses, and all the curious fruits of Barbary
and Spain, "treasures the like of which no hearer ever
heard of before, and no beholder ever saw before his
eyes."[1] It renewed the triumphs of the Roman emperors, and the reports which reached Damascus could
not fail to fan the flame of jealousy already kindled
at court. The Khalif Al-Walid indeed was in a dying
condition, and thus removed from such concern; but
his brother Suleyman, the eager expectant of the
throne, was treasuring his anger and cupidity against
the day when the unwary Musa should fall into his
power with all his treasures.

---

[1] Al Makkari, I. app. lxxix. et sup. The work from which this
account is taken is called "Traditional Stories, relating to supreme
Commanders and wise Rulers." The authorship is doubtful; it has
been ascribed to Ibn Koteybah Ad-dinawarí, in the beginning of the
tenth century. — CONDÉ, I. ch. xvii.

In Egypt, in obedience to the orders of Al-Walid, Musa had a grand reception from Kowah Ibn Sharík, the commander of the Egyptian army; and more like a sovereign than a subject he received the salams of the principal men, bestowed gifts, and forgave debts long owed to him personally. He made, likewise, plentiful presents to the sons and relatives of Abdu-l-'aziz, Ibn Meruan (the son of the former Khalif), his ancient benefactor, so that they all came up to him from every part of Egypt, and Musa showed great affability to them all. [1]

Musa's grand procession reaches Egypt.

In Palestine he remained some time, pitching his tents with the Beni-Ruh, and generously requiting their hospitality to himself and his suite, by the gift of male and female slaves and many other things, the fruits of his conquests.

Thus, with his grand array, he entered Syria by slow marches, with frequent halts, and had reached Tiberias, on the sea of Galilee, when he received a private letter from Suleyman, the brother and heir-presumptive of the Khalif Al-Walid, informing him that the monarch was very ill, and that his illness was mortal; that he could only survive for a few days, and was not in a condition to receive him. He therefore desired Musa, with a show of authority, to halt with his train, until proper arrangements could be made for his reception. There can be no doubt that he desired to grace his accession to the throne with the incoming and novel splendors of the Spanish conquest. For Musa, the case was a difficult one. He could not know the

The despatch from Suleyman, the Khalif's brother and heir.

---

[1] Al Makkari, I. app. lxxx.

truth of the statement: the Khalif was not dead —
might not die. Justice and loyalty required him to
proceed, and even policy did not clearly point out the
prudence of delay. "God forbid," he said, when he
saw the letter, "that I should be guilty of such a
crime! By Allah! I shall neither delay my march,
nor stay on the road. On the contrary, it is my
intention to proceed at the usual speed. If I arrive
before the death of my sovereign, I need not dread
his brother's vengeance; if he should die, Musa disre-
before my arrival, I leave my destiny in the gards it.
hands of God."[1] No sooner had he made this decision, than the dying Al-Walid, hearing of his near
approach, and also of the letter of Suleyman, wrote
Musa to hasten his march, and present himself without a moment of unnecessary delay, before his throne.
Musa, eager to excuse and ingratiate himself, hastened
in person to Damascus, hurrying his train, and craved
an audience.

It was now the fifth of Jumada, A.H. 94 (February,
715); he had left Spain in the latter part of August,

---

[1] Al Makkari, I. app. lxxxi.   There are in this, as in most other
parts of this story, conflicting or, rather, contradictory accounts.
Al Makkari quoting from Ibun Hayyán, says Al-Walid was not
alive when Musa reached Syria.   Cardonne says, "Mousa étoit à
la Tibériade, lorsqu'il reçut la nouvelle de la mort de Vélid." — I. 98.
But again he says, "D'autres historiens assure que Vélid vivoit
encore à l'arrivée de Mousa." — Ibid. 99.   The mass of proof is in
favor of the narrative as given.   Condé says (I. ch. xvii.) that
Suleyman was at Ramla when he wrote to Musa; if so, Musa had
passed, perhaps met, him on the way north.   While the principal
facts are sufficiently clear, the details seem to have been left very
much to the fancy of the Arabian historians, who are at once chroniclers and raconteurs.

713, one year and a half before. His magnificent triumphal procession, occupying thus eighteen months, and extending from the farthest Spanish conquest on the shores of the "Green Sea" and the Atlantic along an uninterrupted tract of conquered lands for two thousand miles, presented the grandest manifesto yet set forth of the success of Islám. The appearance in Syria of the commander, to whom and to whose troops the conquest was due, with the living and shining testimonies of the solid value and the romantic glory of his acquisitions, excited in the enthusiastic oriental mind great wonder and curiosity. The very fact that he had been recalled in the flush of his success gave him additional interest in the popular mind. He was a real hero of romance, rivalling the creations of eastern fiction. From the day when he had received the government of Africa, in May, 698, to that on which he presented himself before Al-Walid at Damascus, nearly seventeen years had elapsed, during which he had constantly been heard of as valiant, devout, and marvellously successful. He had constantly been in the van of western progress. A generation of young men had grown up to hear of him, to believe in him, to emulate him.

CHAPTER II.

THE PUNISHMENT OF MUSA.

THE scene of Musa's presentation to the Khalif is so dramatic that there can be but little doubt that its parts were cast and its surroundings artfully prepared. In the mosque of Damascus, Al-Walid was seated in the minbar or pulpit on Friday, the day of assembly. Although very much reduced by disease, and suffering at times great agony, he had rallied all his strength for the occasion, and had been preaching to the assembled congregation. He had scarcely finished his sermon, when a murmur arose among his hearers, and soon voices were heard outside, shouting, "Here comes Musa Ibn Nosscyr! here comes Musa!"

Musa appears before Al-Walid.

Ushered by these shouts, Musa entered, at the head of a brilliant train. There was a judicious collection of the curious persons and things in his train for the occasion. There were thirty of the handsomest among his noble Gothic captives, in royal robes and crowns; there were a few of the Berber princes, kings, and sons of kings, arrayed in the costumes of their respective countries, with gold diadems on their heads. The principal treasures collected during his conquests —"the jewels, the pearls, the rubies, the emeralds, the mother-of-pearl, the splendid carpets, the robes of gold and silver tissue, sprinkled with pearls and rubies and emeralds," — were placed in rich profusion before the Khalif.

Musa advanced with proud step towards the minbar, while his train was drawn up in two lines, — on the right and left. Then the Khalif offered thanks and praises to God for the victories achieved by the Moslemah; after which he delivered a speech, " the like of which," says the chronicler, " no human ears ever listened to." Thus he protracted the interview until the hour of prayer had again arrived, when the pageant was fitly varied by a solemn interruption, and all the congregation again joined in *He receives* the stated service. This over, he sat down, *him with* *kindness and* and directed Musa to approach. He was *enthusiasm.* overcome with delight. Removing his royal mantle, he placed it three times upon the shoulders of Musa, presented him with fifty thousand dinars, granted pensions to all his sons and to five hundred of his principal *maulis*, and distributed gifts and honors among the faithful Moslemah of Arabian blood who had returned with Musa from the seat of conquest. The reception could not have been more cordial. The spirits of Musa rose; he considered his future as secure, and was full of grateful wonder at the moral conquest which, in spite of all his forebodings, he had achieved at Damascus, — to him of greater present value than that which he had made in Andalus; for it alone could confirm that conquest.[1] He was greatly mistaken.

[1] The details of this narrative are taken from the anonymous history found in the appendix to the first volume of Al Makkari, and

The true ordeal was yet to come. Forty days after this encouraging reception Al-Walid died, and was succeeded by his brother Suleyman, but, during the forty days, the inquiries of Suleyman had been significant of his intentions, which the condition of Al-Walid rendered it no longer necessary for him to disguise. In an interview with Musa, he asked, "Whom didst thou appoint to command in thy name in Andalus?"

Death of Al-Walid and accession of Suleyman.

"My son Abdu-l-'aziz," answered Musa.

"And who is thy lieutenant in Africa proper, Tangiers, and Sus?"

"My son Abdullah," was the reply.

"Thou seemest to me to entertain a very favorable idea of thy sons, since thou didst appoint them to such trusts."

"O prince of the believers," answered Musa, "who is there in thy dominions who can boast of having sons more accomplished than mine?"

He then recounted the exploits of his sons, showing their claims to the high regard of all who had served with them, and to such honors and powers as he had bestowed upon them with the general approbation.

As soon as Suleyman ascended the throne, he held frequent interviews with Musa, and commenced a systematic investigation of his conduct and his man-

improperly attributed to Ibn Koteybah, of which Gayangos says, "It is not only valuable for its great antiquity, but also for the numerous details it gives upon events which have been treated with great brevity by the historians of most repute among the Arabs." He adds, "The author's account of Musa, of his conquests in Africa and Spain, of his arrival at Damascus, &c., is really invaluable."

agement of affairs in Spain. At first, and for some time, while collecting information, he restrained his anger. He asked him numerous questions about the countries and the people he had conquered: Musa's answers to which may be combined and epitomized.

Of his own Eastern troops, he said that the Arabs of Himyar were the bravest, and that among their horses the bays were the best. Of the Greeks, that mixed population of Romans and Vandals, whom the Arabs in their westward progress found occupying the towns on the northern coast of Africa, he said they were "lions within their castles, eagles on their horses, women in their ships: if they see an opportunity, they immediately seize it; but, if the day turns against them, they are goats in ascending their mountains, and so swift-footed in their flight that they scarcely see the land they tread,"—a speaking picture of this motley crew, the successive overflowings of Europe, who had contested the possession of the northern coast.

Of the Berbers he gives us an equally vivid glimpse, an elucidation of the ready combination between themselves and their Moslem conquerors. "They are," he said, "of all foreign nations, the people who most resemble the Arabs in impetuosity, corporeal strength, endurance, military science, generosity, only that they are the most treacherous persons on earth;"—he might have completed the parallel.

The Goths were, in his opinion, "luxurious and dissolute lords; but knights who do not turn their faces from the enemy."

His judgment of the Franks was based upon rumor

rather than on actual knowledge; but every breeze from the north told him that they had "numbers, resources, strength, and valor."

In answer to the question whether he was ever defeated by any of these people, Musa proudly replied, "Never, O Commander of the Faithful! Never did a banner turn away from me, nor a troop under my orders show their backs to the enemy; as long as I commanded, the Moslems were never defeated; never, from the moment I entered upon my fortieth year, until the present moment, being upon my eightieth. Nor have my Moslemah once hesitated to meet them, even though they came upon us as eighty to forty."[1]

Such success in the cause of Islám, and in extending the Khalif's dominions, should not only have weighed against Musa's faults and mistakes, but should have been rewarded with the highest honors: he had for seventeen years been in the van of western conquest, and had never lost a battle; he was over eighty years old, and was incapacitated for further schemes; he had relinquished his command, and put himself and his possessions in the power of the Khalif; but the cruel and crafty Suleyman took counsel only of jealousy and revenge; Suleyman's vengeance and cruelty.

[1] This conversation between Musa and the Khalif is substantially given by most Arabian writers: by Condé (I. ch. xvii.); by Al Makkari, in the text (I. 297); by the anonymous historian already quoted (Ibid. app. lxxx.). If it owes its form to the poetical element, it is pithy and vivid, and deserves to be quoted as a philosophical statement and a historical delineation. It concludes with admirable causality in exalting the power, skill, and valor of Musa at a time when he needed all the evidence he could collect to defend his desperate case.

he saw in the brilliant exploits of Musa and his sons
an eclipsing fame, and he determined to destroy them.
He was now ready to act.

The ostensible charges against Musa were rapacity,
family aggrandizement, injustice to Tarik ; and to these
was added what, in the mind of Suleyman, was the
gravest of all, his refusal to wait for the death of Al-
Walid before making his triumphal entry into Damascus ; which, from his new seat of power, Suleyman
chose to call "disobedience." Unfortunately, there
was more than a shadow of truth in these charges ;
and, fortify his cause as he might be able to do, to
substantiate these charges eminent witnesses were at
hand. Mugheyth Ar-rumí was there, whom the
Khalif Al-Walid had sent to deprive Musa of his
command, and whose friendship had been long alienated by an act of arbitrary injustice.[1]

Tarik was there: he had already given a general
answer to the allegations of Musa, and was working
Musa is con-fronted with Tarik. and hoping to be restored to the command
of the Andalusian army. Indeed, he would
have been, but that Mugheyth praised him too highly
to the envious Khalif, declaring, to show his popularity, that "had he ordered the Moslems to turn

---

[1] The story is, that Mugheyth had captured the governor of Cordova with his own hand, when that city was taken, and wished to
present him to the Khalif. Musa demanded him, and upon the refusal of Mugheyth, he sprang forward and tore the prisoner from
his hands : when Mugheyth declared he would claim him in the
presence of the Khalif, Musa ordered the noble captive to be beheaded. Another account says that Mugheyth slew the Goth
himself that Musa might not have him. The truth of such a quarrel
is all that concerns us in these new circumstances.

themselves to any other point than the *Kiblah* in their prayers, they would have obeyed his commands, without considering that they were infringing the laws of our Holy Prophet, and committing an impious act."[1]

Having thus deliberately prepared his case, and secured his witnesses, Suleyman summoned Musa again to appear before him. Tarik was also directed to present himself; and the rival veterans were placed face to face, feeling that each had, to a great degree the fate of the other in his hands.

Distinguished among the treasures which Musa had presented to Al-Walid, was the splendid table of Solomon, which has been already described, and of which Musa had declared himself the original captor. It now lay before the Khalif's throne, and Suleyman asked Tarik if he knew whence it came.[2] "*I* was the finder of it, my lord," said Tarik; "let us see if there be any defect in it." Upon careful examination, it was discovered that one of the prin- The table of Solomon cipal legs of emerald had been taken out again. and replaced by one of gold. "Ask Musa," said Tarik, "whether the table was in this condition when he found it?" "It was just so," answered Musa.

---

[1] Al Makkari, I. 16. Tarik, some days after, met Mugheyth, and said to him, "I wish, O Mugheyth, thou hadst described me to the Khalif as a man whose authority was resisted, instead of saying that the people of Andalus were so obedient to me."

[2] Condé makes Al-Walid, not Suleyman, the person in whose presence the finding of the table was inquired into. I have chosen the other narrative, as Al-Walid was in a moribund condition when Musa arrived; and the inquisition takes a very probable place in Suleyman's scheme for destroying Musa. — *Dominacion de los Arabes,* I. ch. xvii.

Upon this Tarik produced from under his mantle the
original leg, which he had been sagacious enough to
remove, and which entirely corresponded with the
other. Thus the deception of Musa was manifest.
His word, invalidated in this instance, lost value in
his other assertions, and his claims in all respects
were greatly damaged: the Khalif refused to believe
even what was true.

Then the angry Khalif turned furiously upon him
with bitter reproaches and abuse. " Thou hast run
against my will, and disobeyed my orders ; and, by
Allah ! I will cut off thy resources, scatter thy friends,
and seize upon thy treasures; I will deprive thee of
all the honors conferred upon thee by the sons of
Abú Sufyán and the sons of Meruan, those whose
benefits thou hast repaid with ingratitude, betraying
the hopes they placed in thee."

The flood-gates of vengeance were fairly opened.
Musa's meek disclaimers were vain. " By Allah !
O Prince of Believers ! is this my desert ? Is this
the reward of a man who, like myself, has been so
meritorious in the service of God, and who has,
through his exertions, been the cause of pouring
boundless wealth on the Moslems; of a man who
has so faithfully and honorably served thy ancestors ? "

" Thou liest," said Suleyman ; " may God kill me,
if I do not put thee to death, and cause thee to be
crucified ; " and he repeated in his rage, " May God
kill me, if I do not put thee to death ! "[1]

[1] The narrative of the interviews between Musa and Suleyman
may be found in the anonymous history (Al Makkari, I. app. lxxxv.),

The old warrior, rejecting the counsel of his friends, — and especially, of Omar, the Khalif's brother, that he should consult his safety in flight, — went to his house, washed and perfumed himself, and waited for his summons to the cross. But the punishment seemed, even to the mind of the Khalif, too extreme ; or, perhaps, his cupidity influenced him at least to spare the man, that he might extract from him all his gains, and hold him as a living example of his vengeance.

It was sultry summer weather, and he ordered that Musa should be exposed to the sun for a whole day ; saying to his brother, " O Omar ! I shall not be satisfied unless thou go out and see that my orders are faithfully executed." Thus under a scorch- *Musa's exposure and humiliation.* ing sun, the old warrior, bearing his fourscore years, corpulent to obesity, and afflicted with the asthma, stood until his blood was on fire and his strength exhausted : he sunk upon the ground, and " was on the point of being suffocated several times ; " death would have soon relieved him, but that Omar, declaring " that he had never passed a worse day in all his life," took compassion upon his sufferings, and gained from the Khalif an order to abridge his punishment.[1]

The ruling passion was still strong in Musa; he

which has a *prima facie* air of truth, not impaired by the dramatic cast. The words put in the mouths of the interlocutors seem, as near as possible, exactly what they must have said.

[1] " Whoever prevents me," said Omar, " from speaking as I do in his favor, I deny him all allegiance, and I shall hate him for it ; " fearless words, which deserve to be held in remembrance. — AL MAKKARI, I. app. lxxxiii.

knew that the Khalif would strip him of his wealth, and he expressed his willingness to give up all that he had, if only four things should be granted him. The first was that his son Abdullah should not be removed from the government of eastern Africa for two years; the second, that Abdu-l-'aziz should not be removed from the Amirate of Spain; the third, that what these two sons had themselves taken from the infidels, as their proper share, should not be confiscated; and the fourth, that his refractory *mauli* Tarik with his property should be delivered into his hands. On these conditions, Musa was ready to surrender all that he had.

But he was not so situated as to make conditions; he and his sons Meruan and Abdu-l-'ala were in the Khalif's power, and, as for Tarik, the tables had been turned; the son of Zeyad had conquered in the controversy with the son of Nosseyr; if victory that might be called which resulted in neither public honor nor reward. He simply was vindicated, but was to expect nothing more.

To serve his own purposes, however, Suleyman, while refusing to deliver Tarik and his treasures into Musa's hands, granted, but only in form of words and for a very brief time, his request that his sons Abdullah and Abdu-l-'aziz should remain in command of their respective governments for two years; but the reason of this was that he imposed upon him an enormous fine which he hoped these sons would aid him to pay. After this, they would have little to expect.

The whole amount of the subsidy was four millions

and thirty thousand dinars.[1] On account of this
sum, Musa had already paid only one hun- The enor-
dred thousand dinars. The remainder of mous fine.
the sentence may be most clearly stated in the words
of the Arabian historian: "The Commander of the
Faithful grants Musa a term during which a messenger shall be despatched to Andalus to procure the
said sum from his son Abdu-l-'aziz. The messenger
will present the order to Abdu-l-'aziz, to wait one
month for its fulfilment; at the expiration of which
time, without waiting one day more, he is to return
with or without the money, and go to Africa and do
the same with his son Abdullah. Musa shall not
consider as part of the payment of that fine the sums
which he may have collected in his various governments since Suleyman's accession to the throne,
whether proceeding from the capitation-tax, paid by
the infidels, or from the ransom of cities threatened
with the sword, or from any spoil gained on the field
of battle; since all those sums the Commander of the
Faithful considers his own, and takes possession of
them."[2] The decree, which was also of the nature
of a compact, of which this was an extract, was
witnessed by thirteen of the principal men at court,
and was carried out to the letter.

By giving up his own fortune, by obtaining the
aid of his sons in Spain and Africa, by a voluntary

[1] The dinar is computed at ten shillings, English; in round
numbers, two and a half dollars of our money, which would make
the sum about $10,000,000. At that time the amount seems in-
credible, but Musa was supposed to have the lion's share of the
spoils of the Peninsula.

[2] Al Makkari, I. app. lxxxvii.

contribution of the tribe of Lahm, and doubtless by the assistance of other friends, the enormous sum was made up; and then Musa was banished from the Court to his birthplace at Wáda-1-Kora, that his fellow-countrymen might see his humiliation and despise him. He was a ruined man, and yet his punishment was not complete. The vengeance of the Khalif was not satiated; he determined to destroy the family of Musa, root and branch.

The sins of the father were to be visited upon the children; but, to the vengeful eye of the Khalif, the sons had sins of their own to answer for. Grave charges had been already made against Abdu-l-'aziz, and the Khalif, already so bitter against the father, was ready to prejudge any complaint against the sons.

CHAPTER III.

THE SAD STORY OF ABDU-L-'AZIZ.

THE story of Abdu-l-'aziz is of such deep interest and pathos, that it has fallen into the hands of legendists and poets, and it is difficult to relegate it to the domain of sober history. It combines all the elements of the most sensational modern fiction, — the most romantic love, suspicion of treason, intrigue, assassination; and thus the real story needs no garb of fiction to enhance its interest.

After the departure of Musa from Spain, Abdu-l-'aziz, left in chief command, displayed great and systematic energy in his government, showing clearly to all that, if his father had exposed himself to the charge of nepotism, he had placed a thoroughly competent man in the seat of power. In the words of Al Makkari,[1] "He collected together the scattered forces of the Moslems, fortified the frontiers, and greatly contributed to the consolidation of the Mohammedan power, and to the extension of the limits of the conquest, by subduing several important fortresses and cities which had hitherto escaped the eyes of his father and Tarik." Thus he displayed himself as a military leader, both sagacious and adventurous.

Although he remained in person most of the time

---

[1] Mohammed on Dynasties, I. 30.

at his seat of government, in the vigorous discharge of his administrative duties,[1] his armies pursued the conquest in the north, "to the extreme of Lusitania and the coasts of the great ocean, his captains overrunning all the land of Alguf (the north), Pampeluna and the Albaskinse Mountains (that portion of the Pyrenees bordering the Basque country.)"

He made a regular and equitable system of revenue collections. Every province of Spain and Africa had its receiver-general, whose funds were sent to the common coffer, and thence transmitted to the treasury at Damascus.[2] To convey this accumulated treasure to the seat of government, Abdu-l-'aziz, yet in ignorance of his father's misfortunes, selected ten of his most honorable and trusted councillors, the first of whom was Habib Ibn Abi-Obeydah Al-Fehri, the general just referred to, who had entered Spain in the suite of Musa, who had been one of the witnesses to the treaty of Orihuela, and who was yet to play a prominent and unenviable part in the drama which was about to be enacted.

The equitable government of Abdu-l-'aziz.

Abdu-l-'aziz established magistrates in the towns, like the Eastern Kadis, afterwards known as *Alcaides* or *Alcaldes.* He left to the Spanish people their own judges, bishops and priests, their churches and ceremonies; holding them only as tributaries and not as

[1] Al Makkari, II. 403, note 1. His purpose seems to have been to confirm the conquest in the north. Al-Fehri invaded Galicia, and Mugheyth (who had returned to Spain) carried on the war against Aragon and Navarre.

[2] Condé, Dominacion de los Arabes, I. ch. 18.

slaves.[1] The Christian people who remained under this clement government were called Mostarabes or Mozarabes; they adopted the Arabic languages and customs, and the name was afterwards applied to the Christians of Cordova, Seville, Toledo, and the other large cities, and especially to their religious ritual.[2]

The greedy Khalif received the treasure sent him from Spain with great satisfaction, and with it the accounts of the excellent administration of the Amir; but so far was this from staying his vengeance, that it only confirmed him in his bloody purpose. He would smite the family of Musa, root and branch, and place a creature of his own in the Peninsula, of whose loyalty he could have no suspicion.

Unfortunately for Abdu-l-'aziz, there were not wanting direct charges against him, which, if they could be proved, would warrant the Khalif in deposing him, and give his vengeance the cloak of justice.

Charges against him based upon his marriage.

It has been seen, that upon the death or disappearance of Roderik, he had left a queen, called in the

---

[1] Of this course La Fuente says, "Indulgencia admirable, ni usada en las anteriores conquistas, ni esperada de tales conquistadores."—*Historia de España*, III. 42.

[2] The word is from the Arabic *musta'rab*, which means one "who tries to imitate or become an Arab in his manners and language, and who, though he may know Arabic, speaks it like a foreigner." For other far-fetched derivations see the note of Gayangos, Al Makkari, I. 420. When Alfonzo VI. reconquered Toledo in 1085, he found an Arabic version of the missal in use among the Christians, which has been called *el officio Muzarabé*, and which they were quite unwilling to abandon. The language had become their vernacular, and the modern Spanish had not yet been formed, or rather was in the slow process of formation.

Spanish histories Egilona; in the chronicles and legends Ulaca; and in the Arabic narratives Ayela. She is the same, too, who figures in the "Perdida de España" of Abul-cacim Tarif, and in the drama of Lope de Vega, as the young Moorish princess, who had been shipwrecked on the coast near Denia, when Roderik was rising to power; who had been baptized as a Christian, and had married that monarch. Fiction has decked her in as many fanciful garbs as names, and nothing can be more romantic than the narrative, attributed to Rasis, of her insinuating conversations with the new Amir of Spain. But with all this poetry she is a real historic character. Taken prisoner at Merida, she was the most notable among the captured treasures. She had obtained security by paying tribute, and was living unmolested. She was still young and beautiful; she was a widowed and captive queen. She was a Moor, and had become a Christian. She was thus a very heroine of romance, while, as a historic character, she is full of interest.

Abdu-l-'aziz was a handsome and gallant man, in the prime of life. As her conqueror he had power to command; but when he saw her he became her lover, and it needed but a persuasive tongue like his to induce her to resume her royal seat, and to become the mistress of Moorish, as she had been the queen of Gothic, Spain. She became his wife, and the queen of his affections. He distinguished her above his other wives; he permitted her to retain her Christian creed, and called her by an endearing name — *Ummí-'Assém.*[1]

with Egilona, the widow of Roderik.

[1] This is corrupted into *Omalisman* by the Spanish chroniclers, and has been translated *the lady of the necklace.* It is just to say

The marriage was as happy as it was romantic; and, had there been no Khalif at Damascus to fear and to propitiate, it would have been conducive to the concord and stability of the Moorish government in Spain; but it gave to Suleyman and the faction opposed to Musa and his sons, a new pretext for destroying Abdu-l-'aziz. It might well seem in their eyes a potent instrument of treason.[1] Her history, her station, and her Christian influence, might well suggest danger to the suspicious Khalif.

It does not seem to have entered into the mind of Musa or his sons, at any time, to rebel against the power of the Khalif, or to form an independent empire in Spain; but it was easy to induce the belief that the ardent spirit of his son Abdu-l-'aziz may have entertained such a thought. The Gothic queen whom he had espoused could not forget her former dignity and power, and she used all her attractions to regain it. It is stated, on the authority of the "Coronica General" of Alonzo el Sabio, and the story is corroborated by a study of human nature, that she beguiled her husband into wearing a golden crown, which she had made with her own hands, of her own gold and precious stones. This show of royalty, a departure from the Mohammedan customs, at once gave

that Gayangos denies that *ummt-'assém* has that meaning. He says it is a common household name for women at the east. — AL MAKKARI, II. 404.

[1] With regard to the authenticity of the marriage, there can be no doubt. Isidor Pacensis, one of the very few contemporary writers, declares it. "Abdalazis omnem Hispaniam per tres annos sub censuario jugo pacificans . . . cum Regina Hispaniæ in conjugio copulata, &c." — *España Sagrada*, of Flores, VIII. 302.

his enemies a ground of complaint, which was greatly
exaggerated by the time it reached the ears of the
Khalif. But Egilona was not content even with this.
She bowed in her husband's presence, and did him
homage as a potentate ; and, in order to force the nobles to do the same, she prevailed upon him to have the
entrance into the audience chamber made so low that
every person who went in must bend in doing so, and
thus make an involuntary salam, as if to a monarch.

She tried to convert him to Christianity; and the
chronicle tells us that she had a low door made also to
She tries to her oratory, so that, whoever entered, would
make him a seem to bow to the cross, the image of the
Christian
and a king. virgin, and the shrines of the saints.

Whatever may be the truth of these details, there can
be no doubt as to the general charges which reached
Suleyman, already burning to destroy the unsuspecting
Amir. He was told that Abdu-l-'aziz had determined
to shake off his authority, and establish an independent Khalifate, and was already wearing a royal
crown ; that he was an apostate from the faith; that
he had made an alliance with the fugitives of Galicia;
and that he was meditating the massacre of the Moslems ; in partial proof of which it was asserted that
he was worshipping the Christian images, bending
low before strange gods, and despising Islám and the
Prophet.[1]

[1] We have again the satisfactory authority of Isidorus Pacensis,
— "Quasi consilio Egilonis Regiæ, conjugis Ruderici regis, quam
sibi sociaverat, jugum Arabicum a sua cervice conaretur avertere, et
regnum invasum Hiberiæ sibimet retemptare." — FLORES' España
Sagrada, VIII. 302. See also the note of Gayangos, Al Makkari,
II. 404. The cruelty of Suleyman is somewhat palliated when the
accumulation of charges, with plausible proofs, is considered.

Nor was it only to the Khalif that such a story was related. It spread among the people in Spain; and, although they liked the Amir and his clement rule, they were not unprepared for the cruel order which was soon to be made public, nor unwilling to see it executed. The matter was still further complicated; for Abdu-l-'aziz now began to receive news of the cruel treatment his father had received, and resented it in angry words, which were at once reported to the Khalif.

After the deputation of ten councillors had gone to Damascus with the revenues of Spain, Suleyman had sent six of them back to Abdullah at Kairwan, to await his orders there, informing them that they would receive directions later, to proceed to Spain, and what they were to accomplish there.

Among these were Habib Ibn Abi Obeydah Al-Fehri already referred to, and Zeyd-At-temamí; both friends of Abdu-l-'aziz, but greater friends to Islám.

Not long after their arrival in Kairwan, Abdullah received open despatches, ordering them to proceed to Spain, and report to the Amir; but, with these orders sent through Abdullah, they received secret directions to confer with *Envoys are sent by the Khalif to slay him.* conspirators in Spain, and to use their judgment as to the best mode of destroying Abdu-l-'aziz. Habib was the first to open the bloody despatch, and he recoiled with horror from the deed required of him. He was astonished at the envy and hatred exhibited by the Khalif: he was amazed at his ingratitude for the brilliant deeds and faithful service performed by

Musa and his sons.[1] But his loyalty was stronger
than his pity. "God is just," he said ; "He has commanded us to obey our sovereign, and we have no
choice but to do so." They first applied to Ayúb, the
lieutenant of the Amir, who, desirous of personal
aggrandizement,[2] anxious to exculpate himself from
any participation in the errors of his chief, and perhaps sharing the sentiments of devotion to the
Khalif expressed by Habib, declared his readiness to
take part in the execution. Ayúb was the cousin of
the Amir.

They next approached, Abdullah-al-Ghafekí, "the
most eminent and most conspicuous person in the
army by his talents, his generosity, and his virtues ;"
but he was proof against bribery or threats. He declared that the Commander of the Faithful had been
deceived. The Amir was neither disobedient nor
treacherous. The Khalif, he said, could not, at such
a distance, know the truth of such reports ; "but,"
said he, "you can; and it is for you to decide whether
he deserves death or not. Follow my advice ; give
up your purpose, and write to the Khalif that you
cannot put his orders into execution." [3]

But his just speech found no echo in the hearts
already steeled to perform the cruel mandate. The

---

[1] Condé, Dominacion de los Arabes, I. ch. xix.

[2] The delegates went to see Ayúb, and offered him, in the Khalif's name, the government of Andalus, if he would assist them in
the undertaking. — AL MAKKARI, II. app. iv.

[3] Ib. "The delegates, however," says the author of the anonymous history, "Traditions of Commandments of Government,"
"disregarded his words, *for the love of the Sultan*, and went about
their business."

secret could no longer be kept; the people of Seville
were in commotion, and divided in opinion. The
troops, and especially the body-guard, were determined to defend the Amir at all hazards, but they
were harangued by Zeyd-At-temamí: the precept
of obedience to the successor of Mohammed prevailed over their attachment, and Abdu-l-'aziz was
abandoned to his fate, even when surrounded by pity-
ing friends.

On a farm, in the neighborhood of Seville, the Amir
had built a villa residence, called Kenisa-Rebina,
because it was on the site of a former synagogue of the Jews; and near it had erected a
mosque.[1] There, in the intervals of business,
he spent his leisure in domestic retirement,
and in the duties of religion; and there, in entire
ignorance of the plot which was now ripe for execution, he was recreating from the cares of state in the
society of his beloved Egilona.

The conspirators left Seville before the dawn, with
a number of attendants, and proceeded to this sub-
urban palace; they waited at the gate until he
should go to the mosque to attend morning prayers.
They had not long to wait. At the appointed hour
he left the palace, and, entering the mosque, proceeded
to the sanctuary and began to read the Korán. He
had just finished the introductory chapter, when he
heard a confused noise at the door; and, in a moment,
the conspirators made their appearance.

[1] Condé mistakes *Kenisa-Rebina* for the name of the place:
it means the *synagogue of the Jews.*—See note of Gayangos, Al
Makkari, II. 404.

Before he had time to divine their purpose, his former friend, Habib, rushed upon him, like Brutus upon Cæsar, and dealt him a blow, but without effect. He passed quickly into the body of the mosque seeking shelter, but the other executioners, led by Zeyd At-temamí, fell upon him with numerous and repeated strokes, and his life was soon extinct.

He is decapitated. His head was at once severed from his body, and, after being hastily embalmed, was borne with as little delay as possible, by the emissaries in person, to be presented to the expectant Khalif.[1]

Although, through the eloquence of Zeyd-At-temamí, the people immediately around the Amir had been won over to the purpose of the assassins, and had even "broken into his rooms in wild and cruel emulation, each eager to deal his blow," [2] yet, as the news spread, the mass, who had not been in the secret, were stunned and enraged. Even the production of the Khalif's letters, and the recital of the charges, did not justify "the deep damnation of his taking off."

A wild commotion followed, and the populace, incensed against Ayúb, turned for a moment to Abdullah-al-Ghafekí, who had spoken in favor of the Amir, and had endeavored to shake the purpose of the assassins. And this may be regarded as the first display of public resistance to orders from Damascus; the first, almost unconscious, effort at the indepen-

[1] Another account, ignoring details, says that Abdu-l-'aziz was put to death by the army.

[2] Condé, Dominacion de los Arabes, I. c. 119.

dence of the Spanish Arabs.[1] It was faint, but it was a precedent.

The memory of the unfortunate Amir was long cherished in the Peninsula: in the suburbs of Antequera, there is a valley known to-day as that of *Abdelaxis*, named in his honor.[2]

The Khalif's purpose was now completed. Abdullah was removed from the government of Africa; his after history has been lost. So, too, the fate of Egilona is unknown. Some say that she was slain with her husband: it is more probable that she returned to that privacy of which history retains no record, where she might moralize, not without pride, upon the great events in her checkered career.

It is natural and instructive to consider those historic parallels which display human character as the same in all ages, and which thus bind with living ligaments the men of one age and creed and country to those of different periods, diverse religions, and distant lands.

Parallel between Abdu-l-'aziz and Thomas à-Becket.

Thus the reader will revert to a similar scene enacted in England in the twelfth century. Norman-English conspirators, at the real or fancied request of the first of the Plantagenets, swiftly crossed the English Channel, and slew a Saxon Archbishop of Canterbury on the steps of the altar, because the monarch feared his power. Like Abdu-l-'aziz, Thomas à-Becket,

---

[1] Al Makkari, II. app. v.

[2] En las inmediaciones de Antequera hay un valle, que llaman todavia de Abdelaxis, nombre sin duda conservado por los Arabes en memoria de aquel desgraciado emir. — LA FUENTE, *Historia de España*, III. 45.

although nominally a priest, really held important political power,—representative at once of the church and the Saxon people; and Henry II. was restraining the statesman and exalting the prerogatives of Norman-English royalty while he was gratifying personal revenge.

Both acts were to meet with historical retribution. The murder of Becket canonized a saint, shook the Plantagenet prestige, and led to the humiliation of John and the establishment of the Great Charter. The assassination of Abdu-l-'aziz preyed upon Suleyman as a crime deserving retribution, and was the first blow against the Khalif's supremacy in Spain. Future Amirs would so frame their plans that such an assassination would be impossible.

Habib Ibn Obeydah and his colleagues proceeded without delay to Damascus, and appeared before Suleyman with the embalmed head of Abdul-'aziz enclosed in a precious casket. The sight of that casket should have satisfied the Khalif's vengeance, but his cruelty was of a tougher fibre. He sent for Musa, and making him sit behind the people, he caused the casket to be opened in the presence of a multitude as spectators of the tragic scene; and when the waxen features of the Amir were displayed, he turned to the unhappy father, and exclaimed, "Dost thou know whose head that is?" The earlier Arabian chroniclers have ventured to give the exact words of Musa and the Khalif in this interview, and they have been quoted universally by later writers. Whether they be true or not, I can only say that, for simple pathos their account of the scene has

The Amir's head sent to the Khalif.

no rival in literature, except perhaps the Homeric picture of Priam begging the dead body of Hector from Achilles, — to which, indeed, it bears a striking resemblance. "Yes," answered Musa, "I do. That is the head of my son, Abdu-l-'aziz." Then he rose from his seat, and first folding his hands in prayer, he added : "O Commander of the Faithful, thou art revenged ; but, by the life of God, there never was a Moslem who less deserved such unjust treatment ; for he passed his days in fasting, and his nights in prayer ; no man ever more loved his God or his messenger Mohammed ; no man ever performed greater deeds to serve the cause of the Almighty, or was more firm in his obedience to thee ; or showed a milder disposition to the men under his orders. . . . Abdu-l-'aziz is no more (may God forgive him his sins !) ; for, by Allah ! he was neither avaricious of life, or fearful of death. None of thy predecessors — neither Abdu-l-malek nor Abdu-l-'aziz, nor even Al-Walid — would have treated him thus, or reduced him to this plight. Thou even wouldst never have done what God saw thee do with him, had there been any justice in thee."

Suleyman stopped him, calling him a liar and a dotard. Musa attempted to retort. "I am no dotard. . . . I speak as the honest slave ought to speak to his master ; . . . but I place my confidence in God, whose help I implore and beseech —" Paternal grief and anger would have conquered his prudence, but he broke down in his attempt, and could only say, "Grant me his head, O Commander of the Faithful that I may shut the lids of his eyes." Suleyman said, "Thou mayst take it."

Then Musa took the precious head, and rolled it up in a corner of his tunic, folding it " twice backward." He did not perceive that in doing so the tunic had been detached from his person, until a bystander endeavored to replace it. Musa refused the assistance, and tottered out of the presence, his sorrow and disorder touching, at the last, even the hard-hearted Khalif, who said, —

" Let Musa alone ; he has already been sufficiently punished ; " but, as he departed, he added, " That old man's spirit is still unbroken." The last words were not true ; there was needed no other drop to fill the cup of misery. He retired from the court to Merat Dheran or Wadi-l-Kora, where, according to some authorities, he depended upon public charity for his subsistence. There, it is said, he predicted his own death. " Before two days," he said, " there shall die in this town a man whose fame has filled the east and the west."

" We all thought," says the author of the tradition, " that he meant the Khalif ; but on the morning of the second day, as we were saying our prayers in the mosque of the Messenger of God, we heard the people say, " Musa, the son of Nosseyr, is dead." His long and checkered life came to an end in September, 716.[1]

Musa's death.

---

[1] The story of Musa is so enveloped in traditions that it is difficult to be sure of details. It is, however, wonderfully circumstantial. Al Makkari says that he begged for his subsistence among the Arabian tribes, and was accompanied by a faithful mauli, I. 296. Ibn Kiyan, quoted in the appendix to vol. I. (lxxxix), makes the improbable assertion that he was taken into favor by Suleyman, and accompanied him in a pilgrimage to Mekka, riding, on account of

The fate of Musa and his sons, while it is a proof, one among many, that Islám was the law of submission, but not of charity, has a larger significance. It shows that the great services of subjects become a burden, which human dynasties seek to fling off and to consign to oblivion. History, however, magnifies them, and the ingratitude of monarchs is the dark background which throws such services into grander relief. Fame is the tardy recompense for royal injustice.

Before closing this account, I wish to suggest again that the conduct of Suleyman toward this family, exerted a strong influence, detrimental to his power, upon the Moslems in Spain. When Musa found himself in the power of Suleyman, he begged Yezid, who had been successful in spreading the Mohammedan power in the east, and who was a great favorite with the Khalif, to intercede for him. Yezid could not disguise his astonishment that so bold and sagacious a man, after conquering Andalus and putting a boisterous sea between him and the Khalif, should have been so unwise as to come and deliver himself up. Why did he not send the treasures instead of bringing them? He had an empire in Spain. Why did he not remain, and even resist the Khalif's order?

"By God!" replied Musa, "had my intention been

The conduct of Suleyman alienates Moslem Spain.

his age and feebleness, upon a pregnant camel, whose gait would be cautious and easy. Adh-dhobi, whose history may be found in the Bibliotheca of Casiri, refers to a history of Musa and his exploits, written by his grandson Mo'arek-Ibn-Maron, which, if still extant, would throw great light upon this period. As it is not quoted by the chroniclers, it is probably lost.

such, you would never have seen a single thing of the many treasures you have received from Andalus, never until the last day of judgment; but I swear to God that it never entered my mind to deny obedience to the Khalif, and desert the cause of the people;" and, after Yezid left him, he said to the company, " By Allah! had I had Yezid's good sense, I should not be reduced to this condition. Hast thou not heard of the lapwing, that is enabled to see [the] water at a great depth underground, and yet falls into the snare which is in sight of his eyes?" [1]

What Musa had not seen, the Moslemah in Spain could no longer fail to see. They were eager in the cause of Islám, and loyal to the Khalif. They were ready for action, but they would work for no such recompense as that meted out to Musa and his sons. The Khalif might recall, but not to martyrdom at Damascus; and delegated assassins in Spain would thenceforth pursue a dangerous trade. The first feeble steps towards the independence of Moslem Spain had been taken by the Khalif himself, even while he thought to check its incipient signs.

The fate of Suleyman is regarded by some of the romantic Arabian historians as a retribution: his conduct to the family of Musa was considered in the light of " a crime, which God Almighty did not leave unpunished; it was afterwards visited on the head of Suleyman, who died in the flower of youth, and whose reign was attended with great commotion and strife." [2] After his angry vengeance was appeased,

[1] Al Makkari, I. 295 ; and app. lxxxiv.
[2] Al Makkari, I. 297.

he made cooler inquiries into the charges against
Abdu-l-'aziz; and, when men knew that he was willing to listen to the truth, he heard it, and found that
he had been grossly deceived. That Amir had not
swerved from the path of loyalty and obedience, but
had been a model of virtue and good administration.
Then, with his repentance, arose anger against Habib
Ibn Abi Obeydah and the other messengers, whom
he banished from the court for their want of judgment and discretion in carrying out, when they might
at least with propriety have delayed, the execution
of his instructions.[1] The authority used by Condé
decks the story in a romantic garb. Young and handsome, the idol of his harem, the Khalif was one day
admiring himself in a mirror, and turning towards
his women, exclaimed, "Verily, it is I who am the
King of youth!" One of his gifted wives replied to
him, in impromptu verses, "Thou art handsome;
yea, none can deny it, but all human beauty hath
this defect, that it will not remain; and thine shall
pass away as the flower of the meadow, as the shadow
that crosses the sun."[2] If the story be true, whether
it was a platitude or a prediction, the Khalif is said
to have fallen into deep melancholy, and pined rapidly away. He passed to the Great Assize The death of
within a year after the assassination of Suleyman.
Abdu-l-'aziz and the death of Musa. The remorse
is romantic; a simple historic record is that in the
year 717 (21 Safir, A. H. 99) he was defeated before
Constantinople and died of grief.[3]

[1] Al Makkari, II., app. vi.
[2] Condé, Dominacion de los Arabes, I. ch. xix.
[3] There is, however, another story, and *prima facie*, a true one,

With his reign closed one great act of the Spanish drama, a tragedy in which all the important *dramatis personæ* disappear from the scene. Of Tarik no further mention can be found; he does not even re-appear as the hero of romantic fiction.[1]

Of Mugheyth some writers say that he settled himself at Damascus, and died there; others, that he returned to Andalus, and lived in splendor at Cordova, in a palace afterwards called "Balátt Mugheyth," and that he was the father of the distinguished family known in the later history as the "Beni Mugheyth," who became the centre of wealth, dignities and power in that city, their importance and consideration reaching the highest pitch.[2]

which destroys both the romance and the grief. It is that he was a victim to gluttony. After speaking of his feats in that respect, on a former occasion, Abulfeda tells us that his death was brought on by eating from two large baskets eggs and figs alternately, and by finishing the repast with marrow and sugar : "unde nata cruditas in gravem denique morbum aucta eum strangulavit." — *Annales Moslemici*, I. 126. Ockley's History of the Saracen, Bohn's Edition, Tabular Statement at the end.

[1] Al Makkari, II. 398, note 5.

[2] Although the latter is the more probable story, it may have been a son of Mugheyth who was the founder of the family at Cordova.

BOOK V.

THE GERMS OF THE RECONQUEST AND THE NORTHERN MOVEMENTS OF THE MOSLEMS.

——◆——

CHAPTER I.

THE CONGERIES OF FUGITIVE CHRISTIANS IN THE NORTH-WEST, — PELAYO.

THERE is perhaps no chronicle which bears its philosophy more openly upon the surface than this story of the conquest of Spain. It may be regarded as an allegorical drama, in which real events and persons have a double significance, idealizing virtue and vice, crime and misfortune, in a curious tissue of historic relations and consequences.

The first blow had stunned Gothic Spain; and, before she could recover her consciousness, the skilful hands of the Moslemah had bound her, hand and foot. From the first stupor they were not allowed to recover. The very clemency of the Moslems robbed the Christians of argument. If their swords were sharp, their conduct after battle was far better than the inhabitants had any right to expect, far better than that of the Roman or Gothic conquerors had been, when they invaded Spain. Their religion, the defence of which might have been the last rallying-point, was respected under easy conditions; their lives rendered secure and comfortable; they were under tribute, but a tribute no more exacting than Roman taxes or Gothic subsidies; their treaties were generously drafted, and inviolably kept. If the Gothic dynasty had been destroyed, the people of Spain did not seem to be losers, except in the humiliation of bearing a foreign and an infidel dominion. It was the Gothic element, and not the Hispano-Romans, that felt the humiliation most. It would be vain to look for numbers and statistics of the Arab-Moors in Spain, up to the deposition of Abdu-l-'aziz. The Arabian troops, who had entered with the armies of Musa, were largely recruited with Berbers, and other North-African people; and a small but constant stream of Arabians had been coming from the east to give tone to the mass and to keep moral communication with the Khalif; but when the conquest was sheathing its sword for " lack of argument," when determined resistance was at an end, and the great work was declared achieved; when all the provinces of Andalus were reduced to the obedience of Islám, "many individuals of the best and most illustrious among the Arabian tribes left the tents of their fathers, and settled in Andalus, thereby becoming the stock of the many noble families whose luminous traces are visible throughout the annals of that country." [1] The migration to colonize was greater than that to conquer.

They came chiefly from Syria, into which an immense concourse had gone from Arabia; and from this time the land of the prophet lost its prestige, the seat of the Khalifate being the centre of attraction. Mecca

[1] Al Makkari, II. 20.

and Medina, the birthplace and the burial-place, retained indeed, for all time, their special sanctity, which
could turn the faces of believers every- Colonists
where to the former at the hour of prayer, pour in from Arabia and
and demand the pilgrimage of the faithful Syria.
annually; but Damascus and Bagdad for the east,
and Cordova for the west, were the spots to which
the adventurous of all the Moslem world were attracted by ambition, by pleasure, and by the hope of
gain. Especially was the latter proclaimed as the
centre of an earthly paradise, and even the glories of
Damascus .could not retain those who heard of its
charms of nature, and its abundance of wealth. The
sons of Ummeyah and others of the Koreish; the
sons of Adnan, of Khandaf, of Hammud and of Zoh-
rah; the Beni Zehr, the Beni Makhzum, and the
Beni Kenanah, — were few among the many who
crowded to Spain, and had land allotted to them according to their dignity. This new Arabian element
was to be of great influence in the future history.

Meanwhile, the death of Abdu-l-'aziz had left the
Faithful in the Peninsula without a head. The mass
of the people, in their first excitement, The new
proclaimed Abdullah-al-Ghafekí, but such a Amir of Spain, Ab-
choice could not stand against the prestige dullah-al-Ghafeki.
of the Khalif's power. The death of the Amir had
devolved the temporary administration of affairs upon
his cousin and lieutenant, Ayúb, until a permanent
successor could be appointed by the Wali or Viceroy
of Africa; for to the hands of this officer the appointment was confided, subject always to the confirmation of the Khalif.

Ayúb, the son of Musa's sister, who, though he had consented to his cousin's death, had been appointed by Musa, and therefore shared in the opprobium of the family, could not expect to retain his power for any length of time; but, while he wielded it, he employed himself diligently during his brief dominion. He had experience and skill. He divided the country into four great provinces, north, east, south, and west; he transferred the seat of the general government from Seville to Cordova, as a more central point, and perhaps, too, to make one remove farther from Syria, which was becoming dangerous. He travelled over his Amirate, quelling disorders and administering justice, and between Toledo and Saragossa, on the ruins of the ancient town Bibilis, which he razed, he erected a strong citadel, which long bore his name, "Kalat Ayúb."[1] He was a prudent and successful governor; but, although he had given his assent to the murder of his cousin, the Khalif was unwilling that a nephew of Musa should remain in power; he therefore sent orders to Mohammed Ibn Yezid, the Viceroy of Egypt, to depose him. This functionary was the same who had received the instructions which caused the removal of the sons of Musa.[2] Thus, after the brief administration of six months, Ayúb was superseded.

The general appointed to succeed Ayúb was Al
Al Horr Horr Ibn Abdi-r-rahmán-Al-Thafeki, the
appointed
commander Alahor of the Christian chronicles. To An-
of the
troops. dalus the change was not a happy one. The new Amir was covetous and cruel, and made the

---

[1] Condé, Dominacion de los Arabes, I. c. 20. [2] Ibid.

Moslemah as well as the Christians feel his exactions : he violated the clement regulations of the first conquerors, — the true policy of Islám ; he imprisoned the Alcaldes and the rich citizens to make them give up their treasures.   But he made some amends for his avarice by his zeal in pushing the conquest ; and he vindicated the propriety of his appointment by being the first to organize a formal expedition to plant the standard of Islám beyond the Pyrenees. He ruled for two years and eight months, during which period his cruelties and his avarice were so clearly demonstrated to the Khalif, that he sent orders to depose him ; so that, at the close of the year 719, he was succeeded, by order of the viceroy of Egypt, by Assamah Ibn Maleki al Khaulani, a distinguished general then in command of one of the armies in Spain.   He also was to rule for a brief period, and to give way to a successor.   Change in office was the order of the day.

It was during the reign of Al Horr that an event of the greatest significance took place, which we must now turn aside to consider.   I refer to the The rising rising of the Christians in the Asturias, and of the Christians in the their desperate and successful resistance Asturias. to the attempts of the Arab-Moors to subjugate them in their mountain retreat.   It contains the germ of the reconquest, which eight centuries were required to bring to perfect growth, but which was in constant progress during the entire period.

The history is now naturally divided into three parts, each of which contains a distinct problem ; and yet all are so connected and correlated that no

single one can be treated of without a knowledge and
The triple an application of the other two. It was a
cord of the
history. triangular duel : each element was in conflict
with the other two, and yet their combination gives
the history of the time.

I. We must keep in view the condition of the
Khalifate in Syria, the heart of Mohammedan power,
and particularly its authority over the men and
measures of the Moslemah in Spain. The medium
of this authority was, generally, the Viceroy of Egypt.

II. We must consider the events and the conduct
of Mohammedan affairs in Spain, — the policy and
action of the Amirs, nominally dependent upon the
Khalif, and yet, virtually, so far removed from the
seat of power that the thunders of Damascus were
not very distinctly heard, and were beginning to be
little heeded. Damascus and Cordova were rapidly
drifting apart.

III. We must now also observe the little band of
Christians who had escaped into the fastnesses of the
Asturias, and who were recovering from their first
overthrow ; they were hardy, patient, and hopeful, determined to resist further encroachments, and were
even meditating the recovery of their independence
and the extension of their territory by possessing themselves of lands which had been unwisely abandoned in
the panic after the first fatal defeat, but not securely
occupied by the invaders. This extension of their
territory was a thought for the future. They could
now hold their own in the corner into which they had
been driven.

Each of these parties, I have said, was opposed to

and by the other two. The Khalif, in his dream of unlimited extension, desired the entire subjugation or annihilation of the Christian Goths; but he desired it for the aggrandizement of his own power. He found himself, therefore, greatly concerned to punish the slack allegiance of the Amirs and to strengthen his control over them.

The Amirs were quite as eager to overthrow and subdue all the remnants of Gothic power; but the treatment experienced by Musa and his sons had awakened in them an impatience of the restraints of Damascus and even of the viceroyalty of Africa.[1]

There were, moreover, rumors of weakness in the dynasty of the Ommeyades at Damascus and of an impending change, which promised an easy solution of the problem in Spain.[2] The dynasty which could not maintain itself at home must be even more powerless to control its distant dependencies. Coincident in time with these conditions, a protecting angel seemed to hover over the little handful of Spaniards in the north, and to reserve them for the great historic purpose of which they were already dreaming.

The later history will abundantly develop the first two of these considerations; at this stage we are immediately concerned with the last, which presents itself in the chronological order.

In view of the fierce incursion of Musa, which had

[1] As a measure of control and of security, the Khalif had constituted Spain a province of Africa, and placed it under the immediate government of the Wali of Africa.

[2] Meruan II., the last Khalif of the house of Ummeyah, was not driven from the throne until 750 ; but the decay of the house had already begun.

paralyzed Christian Spain, the modern historian of
Spain is led to inquire, "Had Spain really
expired as a nation ? Was the God of the
Christians, in all parts, tributary to the God
of Islám ?" To these question he proudly answers,
"No; she still lived, though destitute and poor, in a
narrow corner of what had been a vast and powerful
kingdom." [1]

The condi-
tion of the
Christian
fugitives.

The Spanish Goths, at first impelled by the simple
instinct of self-preservation, had fled in all directions
before the fiery march of the Moslemah, after the first
fatal battle in the plains of Sidonia. They had taken
with them in their flight all the movable property
they could carry and the treasures of the churches.
Some had passed the Pyrenees to join their kinsmen
in Septimania; and others had hidden in the mountain valleys of the great chain-barrier; while a considerable number, variously stated, had collected in
the intricate territory of the Asturias and in Galicia,
where strength of position made amends for the lack
of numbers and organization, and where they could
find shelter and time for consultation as to the best
manner of making head against the enemy. The
country is cut up in all directions by inaccessible,
scarped rocks, deep ravines, tangled thickets, and
narrow gorges and defiles,[2] in which ten men might

---

[1] "Era en todos partes, el Dios de los Christianos tributario del
Dios del Islam ? Habia muerto la España como nacion ? No :
aun vivia, aunque desvalida y pobre, en un estrecho rincon de este
poco ha tan vasto y poderoso reino." — LA FUENTE, *Historia de
España*, III. 57.

[2] La Fuente, Historia de España, III. 58.

stay a hundred; in which no army could manœuvre, and in which cavalry were useless.

They were indeed a motley crowd.   All ranks, many race-types, and all stations, were represented, in a democracy of danger.   There were bishops and priests, monks, husbandmen, artisans, and soldiers; men, women, and children clinging like shipwrecked mariners upon a steep coast-rock, to be out of the reach of a devastating flood.

It was a sad outlook!   The Moslems in the arrogance of unchecked victory, and angered by the slightest opposition, had begun to depart from *A sad outlook.* the leniency of their first terms.   The women of Spain were at the mercy of their conquerors as slaves and as favorites.   The men were under tribute, which became more grinding from day to day; the children were snatched from their mothers' arms and destined to slavery.[1]   The young were exposed to the insidious snares of all-conquering Islám.   The shrines were profaned; the Christian churches were, many of them, battered down or burnt, or, worse still, turned into Mohammedan mosques; the images hacked to pieces, and the ornaments and treasures carried away as spoils of war.

Those who seek for a poetical description of this period will find it, at once eloquent and truthful, in the chronicle of Alonzo the Wise, written five centuries afterward.   He calls it the "Mourning of Spain" (*el Llanto de Espana*).[2]   It is a nation's cry of despair: all was lost, and there was no hope!   Not so.

[1] Cardonne, Histoire de l'Afrique, &c., I. 94.
[2] Corónica de España, 202.

To stay the Moorish advance, to assert the uncon-
quered independence of Spain, to recover the lost
nationality, to elevate the standard of the faith, —
these were the grand thought — *el pensamiento grande*
— of the small band of Christians now huddled into
a little corner of the northwest.[1]

Such was the condition of affairs immediately after
the conquest of Tarik and Musa. The organizing
administration of Abdu-l-'aziz had given him no
time to attempt an expedition into the Asturias; but
Ayúb, in his brief Amirate, had sent his troops to
reconnoitre, and, finding in the more open parts of
the territory no show of resistance, he had contented
himself with passing around the mountains to the
coast and taking possession of several ports on the
Bay of Biscay. He left at Gijon, as governor of that
coast region, Othman Ibn Abu Neza, the Munuza of
the Chronicles, who will appear again in this history.
Thus the Christians were encompassed by their enemies; but this was an additional incentive to their
prompt action. They did not fear the invasion of
their rocky retreat; but they must burst through the
circle of fire.

In 717, on the deposition of Ayúb, Al Horr, as has
been seen, became Amir; and while with fresh enthusiasm he was preparing to penetrate into
Gothic Gaul, a rumor came to his ears that
the Christians were stirring in the Asturias.
They had just conceived *el pensamiento grande:* they
struck their shields, as it were, to allure the Moslemah.

*Al Horr be-
comes Amir
as well as
general.*

---

[1] " Nació el pensamiento grande, glorioso, salvador, temerario
entonces, de recobrar la nacionalidad perdida," etc. — LA FUENTE,
II. 69.

To this pitch of valor and defiance they had been raised by the appearance of Pelayo as their leader.

And here it is necessary to pause, — to rescue, if possible, the historic facts from the tangled mass of romantic fiction. Who was Pelayo? Is he but a hero of romance?

Whately, in seeking an illustration for the nebulous philosophy of the day, likens it to "a mist so resplendent with gay prismatic colors that men forget its inconvenience in their admiration for its beauty, and a kind of nebular taste prevails for preferring that gorgeous dimness to vulgar daylight." No figure could more accurately and felicitously express the taste of the monkish chroniclers and the atmosphere of the stories which they relate. As to the specific actions and the portraitures of the prominent actors of the time we find ourselves, when investigating this rising of the Spaniards, enveloped by the mists of fable, parti-colored and shining, but distorting individuals and groups, and concealing the beautiful landscape; and these fables have been wrought into such attractive pictures that the true history seems tame by comparison.

With this preliminary thought, we return to the king or chief elected by this forlorn hope of Christians in the Asturias to consolidate their power and lead them to the perilous attack. He was, say most of the later chroniclers, Pelayo or Pelagius, and those who do not mention him present no other personage in his stead.[1]

---

[1] Even as to the persons engaged in this conflict, and the date of its occurrence, there is a great diversity of statement. Cardonne

The first inclination of the historical student, as he is met by the vague and conflicting stories, is to re-
Question as to the personality of Pelayo. ject the claims of Pelayo as a real personage; but a more careful examination of the authorities leads him, step by step, to a different opinion, — that such a person did live and perform the great task, and that he bore that name. Many apparent discrepancies are readily explained, and the great fact demands such a belief for its full elucidation.

Mondejar says that up to the year 753 the Spanish Goths had no king, but only chiefs (*caudillos*). In considering that early period we may consider the terms "king" and "chief" as interchangeable, and call Pelayo the first of their kings.

Isidor de Beja, who completed his Cronicon in 753–54, makes no mention of Pelayo; and, as he was one of the very few contemporary writers, this silence would seem to throw a very grave doubt upon the subject. But he celebrates the fortitude and valor of Theodomir and Athanagild, who were successively "caudillos de los Christianos desde el principio de su opresion." It has been suggested that the silence of Isidor concerning Pelayo, and his casual mention of Theodomir and Athanagild, are by no means conclusive, as he may have written a special chronicle upon

(I. 105) ascribes the advance of the Moors to Abdu-l-'aziz. Others place it in the time of Anbassah, the successor of Al Horr. (Al Makkari, II. 407). But Adh-'dhobi, quoted by Gayangos, says, "In the year 99, Al-Horr sent his general Alkama, who was defeated and killed." The "Chronicon Complutense or Annals of Complutum," uses these words, "Antequam Dominus Pelagius regnavit, Sarraceni regnarunt in Hispaniam, *annis quinque*," i. e., from 712 to 717, A. D.

the Christian successes in the Asturias, which has been lost. He refers to an *Epitome of the Arabs*, which he had written, but which is no longer extant, and which might have thrown greater light on the subject.[1]

We leave this hopeless fancy for a better suggestion. Theodomir and Athanagild may have been the chiefs under whom the first, almost helpless, rally was made, and Pelayo, the third, the man who brought order out of chaos.[2] Such a leader did arise, whatever his real name.

The story of Pelayo became current among Arabian chroniclers. Ibun Hayýan, who wrote three centuries after these events, had adopted the earlier accounts. With no hesitation as to his personality, but with a curious moral contradiction in his estimate of the man, he says, "During Anbassah's administration, a despicable barbarian, whose name was Beláy, rose in the land of Galicia, and having reproached his countrymen for their ignominious dependence and their cowardly flight, began to stir them up to revenge their past injuries, and to

The Arabian writers accept him as a real personage.

---

[1] "No pudiera ademas el Pacense haber escrito a parte los sucesos de Asturias, y haberse perdido su obra, como desgraciadamente sucedió, con el Epitome de la Historia de los Arabes, de que el mismo Isidoro, nos habla en el n. 65 de su cronica?" The dependence upon works, known to be lost, is weak enough; but it requires a longer credulity to hope for facts in a work not known to have been written, and thus doubly lost to the historian.

[2] This is the opinion of Masdeu, who begins his catalogue of kings with these three names. Pedro de Marca offers another solution of the difficulty, by proposing that Pelayo was but another name for Theodomir. Out of the hurly-burly of opinions rises, with unmistakable identity, the chief whom history, at least, has called Pelayo.

expel the Moslems from the land of their fathers.
From that moment the Christians of Andalus began
to resist the attacks of the Moslems on such districts
as had remained in their possession, and to defend
their wives and daughters ; for, until then, they had
not shown the least inclination to do either. The
commencement of the rebellion happened thus : there
remained no city, town, or village in Galicia but what
was in the hands of the Moslems, with the exception
of a steep mountain, on which this Pelayo took refuge, with a handful of men. There his followers
went on dying through hunger, until he saw their
number reduced to about thirty men and ten women,
having no other food for support than the honey
which they gathered in the crevices of the rock,
which they themselves inhabited like so many bees.
However, Pelayo and his men fortified themselves by
degrees in the passes of the mountain, until the Mos-
His little lems were made acquainted with their prep-
band in-
creases, but arations ; but, perceiving how few they were,
is despised
by the Mos- they heeded not the advice conveyed to
lems. them, and allowed them to gather strength,
saying, ' What are thirty barbarians, perched upon a
rock ? They must inevitably die.' "

In the chronicle of Abeldum, Pelayo is mentioned
as the son of Veremundo, and the nephew of Roderik.
In that of Sebastian of Salamanca, he appears as the
son of Favila, Duke of Cantabria ; in that of Oviedo,
his father is called the Duke of Alava. As Alava was
a province in the Cantabrian mountains, the two latter
statements are reconciled.

Whatever slight discrepancies exist in names and

dates, it seems clear that Pelayo was of noble birth, of the same lineage with Roderik; and it is very easy to believe the assertion that he had been one of the chief sword-bearers of that monarch, and had fought valiantly under his banner in the battle near the Guadalete, although at that time not of age or station to be specially mentioned.[1] And, above all, the important fact of such a leader and his exploits remains as clear as if it were of yesterday. Immediately after the great invasion of the Arab-Moors, a small band of Christian Spaniards, did collect in the mountain region of the northwest : this became a nucleus for other fugitives from all parts of Spain. They were guided and governed by a *caudillo* or chieftain, who may well be called a king. He was a famous man, prudent, constant, judicious, patient, and valiant. Thus Pelayo presents himself to history divested of the fables and the marvels with which chronicle and legend have endued him, and demands the acceptance, the sympathy, and the admiration of the historical scholar.

It has been seen that Musa had passed along the coast of the Bay of Biscay, and had left, here and there, small garrisons to watch the movements of the Christians, and that Ayúb had appointed Othman Ibn Abí Nesa as Moslem governor of Gijon; and it was doubtless intended that a strangling cordon should thus be drawn around the little band of Christians. So strange were the actions of this governor, that he

---

[1] " Habia sido Pelayo Conde de los Espatarios . . . habia peleado heróicamente en la batalla de Guadalete."— LA FUENTE, *Historia de España*, III. 60.

seems to have been an enigma to the chroniclers. They have differed even as to his nationality and his creed. Ambrosio Morales calls him a captain of the Arabs named Munuza.[1] The editor of Mariana speaks of him as in reality a Christian, but a confederate of the Arabs.[2] This conflict of accounts does not at all affect the tenor of the history, but it displays the vacillating and treacherous character of the man. His double dealing has received, as it deserves, the reproach and contempt of both parties in the history.

The ambition of Munuza.

Mariana, using the doubtful authority of Roderik of Toledo, continues his delineation, in very severe terms. "There was nothing of the man about him, except the form and appearance, nor of the Christian but the outer garb."[3] Whatever his creed, self-aggrandizement was his purpose, and he sought his profit on both sides. Even of the town of which he was governor, there seems to be a doubt. La Fuente, who carefully considers the question, calls attention to a probable, because not uncommon, error in the spelling of geographical names, and suggests that he was governor, not of Gegio, the modern Gijon on the bay coast, but of Legio, now Leon, just south of the Asturian range. Now this name Legio or Leon, so long borne by a province and by its chief city in Spain, is

---

[1] A contraction and corruption of Abi Nesah. "Un capitan de ellos (los Alarabes) llamado Munuza." — MARIANA, III. 4, note.

[2] "Cierto general llamado Munuza, constantemente Christiano, aunque confederado de los Arabes." — MARIANA III. 4, note.

[3] "No se via cosa de hombre fuera la figura y aparencia, ni de Christiano sino del nombre y habito exterior." — *Historia de España,* III. 4.

derived from the old Roman *Regnum Legionis* (Kingdom of the Legion).[1]

But, in reality, it matters little what place was the
seat of Munuza's government. He was sufficiently near
to the Christians' retreat, at either point, to harass
them if determined to push the conquest to extremity, or to relieve them by an unwonted lenity or by a
tempting policy. But the gorgeous mist is not yet
entirely dissipated. Again the chronicles have recourse to woman's influence. He became enamored,
they say, of the sister of Pelayo, and struck a truce
with the Christians for her sake.

We shall see, farther on, that when this purpose is
served, the chronicles do not scruple to give him another Christian alliance — with Count Eudes and his
Aquitanians — by marriage with the daughter of the
count. We shall refer to this story in its proper
place. Mariana, accepting either account, attempts to
establish a curious but doubtful parallel between the
romantic event which led to the Moslem invasion of
Spain, and its loss in the initial battle, and this alliance
of Munuza with a Christian maiden, which strengthened the first stand of the fugitives in the Asturias
against the devastating torrent of the Moslems. The
downfall of Roderik was due at last to his amour with

---

[1] In Spruner's "Historisch-Geographischer Hand-atlas (Europa),"
the map of Spain illustrating the period from 711 to 1028 is marked
in all the northwest as Reg. Legionis. The next map is like it.
The third, for the period from 1257 to 1479, has a part of that territory set off as R. Leon. The guttural sound of the *g* would make
its pronunciation somewhat like *Leon.* A blind heraldry, accepting
the Spanish pronunciation of *legion*, gave to the province for cant-
ing arms, — *lions rampant.*

Florinda. The infatuation of Munuza with the sister of Pelayo, or the daughter of Eudes, gave shape and strength to the first faint gleams of the reconquest.

Whatever other causes may have operated upon this little congeries of Christians, their main hope seems to have been in their leader. When he appeared, they were in a prostrate condition. The old Gothic spirit seemed extinct. At the first there was not the shadow of a thought to retrieve the past and restore the former glory, but only to find a safe hiding and to lead a torpid life. It was in this conjuncture that Pelayo appeared to the terror-stricken fugitives as an angel visitant. In every possible respect, he was the man for the time and the need.

Of the blood royal, of high rank and command, he was young, handsome, and heroic. His misfortunes commended him to their sympathy. He had suffered before the war from the unjust suspicions of Roderik; he had vindicated his patriotism in the fatal battle. At the alarm of the invasion, he had forgotten private grievances in devotion to the national welfare; he had lost everything in the general devastation; he had been detained by the Arabs as a hostage at Cordova, whence he had escaped to his native mountains.[1]

Pelayo's name and character a rallying-point.

He now joined them in a common cause, and, added to all these incentives, in the purpose to uphold the Christian faith, which now seemed threatened with complete overthrow. I do not wonder

[1] Al Makkari, II. 260. The appearance of Pelayo in his character as a leader, was in A. D. 717, six years after the battle of the Guadalete.

that such a person should have been made the hero of romance : his historic character warrants it.

From his temporary hiding-place in Biscay, after his flight from Cordova, he heard the feeble call of his countrymen, and, with a few adherents, he moved cautiously among the mountain passes to inspect the numbers and condition of the people who had taken refuge there. The work was, at first, slow and painful; but it was not for a moment intermitted or slackened. A few were as determined and hopeful as himself; but the majority feared, by assuming the offensive, to draw the Moslemah upon them. Pelayo took counsel of his own brave heart, and in the mountain valley of Caggas de Onis, on an eventful day in the Spanish annals, he had the drums beaten and the old standard *The Christian drums beat at Caggas de Onis.* erected. Emissaries were sent in all directions to bring in the people, and they soon began to flock to the protection of his banner. Thus it happened that the little band on the mountain side, of whom the enemy had said, " Let them alone, and they will die," did not die, but soon became a thousand, and were then ready, in knightly style, to invite and hurl back the attack to which the Moslems had recourse when they found that starvation would not do.

And thus we approach the first success of the Christians, since the conquest, at the ever-memorable cave of Covadonga. However vague the personality of the actors and even the details of the events may still appear, the field of the conflict is accurately determined, and aids the traveller to renew, almost at a glance, the scene which was enacted there more than eleven centuries ago.

CHAPTER II.

LA CUEVA DE COVADONGA.

THE Principality of the Asturias (el Principado de las Asturias) comprises a narrow strip of territory on the Bay of Biscay, containing about three hundred and ten square leagues; it is separated from Leon on the south by the Asturian mountain range, while on the north a narrow fringe of hills carries the elevated terrace down to the bay coast. Its inaccessible and remote situation had made it one of the last regions of the world penetrated by the Roman eagles, and it was always indocile to the dominion of the Goths. It was in this territory that Pelayo gathered from the scattered defiles and rock crevices the material for his new army. It was motley in the extreme, — the representatives of every race that had lived in Spain, speaking a jargon of dialects, but with that cordial understanding which springs from a community of danger. Here were the representatives of the ancient Celtic blood and the more ancient Iberian, commingled in the Celtiberian; here were the descendants of the Roman conquerors, sons of the Legion Gemina, which gave its name to the territory.

With them were scattered families of Suevi and Alans, and many sons of the fair-haired Goths, who

*The princi-
pality of the
Asturias.*

had conquered all the conquerors and ruled the land
for three centuries. Among them were gigantic warriors, bearing Gothic swords which had been rusting
since the battle at the Guadalete, and mountaineers
armed only with rude spears, axes, and scythes.
Thus the reconquest was to be made, not by the
Goths or by any one people, but by the conglomerate
Spaniards.

Midway between Oviedo, the capital, and Santan-
der, lies Caggas de Onis, or Canicas, which Pelayo
had made his place of rendezvous; and The cave, or
about a league and a half to the east is the grotto, of
Covadonga.
singular and celebrated grotto of Covadonga. The
approach to the latter place from the west is by a
river defile, which grows narrower, the banks rising
at its narrowest part like perpendicular walls, until at
last it opens out into a small *cuenca*, or hollow shell of
punch-bowl form, limited by three mountain peaks.
Of these the western peak, Mount Auseva, is nearly
four thousand feet high; at its base is a detached
rock, one hundred and seventy-five feet in height, in
the centre of which is the famous cave or grotto. At
its foot rushes the rapid river Diva, which, issuing
from Monte Orandi, leaps through the narrow defile
in picturesque cascades, one of which has a fall of
seventy-five feet. The rock projects in the form of
an arch, and is connected by a succession of eleva-
tions with the mountains behind. The cave is
twenty-five feet deep, forty feet wide, and twelve
feet in height. This was the head-quarters of the
band, with which Pelayo watched the passages of
the Asturian mountains, and to this nest of insur-

gents the lieutenant of the Amir was now directing
his march, with an arrogant certainty of destroying it.

As soon as Al Horr had heard of this impudent
gathering, he had despatched his trusty general Al
Kamah from Cordova, to crush the presumptuous rabble who dared to limit the Moslem conquest with
arms in their hands; and, as soon as Pelayo heard of
his approach, he collected his scattered forces, left
Caggas, and moved to the valley of Covadonga.
Himself and his staff, with a small number of picked
men, occupied the cave. The women and children
were hidden in safe quarters. The rest of his force
he posted along the chestnut-trees which cover the
heights enclosing the narrow valley of the Diva.

Little suspecting the danger into which he was
about to thrust himself, Al Kamah came with what
Al Kamah's was deemed an adequate force, and entered
march
against the the narrow valley. Tradition hints, but his-
Christians. tory does not bear out the statement, that
Oppas accompanied the Moslem army to entice his
relative Pelayo to lay down his arms.[1] The tradition has not *prima facie* evidence of truth: the temper of the Moslems prompted to destruction rather
than compromise, and the destruction seemed certain
and easy of achievement.

To allure the invading army into the snare, a
small force of Christians, posted in the defile, retreated with precipitancy before the enemy. This
apparent retreat of Pelayo gave a fatal confidence to
the Moslem host: they pushed forward in the narrow

[1] Cardonne, I. 108.

pass, skirting the little ledgy border of the Diva, and soon came to the broader track opening into the narrow valley of Covadonga. Thus they were caught in a complete *cul-de-sac*; numbers gave no advantage. A very small force could hold a large army at bay in that narrow pass, while the excluded flanks and the rear were exposed to the missiles launched by the unseen hands of those posted in the woods of the heights on the right and on the left.

The Christians showed no signs until the troops of Al Kamah had emerged into the valley in front of the cave. Then the famous battle began, fa- The battle mous not for the numbers engaged, but for and its un-expected the issues at stake and the completeness of issue. the overthrow.

The bolts and arrows of the Moslems rebounded from the rocky sides of the cave,[1] while a storm of missiles assailed them at short range, and soon threw back the advance upon those behind them. In the midst of the confusion thus produced, Al Kamah ordered a retreat; but, when that was attempted, the Christians posted on the eminences hurled down huge rocks and trunks of trees upon the choking defile, and thus caused a terrible destruction. The panic was complete: they could not fight, and they could not fly. Then the reanimated Christians, commending themselves and their cause to the Virgin, advanced on all sides. Issuing from the cave, Pelayo

---

[1] The story told by most of the chroniclers, that the shafts wounded many of the assailants in their rebound, savors of poetical and romantic description.

bore aloft an *oaken cross*, with the cry that the Lord was fighting for his people.[1]   This was irresistible.

Unable to retreat, Al Kamah endeavored to shelter his force under the brow of Monte Auseva; but even the elements seemed to conspire against him. A furious storm arose, and augmented the terror and confusion of his troops.[2]   The thunder reverberated through the mountain gorges; amid the torrents of rain which blinded their view, the rocks and missiles came tumbling down from the mountain sides.

The waters of the Diva rose rapidly, and many of those crowded back were drowned in the swift flood.

The entire destruction of the Moslem army. The footing was slippery with mud; the very earth seemed in league with the sky to destroy them, and the mountains seemed falling on them.   So complete was the destruction that, according to many chroniclers, not a single Moslem escaped to tell of the disaster.[3]   This is the usual exaggeration, but indicates the terrible nature of the defeat.

It is hardly probable; but the Christian triumph was complete.   The first great stand against the Arab-

---

[1] This cross, or one in its stead, was preserved at Oviedo, and believed by superstitious people to have fallen from heaven.   It was ornamented with gold and enamel in the year 908.

[2] La Fuente, Historia de España, III. 63.

[3] Sebastian of Salamanca makes the invading force *one hundred and eighty-seven thousand!*   Roderik of Toledo destroys, at the first fight in the cave, twenty thousand, and far more in the attempt to retreat.   The reader is impatient of such gross statements.   The real numbers cannot be known.   "Those who now tread these narrow defiles of Covadonga," says Ford, "will see the impossibility of moving, not five hundred thousand men, but twenty thousand. The true solution of all these *cuentas* will be to read hundreds instead of thousands."

Moors had been made; and thus, in 717, only seven years after the landing of Tarik, and in the very flush of the Mohammedan conquest, the germ of the reconquest was firmly planted, and was to grow slowly, but steadily, until it should overshadow the whole land. In Christian Spain the fame of this single battle will endure as long as time shall last; and, La Cueva de Covadonga, the cradle of the monarchy, will be one of the proudest spots on the soil of the Peninsula.

> " Yace de Asturias, donde el sol infante
> Sus montes con primeras luces baña
> De Covadonga el sitio, que triunfante
> Cuna fue en que nació la insigne España . . . " [1]

There are several important inferences to be deduced from this historic event.

The first is, as has already been hinted, that the Spanish success was not a resuscitation of the Gothic dominion, but a fusion of all the elements in the cradle of a new Spain. The very antecedents of the conquest showed clearly that the old rule was effete: it had reached its end. This little rising in the Asturias was the indication of a new life, new interests, a healthier combination; it was the little bead of pure gold which had come out of the furnace seven times heated.[2] Pelayo was the usher and the representative of this new order, and the Christian king-

---

[1] *El Pelayo* of the Conde de Saldueña, Canto II.

[2] "La religion y el infortunio han identificado á Godos y Romano-Hispanos, y no formanza sino un solo *pueblo*, y Pelayo, godo y español, es el caudillo que une la antiqua monarquía goda que acabó, en Gaudalete, con la nueve monarquía Española que comienza en Covadonga."— LA FUENTE, III. 68.

dom of Oviedo was its first theatre. The stage was
to expand steadily in the coming years.

Again, it is due to the character of this combination
that individual independence was established in
Individual
liberty inau-
gurated. Spain, and kept the new kingdom, in its
civil and secular relations at least, the most
democratic of monarchies. "Conquerors and conquered, strangers and natives, all united by the same
misfortunes, forgot their ancient feuds, aversions, and
distinctions; there was but one name, one law, one
state, one language: all were equal in this exile."[1]
Other causes in the later history have led to the
oppression of the Spanish people; but the poorest
mountaineer still calls himself a *hidalgo*, and addresses his penniless companion as *Don*, a Latin title
of courtesy, which marks no distinction of blood or
station.

It is also worthy of special observation that,
in the cave of Covadonga, we may faintly dis-
The obscure
birth of the
Spanish lan-
guage. cern the origin of the modern Spanish language. In the words of Ticknor, "There
indeed the purity of the Latin tongue which
they had spoken for so many ages was finally lost
through the neglect of its cultivation, which was a
necessary consequence of the miseries that had oppressed them."[2]

The numerous dialects of the congeries of fugitives
were combined into one, and give beauty and variety
to that noble Castilian, which has no peer among
modern languages for its simplicity and harmony.

[1] Augustin Thierry, Dix Ans d'Études Historiques, Essay XXVI.
[2] History of Spanish Literature, I. 7.

Thus Spanish philology presents a most curious and interesting problem in the science of language.

The scope of this history does not permit us to follow the fortunes of this new Christian kingdom. The battle of Covadonga, in which it had its origin, cleared the whole territory of the Asturias of every Moslem soldier. The fame of its leader, and the glad tidings that a safe retreat had been secured, attracted the numerous Christians who were still hiding in the mountain fastnesses, and infused a new spirit of patriotism throughout the land. They came out to meet him with grateful acclamations, and day by day his little band grew in proportions and in power to advance. The sneers of his enemy were turned to impotent anger and vain regrets. "The contempt," says Ibnu Said, " in which the Moslems of those days held that mountain, and the few wretched beings who took refuge upon it, proved in after times the chief cause of the numerous conquests, which the posterity of that same Pelayo were enabled to make in the territory of the Moslems."[1]

Pelayo was now king in reality, as well as in name. The Saracens may have still affected to doubt his importance; in addition to this they wanted all their available men to confirm their own possessions, and to invade Gaul. Be this as it may, they let him and his people alone; and, with commendable prudence, he contented himself with securing and slowly extending his mountain kingdom by descending cautiously into the plains and valleys. He gave to it an organization, at once civil and military, such as

---

[1] Al Makkari, II. 35.

its necessities demanded. All the men were drilled in military exercises. Industry was aroused: they began to plant and build and fortify. Adjacent territory, abandoned by the Moslems, was occupied and annexed; and thus the new nation was made ready to set forth on its reconquering march.

The Christians advance slowly but surely.

Pelayo, it is said, died at Caggas de Onis, in the year 737, after a reign of nineteen years, and was buried with great pomp in the church of Santa Eulalia at Abamia, the ancient Velamia, beside the body of his wife, Gaudiosa. Later, a nobler and more fitting resting-place was found for his remains, which were removed to, and still occupy, a tomb in the Cueva de Covadonga, in the company of his son-in-law, and second successor, Alfonso I.

The death of Pelayo and establishment of the succession.

The authority which Pelayo had so strongly established descended to his son Favila, with the consent of the principal warriors; but this monarch did nothing in his short reign of two years worthy of mention, except the erection of the church of Santa Cruz, near Caggas, in honor of the victorious cross which Pelayo elevated in front of his band. The chase was the absorbing passion of Favila; and he came to his end in attacking a bear.

Among the curious carvings in the church of Santa Cruz is one capital, made at a later day, which depicts the manner of his death, so ignoble as compared with the mighty exploits of his heroic father.

With the name of his successor, the new monarchy emerges into a brighter light. Favila left two sons;

but they were both too young to undertake the responsibilities of the throne. Another choice must be made, and the chiefs decided in favor of Alfonso, a noble Goth, fitted by nature and experience for the position, and especially acceptable in that he had married Ermesinda, the daughter of Pelayo. It is stated by Mariana, but cannot now be proved or disproved, that he had been named by Pelayo as his successor in his will. He was a man of strong mind, inclined to war, enterprising and daring, and especially needed, after the torpor of Favila's reign, to carry out the plans of Pelayo. He inflamed the Christian zeal and the patriotism of his people, and urged them to undertake a war of aggression to spread the faith and recover the country.

It is not to my purpose to pursue the Christian successes, except so far as they concern the Moorish conquest: their energy was never relaxed. In the year 801 the Spaniards were masters of a considerable portion of Old Castile, to which their numerous castles gave its name; and when a hundred years more had rolled away their outposts had reached the chain of the Guadaranna Mountains, which separates New from Old Castile.

In verification of the story of Covadonga, there were, as the later history informs us, many relics and souvenirs of this celebrated battle, some of which remain to this day. Caggas de Onis, stately in its natural features, expands into the court of Pelayo, and the imagination reproduces the palace and pantheon of its early monarchs. The Cueva de Cavadonga containing the remains of the first kings, then accessible by a ladder, is now entered by a marble staircase. The inhabitants still point out to the traveller the little streams that ran red with Moslem blood, and even the huge rocks which were hurled down upon them.

The chapel of Santa Cruz in the Vega renews the story of Pelayo's cross. Tradition tells us that, for a

Relics of Pelayo. long time after, the freshets in the Diva, washing away its banks, uncovered the bones and pieces of armor of the Saracen troops who perished there. Adjacent to the cave is a field, called to-day Repelayo (Rey Pelayo), in which the first proclamation of that monarch was made,[1] when his people, according to their mode of election or adoption, elevated him upon a shield.

At a short distance is a field called El Campo de Jura (the field of the oath of office), whither, up to the present century, the judges of the confederate parishes of Caggas proceed to take possession of the staff of justice.[2] " Respectable and tender traditional practices of the people," says the Spanish historian, " which remind us with emotion of the humble and glorious cradle in which the legitimate principle of authority was born." [3]

This is true ; but it should be added that it was authority delegated by a brave people, and based upon

---

[1] " A la salida de este celebre cueva hay un campo, llamado todavia de Repelayo (sincope sin duda de Rey Pelayo), donde es fama tradicional que se hizo la proclamacion levandandole sobre el pavés." — LA FUENTE, III. 68.

[2] " Los jueces del concejo : The *concejo* in the Asturias is a district composed of several parishes, and controlled by a *juez de concejo*." — BUSTAMENTE, *Spanish Dictionary*, voce *Concejo*.

[3] Historia de España, III. 69.

their independence. It was a popular movement, guided by a noble leader. It could boast that the part of Spain in which it had its rise had never succumbed to the infidel invaders : that, while they were vaunting their conquests as complete, Christian Spain had never lost its existence or its identity; but in the most evil days had been like an unfortunate man whose house had been besieged and assaulted, and whose estate had been pillaged, leaving him only a sad and dark corner, into which the robbers were unable to penetrate, but from which he might with renewed strength sally forth to dislodge and drive them away from his entire domain.

Here we leave the new Hispano-Gothic kingdom, and return to consider the plans and fortunes of the Arab-Moors, in consolidating what was securely in their possession, and in their ambitious invasion of Gaul. Commanding the roads leading through the eastern and western "gates" of the Pyrenees, the Moslemah might safely leave the kingdom of Pelayo behind, or rather on the west, as a matter rather of future consideration than of present concern; and feeling sure that a firm foothold at the north would give them additional strength when they should find themselves again in condition to attempt its destruction.

CHAPTER III.

MOVEMENTS BEYOND THE PYRENEES.

WE now return to consider the rapid and disadvantageous changes which were occurring in the government of Spain, and the consecutive steps of the ambitious Amirs, in the invasion of France.

For twelve years — from 719 to 731 — we find a sad record of internal dissensions, due to many causes. The cupidity of the Arabian tribes, and the causes of controversy between the Arabs and the Berbers, led to fierce fighting among the Moslemah. Avaricious Amirs succeeded each other.   The death of a Khalif, or a change in the viceroyalty of Eastern Africa, which controlled the appointments in Spain, caused sudden depositions.   Plans for northern invasion were left inchoate.   On the death of an Amir, the soldiers, like the Prætorian guards in Rome, appointed in the interim, according to their own views of aggrandizement, a provisional successor, who, in most cases, was not confirmed by the Wali of Africa, but who appears

Provisional Amirs appointed by the Moslem troops. on the list of Amirs, and really exercised the authority during the brief period of command.   Such are the elements which confuse the history, and render the dates of accession and tenure difficult to decide.   The principal facts, however, are sufficiently discerned; and, although not of

much interest or importance, it is necessary to present
them briefly, in order to the continuity of the
history.

It will be remembered that Al Horr, who succeeded
Ayúb in 717, was an avaricious and cruel man, laying
heavy exactions upon the Christians, and plundering
his own people.   He would, doubtless, have been
sooner removed but for the sudden death of the
Khalif Omar at Damascus by poison.   That Khalif was
succeeded by Yezid, who made a change in the government of Egypt.   But the generals of Al Horr renewed their complaints to the new Wali of Africa, and
one of them, Assamah, was appointed in his stead.   The
new Amir at once, and with enthusiasm, followed up
the movements of his predecessor in Gaul.   Here
everything was confusion and terror.   The helpless
inhabitants of the mountain-slopes and passes of the
eastern Pyrenees had permitted the Moslem recon-
noissances, and the way was open and easy for their
incursions into El Frangat — or "La Grande Terre" as
Aquitania was called — on either hand by the Moors
and by the Aquitanians; partial incursions, which
preceded and announced a war of conquest.   Assamah
advanced to Narbonne, which had already been occupied and abandoned by the Moslemah, and he put it
in condition to be a strong base for his future operations.   The geography and topography of the place
gave it great importance.   On the site of an old
Gaulish town, eight miles from the sea, and commanding splendid distant views of the Pyrenees, the
Romans had built a stronghold, which they called
"Narbo Martius."   The beauty of its surroundings

won for it from Martial the distinction of "Pulcherrima Narbo."[1]   It gave its name to that extensive southern province extending from the Alps to the Pyrenees, known as Gallia Narbonensis.

The importance of Narbonne.   Its strategic importance is manifest: an easy coast-road leads from it to the valley of the Rhone, through Montpellier, Nismes, and Avignon; while in the valley between the Pyrenees and the Montagnes Noires, along the route of the present Languedoc canal, it has secure communication through Carcasonne with Toulouse and all Aquitania.

Former attacks upon Narbonne had been partial efforts made by small reconnoitering detachments. The capture by Assamah was complete and permanent; and it was attended with ferocious cruelty.   To the men no quarter was given; the women and children were carried as captives into Spain.   The booty was immense.   The churches were pillaged and then destroyed; there was not a shadow of the humanity which had prompted the actions of the first Moslem conquerors.   The chronicle speaks of seven massive equestrian statues of silver which the Amir found in Narbonne, of which the traveller of to-day may form some idea from the mounted image of Santiago, which

---

[1] The glory of Narbonne is of the past.   Charles Kingsley says, "Now a dull, fortified town, of a filth unspeakable.   Stay not therein an hour lest you take fever or worse; but come out of the gate over the drawbridge, and stroll down the canal.   Look back a moment, though, across the ditch.   The whole face of the wall is a museum of Roman gods, tombs, inscriptions, bas-reliefs, — the wreck of Martial's Pulcherrima Narbo." — *Prose Idylls from Ocean to Sea*, p. 218.

literally prances out of the wall in the cathedral at Granada.[1]

The capture and occupancy of Narbonne were by no means the limit of Assamah's ambition. In the early months of the year 721, he marched through Carcassonne, which offered no resistance, and vigorously besieged Toulouse, in which the affrighted Christians of Aquitania had fled for security from the dreadful ravages of the surrounding country. The siege promised entire success: many partial advantages had been gained, and everything was in readiness for a final assault, when news reached Assamah that the king of Afranc, with an immense army, was approaching to relieve the town. It was in reality Eudes, the king or duke of Aquitania, with a hasty levy of Aquitanians and Gascons; so much confusion magnified the foe.

Without a moment of hesitation the Moslem commander advanced to meet this new force, and was thus between the city and the relieving force. He rode through the ranks, and with fiery words inspired his men. In describing his conduct, the chroniclers deal in superlatives. "Fear not," he cried, "this multitude: if God is with

The battle between Eudes and Assamah.

---

[1] Among the confused statements of Musa's progress to the north, one is that he occupied Medina Narbona, "where he took possession of seven idols of silver, all being figures of men seated on horseback, which he found in one of the churches." — CONDÉ, I. ch. xvi. In this brief but confused period, in which the command was so constantly changing, the deeds of one Amir are frequently accredited to another. The cruel capture of Narbonne, here ascribed to Assamah, is, by some historians, placed in the Amirate of Al Horr, whose revolting character it would seem to corroborate.

us, who can be against us ?" "The exploits he performed," says Condé, "would seem incredible if here
related. The blood of the enemy distilled from his
arms at all points, as it flowed from his raised sword
like a torrent ; and whenever he appeared the opponents sank beneath his glance." The enthusiasm of
King Eudes was equal to that of Assamah. He, too,
harangued his men, and distributed among them small
pieces of the holy sponge, blest by Pope Gregory II.,
which had wiped the communion tables of the Roman
bishops.[1]

The battle was long doubtful ; but was at last decided
by the fall of the Arab leader: a Christian lance pierced
him through ; and when he went down the Moslem
cavalry, struck with panic, fled from the field, cutting
their way through the Christian ranks, and were soon
followed by the remainder of the army, who did not
pause in their hasty march until they were sheltered
under the walls of Narbonne. This defeat took place
on the 10th of May, 721; it was a new indication
that the tide of Arabian success had reached
its height, and that further northern conquest was to be painful and costly. The
Moslemah acknowledged the disaster, and
called the field Balattu-sh-shodada, *the pavement or
causeway of the martyrs.*[2]

Assamah is slain, and the Moslems acknowledge a total defeat.

[1] Historia de la Dominacion, I. ch. xxi.

[2] They gave the same name afterwards to the place of defeat between
Tours and Poitiers ; it seems, therefore, of general application. It
has been suggested, that it was given at Toulouse, on account of the
Roman causeway, Balatt being a corruption of Platea, near which
the battle was fought. (See the note of Gayangos, Al Makkari, II.
406, 407). It is not unlikely that it was afterwards adopted for any
field of disaster.

According to Anastasius (le Bibliothécaire), the number of the Moslem slain was three hundred and seventy-five thousand, while the Christians lost only fifteen hundred : not only is this simply incredible, but it is also repeated at the greater battle of Tours, which was to follow eleven years after.[1]

The fall of Assamah was a great loss to the Moslem cause. His large and liberal mind was as useful in political administration, as his valor and enthusiasm were in war. He projected and began the celebrated bridge at Cordova, which was finished by Abdu-r-rahmán.

While such vigor and energy were being displayed in Spain, it is curious to observe the effects produced upon the mind of the Khalif by the accounts he received at Damascus. This can best be expressed in the following quotation from Al Makkari, who finds his authority in Ibun Hayyan : " He (Assamah) brought instructions from the Khalif . . . to write a description of the cities, mountains, rivers, and seas of that country ; and this Omar caused him to do, and to send to him that he might the better gain a knowledge of the countries conquered by the Moslems, and estimate their resources, for he intended to make them evacuate Andalus, dreading the dangers to which they might be exposed in a distant country, away from their brethren in religion, and from the people speaking their language.[2] We may see, in this curious pur-

---

[1] Not one of those who had received a piece of the holy sponge was among the killed.

[2] If our former authority is correct, Yezid had already succeeded Omar ; but the project was undoubtedly that of Omar. — AL MAKKARI, II. 32.

pose, not the suggested paternal solicitude of the Khalif, but his concern for his own power. His remoteness from the Peninsula made his authority there little more than nominal; and he could already see the day approaching when Spain would be a rival Khalifate to Damascus.

Upon the fall of Assamah, the temporary command of the Moslem forces devolved upon Abdu-r-rahmán al-Ghafeki, who was afterwards to figure so brilliantly in the invasion of France. It was he who rallied the fugitives and conducted their hasty march to Narbonne. He was the idol of his troops, and, by a show of election by the army, he was constituted, temporarily, Amir of Spain.

The new Amir, Abdu-r-rahmán.

But his generosity and popularity caused both the Khalif and the Wali of Africa to doubt the expediency of retaining him in power; and he only retained the command until relieved in the same year by Anbassah Ibn Sohaym Al-Kelbi; after which, paying his compliments to the new Amir, and congratulating him upon his promotion, he gracefully retired to his military command,[1] where, indeed, he was of chief value to the Moslem cause.

The great battle of Toulouse seems to have established a temporary truce, or, at least, cessation of hostilities between the two hosts. The Christians, indeed, advanced to Carcassonne, and fortified it; but the hostile relations between Count Eudes and Charles Martel, kept the former from following up his success against the Moslemah, while they, on the other hand, were temporarily paralyzed by the great defeat, and were obliged to take time for new preparations.

[1] Condé, I. ch. xxii.

In the mean time, Anbassah turned his attention vigorously to the interior administration. He put down an insurrection at Saragossa, and razed its walls. He made a new and equitable distribution of the conquered lands; he revised the laws of tribute; and was especially lenient to all who accepted the faith. He administered justice to Moslems and Christians alike; and for four years he ruled Spain in a manner acceptable at once to his superiors and to his people. At last he undertook to retrieve the disaster of Toulouse, and to avenge the blood of its "martyrs."

With a strong and thoroughly organized force, he advanced upon Carcassonne which had become the strongest place in Septimania. He took it from the Christians by storm, and then, leaving a competent garrison as a *point d'appui* when he should be ready to assume the offensive, he turned aside to make an incursion into Provence, which appears to have been less guarded against the Moslem incursions. The march of the generals of Anbassah was tracked by devastation; their squadrons ravaged Nismes, and penetrated to Lyons and Autun.[1] Everywhere were seen flames, and were heard shrieks of mortal agony. The monasteries and churches were pillaged, the monks were killed, the cities given over to sack; and then the victorious Moslems returned, laden with rich booty. The ease of their successes invited them to constant renewals. They could no longer doubt the realization of their wildest dreams, — the subjugation of all Europe to Islám.

[1] La Fuente, Historia de España, III. 50 ; Condé, I. ch. xxii.

But in one of the latest actions Anbassah received a mortal wound; and his death, which occurred in December, 725, or January, 726, checked the further progress of his followers.[1]

Just before his death, he appointed as his temporary successor, Odrah Ibn Abdillah al Fehri, — one of the most distinguished of the Arabian commanders, whose probity and courage had been manifest ever since the conquest. His appointment, however, was not ratified by the Wali of Africa, who sent from Africa, Yahíya Ibn Salmah Al-Kelbí in the place of Anbassah. Thus Odrah was only three months in power, and the plans of Anbassah, now fallen into the hands of a stranger, were no longer pursued; while the rapid change of Amirs thenceforward did not allow the organization of any well-devised scheme for the occupancy of French territory. Nor were the Amirs who followed, until Abdu-r-rahmán-al-Ghafeki capable of originating such plans.

New hopes of the Moslems for northern conquest.

The extreme rigor of Yahíya soon alienated the hearts both of Moslems and Christians, and caused them to unite in a petition to Coltum Ibn Aam, the new governor of Africa, for his removal. After a rule of six months — from March to September, in 726 — he was deposed. A doubt now arises as to his immediate successor, most of the chroniclers naming Othman Ibn Abi Nesah; but a reliance upon the

---

[1] Some writers (Al Makkari, II. 35) say he died a natural death while conducting this campaign. Condé (I. ch. xxii.) says he received several wounds; and some of them were so severe that he died thereof not many days after.

authority of Isidorus Pacensis leads us to interpolate
another Othman — Ibn Abda — for the fourteen
months, from September, 726, to November, 727.   He
was one of the men who had signed the treaty with
Theodomir : his identity is assured.   Isidorus says he
ruled for five months, and was succeeded by *another
Othman*, whom we know to be Othman Ibn Abu
Neza.[1]   Doubtless, Othman Ibn Abda was a usurper,
who took advantage of the confusion to raise himself
to power.   We thus renew our acquaintance with
Munuza, not without some misgivings as to the accounts we have already received of his character.

After the defeat of the Arab-Moors at Covadonga,
he had fled from Gijon into northeastern Spain ; and,
in the period of confusion which followed, had maintained himself by his intrigues ; and, at last, had
caused such representations to be made in his behalf
to the Wali of Africa, that he received the appointment of Amir.   I have spoken of the disastrous
changes in the Amirate, and the absence of proper
organizations for further conquest.   The period of
three years between the accession of Yahíya and the
coming of Al Haytham Iyám-u-l-fitnah may be truly
called the days of confusion.

The Arabs from Yemen, and those from Modhar,
fought against each other for the supremacy.   The
Berbers fought against all of Arabian lineage.   It

Hic (Autuman) ab Africanis partibus tacitus properat.   Hic
quinque mensibus Hispanias gubernavit ; post quos vitam finivit, et
missus est *alius Autuman nomine.*   Gayangos, in the corrected list
of Amirs, makes the period of his rule fourteen months, instead of
five.   See Chronological Table at end of this volume.

matters not what the question, — the division of lands
Strifes be- of spoils or the nomination of an Amir.
tween the
Arabs and Every tribe had its petty faction, and Arabia
the Berbers. and Africa were arrayed against each other,
while both were supposed to be arrayed against
Christian Europe.

The elevation of Munuza seems at first to have
been acceptable to the factions of Spain, but it was
only for a time. " The same persons who had sought
his elevation, dissatisfied with his proceedings, and
disappointed in the vain hopes and extravagant expectations of advantage to themselves which they
had formed, sent repeated complaints against him [to
the Wali of Africa], who wrote to the Khalif, asking
him to name the General Hodheyfah Al Kaysi Amir
of Spain." [1]

This general, who was appointed to the command
in the latter part of the year 728, found neither time
nor scope for his powers. He was deposed in April,
729, the government temporarily reverting to Munuza
until a successor should be named.

In the latter part of 729, the new Amir appointed
by the Khalif arrived in Spain, — Al Haytham Ibn
Al-Haytham 'Obeid Al-Kelábi. He was a Syrian, whose
appointed
Amir. cruelty and avarice soon caused him to be
greatly detested by all the people. Unlike most of
the former Amirs, who had gone in person to the
frontiers and displayed their valor in the van of the
army, he remained in Andalusia, and left the military
conduct of affairs in the north to Munuza, who, as
former Amir, was ambitious of power, and who had

---

[1] Condé, I. ch. xxiii.

given symptoms of wavering in his loyalty to the Moslem cause, for the reasons already mentioned.

The chiefs of the Moslemah conspired against Al Haytham, but he discovered their complots, and punished innocent and guilty alike with imprisonment, torture, and death. The misgovernment and injustice of Al Haytham were so flagrant, that they soon reached the ear of the Khalif's lieutenant in Africa. The friends of a noble and distinguished citizen, Zeyad Ibn Zaide, whom he had imprisoned, sent an account of his cruelty, which was transmitted to the Khalif. It ended with these words, "Turn to thy people, O Commander of the Faithful! for within reach of this tiger they cannot live for a moment in security." The petition was heeded; the Khalif Hisham sent at once, as a special envoy plenipotentiary, Mohammed Ibn Abdillah to investigate the matter discreetly and impartially, and, during the investigation, to suspend Al Haytham from the command.

The result of the investigation was found to be that the charges were in the main just, and the maladministration clear. Vested with the But is soon authority of the Khalif, Mohammed deposed deposed for his cruelty. the Amir, and appointed in his stead Abdu-r-rahmán-al-Ghafeki, to whom all pointed as the man for the post, who, by his generosity, valor, skill, and prudence in military command, and as temporary Amir before, was worthy to govern the Moslemah in Spain.

We thus reach one of the noblest names among the conquerors; it shines out of this confused and desultory record, like a bright star in the darkness.

Abdu-r-rahmán Ibn 'Abdillah-Al-Ghafeki was, as the name indicates, of the noble tribe of Ghafek. He had entered Andalus with Musa, and had been indefatigable ever since in the field, in the Divan, and in public works; he had completed — or, for the most part constructed — the magnificent stone-bridge, of seventeen arches, across the Guadalquiver at Cordova. He had made himself beloved by all the dwellers in Spain. Entirely unselfish, he had accepted power without ambition, and laid it down without a murmur. His unparaded liberality had endeared him to the people; his cheerful abandonment of authority had removed the jealous fears of the Khalif. Such a man was trusted by all.

The brilliant record of Abdu-r-rahmán Al-Ghafeki.

The inquiries of Mohammed had only lasted from August, 731, to October; and when he returned to Africa to make his report, he left Abdu-r-rahmán to his well-earned dignity as Amir of Spain.

The torpor and the confusion disappeared like a mist before the wind; he entered at once upon a career of enterprise and adventure unsurpassed in the annals of Mohammedan Spain; he gave the last and greatest impulsion to the northern movements into Gaul.

To repair the evils wrought by Al Haytham, he began a rapid tour of all the provinces; investigating personally all grievances; rights that had been infringed were protected, wrongs were redressed. The cruel and oppressive subordinates who had been the instruments of Al-Haytham's misrule were removed and punished; the stipulations of treaties made with the Christians, which of late had been entirely violated, were rigorously observed.

While he was thus restoring order, he was not for a moment relaxing his preparations to invade France. He saw the necessity of a large and thoroughly organized army, if he would hope to reap the advantages of success. He prepares to invade France.

To increase his force to such numbers, he had written several letters to the Wali of Africa to send him large re-enforcements. His plan and his request were received with great favor, and awoke an extraordinary enthusiasm, outside of Spain. Whole tribes from Arabia and numerous recruits from Syria, came, with rapid march, to join the Berber contingent enlisted on the slopes of the Atlas and in the Land of Dates. The new expedition into Gaul had become a rallying-cry for the large force which crossed the Strait, in successive detachments, more numerous than any band since the invasion of Musa. As these re-enforcements arrived, he quartered them for subsistence and tactical instruction in different parts of the territory until he should be ready to mass them, in order to carry out the chief purpose of his ambition, — to hurl an invincible column into the heart of Gaul, and to spread the faith of Islám into the seats of Christian Europe. According to many historians, he almost achieved this: the purpose at least was grand.

The appointment of Abdu-r-rahmán seemed to have thus united all interests, and silenced all factions; but there was one man who regarded it with great dissatisfaction, for it foreshadowed the frustration of his designs, and the disclosure of his in- The dissatisfaction of Munuza.

trigues. That man was Othman Ibn Abi Nes'ah-
Munuza. When he had been superseded in the Amirate by Al-Haytham, he had returned to the military
command in the eastern Pyrenees, not without hopes
that with the rapid turn of the wheel of fortune, he
would again contrive to come into power.

He had married, say the chronicles, in speaking of
this period, the daughter of Count Eudes of Aquitania — *la bella Lampégia* — and had entered into a
secret alliance with her father for mutual support.[1]

In the struggle of the Moslem factions, he seems to
have enlisted and represented the Berber interests
against the Arabians. Abdu-r-rahmán was thus triply
opposed to his plans, — as an Arabian, as the new
Amir, and as a faithful son of Islám, who would not
permit the shadow of composition with the Christians,
of which Munuza was charged.

Just before the appointment of the Amir, this Othman had made an indefinite truce with Count Eudes,
and then, claiming that he had acted discreetly in so
doing and for the best interests of the Moslemah, he
wrote a letter to Abdu-r-rahmán, strongly dissuading
him from the project of invasion.[2]

---

[1] Speaking of the rising of the Christians in the Asturias, some of
the chroniclers, as I have already said, declare that he was infatuated
with the sister of Pelayo ; and afterwards that he had fled to eastern
Spain. One account informs us that he was rapidly followed and slain
by Pelayo himself. There is more causality in the present story, —
that he was in alliance with Eudes, through the marriage with his
daughter. Lampégia is also called in the Spanish histories, *Menina*,
and *Numerancia*. H. Martin says (Histoire de France, II. 107)
that the marriage was scandalous to the faithful of two religions.

[2] According to Isidorus Pacensis, " he made haste to conclude
a peace with the Aquitanians, and projected to usurp the sovereign
power over the Saracens of Spain."

But the new Amir saw at once through the flimsy pretexts; he was thoroughly acquainted with the character and the situation of Othman.

He sent him instructions to declare the armistice at an end. It could not bind *him*, for it had been made without his knowledge, and before his appointment to the government. Moreover, he directed Othman to hold himself and his army in readiness to move at once, with the new force now organized, upon the Aquitanians and the Franks.

The love and the jealousy of Othman overpowered his judgment, and led him to an act of open treason. He at once sent to give the Christians information of the Amir's purpose, and warned them to put their territories in a state of defence. And then he sent the insolent message to Abdu-r-rahmán, that neither he nor his troops would march into *la grande terre*, in violation of the truce, which he had a right to make.

The Amir was by no means surprised nor disconcerted at these tidings : they made his way clear. He could deal better with a declared traitor than with an undermining rival. Losing not a moment, he despatched a strong force under Ghedhi Ibn Zeyyan, with instructions to find Othman wherever he should be, to inquire into the reported treason, and, if the accounts should be found true, to take him alive or dead.

The march of Ghedhi was made with such celerity and caution that it took Othman entirely by surprise. He had no time to organize a defence : he could only fly before the avenger with his wife and family, and a handful of followers. They passed rapidly through

Puicerda (Medina-al-bâb, *the city of the gate*), and took refuge in one of the Pyrenean passes. Among the jumbled spurs behind the pass he might hope to secrete himself. But his adversary was at his heels, following as rapidly as he fled. While detachments occupied and examined the adjacent passes, the main body came up with the fugitives in the little valley of Livin.

There, thinking he had distanced pursuit, and deceived the pursuers, feeling sure that, in one more rapid journey, he could find security at the advanced post of Count Eudes's army, the weary Othman and his terrified wife had halted beside a fountain overshadowed by high jagged rocks and shaded with dense foliage. The murmurs of the waters, and the voice of his wife's endearments, shut out other sounds from his ear. Suddenly, his attendants heard the sound of distant footfalls, and the voices of a coming band. Struck with panic, they deserted their hunted chief, and saved themselves in every direction. He sought for some cave or crevice in which he might hide himself and the ill-fated woman, who was the innocent cause of his merited fate. But before he could find a refuge the pursuers were upon him with a shout. He turned at bay, and fought with desperation. Some accounts say that he fell pierced by the lances of the pursuers with numerous wounds; others, that when he found defence vain, he threw himself

Munuza slain, and his wife sent to the Khalif. from the mountain precipice and was instantly killed. Whichever story may be true, in accordance with custom, the pursuers cut off his head, and carried it, with the beautiful Lampégia, whose love had inspired his treason, and thus caused his death, to show the Amir that the chief obstacle to his advance was summarily removed.

The fair captive, a beautiful stranger with a romantic history, Abdu-r-rahmán sent to grace the harem of the Khalif at Damascus.[1]

The chief rendezvous of the Saracen army of invasion was along the upper Ebro. The failure of Othman's scheme and of his protecting truce had spread terror and confusion in the southern provinces of Gaul, and had sounded an alarm on the Loire and on the Seine. But Count Eudes, no longer fearing the encroachments of the Franks from the north, but soliciting their co-operation, immediately gathered all his troops to contest the Moslem advance, which was now imminent. At last it came like a torrent; it was led by the Amir in person.

Instead of entering Aquitania through Septimania and along the old line, he advanced through the western passes, — through Pampeluna and along the Bidassoa; through Roncesvalles they *Abdu-r-rahmán enters France.* poured in several columns, and then spread through the fertile valleys of Bigorra and Bearn. Nothing seemed able to stem the fierce flood. It rolled up and cast aside the Basques and Gallo-Romans hastily collected to oppose his march; the Amir devastated farms, used or destroyed the crops, and found large spoils.

It was now the month of May, 732. Marching by both banks of the Garonne, he advanced upon Bordeaux, towards which the principal forces of Count Eudes

---

[1] Isidorus Pacensis.

had fallen back. That governor did not await, behind the ramparts of the city, the assault of the Moslems, but concentrated his forces at the confluence of the Garonne and the Dordogne. Burning to avenge the loss of his daughter and the devastation of his territories, he fearlessly marched out to meet them, and risked the fate of his capital on a pitched battle in the open field. But his valor was ill requited: the result was not long doubtful; his army was crushed and scattered; and in a single day he lost the fruit of fifty years of glory. Bordeaux was stormed and taken: a general of high rank, incorrectly supposed to be Eudes, was killed and beheaded; the rich churches pillaged; the houses sacked; and the Arab hosts spread without further resistance through all parts of Aquitania.[1]

Captures Bordeaux.

The fugitive Eudes, halting for a moment on the right bank of the Garonne, beheld the mounting flames which enveloped the steeples of his capital. Roving bands of cavalry even crossed the Loire at different fords, and spread devastation and terror into the towns of Orleans and Auxerre. One detachment appeared before Sens, only sixty miles from Paris, meeting there the only rebuff since the storming of Bordeaux. And all these Moslem bands were within call of the main body, whenever — if ever — a firm front of Christian troops should require their concentration for a decisive battle. Surely it was high time that this destructive invasion should be checked. The check was at hand.

And routs the army of Eudes.

---

[1] Isidorus Pacensis exclaims with vague sorrow, "God alone knows the number of those who fell on that day."

We must now leave the narrative at this interesting point to glance for a moment upon the general condition of Europe, thus arrogantly. threatened, and especially to consider what had been transpiring in Gaul while the Saracens had been thus effecting the conquest of Spain.   This is necessary to a proper intelligence of what follows.   In what condition was the congeries of kingdoms in Gaul to meet and hurl back the advancing tide of the Moslem invasion ? What force could be collected ; what mighty man was there who could save Gaul, and, perhaps, Europe, from the impending destruction ?

CHAPTER IV.

THE CONDITION OF EUROPE. — CHARLES MARTEL.

THE irruption of the northern barbarians upon the Western Empire, which had given a Gothic dynasty to Spain, has been likened to a great flood which submerged Roman civilization, and which seemed to promise no ebb, the subsiding waters of which should again uncover its relics and its wrecks, and make them available in creating a new civilization. But the inundation slowly subsided, and the buried world emerged from the waste of waters, to be reinspirited and reconstructed. Even at the early period of which we write, this reconstruction was in vigorous progress.

At the time when the first successor of Mohammed led his army of believers into Syria, the weak and irresolute Heraclius sat upon the throne of the eastern empire of Rome. That empire, founded by Constantine the Great, and owing its later name Byzantium to the ancient city, upon the site of which he had built Constantinople, had long since reached the culmination of its fortunes. While western Rome was falling beneath the Gothic assaults, Justinian had appeared in 482, and his sagacious brain and vigorous hand, overcoming many obstacles, had made the eastern capital a city of refuge for the art, literature, and general culture, which the Eternal City could no longer protect. To Justinian is due the establishment of such a system of laws and government as *The policy of Justinian.* could give a thousand years of life, checkered and declining indeed to the Byzantine empire. He guarded it by fortresses against Europe and Asia ; he made the dome of St. Sophia a beacon of Christianity.

His diplomacy with Persians, Turks, and Abyssinians was acute and skilful ; his master-hand was extended over Italy. Under his direction, Belisarius conquered the southern portions after crushing the Vandals in Africa ; and, above all, he digested that body of laws, the Code, the Pandects, and the Institutes, which, sifting out all that was worthy of preservation in the old royal statutes, the twelve tables of the Decemviri, the people's laws, the decrees of the senate, and the edicts of the prætors, may be said still to rule the world. The *corpus juris* passed from Constantinople to Italy, from Italy to Spain and Gaul, from Gaul to England ; from the middle age to the modern, until it appears in the legislation of all the civilized nations of Europe.

Such was the heritage of power and its sanction, which the successors of Justinian scattered and threw away with the folly of a crazy spendthrift.

From the time of Heraclius the decline was rapid. To the Saracens the eastern empire was no longer an enemy to be feared, but a weak neighbor to *The decline of the eastern empire.* be harassed and despised. A glance at that chapter of Gibbon's great work saddens and irritates the student. We see Constantine Pogonatus punishing the intrigues of his brothers by cutting off their noses. We see Justinian II., who assumed the purple in 685, himself suffering a similar amputation, exiled, restored, and brutally torturing his rivals. In 711, the very year that Tarik was crossing the strait, the effete but brutal dynasty of Heraclius came to an end, and in the eight years of interregnum, up to 718, three usurpers rose and fell, until the Isaurian dynasty appears in the person of Leo III. I need not dwell upon the merits and the superstition of the Image Breaker, who reigned for thirty-two years. It is worthy of record that the Saracens had the assurance and the power to threaten the latter part of his life by themselves investing a usurper with the imperial purple, — one Tiberius of Pergamos, whom they declared to be a son of Justinian II. The fraud was too flimsy to succeed ; but it displays at once their power and their contempt. We leave the empire in the hands of Constantine, who was so dissolute, cruel, and filthy, that he has been named in history Copronymus.

At one remove we pass to Italy, chief seat of the subverted empire of the west. Here, as might be expected, the confusion was greater than elsewhere. The Gothic rule, which had begun with Odoacer, had been strengthened by the forcible accession of Theodoric, who was the friend and nominal tributary of the eastern emperor. In the north, after a period of sixty years, it had succumbed to the Lombards, who, pouring like a lava stream through the Alpine passes, had occupied the beautiful country on the banks of the Po, long afterwards known as Lombardy. But at the time of which we write the Lombards had become enervate. The eastern empire still contested the dominion of Magna Græcia. The forged decretals of Constantine had not yet appeared, but the fact which they were to sanction was already manifest.

The Bishop of Rome had become the greatest Metropolitan in Europe : above all other Bishops or Papas, he had become the Pope by pre-eminence; *The papacy firmly established.* the withdrawal of Constantine, and the new capital which he founded in the east, had resigned to him a spiritual sovereignty in Italy, which demanded corresponding temporalities; and the fiction of an apostolical scribe could no more than legitimate the gifts of the faithful as "the just and irrevocable restitution of a scanty portion of the ecclesiastical state."[1] Thus Italy was a seething caldron, containing many nationalities and many interests, and presenting, even as late as our century, the numerous small territories, kingdoms, dukedoms, and principalities, which so long resisted the yearning and the efforts of the people for a united Italy, so happily effected in our own day.

The Saxon power in England was in process of consolidation in the eighth century. The orig- *The condition and prospects of Saxon England.* inal invasions had formed distinct kingdoms; the claim of the Bretwalda to the control of the Octarchy, was an effort at confederation.[2]

---

[1] Gibbon's Decline and Fall, ch. xlix.

[2] "The exertions of the British against the invaders having failed, *eight* Anglo-Saxon governments were established in the island. This state of Britain has been improperly denominated the Saxon Heptarchy. When all the kingdoms were settled, they formed an Octarchy." — SHARON TURNER, *History of the Anglo-Saxons,* I. Book III. ch. v. Near the close of the sixth century, "Ethelbert of Kent succeeded to that insulary predominance among the Anglo-Saxon kings which they called the 'Bretwalda,' or ruler of Britain." — *Ib.*

The establishment of Oswald of Wessex as king of the four nations, although destroyed by the doughty arm and the rival ambition of Penda of Mercia, marked a step in the progress. Mercia assumed the temporary supremacy; always contested, however, by the power of Wessex. The establishment of Latin Christianity through the efforts of Gregory the Great, at the very close of the sixth century, exerted a salutary influence upon monarchs and people, and brought England into relations with the continent which could have been established in no other way. The laws of Ina of Wessex did much for the progress of civilization, and cause him to deserve, says Sharon Turner, "the gratitude of mankind, in common with every other lawgiver." In the year 721, he resigned his crown, and made a pilgrimage to Rome, where he remained the rest of his life. "The same thing," says the Venerable Bede, "was done through the zeal of many of the English nation, noble and ignoble, laity and clergy, men and women." [1] These numerous pilgrimages doubtless informed the Saxon people, vaguely, of the invasion and conquest of Spain by the Arab-Moors, but it gave them little concern: the country was an unknown land beyond the seas, and the infidel invader could never reach their insular borders. Thus England felt no interest in the Moslem advance.

It is manifest from this hasty glance that the nations mentioned had little part in the struggle which had been going on in the plains of Touraine. It was far otherwise, however, with those peoples

---

[1] Ecclesiastical History, Book V. ch. viii.

who were domiciled in Gaul, and who were now to test the metal and check the fury of the Moslem invaders.

And here let me pause to remove some errors in the very elements of the problem.

The battle, so called of Tours, between Charles Martel and Abdu-r-rahmán al-Ghafeki, has been generally considered by historians as sim- *The philosophy of the contest between the Moslems and the Franks.* ply a contest of creeds, — the desperate and overwhelming assault of Islám against the last entrenchment of Christianity. The rival creeds were indeed involved in the general controversy, and were potent incitements to action on either side; but they were the accidental, and not the essential, elements of the problem. It was a curious ethnic question. The northern barbarians of Teutonic type had come down in successive irruptions upon the soil which Rome had conquered and reclaimed, and they were still making southern progress. The Gallo-Roman had no power to resist them. As Goths, they had overrun and occupied Spain. The southeastern Bedouins of Semitic race had issued from their original seats, under the influence of Islám, to make conquests at the west and north. In Spain and Gaul they met the northern invaders in mid-career, like knights in the lists. Hardy, skilful, and constant, they had both been conquerors. Each had an equally just claim to the occupancy of the Roman territory, — the claim of the sword; but the Northman was far the stronger man, and Shem was once more to recoil before the hand of Japhet.

We come now to consider in what condition the

Frankish territory was, to receive and hurl back the advancing tide of Moslem devastation, which was ready to pour upon it.

The confederated Franks, Teutonic tribes on the banks of the Rhine, the Main, and the Weser, had occupied the northern part of Gaul, and the Merovingian dynasty had been firmly established, under Chlodowig or Clovis, as far as the banks of the Loire. They made southern raids, but returned to this natural line.

Thus a new provincial division had been made of Transalpine Gaul. The northeastern portion, from The division of the Frankish dominion into great provinces. the Rhine to the Scheldt, and extending southward, without very exact limits to the head-waters of the Saone, was called *Austrasia* (Oster Rike), the *eastern kingdom*. It remained in contact and communication with the original seats of the confederation, and drew its fresh strength from the Teutons, who were still pushing westward.

The northwest, comprising the territory north of the Loire, with some significant strips south of that river, and including the Roman Lutetia or modern Paris,[1] was called *Neustria* (Ne Oster-Rike), not the eastern, and therefore the *western kingdom*.

---

[1] Paris was founded by the Senonian Gauls, and from them received the name which was Romanized into *Lutetia*. The tribe of founders called themselves *Parisii*. When it became a city under Roman laws it was called *Lutetia Parisiorum*. Under the Emperor Julian, in the fourth century, it was called *Parisii*. The commonly received derivation of Lutetia, from *lutum*, clay, was an after-thought. It is more probably from the Keltic, *loutow-hesi*, dwelling of the waters. The *muddy* town holds to either derivation.

The valleys of the Saone and the Rhone, with the western slopes of the Alps, including Savoy, received from the northern invaders from the shores and islands of the Baltic who occupied them, the name of *Burgundia*. The remaining territory at the southwest, in which the Goths still held the mastery over the Gallo-Romans, was known as *Aquitania ;* in the southeast was the region called by the Romans *Narbonensis*, and more generally *Septimania*.

There were some subdivisions of these provinces which must be noticed. In the western part of Neustria, formerly Armorica, the independent Bretons, aided by accessions from the Celts, flying from Saxon encroachments in Britain, kept up a distinct individuality in what the Romans called Britannia Minor, and has always since been called *Bretagne* or *Brittany*. In Burgundy, the geographical distinction of the first Roman *Provincia* was maintained, and it has become the *Provence* of later history. The southeastern portion of Aquitania was known as *Septimania*,[1] and the southwestern as *Vasconia*,[2] which has been corrupted into the modern Gascony. It extended south of the Pyrenees. Such were the great geographical divisions during the period of the Merovingian dynasty.

The firmly-established power of the dynasty extended, however, only to Austrasia and Neustria: these

---

[1] " It was principally the Roman Gallia Narbonensis, and comprised the modern Languedoc, with the exception of the dioceses of Toulouse, Albi, Uzes, and Viviers. The name was given because it was colonized by the soldiers of the *seventh* legion." — BESCHERELLE, *Dictionnaire National ;* voce *Septimanie.*

[2] The people and the name were *Basque.*

constituted the actual kingdom of the Franks; but they claimed all the other peoples in the territory of

Austrasia and Neustria.

Gaul as their tributaries, and, in urging their claims, they made constant and inhuman raids upon the Burgundians and upon their Gothic neighbors and cousins; and every organized incursion extended their dominion in the countries south of the Loire, to which I have referred, and increased the terror and the prestige of their arms. Their design was manifest to conquer the whole land, and make it all, in reality and in name, *France.* It is not my purpose to enter into the details of the Merovingian history. Those who desire vivid pictures of that race and its actions will find them in the *Récit des Temps Mérovingiens* of Augustin Thierry;[1] from the establishment of the dynasty to the year 583. It is a history of fierce incursions upon their neighbors, and of fratricidal strifes at home; of outlawries; of church superstitions; of conjugal infidelities; of parricides; of cruelties; of obscenities, worthy of the palmy days of Commodus, Caracalla, and Heliogabalus.

While numerous fierce bands, under petty princes, were fighting for lands and spoils at home and abroad,

---

[1] "It has been said that the object of the historian is to narrate, and not to prove . . . I am persuaded that the best sort of proof in history — that which is most capable of striking and convincing all minds, that which admits of the least mistrust and which leaves the fewest doubts — is a complete narrative, exhausting texts, assembling scattered details, collecting even to the slightest indications of facts and of characters, and from all these forming one body, into which science and art unite to breathe the breath of life." — *Sixth Narrative.* No work better deserves such an eulogium than his own, from which this is quoted.

the evil deeds of the Merovingian dynasty were working out its ruin. The dominion established by Clovis in Neustria had been slowly but steadily declining for two centuries under the constant action of several forces. The men of that race, whose chief had proudly said, when he heard of the crucifixion of Christ, " If I had been there with my Franks, I would have known how to defend Him," could no longer defend themselves. They had become enervate in their new and pleasant seats, while they were called upon to contend with a constant infusion of fresh blood, physical and mental vigor from the northeast, the bracing atmosphere of those seats from which the confederate Franks were still marching down to conquer the enervate Franks.

Thus, while the Neustrian monarchs — nominally kings of the Franks — and the conquered inhabitants had become luxurious and lazy, the Dukes of Austrasia governed a people who had continued to lead a rude and adventurous life, who were physically strong and mentally quick, and who coveted the well-watered and fertile farms and the gathered stores of their degenerate brethren in Neustria. The contest for power between the Old Dynasty and the Austrasian aspirants gave scope to individual ambition, and recognized and rewarded individual superiority. The first step was to gain a foothold in the palace. The Dukes of Austrasia became mayors of the Neustrian palace, and wielded the royal power without the title and without the responsibility. The stewards usurped the wealth and power of the lords.[1]

[1] " The *maires-du-palais* were originally stewards, or head-ser-

It was not only the personal type which had degenerated in Neustria; it was the system which had
Les rois
fainéants. lost all respect from the people. The condition of these *rois fainéants* is sad to contemplate. The power had been transferred to the Austrasian dukes; the people sided with the power which led them to battle and conferred the spoils of war; the church sanctioned it. The little show of regal authority was prescribed, and the monarch could not break down the hedge of prescription. A *fainéant*, whatever his endowments of mind and body, could be nothing else.[1]

At the period of which I am writing the decline was complete in fact, if not in name, and its rapidity
The mayors
of the palace
and dukes
of Aus-
trasia. seems due to one family more than to the prestige of rank or power. Peppin, of Landen, was mayor of the palace under Dagobert; failing of a male heir, he looked to the son of his daughter Begga to succeed to his fortunes. This grandson was Peppin, surnamed Heristal, from his villa near Liege: he was so successful in further

vants, appointed by the monarch. They were afterwards elected by the *leudes.* Their next step was to crush the nobles, and, considering the dignity to be hereditary, to associate their sons with them, and thus transmit the office." — BONNECHOSE, *Histoire de France,* l. i., ch. iii.

[1] "Except this vain name of 'king,' and an annual stipend not well assured, he possessed nothing of his own but a farm of moderate revenue, which furnished him a dwelling and a small number of servants. . . . If he wished to go anywhere, it was in a car drawn by oxen. . . . It was thus that he went to the palace and to the general assembly of the people, held yearly for public business. As for the administration of the kingdom, the measures and dispositions to be made within and without, the mayor of the palace had the entire charge of them." — EGINHARD, *Life of Charlemagne,* ch. i.

trammelling the royal power as to prepare the way for his more renowned son, — the child of a concubine, whose name was Charles, and who, from the strength of his strokes in battle, has come down in history as Charles Martel, or the *Hammer.* No greater name than his, but one, appears in the Frankish Annals. The large renown and the greater empire of his grandson Charlemagne have somewhat eclipsed his fáme and hidden the causes of future events. Men value effects, while they undervalue causes; and, even when history does not foster the error, the later and greater personality throws the former into an inexorable shadow.

Charles Martel is, indeed, one of the most illustrious names in history. Like the great kings before Agamemnon, he lacks a biographer and a poet. He governed the Franks absolutely without *Charles Martel.* a legitimate title. He permitted the nominal rule of the sluggard kings that he might use whatever of moral power still clung to the title. He befriended the church in Gaul, and entered into a treaty with the Pope concerning Boniface, the apostle to the Germans. All this had rendered the alliance between his son and the Pope easy, by frightening the church into submission, and by daring, in a superstitious age, to use the treasures attached to its lazy dignities to maintain his army.[1] It was he who gave practical establishment to the feudal system as a powerful in-

---

[1] "Une impérieuse nécessité, et non la passion ou la colère l'avait poussé à l'invasion violente des dignités et des biens ecclésiastiques : avec quoi eût-il soldé le devouement interessé de cette formidable association militaire dont il était le chef ?"— H. MARTIN, *Histoire de France,* II. 136.

strument of organization, and firmly to establish the new order. He erected the throne of the new dynasty, not for himself, but for his son Peppin, whose mission it was to strengthen and expand it so that it might befit the proportions of Charlemagne.

At the south he claimed the Duke of Aquitania as his vassal; and, resenting his adoption of the kingly title, he ravaged his lands and spoiled his goods. He subjected Burgundy to tribute, and kept it in virtual subjection. And, while thus establishing his power throughout the territory of Gaul, he was constantly concerned with the frontier relations of the kingdom; for Gaul is the most indefensible by its natural features of all the countries of Europe.

His northern campaigns are not within the scope of this history. Previous to the invasion of Abdu-r-rahmán, he had quelled and punished the barbarous Saxons in three vigorous campaigns, in 720, 722, and 729.

In 725, he had invaded German Suabia and Bavaria. In 730, he had made a campaign in Allemania. On the northern line, he was feared as an almost supernatural hero.

The coming Moors were not, up to this time, in his judgment, a pressing problem. He knew that before

He keeps the Moslems in view and makes cautious preparations.

they could reach the Loire they must subdue Aquitania; and he played upon the fears and hopes of Duke Eudes, and succeeded, by chastisements and by the promise of assistance, alternately, in securing his tribute. Even in 731, the year before the great battle which was imminent in the very heart of Gaul, between Tours and Poitiers, he had made an incursion into Aquitania, ravaged the lands, burnt the buildings, taxed the monasteries, and, without waiting for the counter attack, had hurried back behind the Loire. The unhappy Eudes was in great tribulation; the Arab-Moors were upon him; he had no resource but to submit to Charles, and to act, first as a barrier, and then as a co-operating force against the fiery tide from the south.

Charles Martel appeared upon the historic stage just at the time to be the hero of this great epic. Born about the year 689, when the Arab-Moors first crossed the strait of Gibraltar, in 711, he was twenty-two years old. In the year 716, when that first invasion had secured entire success, he was taken from the cloister prison in which the jealousy of his royal relatives had immured him, and was placed in command of the Austrasian army. In 717, he surprised and defeated the Neustrians at Vincey. From that time, for fourteen years, he had been far-seeing and vigilant concerning the progress of the Saracens in Spain : and even a duller mind than his must have guessed their intentions. It has been the opinion of several historians that, when the great emergency came, Charles was surprised and unprepared; that he was compelled, at the last moment, to collect hastily a few troops, as it were to hazard a desperate cause upon a single cast, and that he was fortunate enough to win.

Nothing, I think, can be further from the truth. The facts of history carefully collated prove conclusively to my mind that, when the Moslem force came like a hurricane, it was expected; that Charles,

who, with characteristic prudence, had kept his own
counsel, had been devising and maturing his plans for
succoring Aquitania, and defending the frontier of
Neustria and Austrasia, within which were enclosed
the interests of Christian Europe.

A glimpse of his policy appears at an early day.
Ab-Hijari, an Arabian chronicler of the twelfth
century, in a work entitled "Al-mas'hab," tells the
following story, which displays the opinion of the
His prudence Moslems upon this subject, and is thus far
rebuked. of historic value. When the Arab-Moors
under Musa, son of Nosseyr, had invaded Spain, and
even passed the mountains which divide Andalus
from Afranj, "it is related that the Franks flocked
immediately under the banners of their great king
Karoloh, and said to him, 'What is the meaning
of this our ignominy and shame, which will rest as
a stigma on our posterity? We hear about these
Arabs sprung from the east, and are informed of their
conquests and of their arrival in the west, subduing
the neighboring kingdom of Andalus; and yet these
Arabs, we are told, are scanty in numbers, badly
equipped and provided, and do not wear armor.'
And Karoloh answered them, 'My opinion is, that
we should not oppose these people on their first
irruption, for they resemble the mountain torrent
which surmounts every obstacle in its course; they
are now in the height of prosperity, and, instead of
being abated, their courage is only increased at the
sight of the enemy; their proud hearts scorn the defence of a cuirass. Let them alone, until their hands
are well loaded with spoils; for, when they have set-

tled in this country and established their government, they will vie for command, and fight with one another for the acquisition of it. That will be the time and occasion for attacking them, and I doubt not but that we shall easily vanquish them!' and, by Allah, so it was." [1]

The comment of Gibbon upon this policy is, that "the situation of Charles Martel will suggest a more narrow and selfish motive, — the secret desire of humbling the pride and wasting the provinces of the rebel Duke of Aquitania." "It is yet more probable," he adds, "that the delays of Charles were inevitable and reluctant."

Without noticing the partial contradiction in these statements, we have already shown that the first was an important element in his counsels; he ravaged Aquitania, while Abdu-r-rahmán was concentrating his forces on the Ebro; but the second suggestion cannot be reasonably admitted. The whole course of Charles seems to show that he meant to make his stand in front of the Loire, and that his judgment was deliberate and admirable as to the time and the mode. He did not leave Gaul during that year for a northern invasion.

From the necessity of the case, — the difficulty of keeping a large army together for long periods, and the novel character of the war, — the force with which Charles was to encounter the Moslems was hastily collected, and composed of heterogeneous but powerful materials. Sectional differences were for the time forgotten: it was like a rising *en masse*. In Neustria and

[1] Quoted by Al Makkari, I. 290.

Austrasia, and other parts of his dominion, in marsh and highlands, in field and forest, during the spring and summer, had been heard the blare of Roman clarions, and the bellowing of German horns; and from every quarter men came flocking under his standards. Some were armed in complete steel, some were clothed in skins, many were half naked; but all were inured to hardships and war; all stalwart northern men, determined to do fierce battle against an alien race and a false creed; hopeful of the blessing of the Church, and the rich spoils of the foe. It was a new and holy cause, and the least intelligent among them were made to understand it. Thus they came thronging, some through Tours, but the greater number through Orleans, to the appointed field, and there, marshalled into serried ranks, presented a solid wall of muscular manhood to the Moslem assault.

Pending the serious emergency, all controversy between Eudes and the Austrasian duke was for the time at an end. The former, after the defeat at the hands of the Moslemah near Bordeaux, had fled without preliminary herald, to throw himself and the salvation of his territory upon the mercy of Charles, and he was received with words of kindness and encouragement. The common danger was a bond of union. The scattered forces of Aquitania were collected at safe distances on the Moslem flanks; the fugitives, who had crossed the Loire, were incorporated with the army of Charles, or rallied in his rear to get up a new spirit for the fight.

Charles and Eudes suspend their hostilities to unite against the invader.

The military situation up to this point is one of

unusual interest. All the southwest of France lay prostrate and paralyzed; all hope lay north of the Loire; all men looked to Charles, the martial and sagacious mayor of the palace, as their protector and savior. Much indeed did depend upon him, but I hope to be able to show that behind him lay a magazine of power, capable of reversing his defeat should he be defeated, ten times over. It will also appear, as we proceed, that the prudence of his plans and the *personnel* of his army were such as to render it extremely improbable that he could be defeated.

We return now to the Moslem army. As soon as Abdu-r-rahmán-al-Ghafeki heard that the redoubtable Charles had reached the Loire, he sounded the rally of all his detachments, on the banks of the Charente, between Bordeaux *The movements of the Amir.* and Poitiers, and then moved with his united force to attack the Franks wherever he should find them. His course was marked by unusual devastation; he destroyed the principal houses, and burnt the churches. When he reached Poitiers he found it full of fugitives who had placed the city in a state of defence. He could not stop to besiege it, but he sacked one of the faubourgs, and pillaged and gave to the flames the celebrated church of St. Hilaire, which was held in the greatest veneration. Thence he pushed forward towards Tours; but, before reaching the Loire, he found the way blocked, and was obliged to encamp and study the situation before advancing to the attack of the army which now presented itself before him.

The fighting ardor of his warriors had been somewhat cooled by the ease of their conquests, and more especially by the quantity of booty which they had taken. Heavily laden with the spoils already in hand, and covetous of more, the Moslem soldiers were fast becoming freebooters in place of disciplined soldiers. Nor was this the worst; their greed had produced insubordination. The quarrels of the tribes began again to break out; the trooper neglected his arms, and regarded his horse rather as a beast of burden than a war-steed. Abdu-r-rahmán and other

His army corrupted by the spoils. prudent officers of his command, themselves untainted with the sordid vice, looked with dismay, and not without foreboding as to the issue of battle, upon these evils; and yet found it more prudent to trust to prestige and fortune, and to the incitement of battle, rather than to displease the soldiers, and excite a revolt by ordering them to abandon everything except their arms and horses,[1] which alone could ensure success.

In their camps, the tribes of Arabians and Africans were separated, and were suspicious of each other, and when they issued from their tents to join battle, their hearts were with their treasures rather than in the sweep of their cimeters.

Meanwhile, Charles Martel was already organizing and reviewing the daily arriving detachments of that powerful army which was to arrest their progress and hurl them back upon the Pyrenees in hopeless disorder. Small parties of the two hosts sent out to gather information of each other, could not but engage in slight skirmishes which gave token of that coming

[1] Condé, Dominacion de los Arabes, I. ch. xxv.

conflict soon to be ranked in history among "the decisive battles of the world."[1] It has been justly so considered; the Franks were fighting for their hardly-earned homes and for Christianity in Europe. The Arab-Moors, still eager for bold adventure and new possessions, were inspired by a dream of universal conquest.[2] Charles Martel was already recognized as the greatest warrior who had appeared among the former in their entire history. Abdu-r-rahmán was acknowledged, both as Amir and General, by army and by people, as the best representative of the Moslem power in Spain. If the prestige of advance, which is worth so much in war, was with the Arab-Moors, the vigor of defence was buttressed upon all western Europe, — upon the greater physical strength, the more enduring spirit, the less excitable character of the German, who, not yet stationary in his Gallic seats, might also claim somewhat of the prestige of advance. The great victory which was to test the prowess and the ambition of both parties, and to rearrange the data of the Mohammedan problem, is reserved for the initial chapter of the second volume.

[1] Sir Edward Creary has written a work with that title, in which this battle is described.

[2] " Les Arabes étaient alors dans cet état social mal assis, et dans cette jeunesse passionnée, où les aventures hardies excitent, et attirent les peuples plus que leurs échecs ne les découragent." — GUIZOT, *Histoire de France racontée à mes petits Enfants*, I. 174.

END OF VOL. L

Lightning Source UK Ltd.
Milton Keynes UK

173605UK00001B/231/A